Science Instruction in the Middle and Secondary Schools

Developing Fundamental Knowledge and Skills for Teaching

SIXTH EDITION

Eugene L. Chiappetta
University of Houston

Thomas R. Koballa, Jr.
University of Georgia

PEARSON

Merrill
Prentice Hall

Upper Saddle River, New Jersey
Columbus, Ohio

Library of Congress Cataloging-in-Publication Data

Chiappetta, Eugene L.
    Science instruction in the middle and secondary schools.—6th ed. / Eugene L. Chiappetta,
Thomas R. Koballa.
        p. cm.
    Includes bibliographical references and index.
    ISBN 0-13-191656-4
    1. Science—Study and teaching (Secondary)—United States. I. Koballa, Thomas R. II.
Title.
Q183.3.A1C48 2006
507'.1'2—dc22

2005040824

Vice President and Executive Publisher: Jeffery W. Johnston
Senior Editor: Linda Ashe Montgomery
Associate Editor: Ben M. Stephen
Senior Editorial Assistant: Laura Weaver
Senior Production Editor: Mary M. Irvin
Design Coordinator: Diane C. Lorenzo
Project Coordination and Text Design: Jolynn Feller, Carlisle Publishers Services
Cover Designer: Thomas Borah
Cover Image: Corbis
Production Manager: Pamela D. Bennett
Director of Marketing: Ann Castel Davis
Marketing Manager: Darcy Betts Prybella
Marketing Coordinator: Brian Mounts

This book was set in Galliard by Carlisle Communications, Ltd. It was printed and bound by the Banta Book Group. The cover was printed by Coral Graphic Services, Inc.

Photo Credits: Eugene L. Chiappetta: pp. 2, 28, 44, 56, 88, 124, 136, 142, 162, 214, 230, 262; Thomas R. Koballa, Jr.: pp. 14, 19, 31, 49, 68, 74, 77, 106, 111, 182, 193, 200, 224, 231, 246, 250, 265; Shawn Glynn: p. 174

Pearson Prentice Hall™ is a trademark of Pearson Education, Inc.
Pearson® is a registered trademark of Pearson plc
Prentice Hall® is a registered trademark of Pearson Education, Inc.
Merrill® is a registered trademark of Pearson Education, Inc.

Pearson Education Ltd.
Pearson Education Singapore Pte. Ltd.
Pearson Education Canada, Ltd.
Pearson Education—Japan

Pearson Education Australia Pty. Limited
Pearson Education North Asia Ltd.
Pearson Educacin de Mexico, S.A. de C.V.
Pearson Education Malaysia Pte. Ltd.

10 9 8 7 6 5 4 3
ISBN: 0-13-191656-4

To the many science education researchers whose scholarly contributions to teaching and learning science has benefited this textbook through its many editions.

Preface

Educating students to become the scientifically and technologically literate citizens of the 21st century is the goal set forth for today's beginning science teachers. While achieving this goal is a tremendous challenge, the current science education reform has established expectations that have led to the development of frameworks, such as the *National Science Education Standards* (NSES), for making this goal a reality. Aligned with the expectations and frameworks set forth in the NSES and other reform documents are the *Standards for Science Teacher Preparation*, prepared by the National Science Teachers Association in collaboration with the Association for the Education of Teachers in Science and the National Association for Research in Science Teaching. These standards offer guidance for preparing teachers to teach in ways consistent with reform and what is known about science teaching and learning. A science teacher education program, using the *Standards for Science Teacher Preparation* as its guiding framework, should find *Science Instruction in the Middle and Secondary Schools: Developing Fundamental Knowledge and Skills for Teaching* very compatible with its efforts.

As the *Standards for Science Teacher Preparation* indicate, there is much that is expected of beginning science teachers. The expectations emanate from the science and science teaching communities, school administrators, teaching colleagues, students, and the parents and guardians of these students. The most critical of these expectations are associated with meaningful and measurable student outcomes.

In order for the students of beginning teachers to be successful science learners, we believe there are basic functions of teaching to which beginners must attend. These include *understanding the purpose of science teaching* in America's public schools; *planning science lessons* that are engaging and lead to meaningful learning; *managing the science learning environment* in ways that emphasize student self-regulation and responsibility; *assessing students' science learning* throughout the instructional process and in a variety of ways; and, of course, *teaching students through a process that is both active and personally rewarding*. Only after attending to these basic functions of teaching are preservice teachers ready and able to refine their understandings of other important topics germane to science teaching and learning.

Our initial focus on the basic functions of science teaching is not new nor is it innovative, but it is right for our times. Many beginning science teachers are learning to teach as employees of schools. Fewer and fewer are graduates of traditional science teacher education programs where time is available for exploration of and reflection on science teaching before being engaged as full-time teachers. *Science Instruction in the Middle and Secondary Schools* is designed to provide the initial scaffolding needed by beginning teachers who are attempting to learn about science education prior to employment or while fully employed. Also, the text is designed to extend the learning opportunities of beginning teachers who understand and can enact the basics of science teaching and learning.

New to This Edition

This edition includes several new features. The most prominent of these are the first six chapters. Besides highlighting the initial thoughts and actions of beginning science teachers, these chapters focus on what we view as basic functions of science teaching—purpose, planning, teaching, managing, and assessing. Each chapter begins with a vignette that showcases the experiences of a beginning science teacher related to the topic of the chapter. The vignettes have been written to draw the user into each of the six chapters and to serve as referents for many of the points of discussion.

Three chapters also include tools to help the beginning teacher think deeply about aspects of science teaching and learning. *Chapter 1, "Thoughts and Actions of Beginning Science Teachers,"* includes a Science Teaching Inventory, modeled after an inventory prepared by Carl Glickman for instructional supervisors. Intended to be self-administered and self-scored, the inventory is useful for assessing beginning teachers' beliefs about science teaching and learning. A checklist for beginning science teachers to evaluate their own lesson assessment practices is included in *Chapter 6, "Assessing Science Lessons."* The three sections of the checklist focus on assessment practices that should be addressed before, during, and after a lesson. And, *Chapter 7, "The Nature of Science,"* includes a true-false quiz that addresses a number of common misconceptions about the nature of science, based primarily on the work of William McComas. The answer key for the quiz and explanations that address the common misconceptions also are found in Chapter 7.

Improvements have also been made to the questions that appear in the *Assessing and Reviewing* section at the end of each chapter. These questions have been organized into three categories. The first category, *Analysis and Synthesis,* includes questions that ask students to analyze and synthesize their understandings of important concepts and skills presented in the chapter. The second and third categories of questions reflect areas of priority and are labeled *Practical Considerations* and *Developmental Considerations*—labels used by Glickman, Gordon, and Ross-Gordon in *Supervision and Instructional Leadership: A Developmental Approach.* Practical questions ask students to gather data and draw conclusions from real science teaching experiences or interactions with science teachers about their own teaching and their students' learning. Developmental questions encourage text users to reflect on their own recently constructed understandings of science teaching and to extend their knowledge based on their reading of both classic and timely works and communicating with scientists and science teaching professionals. Additionally, Internet resources have been identified throughout the text to supplement the many print-based sources of relevant science teaching information and activities.

Further improvements have been made to chapters that address teaching strategies, planning, and assessment. *Chapter 8, "Diverse Adolescent Learners and Their Schools,"* has been updated to better address the science learning needs of the diverse population of students found in today's middle and secondary schools. Modifications have been made to *Chapter 12, "Science, Technology, and Society,"* to highlight categories of STS science as described by Glen Aikenhead and how these categories reflect the importance given to STS content in the school science curriculum.

Chapter 15, "Computers and Electronic Technologies," has been rewritten to emphasize the growing uses of Internet-based resources to support science teaching and learning. And, in *Chapter 16, "Long-Term Planning and Assessment,"* the link between assessment and unit planning is made explicit. Discussed in this chapter are strategies for developing teaching units along with a variety of methods for assessing science learning and Web-based sources for locating student assessment tasks and scoring rubrics.

Users of this textbook now have a more compact instructional resource to guide the development of knowledge and skills for beginning and experienced science teachers.

Alignment with the *Standards for Science Teacher Preparation*

Science Instruction in the Middle and Secondary Schools includes information and experiences to support a science teacher education program intent on teachers being able to demonstrate their knowledge and abilities in relation to the *Standards for Science Teacher Preparation.* Resources for addressing the Standards for Nature of Science and the Standards for Inquiry are found in *Chapter 7, "The Nature of Science,"* and *Chapter 9, "Learning in Middle Grades and Secondary Schools,"* respectively. Issues related to science and technology and science-based decision-making, central to the Standards for Issues, are discussed in *Chapter 12, "Science, Technology, and Society."*

The Standards for Teaching are addressed in a number of chapters throughout the text, including the six new introductory chapters as well as *Chapter 8, "Diverse Adolescent Learners and Their Schools,"* *Chapter 11, "Discussion, Demonstration, and Lecture,"* and *Chapter 15, "Computers and Electronic Technologies."* The Standards for Curriculum, which emphasize understanding the curricular recommendations of National Science Education Standards and instructional planning, are specifically addressed in *Chapter 3, "Planning to Teach Science,"* and *Chapter 16, "Long-Term Planning and Assessment."* *Chapter 13, "Laboratory Work and Fieldwork,"* addresses many aspects of the Standards for Community.

Important issues and concepts related to ongoing assessment, multiple assessment tools, and curricular alignment highlighted in the Standards for Assessment are the focus of *Chapter 5, "Managing the Science Learning Environment,"* and *Chapter 16, "Long-Term Planning and Assessment."* *Chapter 14, "Safety in the Laboratory and Classroom,"* covers the Standards for Safety.

Conspicuously absent from the list of standards addressed within the pages of *Science Instruction in the Middle and Secondary Schools* are the Standards for Science Content. While this text is ripe with examples that touch on the science content typically taught in middle and secondary schools, the understandings, skills, and dispositions associated with the Standards for Science Content are best developed in science courses, laboratories, and field work. Indeed, it is these understandings, skills, and dispositions that serve as the foundation for science teacher education.

Acknowledgments

Over the past 45 years, many people have contributed to this science methods textbook. We certainly need to thank Alfred Collette and Walter Thurber for initiating the book with its first edition in 1959. Since that time, many colleagues and students have given their suggestions. Following are some of the individuals to whom we are indebted for the important ideas they provided for the current edition. Marcia Fetters, Western Michigan University; Anita Greenwood, University of Massachusetts–Lowell; Linda Jones, University of Florida; Andrew C. Kemp, University of Louisville; Terrie L. Kielborn, State University of West Georgia; George Ladd, Boston College; William H. Leonard, Clemson University; David W. McMullen, Bradley University; Anita Roychoudhury, The Ohio State University; Barbara A. Salyer, University of South Alabama; Scott Robinson, SUNY–Brockport; Ted J. Singletary, Boise State University; Kathryn Watkins, University of New Mexico; Donald L. Williams, Sterling College; and Heather Wilson, Utah Valley State College.

Coauthor Eugene Chiappetta would like to give special thanks to the following:

Jill Bailer, an outstanding middle school science teacher in the Houston Independent School District, provided many insights into middle school teaching and learning, as well as assistance in obtaining photographs of students engaging in science activities.

David Fillman, Director of Science for Galena Park Independent School District, examined several chapters and offered good suggestions.

The science department at Spring Woods Senior High School, Spring Branch Independent School District, especially the Science Department Chairperson, Virginia Tucker; science teachers Myra Garza, Ann Brown, Deborah Wilkes, and Bruce Ferland; and principal Wayne Schaper, Jr. These educators permitted me to study science in their classrooms, take photographs of students learning science, and teach science methods courses in their science classrooms in order to provide an authentic setting for these experiences for pre-service and in-service science teachers.

Barbara Chiappetta was always willing to proofread yet another chapter and to print many digital photographs for this edition.

Coauthor Tom Koballa would like to thank the following individuals:

David Jackson, University of Georgia, for providing feedback on and offering additions to the "Computers and Electronic Technology" chapter.

Mary Atwater, University of Georgia, for her recommendations on aspects of multicultural science education addressed in the chapter on "Diverse Adolescent Learners and Their Schools."

Steve Thompson, an extraordinary physics teacher, for his insights regarding classroom management highlighted in *Chapter 5, "Managing the Science Learning Environment."*

Lisa Anderson, Kevin McReynolds, Chris Cook, and Kim Harmelink for their assistance with photographs of teachers and students, as well as Shawn Glynn for his guidance and the fine photographs that appear in this edition.

Also, special thanks to Dava Coleman for proofreading and suggesting improvements to several of the chapters.

Discover the Companion Website Accompanying This Book

THE PRENTICE HALL COMPANION WEBSITE: A VIRTUAL LEARNING ENVIRONMENT

Technology is a constantly growing and changing aspect of our field that is creating a need for content and resources. To address this emerging need, Prentice Hall has developed an online learning environment for students and professors alike—Companion Websites—to support our textbooks.

In creating a Companion Website, our goal is to build on and enhance what the textbook already offers. For this reason, the content for each user-friendly website is organized by topic and provides the professor and student with a variety of meaningful resources. Common features of a Companion Website include:

FOR THE PROFESSOR—

Every Companion Website integrates **Syllabus Manager™,** an online syllabus creation and management utility.

- **Syllabus Manager™** provides you, the instructor, with an easy, step-by-step process to create and revise syllabi, with direct links into Companion Website and other online content without having to learn HTML.
- Students may logon to your syllabus during any study session. All they need to know is the web address for the Companion Website and the password you've assigned to your syllabus.
- After you have created a syllabus using **Syllabus Manager™,** students may enter the syllabus for their course section from any point in the Companion Website.
- Clicking on a date, the student is shown the list of activities for the assignment. The activities for each assignment are linked directly to actual content, saving time for students.

- Adding assignments consists of clicking on the desired due date, then filling in the details of the assignment—name of the assignment, instructions, and whether or not it is a one-time or repeating assignment.
- In addition, links to other activities can be created easily. If the activity is online, a URL can be entered in the space provided, and it will be linked automatically in the final syllabus.
- Your completed syllabus is hosted on our servers, allowing convenient updates from any computer on the Internet. Changes you make to your syllabus are immediately available to your students at their next logon.

FOR THE STUDENT—

- **Topic Overviews**—Outline key concepts in topic areas.
- **Activities and Lesson Plans**—A collection of annotated links to a variety of meaningful science lessons and activities available on the Web. This module also includes useful web links related to national science teaching standards.
- **Web Links**—Topic-specific lists of links to websites that feature current information and resources for educators.
- **Electronic Bluebook**—Send homework or essays directly to your instructor's email with this paperless form.
- **Message Board**—Virtual bulletin board to post or respond to questions or comments from a national audience.
- **Chat**—Real-time chat with anyone who is using the text anywhere in the country—ideal for discussion and study groups, class projects, etc.

To take advantage of these and other resources, please visit the *Science Instruction in the Middle and Secondary Schools,* Sixth Edition, Companion Website at **www.prenhall.com/chiappetta**

Educator Learning Center: An Invaluable Online Resource

Merrill Education and the Association for Supervision and Curriculum Development (ASCD) invite you to take advantage of a new online resource, one that provides access to the top research and proven strategies associated with ASCD and Merrill—the Educator Learning Center. At www.educatorlearningcenter.com, you will find resources that will enhance your students' understanding of course topics and of current educational issues, in addition to being invaluable for further research.

HOW THE EDUCATOR LEARNING CENTER WILL HELP YOUR STUDENTS BECOME BETTER TEACHERS

With the combined resources of Merrill Education and ASCD, you and your students will find a wealth of tools and materials to better prepare them for the classroom.

RESEARCH

- More than 600 articles from the ASCD journal *Educational Leadership* discuss everyday issues faced by practicing teachers.
- A direct link on the site to Research Navigator™ gives students access to many of the leading education journals, as well as extensive content detailing the research process.
- Excerpts from Merrill Education texts give your students insights on important topics of instructional methods, diverse populations, assessment, classroom management, technology, and refining classroom practice.

CLASSROOM PRACTICE

- Hundreds of lesson plans and teaching strategies are categorized by content area and age range.
- Case studies and classroom video footage provide virtual field experience for student reflection.
- Computer simulations and other electronic tools keep your students abreast of today's classrooms and current technologies.

LOOK INTO THE VALUE OF EDUCATOR LEARNING CENTER YOURSELF

A four-month subscription to Educator Learning Center is $25 but is **FREE** when packaged with any Merrill Education text. In order for your students to have access to this site, you must use this special value-pack ISBN number **WHEN** placing your textbook order with the bookstore: 013-1954296. Your students will then receive a copy of the text packaged with a free ASCD pincode. To preview the value of this website to you and your students, please go to www.educatorlearningcenter.com and click on "Demo."

Brief Contents

Contents

Chapter 14
Safety in the Laboratory and Classroom 224

Chapter 15
Computers and Electronic Technologies 246

Chapter 16
Long-Term Planning and Assessment 262

Appendices

I n d e x

Note: Every effort has been made to provide accurate and current Internet information in this book. However, the Internet and information posted on it are constantly changing, and it is inevitable that some of the Internet addresses listed in this textbook will change.

Part One

GETTING INTO SCIENCE TEACHING QUICKLY

1

Thoughts and Actions of Beginning Science Teachers

Beginning teachers are faced with many challenges for which they may not be prepared.

Let's look into the classroom of a beginning science teacher who is teaching ninth-grade physical science in a large urban high school. Ms. Melissa Longorio has a degree in biology but was assigned to teach physical science classes in addition to biology, a frequent practice of administrators hiring new teachers. Ms. Longorio is presenting the first lesson on acids and bases, one of the topics in the chemistry portion of the physical science course.

The bell rings, and Ms. Longorio finds herself attempting to get students into the classroom and into their seats. Then, she begins to take roll by calling out students by name:

This logo appears throughout the chapter to indicate where vignettes are integrated with chapter content.

Ms. Longorio: *Martin! Martin, are you here today?*

Martin: *Yes, Ms. Longorio.*

Ms. Longorio: *Juanita!*

Deborah: *She's here at school today. I saw her, but she's not here. You know what I mean.*

Ms. Longorio: *Thanks Deborah, but I need to hear from you only when I call your name. Julio!*

Julio: *A qui.*

Attendance checking continues as the teacher attempts to determine who is present for the day's lesson. As she calls the roll, students are talking and moving about the classroom visiting with their friends. Finally, after several minutes of this activity, Ms. Longorio is ready to start the lesson for the day, which is on acids and bases.

Ms. Longorio begins with a lecture on pH, which she prepared using notes from her college chemistry course. She attempts to explain the mathematical concept of pH, which is the negative logarithm of the hydrogen ion concentration, using the mathematical formula:

$$pH = -log[H^+]$$

The teacher stresses the importance of understanding mathematical relationships in science. She asks the students "What is a log?" This brings some giggling and laughing among the students.

Frankie: *A log is something that you throw in a fire. My mother bought some of those magic logs from Wal-Mart. They make a great fire.*

Ms. Longorio: *Frankie, stop trying to be funny. Who else has an idea of what a log is?*

Janice: *It is something that comes from a tree.*

Ms. Longorio: *That is not the kind of log I'm thinking about. Remember, we're dealing with science and math. I should have said, logarithm. It's a mathematical relationship that we can use to discuss the strengths of acids and bases.*

Angela: *Why do we have to do math in this class, it's a science class? Besides, we have not studied anything about logs or whatever you call 'em in algebra class.*

After a few more minutes of discussion, the teacher realizes that the students do not have a clue about logarithms and feels that she should take up another aspect of the topic. Then, Ms. Longorio decides to give the students a summary of the three theories of acids and bases, which she writes on the board and reminds students to record in their notebooks:

Arrhenius Theory   *An acid is a compound that gives up hydrogen ions [H^+] in solution, and a base is a compound that gives up hydroxide ions [OH^-] in solution.*

Bronsted Lowry Theory   *An acid is a hydrogen ion [H^+] donor, and a base is a hydrogen ion [H^+] acceptor.*

Lewis Theory   *An acid is a substance that can accept a pair of electrons to form a covalent bond, and a base is a substance that can donate a pair of electrons to form a covalent bond.*

As Ms. Longorio provides some details on the similarities and differences among the three theories, the students begin to get restless and talk among themselves. The teacher has to remind the students that this is important material and will be covered on the test. Realizing that this aspect of the topic is not keeping students' attention, she decides to give them the formulas for some common acids and bases and suggests that these are the ones that they should memorize:

Acids: HCl, H_2SO_4, HNO_3, and CH_3COOH

Bases: KOH, NaOH, NH_3, and $Ca(OH)_2$

Before Ms. Longorio can complete her discussion on disassociation of common acids and bases, the bell rings and the students charge for the door. She never had an opportunity to present the material she had prepared on the dissociation of acids and neutralization reactions or to tell the students to read the textbook chapter on acids and bases and answer certain questions at the end of the chapter.

AIMS OF THE CHAPTER

Use the questions that follow to guide your thinking and learning about some fundamental aspects of science teaching:

- What beliefs do many *uninformed* beginning science teachers hold that may lead to ineffective teaching?

- What beliefs do many *informed* beginning science teachers hold that result in successful science teaching?

- What five basic teaching functions must beginning teachers focus on and develop competencies in if they want to be effective in the classroom?

Most people with a college degree feel that they can teach. This view is reasonable because it has been formed as a result of at least 16 years in the classroom. Those who have logged in thousands of hours sitting in classes have formed many ideas about teaching based on a great deal of experience. A common belief among these educated people is,

"I can teach, and probably better than most teachers who have taught me."

However, the truth of the matter is that successful teaching is far more complex and difficult than most people realize.

The stories of classroom veterans as well as people who have quit teaching make it clear—teaching, especially science teaching, is not easy. Beginning science teachers often struggle in the classroom. Their notions of how to instruct students are less effective than they ever expected. This is evidenced by student behavior during instruction and student performance on chapter and unit tests. Students are frequently inattentive and often disruptive in the classrooms of "new teachers." Further, scores on tests and exams are lower than desired.

Stop and Reflect!

- What are some of the challenges that you associate with being a new science teacher?

- Why do you think that beginning teachers find teaching so challenging? Make a list of your reasons.

- Make a list of the beliefs about science teaching that may cause a new science teacher to be unsuccessful in his or her work.

THOUGHTS AND ACTIONS OF BEGINNING SCIENCE TEACHERS

The challenges facing beginning science teachers are many, but they are not insurmountable. The remaining sections of this chapter will highlight critical features of science teaching that beginning teachers should consider. These features are: *purpose, planning, teaching, management,* and *assessment.* To help develop a mind-set for science teaching, the discussion will contrast the thoughts and actions of many uninformed people who are beginning their career in the classroom with those who have reflected carefully about what is required to be an effective science teacher. Please reacquaint yourself with the vignette at the front of this chapter in order to prepare for a discussion of how a beginning science teacher might instruct students.

Purpose

In order to benefit from this discussion, write down several sentences that you think capture the purpose of Ms. Longorio's lesson on acids and bases. Then, let's listen in on a conversation between Ms. Longorio and her school-based mentor, Mrs. Reed, to learn what Ms. Longorio thought about the lesson's purpose.

MRS. REED: Melissa, how do you feel about your lesson?

MS. LONGORIO: It was bad!

MRS. REED: What do you mean?

MS. LONGORIO: Well, you know. These kids didn't get it. They are not interested in this stuff.

MRS. REED: Okay. What was your *purpose* for teaching this introductory lesson on acids and bases?

MS. LONGORIO: I read through the textbook chapter and my college chemistry notes to identify what I thought these kids should know. I wanted them to understand pH, acid-base theories, and dissociation, but you saw what happened.

MRS. REED: Yes, but let's back up and think about teaching science in general to young people. What was your *purpose for this lesson?*

MS. LONGORIO: My purpose was to teach them a certain amount of subject matter, especially the main ideas, and to cover it during the period.

MRS. REED: Do you feel maybe you selected the wrong concepts to teach for this first lesson on acids and bases?

MS. LONGORIO: What do you mean?

MRS. REED: For this lesson, you should consider the district's physical science course syllabus in which the unit begins with a review of the properties of acids and bases. The reason is, we have found that these students need to begin their learning with concrete ideas and to review what they may or should have had in middle school. Therefore, we recommend addressing the properties of acids and bases, which focus on naturally occurring acids and bases, ones that the kids might have experience with such as fruits and household cleaning agents, and how acids and bases react with litmus paper. In this way, you will be teaching a concept or principle in the syllabus that students might connect with and find meaningful. Your intent should be to help students grasp a few concrete concepts before getting into more abstract and complex ideas that may turn them off to the lesson. Also, when you introduce a new unit, it is helpful to provide students with an overview of the content that they will find meaningful.

At this point, it should be evident that the beginning teacher holds beliefs concerning the purpose of the lesson that caused her to be less effective than she and her mentor desired. She thought the purpose for the lesson was to get right to the heart of the subject matter and to make students understand acids and bases—pH, theories, and disassociation—and to be sure to cover this chunk of subject matter during the class period. However, experience has taught Mrs. Reed that introducing a new science topic to adolescents should take a different approach. A more informed teacher's thinking would cause him or her to provide students with a concrete overview of the topic in order to draw them into the instruction, building on what they already know.

The purpose that a teacher has for a science lesson directly affects how she will plan and teach and also what students will learn. We will go into a more in-depth discussion of the purposes and many dimensions of science teaching in the middle and secondary schools in the next chapter.

Planning

Appropriate planning certainly ranks as one of the most important teaching functions. This activity provides a scheme for accomplishing a set of learning outcomes. Teaching plans lay down a blueprint that gives vision, organization, and coherence to classroom instruction and student learning. This activity requires considerable thought and creativity. It is obvious when a teacher, especially a beginning teacher, has not planned well, because the instruction results in a lack of student engagement and little learning.

Science teachers must plan frequently and thoroughly in order to be successful. Further, their purpose must be to engage students in activities that are instructive and meaningful and that help students to construct important concepts and develop useful skills.

Stop and Reflect!

- What do you think was the purpose of Ms. Longorio's lesson plan on acids and bases?
- How was the purpose of the lesson reflected in the teacher's planning?

During the post-lesson discussion between Ms. Longorio and her mentor teacher, it became evident that the beginning teacher's planning needed a new direction. When Mrs. Reed asked Ms. Longorio how she planned the lesson, the response was that she: (a) focused on conveying subject matter from the textbook, and (b) organized the lecture notes over the text material written in the chapter. Mrs. Reed responded to this plan by suggesting that Ms. Longorio take a different approach when introducing a new topic to students.

The mentor teacher emphasized that Ms. Longorio should identify what students might find meaningful in the content of the lesson, then begin with what students can relate to, given their prior experiences inside and outside of school. With this in mind, select more than one instructional activity to engage students. Then, describe the activities in order to project how long they might take, the resources needed, and other considerations. Finally, specify exactly what the students should learn from the lesson. In other words, what should students walk away from the class knowing or being able to do?

Reflect back over this brief discussion on planning and determine the extent to which it matches with what you believe about planning and the thoughts of a beginning science teacher. Your thinking will likely reveal the close link between lesson purpose and how the teacher would plan for the lesson. Later in this textbook, you will find an entire chapter devoted to planning to teach science, which goes into greater depth on this topic and can prepare you for lesson and unit planning in the middle and high schools.

Teaching

Most people consider teaching as *the* major activity of a teacher. Teaching, or instruction, as it is often called, is what people usually think of when they visualize the classroom. Teaching initiates and guides learning. This basic function can take many forms, such as lecture, discussion, demonstration, laboratory work, guided reading, simulation, and so on. Let's return to the conversation between the beginning science teacher, Melissa Longorio, and her mentor, Mrs. Reed, in order to understand what Melissa was thinking about with regard to her teaching.

MRS. REED: Melissa, what was your instructional plan for this lesson?

MS. LONGORIO: Well, I wanted to give the kids some information about acids and bases.

MRS. REED: What methods or techniques did you use in the lesson?

MS. LONGORIO: I used lecture and the board to present the information. I also asked the students questions.

MRS. REED: While I think that the lecture along with questions and answers is a good instructional strategy, you should consider other approaches as well.

MS. LONGORIO: What do you mean? Some of the best teachers that I had in high school and college gave good lectures.

MRS. REED: For many of the students enrolled in middle and high school science in this district,

science is a subject they have to take and school is a place to show up everyday. They do not value learning. Their knowledge of science is poor, as are their reading and writing skills. Consequently, many of us in the district have learned to use a variety of teaching skills and strategies to actively engage students in learning science and to stimulate interest in the subject.

MS. LONGORIO: How would you have taught this lesson?

MRS. REED: First, I would consider using a combination of these strategies: lecture and discussion, demonstration, simulation, and laboratory exercises. Second, I would select two or three of the strategies in order to draw students into the lesson and to keep their attention throughout the period. Third, I would use questioning to determine what students know so that I could build on their backgrounds and preferences. Finally, I would use techniques that encourage students to think deeply about certain aspects of acids and bases.

When we analyze the instruction of this beginning science teacher, it becomes evident that her approach is limited. Presentation of information and asking some questions is not effective. When teachers attempt to orally transmit concepts that are new to students, often the students do not assimilate much of the information.

How might a more informed science teacher approach this lesson? As pointed out earlier, the focus of the lesson should be different. It should be more concrete and engaging. Consider the following recommendations, which might illustrate a more informed approach to science instruction for a beginning teacher:

a. **Question-and-Answers.** Begin the lesson with questions to determine what students know about acids and bases. Ask questions to ascertain prior knowledge about acids and bases, and include some open-ended questions to gain students' perspectives regarding this branch of chemistry.

b. **Chemistry Demonstration.** Provide samples of common household items such as foods, medicines, and cleaning solutions as well as items found in the science laboratory. Call on students to identify acids and bases, discuss their uses, and describe their properties.

c. **Presentation of Information.** Give a brief overview of important acids and bases and their properties in order to organize students' thinking.

The act of teaching is multifaceted and requires careful consideration of students' prior knowledge and their abilities. While there is no best approach to teaching, some approaches are better than others for a given situation, depending on the students and the desired learning outcomes. You will learn more about teaching skills, instructional strategies, and learning techniques in Chapter 4 on teaching science.

Management

Classroom management is the number one concern of beginning teachers. Although they have spent many years learning about the content they will teach and perhaps many years working with the content in a real-world business or industrial setting, they have had little practice at managing the learning of others and dealing with adolescent students who make up today's diverse society. The task of guiding the learning of 25 or 30 middle or high school students in a science classroom or laboratory can be extremely challenging, requiring understanding to make good management decisions.

Many classroom management decisions must be made in advance of the actual lesson as part of the lesson. Others are made in the midst of the instruction. In either case, the teacher's decisions must be directed toward developing a classroom environment where students learn, feel safe, and assume responsibility for their own actions.

Ms. Longorio and Mrs. Reed also addressed issues of classroom management during their post-lesson conversation. Let's eavesdrop in on a part of their conversation:

MS. LONGORIO: I am really disappointed in the students' behavior. Some of them were talking and not taking notes while I was lecturing. And did you see how they all ran for the door as soon as the bell rang? I didn't even have a chance to tell them what I wanted them to do for homework.

MRS. REED: Yes, I observed that and I share your disappointment. You know, it would be so easy to blame the students for their actions and come down on them hard tomorrow, but let's think about some of the things that you could have done to make the class run more smoothly. For instance, you said you didn't have time to give the homework assignment. What could you have done to provide yourself with more instructional time? Begin by telling me how you started the class period.

MS. LONGORIO: Well, I started by calling the roll. It took me exactly 5 minutes. I know it took me 5 minutes because I checked my watch when I got to Jessie Zegato's name, and his is the last one on my grade roll.

MRS. REED: That's quite a lot of time to check attendance, even though you have 32 students in the class. Now, tell me what the students were doing while you were calling the roll.

MS. LONGORIO: Most were taking out their textbooks and notebooks and talking. A couple of students were sharpening pencils, and I saw Kiki and Marvin arguing about something. I had to stop twice and tell Marvin to return to his seat on the other side of the room.

MRS. REED: I hear you saying that the students were not engaged in any learning activities during the first 5 minutes of class. If you check attendance this way every day, you will have lost, let me do the math here, 900 minutes or 15 hours of instructional time by the end of the school year. Is this a good thing?

MS. LONGORIO: Of course not. I never thought of calling roll in terms of lost instructional time. Perhaps I should develop a seating chart and check attendance using it, like I saw Mr. Jefferson do when I observed his biology class.

MRS. REED: Good idea! Checking attendance using a seating chart is exactly what I would recommend. However, this will also take some time. What could students be doing while you're checking attendance?

MS. LONGORIO: Well, I guess I need to give them something to do. But, I'm not sure what.

MRS. REED: One strategy is to have students respond to two to three questions on something you taught about acids and bases the day before. You can write the questions on a transparency in advance, place the transparency on the overhead projector before the tardy bell rings, and instruct students to begin answering the questions. With students engaged, you should have time to check attendance and deal with other housekeeping chores at the start of the period. This means no lost instructional time.

MS. LONGORIO: Hey, I could also write the day's homework assignment on the transparency and tell students to copy it into their notebooks. This would solve the problem of students leaving class without their homework assignment.

MRS. REED: Now you're getting the idea.

You can sense from this exchange that classroom management has a lot more to do with making decisions about classroom procedures and routines than disciplining students who misbehave. When students know what is expected of them and procedures and routines are in place, students often will rise to meet those expectations, resulting in a more effective lesson. More information about how to manage the science learning environment is presented in Chapter 5.

Stop and Reflect!

- If you were in Ms. Longorio's place, how would you have responded to Mrs. Reed's recommendations for improving the classroom environment?
- What recommendations would you add to those offered by Mrs. Reed?

Assessment

Based on their own school experiences, most people think of assessment as testing and giving grades. These are activities that are considered only at the end of an instructional unit. Testing requires administering and scoring a paper-and-pencil test that includes a selection of multiple-choice and true-false items along with a few short-answer or essay questions. Test development may involve choosing items from a test bank provided with the textbook program. And grading is often thought of as a bias-free way of segregating students along the A to F continuum.

In actuality, assessment must be an ongoing activity that is an integral part of the teaching and learning process. A beginning teacher may wish to check on student progress to inform their learning and his or her teaching, or he or she may wish to diagnose students' understanding about a topic before beginning a new unit of instruction. These kinds of assessments provide the teacher with feedback useful for determining which students need help and for improving the quality of instruction. A comprehensive assessment effort couples these kinds of assessments with an overall determination of achievement and grades.

Let's listen in on part of the post-lesson conference between Ms. Longorio and Mrs. Reed in which they discuss issues of assessment:

MRS. REED: Melissa, tell me how you will determine what your students have learned about acids and bases.

MS. LONGORIO: Well, I plan to give them a test next Wednesday. That will give us 4 days on acids and bases, with one of those days spent in the lab. By then, the students should know all I want them to know about acids and bases.

MRS. REED: So, what do you think your students learned from today's lesson?

MS. LONGORIO: I lectured about pH and the three theories of acids and bases. I also gave the students formulas for some common acids and bases for them to memorize.

MRS. REED: That's what *you* did today, but what did your students learn?

MS. LONGORIO: To be honest with you, I'm not really sure what they learned today.

MRS. REED: Okay, let's think about what you could have done to find out what they learned as a result of your teaching.

MS. LONGORIO: Well, I guess I could have given them a pop quiz at the end of the period. But, in order to do that, I would have had to restructure my lesson to allow time for the quiz.

MRS. REED: A short quiz at the end of the period is not a bad idea, and you are right about the need to restructure your lesson to allow time for the quiz. You could do the quiz in 5 minutes or less. Some of the teachers in the department regularly give short quizzes at the end of class. Ms. Bennett, who teaches chemistry, calls the end-of-class quiz the students' "ticket out the door." Her students must hand in their quiz papers before they leave the classroom. Other teachers in our department don't give end-of-class quizzes. Instead, they ask questions throughout their lessons, have students construct concept maps or drawings, or allow students to perform dramatic role-plays to assess learning.

But since you suggested giving a pop quiz, let's think about questions that you might have asked to find out what your students learned. Based on the content of today's lesson, you could have asked, let me think now, "What is the hydrogen-ion concentration for a solution with the pH value of 5?" and perhaps, "How are acids and bases defined by the Lewis theory?" Of course, you would want to have these questions written down before the start of the lesson to make sure that they are worded well and reflect what you expect students to know or be able to do.

MS. LONGORIO: So, from the students' answers to these questions, I can find out what they learned from my lesson. I don't have to wait until the unit test to find out what they learned and didn't learn.

MRS. REED: That's right! The students' answers to the quiz can tell you what they learned and more. Say, 28 out of the 32 students in your class gave incorrect responses to the question about the Lewis theory. What does this tell you about your teaching?

MS. LONGORIO: Well, it tells me that maybe I didn't do such a good job. Maybe I would need to re-teach the Lewis theory and perhaps the Arrhenius and Bronsted-Lowry theories, as well.

MRS. REED: I agree. And, as you think about re-teaching the acid-base theories, you may wish to consider other ways to help students learn the content rather than just teaching it the same way you did today. Try to recall what helped you understand the distinguishing features of the three theories and what made your learning about acids and bases interesting and enjoyable. Doing this may suggest other ways to re-teach this content.

Ms. Longorio: Mrs. Reed, I'm beginning to understand that assessment has multiple purposes. Assessment is not only for giving student grades, but it can help me improve my teaching.

Mrs. Reed: You're right, Melissa, and well-constructed assessments, like the questions we discussed, are most useful when they correspond with the standards or objectives that guide your lessons and when you teach in ways that are in alignment with your assessment.

As Mrs. Reed spoke, she illustrated this final point for Melissa with the sketch shown in Figure 1.1.

As the conversation between Ms. Longorio and her mentor, Mrs. Reed, reveals, assessment is one of the most sophisticated teaching functions. Well-constructed assessments can serve many purposes, including improving instructional practices, reinforcing learning outcomes, and assessing student understandings and skills. As you will learn in Chapter 6, there is no one best way to assess the outcomes of learning. A multitude of assessment methods exist for use in science classrooms.

INFORMED AND UNINFORMED SCIENCE TEACHING

Melissa Longorio's lesson on acids and bases and her post-lesson conversation with her mentor, Mrs. Reed, reveal much about science teaching. Science teaching is much more than the teacher telling students what she thinks they should know. Teaching science in today's middle and high schools also involves considering the

FIGURE 1.1 Mrs. Reed's illustration of the relationships between standards, teaching, and assessment.

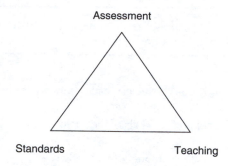

lesson's purpose, planning the lesson well, managing the classroom environment, and assessing student learning.

The post-lesson conversation between Ms. Longorio and Mrs. Reed also highlights differences in understanding and skills associated with science teaching. Mrs. Reed's classroom experience and ability to reflect on her teaching enable her to see potential lesson weaknesses and to make decisions that will likely lead to greater student learning. This knowledge base for science teaching is called *pedagogical content knowledge,* a special amalgam of content and pedagogy that is uniquely the province of teachers (Shulman, 1987, p. 8).

Of course, it is not expected that a beginning teacher will think about teaching and student learning in the same way that a veteran teacher would. However, by carefully considering the five basic elements of teaching discussed in this chapter, the beginner will be more apt to enter the science classroom prepared to meet the many challenges associated with teaching. It is the nature and depth of understanding associated with the five basic elements of teaching that distinguishes the *informed* science teacher from one who is *uninformed.* The thoughts and actions about science teaching commonly held by many informed beginning science teachers and many uninformed beginning science teachers are presented in Table 1.1

TABLE 1.1   A Comparison Between the Thoughts and Actions of Many Uniformed and Informed Beginning Science Teachers

Thoughts and Actions of Many Uninformed Beginning Science Teachers	Thoughts and Actions of Many Informed Beginning Science Teachers
Purpose	
To convey chunks of subject matter from the textbook.	To teach a few concepts or principles from the course syllabus.
To get right into the details of the subject.	To provide a meaningful overview of content to be highlighted: "Why are we learning this?"
To cover a certain amount of material.	To help students grasp a few concepts well and to spark interest.
Planning	
Focuses on covering textbook chapter material.	Identifies what students may find meaningful about the core concepts or principles.
Organizes lecture notes over the content.	Outlines several instructional activities.
Assumes students understand what should be learned.	Specifies the intended learning outcomes for each lesson.
Teaching	
Attempts to transfer information to students.	Engages students in thinking and finding out through use of questions and other means.
Asks students to take notes and to remember what they hear and see written.	Asks students to explain their understandings.
Management	
Attempts to keep students in their seats.	Provides opportunities for active student learning.
Makes students listen and follow instruction.	Gives students opportunities to express their ideas.
Disciplines students who misbehave.	Encourages students to monitor their own behavior.
Assessment	
Rarely checks for student learning during instruction.	Reviews to check on student learning.
Uses mostly paper-and-pencil tests to determine grades.	Uses multiple methods to determine what students know and can do.
Fails to use test results and grades to evaluate teaching effectiveness.	Considers student performance to gauge teaching effectiveness and improve instruction.

FIGURE 1.2   Science Teaching Inventory.

This inventory was developed for individuals interested in a career in science teaching to assess their beliefs about science teaching and learning. The inventory assumes that beginning science teachers believe and act based on recollections of their own science learning experiences and their knowledge of today's adolescent learners, schools, and contemporary thinking about science teaching and learning. The inventory is intended to be self-administered and self-scored.

Directions: Choose either A or B for each item. Even though you may not completely agree with either choice, select the one that mostly closely matches your thinking.

1. A. The purpose of science teaching is to transmit subject matter knowledge to students.
   B. The purpose of science teaching is to help students develop scientific understanding.

2. A. Science lessons should be content-centered and sequential.
   B. Science lessons should be flexible and inquiry-centered.

3. A. The teacher is solely responsible for science lesson and unit planning.
   B. The teacher should solicit input from students when planning science lessons and units.

4. A. The big ideas of science should be the focus of science instruction.
   B. The focus of science instruction should be discrete chunks of content.

5. A. The starting point for instruction should be students' science misconceptions.
   B. When starting a lesson, a teacher should assume that students have no conceptions of the content to be taught.

6. A. The outcome of science teaching is students knowing more content.
   B. The outcome of science teaching is students knowing less content in greater depth.

7. A. The subject matter students learn in science class is applied in the class context, including tests and projects.
   B. The subject matter students learn in science class is used to make sense of the world.

8. A. In science class, assessment is distinct from learning.
   B. In science class, assessment is integrated with learning.

9. A. The purpose of assessment is to understand students' constructions of knowledge.
   B. The purpose of assessment is to measure science learning and grade students.

10. A. The function of laboratory and fieldwork is to verify concepts taught in class.
    B. Laboratory and fieldwork can be used to introduce concepts that students will encounter later in class.

11. A. Student obedience is the centerpiece of science classroom management.
    B. Science classroom management emphasizes student responsibility.

12. A. Sound instructional planning will lessen classroom management problems.
    B. Student discipline problems can be curtailed by establishing enforceable classroom and laboratory rules.

Note: The scoring key can be found in Appendix D.

ASSESSING AND REVIEWING

Analysis and Synthesis

1. Respond to the "Science Teaching Inventory" presented in Figure 1.2. What do your responses tell you about your own thoughts concerning science teaching and possible actions in the science classroom? See how your responses compare with those of other beginning science teachers.

2. Suppose you are in a teaching position similar to that of Ms. Longorio's and teaching the first lesson in a science unit (you pick the topic). Describe your lesson purpose and how you would plan for the lesson. Include in your description some ideas about how you might align your objectives, instruction, and assessment.

3. Most people who choose to become teachers did well in school and have developed an interest in the science content they hope to teach. Think about a science topic that you find particularly interesting. What life events triggered your interest in the topic? How might you go about developing interest in this topic among middle or high school students? What relationship do you see between interest and learning?

4. Read Professor Lee Shulman's seminar article, "Knowledge and Teaching: Foundations of the New Reform" in *Harvard Educational Review* (1987, Volume 57, Issue 1, pgs. 1–22). What is your understanding about the knowledge base for science teaching? How is your understanding similar to and different from those presented by Shulman? Write a report that summarizes your thoughts about the information presented in this article.

5. Write an autobiographical essay in which you discuss your experiences in school and work that led you to consider science teaching as a profession. Conclude your essay by speculating about the influence of your background on your career as a science teacher.

Practical Considerations

6. Prepare for and teach a 10-minute lesson on a science topic that you know a lot about. The students for your lesson could be other beginning teachers or adolescents. (Adolescents willing to collaborate may be identified by contacting leaders of after-school programs and youth centers.) Videotape the lesson and view it by yourself or with a friend. Write a short critique of the lesson. Put the videotape and critique in a place for safekeeping. You will want to view your tape and read your critique several months from now to gauge your development as a science teacher.

7. Make arrangements to observe a lesson taught by a veteran middle or high school science teacher and to speak with the teacher after the lesson. Ask the teacher about the lesson's purpose, planning, instruction, classroom management, and assessment. Write a paragraph about your experience in which you compare your thoughts about the lesson with those of the teacher. Share your paragraph with other beginning teachers.

8. Conduct interviews with two first-year science teachers and ask them about the joys and challenges that they associate with their jobs. Write a report summarizing the teachers' responses and giving your opinion about whether you share their ideas regarding the joys and challenges of science teaching.

9. Interview a science teacher who has served as the mentor for beginning teachers in the past. Ask the teacher about his or her expectations for a beginning science teacher in the areas of lesson planning, instruction, classroom management, and learning assessment. Prepare a report summarizing your findings and drawing conclusions regarding your own preparation for science teaching.

Developmental Considerations

10. The National Science Teachers Association (NSTA) is the largest organization in the world committed to the advancement of science teaching. Access the NSTA website (www.nsta.org) and check out its teacher resources, events for science teachers, and professional journals—*The Science Teacher,* for high school teachers, and *Science Scope,* for middle school teachers. Join NSTA as a student member.

11. Begin a journal of how your teacher education classes and school-based experiences affect your thinking about science teaching and student learning. Make entries into the journal throughout your teacher education program.

12. Start a notebook of science teaching ideas and materials. Organize your notebook into sections (e.g., classroom management, assessment, safety, demonstrations, etc.) and add your reflections regarding the usefulness of ideas and materials included.

References

Shulman. L. (1987). Foundations of new reform. *Harvard Educational Review, 57*(1), 1–22.

The Purpose of Teaching Science

*Understanding the diverse purposes of the
American education system is critical to the
success of a beginning teacher.*

*L*et's listen in on a conversation between Mr. Clark, a newly hired sixth-grade science teacher, and Ms. Roberts, a veteran middle school science teacher and science department head. Mr. Clark has no teacher-education training and was hired by the district on an emergency certification basis because of the need for science teachers. Before taking this teaching position, he worked for an aerospace contracting company. Mr. Clark has gotten off to a bumpy start in his first few weeks of teaching and has been approached by the science department head for some guidance. Before getting into the nitty gritty of Mr. Clark's planning, teaching, and classroom management, Ms. Roberts has decided to give the new teacher an orientation on the American educational system and science education.

This logo appears throughout the chapter to indicate where vignettes are integrated with chapter content.

Ms. Roberts: Mr. Clark, have you had an opportunity to observe middle schools and middle grade students recently?

Mr. Clark: No, as I indicated in my interview for this position, I was with an aerospace company for the past 20 years traveling all over the world. When my daughter was growing up, my wife spent more time with her than I, going to school and church activities, because I traveled so much troubleshooting for my company. When I married my second wife, her children were already in high school. Therefore, I have spent no time in public schools after graduating from high school. I think that I will learn about schools in the alternative certification program in which I am enrolled.

Ms. Roberts: Okay. I am going to give you a crash course on the American school system and the purpose of science teaching. You will need this background to orient your thinking about this school, the curriculum, and the students. So tell me, what is our job with these students?

Mr. Clark: I feel that these kids need to be prepared for college and to learn science, engineering, and computer technology. They need to be taught a lot of science and math so that they can get into the hard stuff and learn to solve problems like I did when I was their age. I don't want them to be flipping hamburgers.

Ms. Roberts: This district has changed greatly over the past 20 years. When I began teaching in this school, the student body was mostly White and middle class. About 60% of the students went on to college. Today, the school is attended by mostly minority students, many of whom are on free or reduced lunch. A large percentage of the students who start the school year in the fall move elsewhere with their family before the end of the year. We worry about these kids staying in school and graduating, let alone going to college. We try to provide a learning environment that will encourage these students to want to come to school. Yes, we would like them to learn science, but we also would like them to appreciate science and how it may lead to job opportunities and even hobbies. The curriculum is broader than I believe you experienced in your schooling. We spend a great deal of time designing science courses that are tailored to the abilities and backgrounds of these students. All of the sixth-grade teachers collaborate to provide our students with a well-rounded education. We try to balance general education goals with subject-matter-specific goals that are related to science.

Mr. Clark: I am here to teach science, not reading, writing, and civics.

Ms. Roberts: I can appreciate your feelings, and I think many people enter the teaching profession with that point of view. Can I lend you my foundations of American education textbook and ask you to read just *the first chapter? This may give you a different perspective concerning general education in the public schools.*

MR. CLARK: *Sure, it can't hurt me to read one chapter.*

After listening in on the conversation between the inexperienced and the experienced teacher, it should be obvious that Mr. Clark must change his beliefs and orientation regarding the purpose of schooling. Without a sense of the broad goals that should be used to guide a general education, the uniformed science teacher will experience more difficulty in his first year of teaching mid-level students. Further, without this orientation to the American public school system, Mr. Clark will be out of line with the expectations of the school and the district in which he teaches.

"The American Public School has always carried a heavy burden of responsibility."
(Hlebowitsh, 2001, p. 4)

AIMS OF THE CHAPTER

Use the questions that follow to guide your thinking and learning about the many purposes of science teaching, from those that are related to general education to those that are specific to science education:

- What are some of the many expectations of the American educational system for all students who attend public schools?

- How does the public school system in the United States differ from those in Western European countries?

- What are some of the goals that have been laid down for science education, which have been set forth by national committees, such as the American Association for the Advancement of Science and the National Research Council?

- How do students in the United States compare with those in other countries in terms of science knowledge?

- After you have studied the contents of this chapter, how would you approach a science lesson or unit?

As stated in the quote by Hlebowitsh, the American educational system asks a great deal from public schools and its teachers. While the general public views education as teaching the "three Rs" along with academic preparation, much more is expected. The system must consider individual and personal growth so that each student can maximize his or her potential, both personally and as a member of society. Therefore, society wants its citizens to understand the democratic process and to be socially active in their communities. In addition, many would like schools to provide vocational education in order to prepare students to take their place as skilled workers in a communication/technology-based society. The list is long regarding the demands that society, especially politicians, have placed on public education.

Indeed, the American public school is a comprehensive system of education. Elementary, middle, and high school teachers are expected to do a great deal for all students. They must increase student understanding of fundamental knowledge and skills related to language arts, mathematics, science, and social studies. Further, teachers are expected to ensure mastery of core content for all students on standardized tests. Many states are implementing testing programs at grades 4, 8, and 11 to determine student readiness to advance to the next grade level and to graduate from high school. Further, teachers are being held accountable for the success or failure of their students.

In contrast to the American system of schooling, the educational systems in other first-world countries are remarkably different from ours. For example, in Western European countries such as Austria, Germany, France, and Italy, vocational as well as academic preparation is a standard option of public education. At fourth grade, students take an examination that determines their educational track for part or all of their mandatory schooling. The system attempts to match the backgrounds, interests, and especially the maturity levels of students with an appropriate educational experience.

Many Western European counties use test results for student placement in the high school, which begins in grade 5 and terminates in grade 12, where an academic curriculum stresses mathematics, science, languages, history, and so on. Those not entering the high school academic track go into the middle school, which extends from grades 5 to 8. The middle school focuses on vocational studies along with basic academic subjects. Middle-grade students can take an examination at the end of the eighth grade for entrance into an academic high school. However, most of the middle-level students continue on in the vocational school for the remainder of their public education.

In vocational schools, students learn practical knowledge and skills related to many businesses and trades. These students can choose to be a bookkeeper, sales clerk, chef, baker, mechanic, electronic technician, and so on. Vocational schools in Europe have been in place for a long time and fulfill their purpose well.

In addition to providing two educational paths, the European educational system attempts to teach less subject matter content over the school year. For example, consider the academic track where students participate in physics instruction throughout the middle and high school grades. The instruction each year addresses a smaller number of topics than one year of physics in the United States. Further, the European textbooks in physics, as well as in the other science subjects, have fewer pages of text than those used in the United States. Also, the major content areas—biology, chemistry, and physics—are taught each year during grades 5 through 12.

The comprehensive nature of middle and secondary schools in America presents a big challenge to inexperienced as well as experienced science teachers. In addition to working in an educational system that requires all students to participate in a comprehensive curriculum and to learn a great deal of subject matter during each school year, teachers are expected to accomplish these varied goals with a diverse student population, consisting of individuals who come from very different ethnic, socioeconomic, and educational backgrounds. Many school districts in large urban areas report over 50 different languages and dialects spoken by students in their schools.

A substantial percentage of students in our society are from low-income families. These children lack the resources of children from middle- and high-income families. You are unlikely to find computers, Internet connections, books, educational magazines, and desks to do homework in the homes of students from low-income families. Many of these children have never visited a zoo or a museum, nor have they traveled to other parts of their home state to visit places of historical importance or educational value. Yet, the American educational system asks the same from the disadvantaged children as from the advantaged in terms of the acquisition of basic skills.

Given the broad and varied purposes of education imposed on the pubic schools by society, what has society asked of science education and science teachers, specifically? As you might expect, science education also has a long list of goals and purposes. Back in the 1940s, The National Society for the Study of Education (1947) put forth many outcomes for science teaching in the *Forty-Sixth Yearbook, Part 1,* which are summarized as follows:

- Facts
- Concepts
- Principles
- Skills
- Attitudes
- Appreciations
- Interests

In the 1980s, Project Synthesis (Yager, 1982) produced a cluster of science education goals that grouped together many of the purposes of science education. The project was carried out to increase science teachers' awareness that there is more to science teaching than focusing on content mastery of the subject matter and organizing courses that stress academic preparation. These four goals are:

1. Personal needs
2. Societal issues
3. Academic preparation
4. Career education

More recently, during the 1990s, the National Research Council (1996), in its publication *National Science Education Standards,* stressed the importance of producing a scientifically literate society. This widely circulated publication emphasizes the importance of educating students to encourage their curiosity about the world in which they live so that they ask questions about nature and answer those questions as the result of their investigative actions. Further, this publication indicates that students should examine science and societal issues in order to become knowledgeable about the interactions between science, technology, and society.

Let's return to a brief conversation between Mr. Clark, the new science teacher, and Ms. Roberts, the experienced science teacher, after the beginning teacher read the introductory chapter in the foundations of American education textbook.

 Ms. *Roberts:* Mr. Clark, did you learn anything from the chapter that might give you a different perspective regarding the purpose of middle school education?

Mr. *Clark:* I think so. Now I realize that we are expected to teach these kids a lot more than the science in their textbook. We need to prepare them for life. Perhaps I'm starting to think about what I teach from a different angle. I realize that I must make the material in the textbook relate to students' entire life and to what they will be doing after they graduate from high school.

Ms. *Roberts:* Good! If you don't mind, I would like to introduce you to science education, which has a long and rich history. This may give you a better idea about the purpose of science teaching in the middle school and secondary schools. However, what I give you to study will focus only on the recent past.

Stop and Reflect!

Before going on to the next section, do the following: List the goals or purposes of education, in general, for grades 6 to 12, that you believe have been set down for our nation's school. To what extent might the general education goals be similar to science education goals that you will read about later?

GOALS AND PURPOSES OF SCIENCE EDUCATION FROM 1980 TO THE PRESENT

The Period Between 1980 and 1989

A great deal of criticism and controversy occurred during the 1980s regarding the status of science education. *A Nation at Risk* (National Commission of Excellence in Education, 1983) states clearly that "our educational system has fallen behind and this is reflected in our leadership in commerce, industry, science and technological innovations which is being taken over by competitors throughout the world" (p. 5). Many of the reports and discussions that appeared in the literature were drawn from a multitude of studies conducted in the 1970s. The more than 2,000 pages of reports from the professional groups were synthesized and interpreted by Norris Harms and other science educators in Project Synthesis (Yager, 1982).

As pointed out previously, Project Synthesis called for a more balanced science curriculum for the nation's youth, which should consider personal and societal needs of students as well as their academic preparation and potential careers. Out of Project Synthesis and many other studies came a movement that has directed science education beyond its discipline base, which is something politicians and others never seem to get beyond. This led to a science education reform aimed at strengthening the economic viability of the nation, which in turn necessitated a scientifically literate populace.

Today, the electronic-, communication-, and information-age society in which we live requires citizens who can develop technology as well as live with it. Science teachers have been given the challenge of educating the youth of America to participate in a technology-based world economy in which they must gather and use information from computers and other electronic devices. However, in order to profit from this information, students must possess a knowledge base that will permit them to assimilate information from printed and electronic sources and to make sense out of it. During the 1980s, as well as today, there is a body of fundamental knowledge that students should master re-lated to biology, chemistry, earth science, and physics in order to use it in their daily lives and in their future workplace.

The Period Between 1990 and 1999

During the 1990s, the education reform gained momentum as it spread across the nation. School systems moved in many directions in their attempt to improve education, experimenting in many areas, from trying to help bilingual students learn content to creating alternative forms of education through charter schools. However, what stands out as most memorable from this period is the sincere attempt to (a) focus on the education of all students, especially students of color and those traditionally underrepresented in all aspects of society; (b) specify higher standards for learning; (c) promote a broader-based assessment process; and (d) establish tougher accountability for teachers and students. These aspects of the general educational reform are evident in the writings of the professional organizations representing the various subject matter disciplines.

With regard to science education, a bold initiative was announced in the 1990s when national guidelines were published that were meant to not only set the philosophical tone for learning science in grades K–12, but to identify the content to be learned. The time had arrived when policymakers believed that a country with 50 states could benefit from the thinking of national committees of educators and scientists. The nation's schools needed goals and directions with more specificity than they had ever had during any period in the past. Now, perhaps, the national policies could better guide local and state boards of education in their attempt to achieve science literacy for all Americans.

Given the number and heterogeneity of the school districts across America, science teachers need standards for subject matter content in order for students to learn a similar body of knowledge by the time they complete their high school education. Adopting commercially produced textbook-based curricula or innovative instructional materials do not offer that direction. This was evident during the science education reform movement of the 1960s and 1970s that relied heavily on instructional materials, funded by the government, to initiate changes in school science. The curriculum materials of the past that went under acronyms, such as SAPA, ISCS, BSCS, ISIS, and HHP, differed significantly in their content as compared to what appeared in traditional textbooks that were used widely in the schools. We are optimistic that the national guidelines of the 1990s will provide a better outline of critical content and a clearer picture of the nature of science than the reform movements of the past half-century.

Three prominent organizations have given the profession sets of standards to guide the science education reform: the American Association for the Advancement of Science (AAAS), The National Research Council (NRC), and the National Science Teachers Association (NSTA). The AAAS produced a large set of reform documents called *Project 2061—Science for All Americans*. The NRC published a booklet called the *National Science Education Standards*. The NSTA calls its project *Scope, Sequence, and Coordination*.

Project 2061

In the mid-1980s, the American Association for the Advancement of Science (AAAS) spearheaded the science reform movement by initiating Project 2061. The central theme of this reform effort is to produce a scientifically literate society by the year 2061, when Halley's comet can be observed from Earth. The AAAS is taking the long view with its reform effort because it posits that important societal changes require a great deal of time to achieve. One of the first documents it produced is titled *Science for All Americans* (AAAS, 1990). As the name implies, the intent is for "all" students to receive an education in science.

The AAAS reform project stresses the critical need to produce a scientifically literate society so that individuals can deal with the problems they will face in the new millennium. Many of the problems with which U.S. citizens must concern themselves are global, such as population growth, destruction of tropical rain forests, extinction of plant and animal species, scarce natural resources, and nuclear war. Science can provide knowledge and understanding about natural phenomena and social behavior that can benefit society. However, it will take an educated society, versed in science

All science teachers should become familiar with the National Science Education reform documents.

and technology, to comprehend societal problems and deal effectively with them. "The life-enhancing potential of science and technology cannot be realized unless the general public can understand science, mathematics, and technology, and acquires scientific habits of mind. Without a science-literate population, the outlook for a better world is not promising" (AAAS, 1990, pp. xiv–xv).

Science for All Americans identifies serious shortcomings of our educational system, which science teachers must address in order for a successful science education reform to take place. It reminds us that a great deal of instruction that takes place in science classrooms centers around learning answers rather than exploring questions. Memorization is emphasized at the expense of critical thinking. Often, reading about science takes the place of doing science. Students are not encouraged to work together on problems or to discuss their findings with others.

> The present curricula in science and mathematics are overstuffed and undernourished. . . . Some topics are taught over and over again in needless detail; some that are of equal or greater importance to science literacy—often from the physical and social sciences and from technology—are absent from the curriculum or are reserved for only a few students. (AAAS, 1990, p. xvi)

The idea that science courses cover too much material is a serious problem. This situation must be changed by focusing on less material and studying it in greater depth, which will actually result in students learning more. The "less-is-more" idea has become a slogan in the reform, and it should be taken seriously by all science teachers.

The recommendations in the *Science for All Americans* document are clear about the education that a student must receive in order to be scientifically literate. Indeed, it is a comprehensive and interdisciplinary education that is proposed. Students must come to understand the nature of science, mathematics, and technology as well as how these enterprises function separately and together. They must be versed in the physical, life, and social sciences from which they gain fundamental knowledge and understanding of reality. Students must study the designed world that has been shaped by human action to further the progress of society. Great importance should be placed upon providing students with a historical perspective of how the fundamental science ideas have evolved, such as the place of the earth in the solar system, matter and energy, fire, the atom, germs, and the diversity of life. Importantly, this reform project places a premium on the development of habits of mind that stress useful values, attitudes, and skills that students must acquire as they become versed in science, mathematics, and technology.

FIGURE 2.1 A sample of a set of learning outcomes in the *Benchmarks*.

CELLS

A Sample of Learning Outcomes from the *Benchmarks* "The Living Environment"

Kindergarten through Grade 2

By the end of the second grade, students should know that:

- Magnifiers help people see things they could not see without them.
- Most living things need water, food, and air.

Grades 3 through 5

By the end of the fifth grade, students should know that:

- Some living things consist of a single cell. Like familiar organisms, they need food, water, and air; a way to dispose of waste; and an environment they can live in.
- Microscopes make it possible to see that living things are made mostly of cells. Some organisms are made of a collection of similar cells that benefit from cooperating; some organisms' cells vary greatly in appearance and perform very different roles in the organisms.

Grades 6 through 8

By the end of the eighth grade, students should know that:

- All living things are composed of cells, from just one to many millions, whose details usually are visible only through a microscope. Different body tissues and organs are made up of different kinds of cells. The cells in similar tissues and organs in other animals are similar to those in human beings but differ somewhat from cells found in plants.
- Cells continually divide to make more cells for growth and repair. Various organs and tissues function to serve the needs of cells for food, air, and waste removal.
- Within cells, many of the basic functions of organisms—such as extracting energy from food and getting rid of waste—are carried out. The way in which cells function is similar in all living organisms.
- About two thirds of the weight of cells is accounted for by water, which gives cells many of their properties.

Grades 9 through 12

By the end of the 12th grade, students should know that:

- Every cell is covered by a membrane that controls what can enter and leave the cell. In all but quite primitive cells, a complex network of proteins provides organization and shape and, for animal cells, movement.
- Within the cell are specialized parts for the transport of materials, energy capture and release, protein building, waste disposal, information feedback, and even movement. In addition to these basic cellular functions common to all cells, most cells in multicellular organisms perform some special functions that others do not.
- The work of the cell is carried out by many different types of molecules it assembles, mostly proteins. Protein molecules are long, usually folded chains made from 20 different kinds of amino-acid molecules. The function of each protein molecule depends on its specific sequence of amino acids, and the shape the chain takes is a consequence of attractions between the chain's parts.
- The genetic information in DNA molecules provides instruction for assembling protein molecules. The code used is virtually the same for all life forms.
- Complex interactions among the different kinds of molecules in the cells cause distinct cycles of activities, such as growth and division. Cell behavior can also be affected by molecules from other parts of the organism or even other organisms.
- Gene mutation in a cell can result in uncontrolled cell division, called cancer. Exposure of cells to certain chemicals and radiation increases mutations and thus increases the chance of cancer.
- Most cells function best within a narrow range of temperature and acidity. At very low temperatures, reaction rates are too slow. High temperatures and/or extremes of acidity can irreversibly change the structure of most protein molecules. Even small changes in acidity can alter the molecules and how they interact. Both single cells and multicellular organisms have molecules that help to keep the cell's acidity within a narrow range.
- A living cell is composed of a small number of chemical elements, mainly carbon, hydrogen, nitrogen, oxygen, phosphorus, and sulfur. Carbon, because of its small size and four available bonding electrons, can join to other carbon atoms in chains and rings to form large and complex molecules.

In addition to *Science for All Americans,* Project 2061 has produced another important document entitled *Benchmarks for Science Literacy* (AAAS, 1993). *Benchmarks* specifies a common core of learning for students to master specific points in their K–12 education. The document lists learning outcomes that all students should know or be able to do in science, mathematics, and technology by the end of grades 2, 5, 8, and 12. The objectives identify fundamental ideas that *all* children can attain. However, the document reminds us that many students are capable of going beyond these outcomes. Further, science teaching can use many methods and approaches to help students achieve these literacy goals. Examine Figure 2.1 for a sample of learning outcomes in the *Benchmarks* pertaining to cells.

National Science Education Standards

The National Research Council (NRC) produced a publication entitled *National Science Education Standards* (NRC, 1996). This document stresses the importance for every citizen to become scientifically literate. Individuals need a background in science in order to evaluate technical information and make informed decisions. They need to reason logically and think scientifically about problems that confront them in their daily lives. The knowledge and skills that are central to science also are necessary for many jobs and careers, whether or not they are in scientific fields. The following quote by the NRC (1996) reflects the intent of the *Standards:*

> The *National Science Education Standards* are designed to guide our nation toward a scientifically literate society. Founded in exemplary practice and research, the *Standards* describe a vision of the scientifically literate person and present criteria for science education that will allow that vision to become a reality. (p. 1)

The *Standards* make it clear that scientific literacy is at the center of the reform movement. A scientifically literate person is identified as one who is curious about the world and desires to ask questions and find answers to those questions. These individuals can describe and explain natural phenomena as well as predict their behavior. They can also deal with science and societal issues by expressing them from an informed point of view, using their knowledge to evaluate the issues.

Knowledge and understanding of science are important guidelines for the realization of a scientifically literate society. Students must learn fundamental scientific facts, concepts, principles, laws, theories, and models. These ideas must be integrated into students' cognitive structures so that they can be recalled and applied in their decision-making activities. Further, students must be able to use this understanding to distinguish between scientific information that is valid and that which is unsubstantiated.

Inquiry is a theme that runs through the *Standards.* This concept is defined relative to scientific inquiry, which centers around humankind's probing the natural world in search of explanations, based on evidence, leading toward an understanding of reality. Scientific inquiry includes both the ideas under study as well as the way in which those ideas come to be known. The *Standards* make it clear that there are many ways to inquire and to find out, from conducting firsthand investigations to reading about what others have found. Further, "conducting hands-on science activities does not guarantee inquiry, nor is reading about science incompatible with inquiry" (NRC, 1996, p. 23). Table 2.1 presents the changing emphases that are recommended by the science reforms regarding how to teach science *as* inquiry.

Science and technology are seen as compatible and necessary to the development of scientific literacy. They are closely tied together and should be part of reform science programs. However, they are different enterprises. The major aim of science is to understand nature, whereas the major aim of technology is to create devices and systems to assist society.

The *National Science Education Standards* provide science teachers as well as the entire profession with important guidelines that they can use to plan, organize, develop, implement, and evaluate science programs, which will make a difference in reforming science education. There are many dimensions to science teaching, and they must be considered in the development of effective science programs that will produce scientifically literate citizens.

Scope, Sequence, and Coordination

During the 1980s, the National Science Teachers Association initiated a science reform project for grades 6–12. The project is called Scope, Sequence, and Coordination (SS & C), and its aim is to change the structure of science curricula in the middle and senior high schools. The rationale for altering the content structure that exists is a belief that teaching the separate disciplines—biology, chemistry, earth/space science, and physics—each year, in a separate year, is inefficient and does not integrate the sciences so that they make sense to the students. With the "layer cake" curriculum that has been in existence for over a century, students take earth science for one year, biology for one year, and perhaps chemistry one year. This year-long, concentrated approach does not lend itself to building upon what the students have studied in previous science courses. Further, the one-year science courses that are traditionally taught are usually textbook-based experiences that are heavy on content and learning large numbers of

TABLE 2.1   Recommendations for Teaching Science from *National Science Education Standards*

Changing Emphases

The *National Science Education Standards* envision change throughout the system. The science content standards encompass the following changes in emphases:

Less Emphasis on	*More Emphasis on*
Knowing scientific facts and information	Understanding scientific concepts and developing abilities of inquiry
Studying subject matter disciplines (physical, life, earth sciences) for their own sake	Learning subject matter disciplines in the context of inquiry, technology, science in personal and social perspectives, and history and nature of science
Separating science knowledge and science process	Integrating all aspects of science content
Covering many science topics	Studying a few fundamental science concepts
Implementing inquiry as a set of processes	Implementing inquiry as instructional strategies, abilities, and ideas to be learned

Changing Emphases to Promote Inquiry

Less Emphasis on	*More Emphasis on*
Activities that demonstrate and verify science content	Activities that investigate and analyze science questions
Investigations confined to one class period	Investigations over extended periods of time
Process skills out of context	Process skills in context
Individual process skills such as observation or inference	Using multiple process skills—manipulation, cognitive, procedural
Getting an answer	Using evidence and strategies for developing or revising an explanation
Science as exploration and experiment	Science as argument and explanation
Providing answers to questions about science content	Communicating science explanations
Individuals and groups of students analyzing and synthesizing data without defending a conclusion	Groups of students often analyzing and synthesizing data after defending conclusions
Doing few investigations in order to leave time to cover large amounts of content	Doing more investigations in order to develop understanding, ability, values of inquiry, and knowledge of science content
Concluding inquiries with the result of the experiment	Applying the results of experiments to scientific arguments and explanations
Management of materials and equipment	Management of ideas and information
Private communication of student ideas and conclusions to teacher	Public communication of student ideas and work to classmates

Reprinted with permission from *National Science Education Standards*. Copyright 1996 by the National Academy of Science. Courtesy of the National Academy Press, Washington, DC.

vocabulary terms. The one-discipline-based science course often results in students memorizing many terms, taking factually oriented paper-and-pencil tests, and remembering very little fundamental science.

Scope, Sequence, and Coordination's recommendation for reforming middle and senior high school science is to teach all four of the major science disciplines—biology, chemistry, earth/space science, and physics—each year in grades 6–12. In this manner, students would be able to connect the sciences and learn through a coordinated sequence the fundamental principles of the four major disciplines of science. Further, if the curriculum adheres to the less-is-more notion that covering fewer topics can help students learn more about a given area, then students will develop a deeper understanding of a given set of important ideas.

The term *scope* refers to the coherence of the curriculum that can be achieved by studying a set of fundamental ideas over 6 or 7 years of school science. The term *sequence* addresses student learning with the belief that students should be taught beginning with concrete ideas and moving toward the abstract as they advance through the grade levels. In addition, science programs should space the learning so that fundamental ideas are studied over many years rather than many days or weeks. Also, the curriculum should provide application of knowledge so that it is relevant to students' lives. The term *coordination* refers to the continuity of studying the four basic science disciplines.

Science teachers should examine the publication *Scope, Sequence, and Coordination of Secondary School Science, Volume 1: The Content Core* for a thorough description of the recommendations that the National Science Teachers Association (1992) has put forth to change the way science is organized in secondary schools. More recently, this project has coordinated its efforts with the *National Science Education Standards,* producing a curriculum framework called *Scope, Sequence, and Coordination: A Framework for High School Science Education* (Aldridge, 1996), which lists content standards and implementation guidelines for reforming science education.

Third International Mathematics and Science Study

During the 1990s, the Third International Mathematics and Science Study (TIMSS) was conducted. The test results for elementary, middle, and senior high school students were reported, comparing the United States with 41 countries. These data show that students in the United States fall approximately in the middle when assessed for their general knowledge about science, as shown on Table 2.2. Following is a summary of a presentation by William Schmidt (1997), one of the TIMSS coordinators. Schmidt's remarks pertain to comparisons of eighth-grade students in the United States with students in other countries around the world:

- The United States is in the middle regarding test performance in earth and life sciences when compared to other countries, and it rates significantly lower in physics.
- In mathematics, the United States does worse than in science.
- Math and science curricula are not the same in each of the countries. The topics are grouped differently in the various countries.
- Achievement scores reflect the curriculum. Students did better in countries where they were tested on ideas taught in science.

- The United States has no single vision for math and science, which appears to be problematic in a country with approximately 15,000 school districts.
- In America, there is grand dialog regarding education, but the results never seem to improve.
- More topics are taught in the United States in a given school year than in many other countries. For example, in Germany and Japan, 10 topics may be covered versus 65 in the United States.
- Most reform ideas merely add to the curriculum rather than replace or reduce subject matter content.
- Teachers seem to do what they believe they are being asked to do, which is to teach all of the topics.
- U.S. textbooks have 700 to 800 pages, while those in other countries might have 150 to 200 pages.
- U.S. textbooks are too long and are not focused on fundamental principles.
- The U.S. educational system needs a set of national standards to specify fundamental principles that all students should learn.

Schmidt's (1997) comment that follows captures well the type of mathematics and science curricula typical in our schools.

> *"U.S. education in math and science is a mile wide and an inch deep. It never gets off the surface level of knowledge."*
>
> *(Schmidt, 1997)*

Science education at all levels has been one that covers too much subject matter at the expense of in-depth study of fundamental principles within a relevant context for students. It is hoped that this situation will change in the new millennium. There are some signs of improvement. The National Assessment of Educational Progress (NAEP, 1998) reports some increase in the average science scores of 9-, 13-, and 17-year-olds. The data show declining scores from 1970 to 1977 with rising scores up to 1992. Performance among Blacks and Hispanics showed a positive trend upward for all three levels from the 1970s up to the 1990s.

With all of the talk about crisis, reform, standards, and test scores, one might get the impression that science education is in a sad state with little hope for change. However, the United States in the 1990s has led the world in scientific and technological advancement. Its economy was exceptional. Consequently, the prosperity of the country does not seem to be exclusively tied to the scientific literacy of the general public nor to the number of scientists and engineers. Much of the prosperity in the communication and technology industry has resulted from factors such as a democratic government, a free economy, global competition, and technically skilled workers from other countries

Table 2.2   Comparisons of U.S. 8th and 12th Grade Students' Science General Knowledge with Other Nations

8th Graders*			
Nation	*Average Score*	*Nation*	*Average Score*
Singapore	607	Thailand	525
Czech Republic	574	Israel	524
Japan	571	Hong Kong	522
Korea	565	Switzerland	522
Bulgaria	565	Scotland	517
Netherlands	560	Spain	517
Slovenia	560	France	498
Austria	558	Greece	497
Hungary	554	Iceland	494
England	552	Romania	486
Belgium-Flemish	550	Latvia	485
Australia	545	Portugal	480
Slovak Republic	544	Denmark	478
Russian Federation	538	Lithuania	476
Ireland	538	Belgium-France	471
Sweden	535	Iran, Islamic Rep.	470
United States	**534**	Cyprus	463
Germany	531	Kuwait	430
Canada	531	Colombia	411
Norway	527	South Africa	326
New Zealand	525		

12th Graders[†]			
Nation	*Average Score*	*Nation*	*Average Score*
Sweden	559	Germany	497
Netherlands	558	France	487
Iceland	549	Czech Republic	487
Norway	544	Russian Federation	481
Canada	532	**United States**	**480**
New Zealand	529	Italy	475
Australia	527	Hungary	471
Switzerland	523	Lithuania	461
Austria	520	Cyprus	448
Slovenia	517	South Africa	349
Denmark	509		

*United States National Research Center. (1996, December). U.S. National Research Center Report No. 7: Summary of eighth-grade achievement results. From Third International Mathematics and Science Study. Michigan State University.

[†]United States National Research Center. (1998, April). U.S. National Research Center Report No. 8: TIMSS high school results released. From Third International Mathematics and Science Study. Michigan State University.

emigrating to the United States to participate in the technological revolution. The present reform is about helping all students to learn about science and technology so that they can appreciate these enterprises and use this knowledge in their everyday lives as well as to make their living.

CONCLUSION

Most uninformed beginning science teachers rarely consider the ideas discussed in this chapter. They are interested in getting right into the subject matter, often teaching as telling, just as they might have experienced during their education. These individuals are intent on covering a certain amount of subject matter during the class period. Unfortunately, beginning science teachers often experience many setbacks and frustrations in their initial teaching because of their approach and mind-set regarding the purpose of science teaching and the nature of public schooling. It is advisable for inexperienced science teachers to reflect on the history and goals of the American public school system, the recommendations from national science education reform committees, and the results of international assessments in mathematics and science. This background provides a good perspective of science education and how to design science instruction to help all students become productive citizens in a communication/information-age society.

ASSESSING AND REVIEWING

Analysis and Synthesis

1. Go back over the first section of the chapter where the American public school is discussed. What did this section reveal to you regarding: (a) the demands that are placed on schools in the United States and (b) how the educational system in the United States differs from that in other countries, such as those in Western Europe?

2. Construct statements that capture the recommendations of national committees regarding the purpose of science education. Place bulleted statements under the following headings that capture the essence of these recommendations:

> The Period between 1980 and 1990
>
> Project 2061
>
> *National Science Education Standards*
>
> Scope, Sequence, and Coordination
>
> Third International Mathematics and Science Study

3. Write a few paragraphs reflecting your thinking regarding the purpose of science teaching for the level at which you are planning to teach (i.e., middle school or high school). In your thinking, consider not only the subject matter content, but also the diversity and ability of the students and the performance of students in the United States versus other countries.

4. Revisit the vignette at the front of the chapter, which describes a conversation between a beginning middle school science teacher and a veteran science teacher.
   a. Do you feel that individuals who are new to science teaching are similar to Mr. Clark in their thinking before being given some orientation by an experienced teacher or from a science education course?
   b. Do you feel that teachers, like Mr. Clark, will change and expand their views regarding the many purposes of science education after reading and discussing them?

Practical Considerations

5. Describe, in a few paragraphs, how you would approach a science lesson that introduces a particular unit of study now that you have studied the goals and purposes of science education.

Developmental Considerations

6. Either borrow or purchase for your professional library some of the science education reform documents, printed in paperback, that were discussed in this chapter and listed in this chapter as Resources to Examine. Read some of the chapters in these books and reflect on the recommendations for science education in the United States.

RESOURCES TO EXAMINE

Benchmarks for Science Literacy. 1993. American Association for the Advancement of Science, New York: Oxford University Press.

Address for ordering: 2001 Evans Road, Cary, NC 27513-2010. Phone: (800)451-7556.

All school science departments should have a copy of this book, which contains general statements of learning for 12 areas of science education, such as the nature of science, the physical setting, the living environment, the human organism, the designed world, historical perspective, habits of mind, and more. The generalizations are arranged into what students should know by the end of grades K–2, 3–5, 6–8, and 9–12. Science teachers can compare what they expect students to learn at the end of their course with these standards.

National Science Education Standards. 1996. National Research Council, Washington DC, National Academy Press.

Address for ordering: 2101 Constitution Ave., NW, Box 285, Washington, DC 20055. Phone: (800)624–6242 or (202)334–3313 (in the Washington area).

This is a 243-page booklet that gives an overview of what should take place to achieve a successful science education reform. It gives science standards for teaching, professional development, assessment, science content, and science programs. All science teachers should have a copy of this booklet for frequent reference.

REFERENCES

Aldridge, B. G. (Ed.). (1996). *Scope, sequence, and coordination: A framework for high school science education.* Arlington, VA: National Science Teachers Association.

American Association for the Advancement of Science (AAAS). (1990). *Science for all Americans.* New York: Oxford University Press.

American Association for the Advancement of Science (AAAS). (1993). *Benchmarks for science literacy.* New York: Oxford University Press.

Hlebowitsh, P. S. (2001). *Foundations of American education: Purpose and promise.* Belmont, CA: Wadsworth.

National Assessment of Educational Progress (NAEP). (1998, September). Long-term trends in student science performance. *NAEPFACTS.* Washington, DC: U.S. Department of Education Office of Educational Research and Improvement.

National Commission of Excellence in Education. (1983). *A nation at risk: The imperative for education reform* (Stock No. 065-000-001772). Washington, DC: U.S. Government Printing Office.

National Research Council (NRC). (1996). *National science education standards.* Washington, DC: National Academy Press.

National Science Teachers Association. (1992). *Scope, sequence, and coordination of secondary school science. Volume 1: The content core.* Arlington, VA: Author.

National Society for the Study of Education (NSTA). (1947). *Forty-sixth yearbook, part 1.* Chicago: University of Chicago Press.

Schmidt, W. (1997, March). *A report on the third international mathematics and science study, conducted at the eighth-grade level.* Speech at the Annual Meeting of the National Association for Research in Science Teaching.

Yager, R. E. (1982). The current situation in science education. In J. R. Staver (Ed.), *1982 AETS yearbook.* Columbus, OH: ERIC Center for Science, Mathematics and Environmental Education at Ohio State University.

chapter

3

Planning to Teach Science

*Beginning teachers must take time for planning
in order to be successful.*

Mrs. Leticia Jones is a first-year biology teacher at a large urban high school. She has had a few education courses and has been given a temporary teaching permit with the expectation that she will complete her certification program in the first 3 years of teaching in the district. Mrs. Jones is working after school with her mentor teacher, Mr. Michael Thanos, who has been a biology teacher in that school for over 30 years. Mr. Thanos has mentored many new teachers during his career and often has a student teacher in his classroom. Let's listen in on a conversation between the novice teacher and the experienced teacher.

This logo appears throughout the chapter to indicate where vignettes are integrated with chapter content.

MR. THANOS: Mrs. Jones, we are about to begin teaching about the cell, which is used as a foundational topic for the rest of the biology course. What are your thoughts on how to teach this unit?

MRS. JONES: I would like to begin by teaching about the discovery of cells, cell structure and function, and cytoplasmic organelles. Then move on to energy, photosynthesis, glycolysis, respiration, and fermentation. If the kids know this material, they can build on this knowledge.

MR. THANOS: How long will you spend on this?

MRS. JONES: I can probably cover this in 6 or 7 days. There is a great deal to cover this semester, and I must cover this material quickly. My friend Alice teaches biology at the other high school, and that is what she does.

MR. THANOS: Yes, I know Alice. She has been teaching for a long time, and I believe the biology teachers in that school have a different approach to biology course instruction than some of us in this school. Further, there is a different student population in that school. The students in this school are much more diverse. There are over 20 different languages and dialects spoken by students in this high school. Do you have time for me to describe how I would approach the cell unit, given the students that you have in your classes?

MRS. JONES: Sure, but I don't have a lot of time this afternoon because I have to pick up my daughter from day care, and then I have choir practice at the church this evening.

MR. THANOS: Okay! Let's get started on this unit. What activity might you begin with to capture the interest of the students?

MRS. JONES: Well, you know, I would draw a cell on the board and ask the students to help me label the structures.

MR. THANOS: I have taken that approach at times. How about an activity that would immediately get the students engaged and connected to what they are about to learn with what they already know? Give this some thought while I go to my classroom and get some materials that you may find useful for initiating the study of cells. Please make a list of instructional activities that would interest your students in learning about cells.

After about 5 minutes, Mr. Thanos returned with a box of folders, handouts, and lab materials.

MR. THANOS: Leticia, what have you come up with?

MRS. JONES: I didn't get very far because my cell phone rang. It was my sister telling me she could not babysit this evening while I'm at choir practice. I will have to find someone else to watch my daughter this evening. Back to my ideas about biology class, I do have one idea. I could demonstrate osmosis. That experiment always gets students' attention.

MR. THANOS: Good, I like that idea. Let me tell you how you might build up to osmosis by beginning with cell structure and function. Here, take this chicken's egg. What is there about this egg that might relate to the structure of a biological cell?

MRS. JONES: *Well, the shell could represent the cell wall or membrane.*

MR. THANOS: *Break the egg into this Petri dish, and let's examine all of the parts that we can observe. What do you see under the shell?*

MRS. JONES: *Oh! I see a membrane under the shell.*

MR. THANOS: *That is correct. It is the shell membrane, and you can demonstrate osmosis with that structure. Can you tell me what the yellow and white materials are and what part of the cell they represent? Also, is there a visible structure that represents the nucleus?*

MRS. JONES: *I never thought of a chicken's egg as a cell. Can we take this up again tomorrow after school when I have more time? I need to hurry and pick up my daughter from day care. Thanks for your help.*

Mr. Thanos waved goodbye to Mrs. Jones as she left the room. He sat quietly, reflecting on how times have changed since he began teaching. Back then, it seemed that new teachers went through a lengthy teacher education program with a full semester of student teaching. Also, new teachers spent more time after school planning and preparing for the next day's classes. There were no cell phones and rushing off to take care of personal matters until long after students left for the day.

———————————— ■ ————————————

AIMS OF THE CHAPTER

Use the questions that follow to guide your thinking and learning about planning to teach science:

■ Why is planning so important?

■ What are the major aspects of planning to consider when making decisions about a course, a unit, or a lesson?

■ What are the basic components of a science lesson plan?

■ How good are you at writing instructional objects for science lessons?

■ Can you plan a science lesson that will engage your peers in the science methods class or students in a middle or high school in a manner that will help them to understand the methods and products of science?

Planning is one of the most important teaching functions. This activity provides a "game plan" of what to teach and how to teach. The process of thinking through a lesson gives you opportunities to sequence instructional events that hold the potential to initiate and sustain learning. Architects use blueprints, conductors follow music scores, and teachers use unit and lesson plans. All teachers plan. However, some plans are more carefully and thoroughly conceived than others.

Those who plan well will likely be more effective in helping students to learn. These teachers will be in a better position to specify learning outcomes that all or most students can achieve. They will be prepared to manage a learning environment where students are expected to be more responsible for their own learning. Further, teachers who plan well can teach for understanding rather than for covering material and rotely memorizing terms.

The most critical ingredient in planning is *time to plan*. Without taking the time to find a quiet place to think about a unit or lesson, it is unlikely that a teacher can orchestrate a coherent set of activities that will engage most students in learning. In this busy, hectic society many beginning as well as experienced teachers seem too occupied with after-school activities to devote the time necessary to meet the challenges of today's educational system. Some teachers have a second job, church activities, young children to care for, coaching duties, cheerleading practice, and so on, all of which detract greatly from planning and teaching.

In addition to after-school and extra-curricular activities, there are related in-school tasks that take away from planning. The paperwork required by the administration can exhaust most teachers. Special provisions must be *provided* and *documented* to show that each special education student is being accommodated by lesson plans that will aid him or her to achieve a given set of learning outcomes. This additional planning also is required for English as Second Language (ESL) students. The amount of testing and student progress reporting has become burdensome for all teachers. The list of noninstructional tasks that face teachers is large and growing, and for these reasons we cannot overemphasize the importance of being prepared when the bell rings to begin class.

An experienced teacher can play a big role in providing an inexperienced teacher with emotional support and ideas for successful planning and teaching. Veteran teachers have acquired curriculum resources that work well in the classroom. They have laboratory exercises, simulations, demonstrations, CDs, PowerPoint presentations, videos, textbooks, Web sites, reviews, tests, and so on, that an individual who is new to teaching must access and incorporate into his or her planning. It is not unusual for a new or even an experienced science teacher to feel isolated (Guarino & Watterson, 2002).

Therefore, it is necessary for new teachers to reach out to those who have been teaching for many years and ask for their assistance with regard to resources, policies, and things to avoid.

The purpose of this chapter is to help plan science lessons that engage students in learning fundamental science concepts in a "stand-up and teach" classroom situation. Laboratory and a more inquiry-based type of instruction will be taken up later in this textbook. Let's begin to organize our thinking about planning for instruction by using the following scheme:

- *What* are you planning to teach?
- *Whom* are you planning to teach?
- *How* are you planning to teach?
- *How* are you planning to manage the learning environment?
- *When* are you planning to assess learning?

WHAT ARE YOU PLANNING TO TEACH?

"When you plan to teach science, just what are you planning to do?"

This question is central to the planning process. When you know what to teach, you are on your way to an effective lesson. First, you must possess the type of mindset that this textbook is attempting to help you develop. Ask yourself: What is the purpose of general education in the United States? If the purpose is to train all students to become scientists or engineers, then you will probably aim to teach a high-powered science course, covering large amounts of subject matter and requiring students to work many word/math problems. If the purpose is to educate all students so that they understand certain fundamental science concepts and develop an understanding of the scientific enterprise, then you will carefully select subject matter and skills for students to master.

The vignettes that open each of the preceding chapters provide examples of the thoughts and beliefs of inexperienced science teachers whose first instinct urged them to cover a large number of abstract science concepts that were presented to them in college science courses or that are presented in a science textbook. If that is your orientation, stop and think! The chances are high that the students in the classes you will be assigned to teach will have a large range of abilities. Some common statements from beginning science teachers regarding the abilities of their students include:

- "What did they teach these kids in science in the earlier grades? They cannot graph."
- "I overestimated the ability of these kids. I thought they could use fractions."

Lesson plans reflect the beginning teacher's best intentions for her teaching and her student's learning.

- "Most of my students flunked the first test and I made it so easy."
- "My students are not able to write a coherent paragraph."

Let's recall the opening vignette in Chapter 1 where Ms. Longorio attempted to begin the acids and bases unit by getting right into pH, acid-base theories, and disassociation. When this approach did not work well, the mentor teacher suggested that Ms. Longorio begin at a more concrete level with properties of acids and bases that the students can observe firsthand. In the opening vignette in Chapter 2, Mr. Clark, the aerospace engineer, was eager to jump into some heavy-duty problem solving with his sixth-grade students until his mentor teacher came to the rescue. Ms. Roberts awakened Mr. Clark to the type of students in their middle school and the purpose of the American educational system.

While we do not want to paint a bleak picture of all students and teaching situations in the middle and secondary schools, we want to inform you of what you can expect in many teaching situations. Most people going into teaching either disregard the recommendations given here or do not take them seriously. Even with students who are enrolled in more advanced classes or attending private schools, you will find students who lack many basic skills. Remember, *you are teaching science for all Americans.*

FIGURE 3.1   Comparison of learner expectations that an uninformed, beginning science teacher might select to initiate the teaching of a topic versus a more informed, experienced science teacher.

Middle Level Integrated Science—Sound and Hearing
- Draw and label the structures of the outer, middle, and inner ear.
- Trace a sound wave from the outer ear to the brain and explain how a mechanical disturbance is changed into chemical and electrical impulses in the auditory cortex of the brain.
- Explain how the inner ear functions and aids humans in keeping their balance.

Or

- Demonstrate and explain how a blind or blindfolded person locates the origin of a nearby sound.
- Demonstrate and explain the difficulty a blind or blindfolded person has in locating the origin of a nearby sound with the use of only one ear to receive sound waves.
- With eyes closed or blindfolded, identify common objects, such as coins that are dropped onto a hard surface.

Senior High Level Biology—Photosynthesis and Respiration
- Trace the flow of energy during light and dark reactions of photosynthesis.
- Show the steps in the breakdown of glucose to carbon dioxide and water that occurs during glycolysis.
- Describe the important steps in the Krebs cycle, beginning with pyruvic acid and ending with ATP.

Or

- Identify and name objects that you see or come in contact with every day that are the result of energy from the sun.
- Write or recognize a basic chemical formula that represents photosynthesis.
- After extracting the chlorophyll from green plant leaves, describe what is taking place when this pigment fluoresces under a UV light.

Senior High Level Physics—Induced Electromagnetic Force
- Explain magnetic flux and how it relates to the strength of a magnetic field.
- State Faraday's law.
- Use a formula to determine the emf induced across a loop of wire or coil of wire with N loops.

Or

- Demonstrate several ways to produce an electric current by moving a loop of wire or a coil of wire across a magnetic field.
- Investigate a range of properties that may or may not affect the electric current produced—such as strength of a magnetic field, size of wire loop, number of loops, speed of motion, angle of the loop with respect to the magnetic field—and relate these findings to Faraday's law.
- Illustrate how induced electromagnetic forces are used in a variety of devices that serve society, such as generators and meters.

You should study Figure 3.1 to orient your thinking regarding what an uninformed, beginning science teacher might choose to initiate his or her teaching of a topic versus a more informed and experienced science teacher. Note the difference in the concrete/abstract nature of the subject matter given in the example of sound and hearing at the middle school level, photosynthesis and respiration at the high school level, and induced electromotive force at the high school level. Further, the approaches differ in that the second set of examples in each subject area implies more hands-on instruction.

Those who are preparing to become science teachers must be educated to teach in a different way than what they usually experienced over many years of schooling (Lederman & Gess-Newsome, 1999). They must learn about *pedagogical content knowledge* and use it in their teaching. Pedagogical content knowledge is a special amalgam of content and pedagogy that is uniquely the province of experienced teachers (Shulman, 1986, p. 8). The knowledge and skills obtained go beyond teaching basic content and explaining that content; they fuse the *what* and the *how* of instruction in a way that facilitates learning.

Following is a short checklist of resources to help you make wise decisions regarding *what* to teach when planning a science lesson or unit:

_____ Course syllabus prepared by the school or district

_____ Teacher and student copies of the assigned textbook, laboratory manual, and ancillary materials

_____ Experienced teachers in the school building, district, and elsewhere

_____ Innovative curriculum materials and other related resources

_____ The Internet for all types of teaching resources and information about science

_____ National science education standards

Stop and Reflect!

Working with a classmate, identify a topic that you are teaching or may teach in the future. List three or four descriptors of the content that you believe a new science teacher might use to initiate the teaching of the topic and contrast this with what a veteran teacher who has had plenty of experience in planning instruction might use.

WHOM ARE YOU PLANNING TO TEACH?

After you have a idea about what you want to teach, stop and think about your audience. You must think twice, three times, or more about the students you teach. How will these young and often immature people receive you as a teacher as well as the instruction you have planned? With perhaps over 100 students a day in your classes you can be certain that there will be many individuals you will not reach unless you plan carefully.

You must continually remind yourself that diversity is the major characteristic of the American school population, and you must deal with this variation in your planning, teaching, management, and assessment. You must think ahead and predict how students will react to your instruction, especially those who are limited in their speaking, reading, writing, mathematics, and study skills. Also, how will you deal with boys and girls who do not participate in instruction because they do not care about school? Will there be students in your classes who are unable to hear you speak or unable to read what you are writing on the board or projecting on

a screen? How will you react to students who enjoy being disruptive and those who are poorly mannered?

Let's think about the realities of the classroom and reflect on the following questions as they relate to your selection of content and instruction for a given group of students:

Language Skills

■ How will you teach students who have recently arrived in the United States from Mexico, Brazil, Russia, Romania, China, Korea, and so on, who barely speak English?

■ How will you alter your instruction for students who have been in the American school system for many years, yet are unable to read at grade level and unable to write a coherent paragraph?

■ How will you plan lessons that require the use of simple mathematical formulas to solve word problems for students who cannot master basic algebra?

Classroom Behavior

■ What behavioral problems should you anticipate when instructing many students each day?

■ How will you react to students who thrive on being disruptive?

■ How will you help students take responsibility for their own learning?

Physical and Learning Challenges

■ How will you modify your teaching plans for students who have difficulty seeing the board or projection screen?

■ How will you accommodate students with hearing problems?

■ Can a dyslexic or attention-deficit student be successful in your class?

Cultural diversity and student attributes will be discussed in more detail in later chapters. Nevertheless, these factors should be considered in your planning to teach science.

HOW ARE YOU PLANNING TO TEACH SCIENCE?

Effective teaching is a complex act that must be based on thoughtful planning and good decisions. If you observe an effective science teacher in action, you will be able to observe certain behaviors that facilitate learning. Figure 3.2 presents a menu of teaching skills, strategies, and techniques that hold great promise for engaging students in thinking and learning. Let's briefly review these aspects of teaching in order to set the stage for planning science lessons that will be taken up later in this chapter.

FIGURE 3.2 A menu of skills, strategies, and techniques to engage students in teaching and learning science for understanding.

Employ Many Teaching Skills
✓ Introduction
✓ Directions
✓ Questions
✓ Feedback
✓ Closure
✓ Assessment

Use a Variety of Instructional Strategies
✓ Lecture
✓ Discussion
✓ Demonstration
✓ Laboratory work
✓ Reading
✓ Writing
✓ Group work
✓ Simulations/games
✓ Recitation

Incorporate Techniques to Enhance Learning
✓ Note taking
✓ Identifying similarities and differences
✓ Graphic organizers
✓ Practice
✓ Reviewing

You must organize your lesson plans to include many *teaching skills* (see Figure 3.2). The plan must have a useful beginning and ending. The introduction must gain students' attention and give them an idea of what the lesson is about. The most problematic aspect of teaching a lesson is the assessment of learning because the end of the class period invariably comes before one can determine what has been learned. Then, there are the questions to be asked during the lesson, which must be planned beforehand so that they are in one's mind, ready to draw students into the learning process at any instant. The art of preparing and asking questions is based on how much you know about the topic at hand and how well you state that knowledge. Feedback during the lesson and closure also are critical components of a science lesson.

We cannot overemphasize the importance of using more than one *instructional strategy* during a class period. An instructional strategy is the manner in which a major segment or an entire lesson is approached. The experienced science teacher often uses several strategies to gain students' attention and to keep them involved in learning (Rosenshine, 2002). They move smoothly from one type of instruction to another. These teachers have learned that to use one strategy during a class period, such as a PowerPoint lecture, is not as effective as using two or more strategies. Consequently, experienced science teachers divide the class period into two, three, or even four segments and combinations of strategies that best facilitate the learning of a particular topic. In Figure 3.2, we have listed many instructional strategies that you must use in your teaching in order for it to be effective.

Educational researchers have learned that it requires more than teaching skills and instructional strategies to facilitate content mastery of subject matter. They have assisted the profession greatly by identifying many learning *techniques* that have shown to increase student achievement (Marzano, Pickering, & Pollock, 2001). For example, note taking, identifying similarities and differences, graphic organizers, practice, reviewing, and explaining are among some of the most powerful techniques to enhance learning in any course. These techniques must become part of your repertoire of teaching and must be built into your planning.

HOW ARE YOU PLANNING TO MANAGE THE LEARNING ENVIRONMENT?

Almost every beginning teacher experiences classroom management problems. While thorough planning will eliminate many management problems, it will not ensure that all students will be on-task and behaving properly. As you plan instruction, begin to reflect on at least these aspects of classroom management:

- Creating a positive learning environment
- Managing students to learn
- Dealing with student misbehavior

Is your lesson planned so well that you will be able to interact with the students during the instruction? Effective teachers know all of their students by name and call on them to answer questions and to take part in the instruction. They have high expectations and communicate this to the students. These teachers focus on the students they are teaching as well as the subject matter they wish students to master.

Can you visualize the classroom setting where the instruction will take place? Think about the seating arrangement, the laboratory benches or tables, the writing board, projection screen, and where you will position yourself throughout the lesson. These considerations and other aspects of the instructional environment should facilitate the learning that you envision for the students. And, of course, be sure to have all of the materials on-hand and ready to go before the lesson is to be taught.

Later in this textbook you will find a complete chapter devoted to managing the science learning environment. However, you might give some thought to dealing with disruptive students and how you would react to individuals who horse around during lessons. Will you ignore this type of behavior, signal students to stop, move closer to them, speak directly to the situation, send the students to the office, or take some other action? Your goal is for the entire class period to run smoothly.

WHEN WILL YOU ASSESS STUDENT LEARNING?

All lessons must include assessment. Although we often think of assessment as a test that comes at the end of a lesson or unit, assessment should occur frequently throughout the lesson as well as at the end. Effective assessment provides the teacher and students with information concerning how well learning is taking place, which in turn can be used to modify the instruction and gauge teaching effectiveness.

Your effectiveness as a science teacher can improve by using alternative as well as traditional assessment techniques, some of which are listed here:

Traditional Assessment Techniques

- Paper-and-pencil tests
  — quizzes
  — tests
  — exams

Alternative Assessment Techniques

- Performance tasks
- Word problems
- Graphic organizers
- Observations
- Interviews
- Journals

Before studying assessment in more depth in a later chapter, you must consider using some of the techniques just listed in the closure and review of a lesson that you will be planning to teach during this methods course and for teaching students in middle and high schools. Effective teaching should have a beginning, a middle, and an end.

CONSTRUCTING INSTRUCTIONAL OBJECTIVES

Instructional objectives are an integral part of a lesson plan and should specify the learning outcomes for a particular national, state, or school district curriculum standard. These succinct statements zero in on what the learner should know and be able to do as a result of the teaching and learning process. Instructional objectives provide a focus for what is to be taught and what is to be assessed. Some educators refer to instructional ob-

jectives as performance objectives; others call them behavioral objectives. Regardless of the name, most educators agree that instructional objectives should be an essential component of any teaching plan.

Instructional objectives can be placed into three categories or domains—cognitive, affective, or psychomotor. Objectives in the cognitive domain relate to intellectual abilities and skills such as recognition, recall, comprehension, and problem solving. Most of the objectives in science course work are written in the cognitive domain. Objectives in the affective domain relate to attitudes, interests, beliefs, and values. Objectives in this area are beginning to appear more frequently in science curricula because they relate to critical aspects of school learning. Objectives in the psychomotor domain reflect motor skills and hand-eye coordination. They occupy a special place in the teaching of science, especially in the laboratory.

A good instructional objective must describe a learning outcome that states what the student will be able to do, know, or believe as a result of the instruction. This must not be confused with an instructional activity that indicates what students will be doing during a lesson. For example, engaging students in a laboratory exercise on constructing parallel circuits in order to learn how to wire this type of electrical circuit is not the same as asking students to solve word problems to calculate the current in different branches of a parallel circuit. One way to understand what is meant by a learning outcome or an instructional objective is to determine what students should be able to do, think, or know as a result of the instruction. The teacher should then write these outcomes in precise terms. The teacher should keep in mind several criteria when constructing objectives:

- Center the ideas to be learned on important or critical subject matter content
- Focus on student learning outcomes rather than instructional activities
- Describe what the learner should know, be able to do, or believe
- State learning outcomes that are observable
- Construct objectives that can be measured by a test or other assessment tool

Robert Mager (1984) provides a useful technique to prepare and analyze instructional objectives. He indicates that clearly stated instructional objectives have three characteristics:

1. A *performance* component that specifies an observable behavior that the learner is to exhibit.
2. A *condition* component that specifies the conditions under which the learner will be assessed and what the learner will be given or denied.
3. A *criterion* component that specifies the minimal level of acceptable performance that the learner will be expected to exhibit.

When you use the three component parts, you will most likely produce clear statements of the learning outcomes that are expected of students, which can be used to guide instruction and assessment. In practice you will find that most objectives written by science teachers for daily lesson plans include only the performance component. However, these objectives can be clarified in many instances by including condition and criterion components that will more precisely identify what it is that the students should be able to know and do as a result of the instruction.

Consider a lesson to teach students about chromosomes. Following are two example of objectives. The first is a general objective or state standard. The second is much more specific and understandable; it is called an instructional objective.

> Students should understand the relationship between the macrostructure of chromosomes and the health of humans.

The first question to ask yourself when translating a general objective, such as the one previously stated, into a more specific instructional objective is: What is it that the learner should know about chromosomes? Let's examine the following instructional objective to determine if it includes the three component parts of a clearly stated learning outcome:

> Given a karyotype to examine from a person who has several chromosomal abnormalities, identify one chromosome that indicates translocation has occurred and one that indicates deletion of genetic material has occurred.

In this example, the learner must identify chromosomes that show where genetic material has been broken off from one chromosome and relocated on to another chromosome (translocation) and where chromosomal material has been broken off and lost (deletion), both of which illustrate mechanisms that result in serious physical abnormalities.

The instructional objective stated has the three parts that a clearly written instructional objective should contain. The verb "*identify*" is the *performance* to be exhibited by the students. The phrase "*Given a karyotype to examine from a person who has several chromosomal abnormalities*" is the *condition*, or what the students will be given during their assessment of the learning outcome. The phrase "*one chromosome that indicates translocation has occurred and one that indicates deletion of genetic material has occurred*" specifies the *criterion* component for assessing student performance. How would you judge the clarity of this instructional objective?

There is one other aspect of instructional objectives that science teachers should consider. How *educationally important* are the objectives that students are expected to achieve? Do the instructional objectives suggest that students will be learning skills and acquiring information useful to their lives? We often see instructional objectives that indicate students will be learning long lists of vocabulary terms, which suggests that they are required to learn science topics in needless detail and to regurgitate this knowledge on long paper-and-pencil tests—a recipe for poor science teaching.

Stop and Reflect!

Evaluate the instructional objectives listed here with respect to their (a) clarity and (b) science education importance. For those that are not clearly stated, alter them to include the three component parts: performance, condition, and criteria.

1. Given actual items or pictures of household cleaning products, estimate their pH to within at least two units of their actual pH values.
2. Name the elements of the periodic chart.
3. Find areas of low and high pressures and cold and warm fronts on weather maps.
4. Write a report on stem cell research.

EXAMPLES OF SCIENCE LESSON PLANS

This section will describe three types of lesson plans—those that go into the daily plan book, the short-form, and the long-form. Each type has its own purpose. Nevertheless, the more detailed long-form will be stressed because of its usefulness to beginning science teachers and those preparing to teach science lessons for feedback in teacher education programs.

There is no one accepted format for designing a lesson plan. The sequence, number of elements, and amount of detail in a lesson plan vary considerably. The short-form lesson plan incorporates more detail than that found in the daily plan book. It is usually about one page in length. In contrast, the long-form lesson plan describes all aspects of each lesson in detail, including the handouts, worksheets, and assessments. It contains many pages and gives great detail.

The long-form lesson plan is much more useful than the short-form to analyze and reflect upon the potential effectiveness of an instructional plan. The long-form plan is very helpful for those who wish to develop and teach exemplary science lessons. Whether using the short- or long-form, teachers should recognize that a lesson plan represents their best intention of what should occur during a lesson to achieve the desired learning outcomes. From this perspective, a lesson plan should be viewed as a guide for teaching, not as an inflexible set of rules and procedures that must be followed.

Daily Plan Book

Many school districts require teachers to keep a daily plan book. A daily plan book is often confused with a daily lesson plan, which it is not. The plan book merely presents a sketch of what will occur during each lesson. It provides the minimum detail and number of elements. Usually, school districts require the teachers to briefly outline their teaching plans for each week. This gives the teacher, administrators, or a substitute teacher some idea of what should be taught each school day. Figure 3.3 is an example of a daily plan book for five class sessions of a unit on chemical names and formulas. These lessons are intended for high school chemistry students. Inspection of the example reveals that space is limited to describe the elements associated with the lesson. The elements contained in this particular plan book are as follows: abbreviated instructional objectives, procedures, resource materials, and evaluation. Because so little information is given in the plan book, it is difficult to determine exactly what will take place during the lesson and to critique it for its potential success.

FIGURE 3.3   Daily plan book for 1 week of instruction.

Monday

Instructional Objective: Explain the organization of the periodic table.

Procedure: Students read and discuss Section 5.1 "The Periodic Table." Students locate groups, periods, representative elements, and transition elements.

Resource Materials: Addison-Wesley's *Chemistry:* Chapter 5, pp. 107–108. Transparency of Period Table.

Evaluation: Have students explain how properties of elements vary from the one side of the chart to the other and from top to bottom.

Tuesday

Instructional Objective: Define cation and anion and describe how they are different.

Procedure: Teacher demonstration, 5.2 "Ionization of Sodium Metal." Students discuss demonstration and the production of ions.

Resource Materials: Addison-Wesley's *Chemistry* (TE): Chapter 5, pp. 106B. Na metal, 0.1% phenolphthalein, safety goggles for all students.

Evaluation: Have students explain how the magnesium ion differs from a magnesium atom and how a bromine ion differs from a bromine atom.

Wednesday

Instructional Objective: Distinguish between chemical formula and molecular formula.

Procedure: Students view the video *Chemical Symbols: Formulas and Equations* and practice writing chemical and molecular formulas.

Resource Materials: Videocassette player and monitor video #4FS.

Evaluation: Provide chemical and molecular formulas and ask what information can be obtained from the formulas.

Thursday

Instructional Objective: Infer the charge on an ion from the periodic table.

Procedure: Students construct a table of ionic charges of representative elements by group.

Resource Materials: Transparency of Period Table.

Evaluation: Have students name the ionic charge of an element when given its group.

Friday

Instructional Objective: Learn the names and formulas of polyatomic ions.

Procedure: Students read and discuss Section 5.7 "Polyatomic Ions." Students construct models of polyatomic ions and ion complexes.

Resource Materials: Addison-Wesley's *Chemistry* (TE): Chapter 5, pp. 122–123. Polystyrene balls of various sizes, toothpicks.

Evaluation: Have students match the names and formulas of 3 polyatomic cations and 3 polyatomic anions.

Based on information from Chemistry, *by A. C. Wilbraham, D. D. Staley, and M. S. Matta, 1995, Menlo Park, CA: Addison-Wesley.*

FIGURE 3.4   A short-form lesson plan pertaining to wind and weather.

Class: Earth Science, Section II
Unit: "Wind and Weather"
Topic: Weather Vanes

Instructional Objectives: Students should be able to:
1. Construct a weather vane using simple materials.
2. Determine wind direction using a standard weather vane and a compass.
3. Describe how the size and shape of the weather vane's point and tail affect its operation.

Time	**Activity**
9:15–9:25 A.M.	Use color slides of different weather vane designs to introduce the topic of weather vanes. Ask students: Does changing the size and shape of the point and tail of a weather vane affect its operates? Record student predictions.
9:25–9:40	*(Exploration)* Give instructions regarding use of the compass and have student groups construct several standard weather vanes with the following features: (a) large point and small tail, (b) small circle and large circle in place of point and tail, and (c) squares of the same size in place of point and tail.
9:40–9:50	Students test the different wind vanes and record their results on an activity sheet. Use blow dryers as a wind source if winds are calm.
9:50–10:10	*(Intervention)* Class discussion of results. Guiding questions: How are the compass and weather vane used to determine wind direction? How does the shape and size of a weather vane's point and tail affect its performance? What rule can we state about the performance of weather vanes based on our work?

Assignment
1. *(Application)* Construct a weather vane different from the ones constructed in class. Does its performance provide support for our rule?
2. Ask for volunteers to interview a friend or family member about how a weather vane works, and share the results of their interview in class.
3. Textbook pp. 205–206, "Weather Vanes and Weather Forecasting."

Activity Materials Needed
45 note cards, 15 pairs of scissors, 15 pencils with erasers, 15 straight pins, 15 compasses, 3 blow dryers, 3 rolls of transparent tape

Resources for Lesson
1. Weather vane slides
2. Teacher-made activity sheets
3. Bulletin board with pictures of weather vanes

Short-Form Lesson Plan

The short-form lesson plan includes a moderate amount of detail about a lesson. Figure 3.4 shows an example of a short-form lesson plan about weather vanes that is part of a junior high school earth science unit on wind and weather. It also shows the teacher's intended use of the learning cycle model to have students explore different weather vane designs and to construct an understanding of the important features of a weather vane by means of discussion.

Analysis of this example reveals the advantages and disadvantages of the short-form lesson plan. The time schedule gives the teacher an idea of what to do during each time segment of the class period. This will help the teacher gauge the length of each activity and realize how much can be accomplished during the period. There is plenty of room in this lesson plan to write the assignment, list the materials that are needed, and mention the references that will be used.

This type of plan has two major shortcomings. First, the objectives are usually abbreviated in that only the performance component is given, and the conditional and criterion components are left out because of space constraints. When the conditional component of an instructional objective is omitted, the conditions under which the students will be assessed are not revealed. Using this form, it would be difficult to describe the lesson's beginning, the major instructional activities, the directions for weather vane construction, or the closure. It is possible to provide the necessary detail for these elements, however, by adding additional pages to describe these activities more fully.

Long-Form Lesson Plan

The long-form lesson plan is a complete and detailed plan of instruction that includes many elements. An example is presented in Figure 3.5. The plan may be many pages and provides a thorough description of the instructional plan: purpose, objectives, activities, and so forth. The long-form gives the teacher an opportunity to formulate a thorough and meaningful plan of instruction. This type of plan is often used in teacher education programs because it can be analyzed to determine the extent of the preparation, appropriateness of the activities, the relevance of the learning outcomes, and the continuity among lesson plan elements. The long-form format is ideal for designing a lesson to stimulate student interest and to achieve specific learning outcomes that can be analyzed to determine the extent to which these aims might be attained

or have been attained at the conclusion of the lesson. There is no accepted format for the number of elements and the amount of detail in a long-form lesson plan. The following list suggests elements that the teacher might incorporate in a thoroughly prepared science lesson plan:

- Title
- Purpose
- General Objectives
- Instructional Objectives
- Major Concepts
- Materials and Equipment
- Instructional Activities
  - Introduction
  - Other instructional activities
  - Review
- Assessment of Instructional Objectives

By now, you should realize that planning to teach science requires a great deal of effort, but without it your teaching effectiveness will suffer, as will your ego. The more you practice detailed lesson planning, the easier it will become and the better you will teach. Continue on to the Assessing and Reviewing section of this chapter to reinforce your understanding and ability to plan good science lessons.

FIGURE 3.5   An example of a long-form lesson plan highlighting certain components of this type of instructional organization.

"Why the Nerve of You"

Improving Your Mind and Mood by Better Understanding Nerve Cell Function, Receptors, and Nutrition

Purpose

How you think is critical to how you live. But what does this have to do with biology? Human behavior is centered in biological cells. If this is true, then gaining insight into the structure and function of nerve cells can provide useful knowledge about behavior and well-being.

During this lesson, we are going to begin the study of the cell. However, instead of focusing on the structure of the cell and naming all of its parts, we will begin by examining cellular structures and functions that can add greater meaning to cell biology because of their relevance to everyday living and immediate application of learning. For example, how would you like to learn how to influence your brain in order to get to sleep faster or to energize your thinking so that you are a better problem solver?

State Standard and General Objective

Learn about the structure and function of different types of plant and animal cells.

Instructional Objectives

1. Explain the function of neurotransmitters in facilitating communication between nerve cells. [Assess during the lesson.]
2. Describe and identify the predominant macronutrient (carbohydrate and protein) in common food products and indicate which neurotransmitter (dopamine, norepinephrine, and serotonin) it releases from the axon tip of a nerve cell. [Assess during lesson and at the end of lesson.]

(Continued)

FIGURE 3.5   Continued.

3. Briefly describe or state the specific effect that each macronutrient (carbohydrate and protein) has on mental awareness—that is, whether the macronutrient stimulates or relaxes the mind. [Assess during and at the end of lesson.]

4. Given a diagram and major parts of two adjacent nerve cells, trace the movement of three neurotransmitters—dopamine, norepinephrine, and serotonin—across the synapse between two adjacent nerve cell endings. [Assess during lesson.]

5. Form a spherical model of a cell with modeling clay and create a variety of unique indentations on the surface of the cell to represent molecular receptors. [Assess during lesson.]

6. Create two menus or meal plans, one that will energize you and one that will relax you (which will be used over a 1-week period), reporting the results to the class. [Assess during lesson.]

Major Concepts

Nerve cell, receptor, neurotransmitter, macronutrient, mental stimulation, and relaxation.

Instructional Materials

[This information has been eliminated due to space considerations.]

Instructional Activities

1. Set induction. Engage the audience in the lesson by placing two foods on the demonstration table. Food A should be a carbohydrate and Food B a protein. A box of spaghetti and a can of tuna fish will do.

   Present the scenario: You have had a very hard day at work. There were many problems to solve and you had to stay until 6:30 PM before leaving for home. You will be eating supper at 8 PM, much later than usual and hope to be in bed by 10 PM, because you have to be at work in the morning by 6 AM

   Q: What would you choose to eat for supper in order to fall asleep as soon as possible and perhaps to get a good night's rest?

   Ans: You should *not* eat too much, and you should eat plenty of carbohydrates with modest amounts of protein. **First,** eating too much may keep you awake, as your digestive system may have to work hard to do its work. Eating too much protein might give you too much mental energy and interfere with getting to sleep in less than 2 hours after a meal. **Second,** carbohydrates have a relaxing effect on your mental state and may assist you in winding down after a hard day at work and help you to fall asleep.

2. Place the title of the lesson on the board "Why the Nerve of You." Cover the title with a **sheet of newsprint** and remove it for effect. Give the purpose of the lesson by presenting the information in the **Purpose of the Lesson** on the first page of this plan, followed by the **Instructional Objectives.**

3. In order to better comprehend brain chemistry and how foods and drugs lead to specific responses in our body, let's examine the diagram of the nerve cell shown in the **transparency** with **copies to students.** Pass out a nerve cell diagram to all students.

   Discuss the movement of nerve impulses along the axon:
   a. electrical impulses move along the axon to the axon terminals,
   b. the axon terminals release neurotransmitters that move across the synapse to receptors on the surface of nerve cells (dendrites) or muscles cells, bones cells, or intestine cells, etc., and
   c. the receptors that act as on/off switches for specific responses.

   Direct the students to draw a chemical mechanism that illustrates what takes place at the axon terminal tip/synapse/receptor junction.

   Ask many questions to make this information more relevant to students:
   a. What happens neurologically when you eat a hamburger? (Stimulates brain activity.)
   b. What happens in your body when you take in an opiate like cocaine or eat chocolate? (They make you feel good.)
   c. What happens when you take an antihistamine? (Blocks allergic reactions via receptors.)

4. Let's continue the study of brain chemistry by examining two contrasting types of neurotransmission with the use of an overhead transparency.

→ energizing mind/body responses
→ calming mind/body responses

a. When you eat a protein-based meal, the resulting composition of the blood is such that the amino acid *tyrosine* enters the brain, which in turn initiates the release of the neurotransmitters *dopamine* and *norepinephrine*. This series of chemical reactions produces an energizing effect.

Protein → tyrosine → brain → **dopamine & norepinephrine** → energizing effect

b. When you eat a carbohydrate-based meal, the resulting composition of the blood is such that the amino acid *tryptophan* enters the brain, which in turn initiates the release of the neurotransmitter *serotonin*. This series of chemical reactions produces a calming effect.

Carbohydrate → tryptophan → brain → **serotonin** → calming effect

5. More information about the chemistry of tryptophan and tyrosine. [The rest of this activity has been eliminated due to space considerations.]

6. Ask participants to draw, label, and give the function of the major structures associated with neurons. [The rest of this activity has been eliminated due to space considerations.]

7. Stress the importance of **receptor molecules** that reside on the surface of cells. Neurotransmitter molecules dock onto receptors molecules, which convey chemical messages to the cells, be they nerve or other type of cells of the body (muscle, bone, immune, digestive). Distribute a small piece of **modeling clay** to each participant.

Directions: Form the clay into a ball to represent a cell. Using a pen, pencil, coin, key, or any small object, make indentations on the surface of the cell model to present different chemical receptors.

8. Pass out to everyone a four by six index card. Instruct the class to draw a line down the middle of the card. **Create two meal plans:** (a) one that will energize you and (b) one that will relax you. These meals can be for breakfast, lunch, or dinner. Experiment with the meals several times over the next week and bring back the findings for discussion.

Review of Lesson

a. Form groups of two to four participants. Ask them to draw a diagram or a concept map to illustrate the connection among: various types of foods or macronutrients, the nervous system, and mental moods.

b. When the groups have completed their visuals and placed them on large newsprint paper, display and discuss them. Focus the discussion on the instructional objectives of the lesson and present on an overhead transparency the concept map designed for this lesson.

Post-Lesson Assessment of Selected Instructional Objectives

1. Identify the predominant macronutrient (carbohydrate and protein) in common food products and indicate which neurotransmitter(s) (dopamine, norepinephrine, and serotonin) it releases from the axon tip of a nerve cell.

Food Product	Macronutrient	Neruotransmitter
Rice	_____	_____
Steak	_____	_____
Tuna fish	_____	_____
Potato	_____	_____
Corn	_____	_____

2. State the specific effect that each macronutrient (carbohydrate and protein) has on mental awareness (i.e., whether the macronutrient stimulates or relaxes the mind).

ASSESSING AND REVIEWING

Analysis and Synthesis

1. Consider a science lesson that you might conduct with your peers in the methods class. Write three or four instructional objectives that include a performance, condition, and criterion component. Exchange your list with others and analyze each instructional objective for relevance to the audience and for the inclusion of the three component parts of a clearly written learning outcome.

2. Gather some lesson plans that have been developed by science teachers for their classes. Evaluate each plan for the following:
   a. Relevance for the intended student audience.
   b. Inclusion of important components of a teaching plan, for example, title, purpose, instructional objectives, instructional activities (introduction, variety of activities, questions, review, closure, and assessment).

3. Evaluate the long-form lesson plan example shown in Figure 3.5. Use the component parts of a teaching plan to guide your assessment of the plan.

Practical Considerations

4. Construct a checklist of reminders that you will incorporate into your lesson planning. Organize the list by using the headings that follow. For each heading add several phrases.

   > What am I planning to teach?
   > Whom am I planning to teach?
   > How am I planning to teach?
   > How am I planning to manage the leaning environment?
   > When am I planning to assess learning?

5. Design a long-form lesson plan to be given to the participants in the methods class. The plan should be 50 to 60 minutes in duration, and it should be aimed at teaching the adult science majors some aspect of science that they are not familiar with or have not understood in preparation for becoming a science teacher. The lesson plan should be interesting and meaningful to the participants and challenge their thinking.

Developmental Considerations

6. Identify a few science teachers who are regarded as very effective in their work. Discuss planning with these individuals and ask them for tips on how to prepare lessons in an efficient manner. In addition, ask the teachers to share with you some of their best lesson plans.

RESOURCES TO EXAMINE

The Science Teacher, September 2002.

The entire issue is devoted to helping teachers survive their first year on the job. Here you will find: (a) tips and tricks for success, (b) lifelines to help you stay afloat, (c) organizing the classroom, (d) coping with isolation, (e) working with a mentor, and so on.

The Educator's Reference Desk.   [On-line]. Available: http://www.eduref.org.

This Web site has many lesson plans written by teachers. The site continues to add lesson plans that range from art to social studies. The science lessons include topics related to agriculture, biology, earth science, natural history, physical science, process skills, space science, and technology.

"Cultural Myths as Constraints to the Enacted Science Curriculum."   (1996, February). *Science Education,* pp. 223–241.

Kenneth Tobin and Campbell McRobbie's study of cultural myths identifies beliefs held by teachers that tend to inhibit them from planning and teaching in ways that support the reform initiatives. The beliefs depict constraints that are both personal and social constructions; center on the transmission of content knowledge, teaching efficiency, course rigor, and exam preparation; and have broad support among educational stakeholders, including students, parents, and school administrators.

"Those Who Understand: Knowledge Growth in Teaching." (1986). *Educational Research, 15*(2), pp. 1–32.

Lee Shulman presents his thoughts about pedagogical content knowledge—the unique knowledge base that teachers develop as a result of experience and reflection. This is a seminal paper about the special knowledge that effective teachers possess that combines knowledge about subject matter with ways of teaching that content.

Cases in Middle and Secondary Science Education: The Promise and Dilemmas. 2000. Thomas Koballa, Jr. and Deborah Tippins Eds. Upper Saddle River, New Jersey: Merrill. Go to http:www.merrilleducation.com

This paperback book contains over 30 open cases describing science instruction. Each case is written by a science teacher or science educator and followed by a reflection by a science educator. The text is an excellent resource for beginning and experienced science teachers and for those who are preparing science teachers. It serves as a companion text for this science methods textbook.

REFERENCES

Guarino, F. L., & Watterson, S. M. (2002, September). You are not alone. *The Science Teacher,* 40–41.

Lederman, N. G., & Gess-Newsome. L. (1999). Reconceptualizing secondary science teacher education. In J. Gess-Newsome & N. G. Lederman (Eds.), *Examining pedagogical content knowledge* (pp. 199–214). Norwell, MA: Kluwer.

Mager, R. E. (1984). *Preparing instructional objectives.* Belmont, CA: Fearon Press.

Marzano, R. J., Pickering, D. J., & Pollock, J. E. (2001). *Classroom instruction that works: Research strategies for increasing student achievement.* Alexandria, VA: Association for Supervision of Curriculum Development.

Roshenshine, B. (2002). Converging findings on classroom instruction. In A. Molnar (Ed.), *School reform proposals: The research evidence* (pp.175–196). Greenwich, CN: Information Age.

Shulman, L. (1986). Those who understand: Knowledge growth in teaching. *Educational Researcher 15*(2), 4–14.

4

Teaching Science

*Effective science teachers devise clever ways
to engage students.*

*D*avid Isaacson completed his student teaching during the previous school year and is a new teacher assigned to eighth-grade science at Drake Middle School. The curriculum is an interdisciplinary textbook program. The school is located in a small suburb about 20 miles west of a large city in the Midwest. Most of the children are from middle-to upper-middle-class families. At least 80% of the students who graduate from high school go on to college.

Mrs. Manning is the assistant principal for instruction who has scheduled a visit to David's classroom in order to observe his teaching and to determine how he is getting along as a first-year teacher. The observation session is taking place during the second month of the school year.

After Mr. Isaacson took role, he asked the students if they watched the Public Broadcasting System (PBS) science program last evening about the earth's interior. Four hands shot up with students eager to discuss the program. Mr. Isaacson responded with glee to learn that the students had taken the time to view the program. He called on several class members to give a summary of what they had learned from the 1-hour program. For the students who had not viewed the TV program, Mr. Isaacson told them that he taped it, and they could watch the program after school. He then reminded the class that they were studying chemical and physical changes, and that the PBS program focused on changes in the earth that have occurred over millions of years.

Mr. Isaacson used the next 10 minutes to discuss chemical and physical changes that he hoped students noted during the TV program, asking them to refer to the guide sheet he had prepared and given to them the day before in order to direct their attention to important science ideas during the viewing.

MR. ISSACSON: Brandy, would you mind going to the board to list the physical changes that you recognized during the TV program?

MR. ISAACSON: Franklin, would you go to the board to list the chemical changes that you recognized during the TV program?

Then, Mr. Isaacson thanked the two students and called on the rest of the class to add to the lists of chemical and physical changes. At the conclusion of this segment of the lesson, Mr. Isaacson congratulated the students for being so observant about the science that was illustrated in the program and announced that he was moving on to another aspect of the study of chemical and physical changes.

MR. ISAACSON: Class, I want you to observe carefully what I am doing during this demonstration. Therefore, would you all stand and come a little closer to the demonstration table, but stay about 8 feet away. Okay, thanks.

When the students were in position and ready to view what Mr. Isaacson was about to do, he stepped out in front of the demonstration table and held up a large, rusty nail.

MR. ISAACSON: Look at this nail carefully and tell me what you see.

MARISSA: The nail is rusted.

MR. ISSACSON: Very good, Marissa. Do the rest of you notice the rust and corrosion that has occurred on this nail?

After everyone in the class acknowledged the rusting that had occurred on the nail, Mr. Issacson put on a pair of safety goggles and called a student to the demonstration table to weigh a handful of steel wool. He called on another student to record the mass of the steel wool on the board.

Then, Mr. Isaacson stepped behind the demonstration table, placed the steel wool on a square of aluminum foil, and ignited it by touching the positive and negative contacts of a 9-volt battery to the metal fibers of the steel wool.

The spectacular flame this reaction produced caused great excitement among the students. After the flame went out, the teacher calmed the students down and asked for silence. He asked the class members to make an inference about the change in mass of the steel wool by requesting a show of hands regarding the mass of the steel wool after is was set on fire. Was the steel wool: (a) lighter, (b) heavier, or (c) the same?

Mr. Isaacson called a student to the front demonstration table to place the steel wool on the scale to determine the mass and asked another student to record the mass on the board. Needless to say, the students were stunned to learn that the steel wool was heavier after burning it. Looks and comments of disbelief were all about the classroom. After the talking died down, Mr. Isaacson stated that he wanted the students to explain why the steel weighed more after it was set on fire.

Mr. Isaacson handed out a simple, one-page explanation of the oxidation that occurs when iron is set on fire. He asked the students to study the handout and to make notes in order to explain this puzzling event. After the 10 minutes, Mr. Isaacson announced that the class period would end in 8 minutes. He conducted a short review of the day's lesson and assigned three pages of reading from the science textbook, requesting that the students bring a two-paragraph explanation to class tomorrow that would demonstrate their knowledge of the science involved in burning steel wool.

STOP!

Before going on in this chapter, please do the following: take a sheet of paper and construct an evaluation form to assess the effectiveness of the teaching that occurred in this science lesson. You should use the ideas of good lesson planning that were discussed in the previous chapter, such as those related to teaching skills, instructional strategies, and learning techniques. When you have completed your evaluation of the lesson, discuss it with the instructor and other class members.

AIMS OF THE CHAPTER

Use the following questions to guide your thoughts and actions about teaching science:

- Can you develop assessment procedures to be used during and at the end of a lesson or unit that measure the effectiveness of a science teacher's instruction, including elements related to personal characteristics, teaching skills, instructional strategies, and techniques to enhance learning?

- How well can you analyze and evaluate the effectiveness of science teaching in a manner that would result in agreement with other pre-service or in-service science teachers who have studied this chapter and other chapters in this methods textbook?

- On a scale of 1 to 10, what teaching effectiveness score would you receive from your instructor or peers if you taught a science lesson to middle school and high school students or to adults preparing to become science teachers?

The act of teaching is familiar to all of us. After 16 or more years of schooling, all college graduates possess knowledge of how to instruct students because they have observed and participated in thousands of hours of instruction. Further, we would venture to say that most individuals with a baccalaureate degree believe they can teach well. The time has come for you to test this assumption. However, before going on, you must perform the following task.

Stop and Reflect!

Go no further until you have constructed an evaluation form and analyzed the vignette at the front of this chapter. You will need your assessment of Mr. Isaacson's teaching effectiveness in order to continue with the reading and exercises in this chapter.

In the writing exercises that follow we will concentrate on helping you to become a more effective science teacher, one who is informed about good teaching practices, knowledgeable enough to recognize them, and able to use them. The focus will be on teaching in front of students in grades 6–12, as well as with adult peers in the science methods class. Teaching science as inquiry is our philosophical position with regard to instruction, which includes a variety of skills, methods, and techniques (National Research Council, 1996). Later in this textbook, you will encounter entire chapters that address: (a) managing the learning environment, (b) assessing student learning, (c) inquiry-based instruction, (d) laboratory exercises and fieldwork, and (e) science/technology/society approaches to science teaching. For now, let's examine teaching science lessons by focusing on four aspects of teaching effectiveness: the personal characteristics of the teacher, the use of teaching skills, the implementation of instructional strategies, and the incorporation of learning techniques.

PERSONAL CHARACTERISTICS

The attributes of a teacher are critical to his or her success in the classroom. The most capable science teachers that we have observed possess a great deal of energy that translates into their work. These teachers are more likely to engage students in effective procedures and *teach science as inquiry* than those who expend a minimal amount of energy in their planning and teaching. Instead of presenting students with a large body of organized information, the more experienced and informed science teachers engage students in a variety of thinking processes and ways to help them construct their own science understanding and consider how these understandings can be used to enhance their lives.

A competent science teacher must possess a good *understanding of the subject* he or she teaches. Only with this level of knowledge will a teacher be able to ask good questions, probe for student understanding, and stimulate class discussion. The body of scientific knowledge is large, and comprehending even a small amount of core content in the fields of science you are assigned to teach requires a good background. Students quickly realize when their teacher lacks subject matter competence. Therefore, all science teachers must maintain continuous study of science, especially in the areas they are assigned to teach.

An individual who can *make the subject interesting and relevant to the audience* holds the potential to engage them in learning and remembering the content under study. The teacher with a baccalaureate degree in science who attempts to merely cover the content of a science lesson does not fare well in his or her teaching. Lessons need to be tailored to the prior knowledge and abilities of the audience. You are expected to bring your own special twist to teaching a given topic, which must include minds-on activities as well as information.

Teachers who are *enthusiastic* about teaching science are apt to motivate students. Their understanding about natural phenomena and the stories about how this knowledge has been constructed over time are made fascinating by their interest in teaching as well as the topic under study. And, of course, the very experienced, exceptional science teachers are passionate about their work. These educators exude their knowledge and understanding of science, which in turn infects their students.

You must be "withit" in order to be successful in the classroom. "*Withitness*" is the ability to teach students and to know what is taking place in all areas of the classroom (Brophy, 1983). Teachers who exhibit this ability can manage student activity and instruct at the same time. They know if students are misbehaving and off-task, and students are aware that the teacher knows what they are doing at all times. Therefore, you must be prepared to move from one instructional strategy to another, keeping your eye on all students and engaging them in learning. Withitness is a personal characteristic that may be difficult to develop, but nevertheless it is essential to managing a productive learning environment.

You must show *interest in helping students to learn,* not merely in communicating what students should be learning. Audiences of all ages can sense the difference between a teacher who covers the subject matter and one who is focused on how well they are grasping the ideas under study. An effective teacher is a guide and a facilitator, encouraging students to learn and to be successful (Rogers & Freiberg, 1994).

Stop and Reflect!

Return to the scenario of the first-year teacher described at the start of this chapter and to your analysis of his teaching. Considering the personal characteristics of an effective teacher, how would you describe and rate Mr. Isaacson on these elements? How interested is the teacher in teaching science to young people and helping them to be successful in learning science? Does Mr. Isaacson make the subject matter relevant? Is he withit?

TEACHING SKILLS

Teaching skills are specific behaviors that teachers use to conduct lessons and implement instructional strategies. These skills are needed to introduce lessons, ask questions, give directions, provide feedback, interact with students, and end lessons. Teaching skills must be developed in order to conduct effective science lessons. These are the behaviors that promote student engagement during instruction.

Introduction

The introduction prepares students for learning. It focuses attention on what will be taught and attempts to interest students in the lesson. Other labels given for the lesson introduction are: set induction, anticipatory set, and attention grabber.

Directions

Directions communicate what is expected and guide students to proper and productive behavior. Directions are given in a manner that ensures that all students know what to do and how to perform. Directions are generally given orally and written on the board. Questions asked by the teacher can be used to determine how well students comprehend what it is they have been directed to do.

Questions

Questions involve students in learning by causing them to think and respond. Students' responses to questions aid in the development of their understanding. Teachers can ask many types of questions beyond the one-answer type, such as higher-order, open-ended, and probing questions. They can use questions that encourage students to: be *engaged* in the lesson, *explore* their own thinking, *explain* their ideas, *evaluate* their findings, and *elaborate* on what they have learned. Further, teachers can demonstrate appropriate wait time, giving students opportunities to think about the question posed and the responses given by other students.

Teaching Aids

There are many teaching aids that facilitate the presentation of ideas and information and promote student learning. These instructional devices, when coupled with good questions and clear explanations, are very effective. The chalkboard and whiteboard, found most often at the front of the classroom, are common fixtures in most classrooms. The overhead projector may also be found in the classroom. Teacher-made posters are effective teaching aids. Today, some schools have placed electronic projection systems in classrooms to show pictures and text computer files, PowerPoint presentations, and commercially prepared CDs.

Management

Good classroom management includes everything that a teacher does to create and sustain a productive learning environment. The skills that lead to a productive learning environment can be observed in teachers who develop positive relationships among all students and between students and the teacher. It can also be observed in those who transition efficiently from one activity to another.

The good classroom manager keeps students on-task and is quick to address disruptive behavior. Further, these teachers consciously position themselves in the classroom in order to maximize student engagement.

Closure

The closure brings a lesson or a teaching segment to an end. This act helps students to review what has been presented and to reinforce main ideas. Student achievement of the intended learning outcomes also can be ascertained during closure. Asking students to respond orally to questions, complete a worksheet, or construct a diagram or concept map are effective ways to both assess and reinforce learning.

Assessment

An essential aspect of a successful teaching and learning experience for students is to measure and evaluate their learning often during the lesson. When all is said and done with regard to a teaching session, a legitimate question is: To what extent did the students achieve the instructional objectives? A complete teaching and learning experience should provide evidence of student learning, whether it takes the form of questions to answer on paper, a paper-and-pencil quiz, or drawing a concept map. The assessment process should provide both the teacher and students with a clear idea about the success of the lesson and what future lessons should address.

The effective use of many teaching skills during a period of instruction, while seemingly simple and straightforward, is not easy to carry out well. The development of these skills is a life-long pursuit. In busy, complex classrooms, many teachers are not aware of how well they open a lesson, engage students, close the lesson down, and so on, because: (a) "classroom events are complicated, (b) communication is rapid, (c) teachers generally do not study their classroom behavior (d) rarely do they receive good, objective feedback" (Good & Brophy, 2000, p. 23).

Stop and Reflect!

Return to your assessment of the lesson of Mr. Isaacson. Examine the teaching skills that you noted in his teaching.

- Which teaching skills were used in the teaching session?

- How would you judge the effectiveness of this beginning science teacher with regard to his use of specific behaviors to conduct the lessons?

- Do you think that this teacher uses teaching skills automatically, or does he make a conscious effort to use them in lessons?

INSTRUCTIONAL STRATEGIES

An instructional strategy designates the way a major segment or an entire lesson is approached. It is the general teaching plan for achieving a given set of learning outcomes. Some lessons are planned around the presentation of information, and thus the lecture may be used. Some lessons are planned around activities that require students to develop abstract ideas from firsthand experiences. Some lessons are planned around the illustration of science principles or laws through the use of a demonstration. Some lessons are planned around reinforcing what has been learned over several lessons by recitation that incorporates questioning and reading selected passages from the assigned textbook, while other lessons are designed around two or more instructional strategies.

Let's review the instructional methods discussed earlier in this textbook so that you will get into the habit of carefully selecting, planning, and implementing these approaches in your science lessons.

Lecture

Lectures involve the presentation of information. Lecturing is an efficient way to instruct a large group of students. It should involve carefully organized information communicated in an articulate manner. Further, a good lecture should be interesting and informative, advancing the audience's understanding of the topic, not merely covering large numbers of terms to be memorized. Lectures should be planned based on the attention span, background knowledge, and interests of the audience.

Discussion

Discussion permits students to express their views and clarify their ideas. This is a good strategy for promoting student involvement in the classroom. Discussion groups can be organized with the entire class, small groups, or in student pairs. However, in order for discussions to be productive and focused on the intended learning outcomes of the lesson, their purpose must be made clear. Students must listen carefully, and respondents must focus on the important content that is being discussed. Panels can be organized in order to debate and discuss issues. Also, informal discussion groups can be formed for the purpose of brainstorming to generate ideas.

Demonstration

Demonstrations illustrate ideas through concrete means. They focus attention on key aspects of a concept and can be an effective means for guiding student thinking. Demonstrations are often of high interest to students. This is a strategy that teachers can use to illustrate science concepts or principles that may not be desirable to study in the laboratory because of expense or safety.

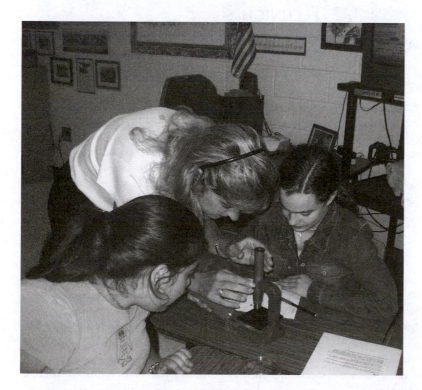

Good teachers are not born, but develop their skills and understanding through practice, reflection, and interaction with knowledgeable others.

Laboratory Work

The laboratory involves students in firsthand experiences to study natural phenomena. Laboratory exercises also are used to teach students laboratory techniques and inquiry skills. This strategy can be approached in a variety of ways, such as initiating laboratory experiences with an inductive or a deductive activity or by focusing on a problem to be solved. Laboratory exercises should be used frequently throughout a science course to promote science learning.

Reading

Reading is a way to promote many aspects of science by forming ideas and grasping meaning from the printed word. Directed reading activities in science textbooks or other printed materials can be implemented frequently as a whole-class, small-group, or independent activity. One type of content reading strategy might include the following activities: (a) pre-reading exercises to identify what students know, (b) during-reading exercises that focus on key words and passages, and (c) after-reading exercises that summarize what has been learned.

Group Work

Group work is an excellent way to engage students in learning science. This strategy encourages students to work together, sharing ideas and working cooperatively at tasks that lead to a common product. Cooperative grouping is designed to assign different roles to individual students with guidelines to carry out their tasks. This can be a powerful strategy to learn science content and process, promote good working habits and cooperation, and build a positive classroom atmosphere.

Simulations and Games

Simulations and games are designed to illustrate events and processes that occur in the real world. They help students visualize objects and events that cannot be observed in the classroom, laboratory, or nearby community. Today, there are many computer simulations that provide rich learning experiences for students. Good, short science simulations should be part of all units and courses of study, but should not to be confused with laboratory work.

Computers and Internet

The computer and the Internet hold enormous potential to engage students in finding out about ideas, answering questions, and solving problems. Students can search thousands of science topics on the Internet and even find scientific data to analyze and study. They can use e-mail to contact scientists and others for information. Many government research facilities and science museums can be accessed for information related to science. Students can use word processing and graphics programs to organize and present their ideas and findings. The instructional possibilities are unlimited with computer and Internet technology.

Recitation

The recitation session requires students to demonstrate their knowledge through their responses to teacher questions. It usually takes place toward the end of a lesson, with the teacher calling on certain students to answer questions that pertain directly to the learning outcomes of the lesson. However, recitation can take place during lessons. Recitation is an excellent strategy for incorporating formative assessment into instruction.

Stop and Reflect!

- List the instructional strategies that were used by Mr. Isaacson during his science lesson, and compare your list with those of other participants in the methods course. How much agreement is there among your analyses?
- Which instructional strategies would you use in teaching chemical and physical changes to middle school students or to high school chemistry students?

LEARNING AND REINFORCEMENT TECHNIQUES

When you teach a science lesson that incorporates many teaching skills and instructional strategies, you may feel confident about the success of your teaching. And indeed, you should feel good about this. However, there is more to the teaching effectiveness equation that must be considered in order to reinforce student learning. Remember, we want students to understand what they are expected to learn and to explain this understanding in an articulate manner. Teaching and learning for understanding is a major goal for science education, just as the aim of science is to understand natural phenomena. Teaching for understanding sets the stage for moving on to applying what is being studied. We believe that students who understand the conceptual knowledge they are expected to learn may perform better on district, state, and national standardized texts.

Today, educators realize that a teacher must get students to use learning techniques that organize and reinforce the knowledge they are constructing. Research on cognitive learning processes has advanced our understanding on how to help students develop knowledge structures that promote understanding and retention of subject matter (Rosenshine, 2002). Following is a discussion of some of the techniques to incorporate into your instruction. While you may not be able to use all of these techniques in a given lesson, you should implement most of them within a unit of study.

Note taking should be a standard practice in science course learning. This process causes students to focus on the important ideas and information. Students must keep a science notebook of useful information that they will commit to memory and refer to when reviewing for tests, doing homework, and completing assignments. Also, you must teach students how to take notes and monitor their note taking so that feedback can be given on how well this is being done.

Writing summaries and short papers to organize ideas is critical to the understanding of abstract science subject matter. Writing requires students to think deeply to recall what they know, organize what they are expected to learn, and organize their thoughts on paper. Students should be required to write often about their science learning. Writing is one of the most powerful mental tasks in which teachers can engage students (Wallace, 2004).

Identifying similarities and differences is a technique that appears to have one of the strongest effects on learning (Marzano, Pickering, & Pollock, 2001). When you call on students to compare science concepts, they must know their attributes and indicate how they are similar and what distinguishes them. It is essential that students possess a clear idea of how fundamental science concepts are similar, yet different, such as mitosis and meiosis, mass and weight, and speed and acceleration. Analogies are powerful tools for helping students to learn abstract ideas.

Concept mapping supports visual learning. It helps students to organize information by showing the relationships among key concepts. This graphic learning technique can facilitate the meaningful learning of abstract and complex ideas when students are actively engaged in forming their own concept maps of important subject matter content. You should frequently ask students to construct concept maps, webs, and diagrams to demonstrate their knowledge of the subject under study.

Practice and feedback must be an integral part of all science instruction. There is always the danger of covering too much subject matter in science courses and not providing enough instruction of main ideas to ensure mastery. Students need to practice the cognitive skill of articulating their understandings of science in order to integrate their knowledge into long-term memory. Teachers must monitor these learning activities and provide feedback to ensure that students are forming ideas correctly and staying on the task of learning.

These and other learning techniques will be taken up in the chapter on Learning in Middle Grades and Secondary Schools. Nevertheless, we hope that you will be motivated to use them in your teaching. Your commonsense knowledge about these techniques will get you started.

Stop and Reflect!

Go back and examine the instruction that took place in Mr. Isaacson's classroom.

- Did Mr. Isaacson include in his lesson any of the learning strategies described?
- How might Mr. Isaacson improve his teaching in order to ensure greater understanding of chemical and physical changes among his students?
- Can you name the learning strategies that you have observed in the classrooms of effective science teachers?

SUMMARY

This chapter has provided a brief description of many aspects of teaching that relate to student learning. You know about these elements of teaching because of the many years you have spent in school. Now, you must incorporate these teaching skills, instructional strategies, and learning techniques into your teaching, and you must become more aware of the personal characteristics of good teachers that also impact student success. Figure 4.1 summarizes these ideas, and you should refer to them often as you plan and teach science lessons.

NOW LET'S TEACH SCIENCE

The time has arrived when you should teach a science lesson and receive feedback and evaluation on your performance. Prepare a science lesson to be given to your peers, adult science majors preparing to become science teachers. (Refer to the previous chapter on planning science instruction.) Construct a lesson plan for a 50-minute period of instruction. Conduct the first 20 minutes of the lesson and receive feedback from your peers and instructor. The instructor can provide the overall rating of the teaching, or this can be achieved by the collective ratings of the peer group. Of course, if time permits, the teaching session can extend for the full 50-minute lesson. Following are some guidelines for this exercise, which can be modified to suit your situation:

1. Design a science lesson to be taught to a group of *peers* that is appropriate for this audience. The lesson must be one that:
   - Actively engages the audience in thinking
   - Is perceived by peers and the instructor to be interesting and meaningful
   - Is challenging for the adult science majors in the audience
   - Focuses on a science concept, principle, law, or theory

FIGURE 4.1   A menu of personal characteristics, teaching skills, instructional strategies, and learning techniques to engage students in learning science for understanding.

Be Aware of Personal Characteristics
- ✓ Inclines toward inquiry-based instruction
- ✓ Demonstrates knowledge and understanding of the subject
- ✓ Makes the subject interesting and relevant to the audience
- ✓ Enthusiastic about teaching science
- ✓ Exhibits "withitness" in the classroom
- ✓ Shows interest in helping students to be successful

Employ Many Teaching Skills
- ✓ Introductions—grabs attention and provides a foundation for the lesson
- ✓ Directions—clear and concise
- ✓ Questions—directed toward students to stimulate thinking and reasoning
- ✓ Teaching aids—facilitate the presentation of ideas and information
- ✓ Management—keeps students on task and minimize disruptions
- ✓ Closure—summarizes and reviews main ideas
- ✓ Assessment—used to reinforce learning and is linked to instructional objects

Use a Variety of Instructional Strategies
- ✓ Lectures that promote organization of ideas and stimulate interest
- ✓ Discussions that stimulate thoughtful dialog among students
- ✓ Demonstrations that spark interest and illustrate key concepts
- ✓ Laboratory work that provides firsthand experiences with laws and principles
- ✓ Reading that helps to build knowledge
- ✓ Group work that promotes cooperation and collaboration
- ✓ Simulations/games that illustrate important concepts and principles
- ✓ Recitation that reinforces learning

Incorporate Techniques to Enhance Learning
- ✓ Note taking that organizes and summarizes information to be learned
- ✓ Writing that stimulates deep thinking and mental processing of ideas
- ✓ Identifying similarities and differences among key concepts
- ✓ Concept mapping to facilitate visual learning
- ✓ Practice and feedback for mastery

- Does *not* involve laboratory work, *nor* does it attempt to teach science process skills or about the nature of science
2. Construct a detailed, long-form lesson plan for a 50-minute class period. The lesson must be typed, single-spaced, and include:
   - Cover page with the title of the lesson and your name
   - Paragraph giving the purpose
   - List of materials and equipment that are needed to deliver the lesson
   - Instructional objectives that state precisely what the peers will learn from the lesson
   - Detailed descriptions of the instructional activities

   Be sure the first instructional activity (often called a set induction or an anticipatory set) grabs the attention of the learners and provides them with a mental set for the lesson. End with a closure and review of key ideas.
   - Attach handouts that will be used in the lesson
   - Actual assessment of the instructional objects at the end of the lesson plan
3. Teach part of the lesson (approximately 20 minutes) to peers. This teaching exercise is only for the first part of the lesson, and the individual teaching must not attempt to teach the entire lesson during this period of time, because it would result in a fast-paced lesson that would minimize learner engagement.
4. Following the 20-minute teaching session, the person teaching can participate in the feedback of the lesson by going to the board and writing the comments of the audience as suggested in Figure 4.2.

FIGURE 4.2   Feedback and evaluation form for a teaching session.

Title of Lesson: _____

Name of Teacher: _____ Date: _____

Rating of Lesson: ------Poor------   ------Fair------   ------Good------   -----Excellent-----
                    6.0   6.5   7   7.5   8.0   8.5   9.0   9.5   10

Elements to Look for During the Lesson

A. *Personal Characteristics*
___ Demonstrates understanding of subject
___ Exhibits enthusiasm for teaching
___ Maintains students' interest
___ Plans a challenging lesson

B. *Teaching Skills*
___ Provides an attention-grabbing introduction
___ Asks thought-provoking questions
___ Gives students time to think about their answers
___ Paces the lesson well
___ Uses a variety of teaching aids

C. *Instructional Strategies*
___ Implements more than one instructional strategy
___ Uses instructional strategies well
___ Results in great deal of student engagement

D. Learning Techniques
___ Note taking and writing is encouraged
___ Explaining ideas is stressed
___ Feedback is given
___ Reinforcement and praise is observed

Notes on Teaching Observed During the Lesson

Summary of Post-Lesson Feedback

Effective Aspects of the Teaching   *Suggestions for Improvement*

5. After reflecting on the lesson for several days, each person who taught should write at least one paragraph stating the strengths of the lesson and one paragraph indicating aspects that might be modified or improved.

Figure 4.2 presents a feedback and evaluation form that can be used for this teaching exercise. The form lists some of the personal characteristics, teaching skills, instructional strategies, and learning techniques that might be used during a science lesson. Note that there is a place for observational notes. In addition, there are spaces at the bottom of the form to list the *effective aspects* of the teaching and *suggestions for improvement*. At the end of 20 minutes of teaching, the individual who taught can place the labels on the board as shown on the form and list the phases given by the peers and instructor. The individual who teaches may also list his or her reflections regarding the teaching.

NOTE: The first 20 minutes of the teaching should be very engaging, interesting, and challenging to the audience, teaching them something that they did not know about the science topic. This segment of the lesson should be a "knock-your-socks-off introduction" that leaves the audience saying: "I did not know that" or "I never thought of it that way." Further, the session should be an invitation to inquiry, whereby the audience wants to learn more about the topic.

Begin the feedback with the effective teaching behaviors that were demonstrated, followed by a list of suggestions for improvement that should have been present during this lesson to this group. Avoid the use of the term *criticism* or a discussion that is critical in nature. List only suggestions for improvement that identify teaching behaviors that were absent and detracted from the lesson. You should not bring up trivial aspects of the teaching or suggestions that pertain to teaching a younger audience. Keep the feedback positive!

The form also has a place at the top to rate the lesson. The rating scale scheme is a holistic approach to assessment, not one where you add up points for each behavior observed. At the end of the session, you form an overall impression of the teaching. This scale can be modified for a 50-point, 100-point, or other range.

All teachers can profit from a short, 20-minute teaching session with feedback and evaluation from adult peers. After success with this short practice teaching approach, lessons can be given to middle and high school students in local school classrooms. The classroom science teacher can provide feedback and a rating score on the lesson.

ASSESSING AND REVIEWING

Analysis and Synthesis

1. Name the four categories of teaching that were discussed in this chapter. Within each category, which descriptors do you feel are most critical to effective science teaching?

Practical Considerations

2. Consider a situation where a colleague or peer asks you to observe a science lesson that he or she will teach and to provide feedback and an evaluation of the lesson. Based on the discussion of science teaching in this chapter, *design* a feedback and evaluation form that you would use in observing your colleague or peer.

3. Make arrangements to observe an inexperienced and an experienced science teacher instructing middle or high school students. Use a feedback and evaluation form that you developed or the one presented in this chapter to make notes and to summarize the teaching behaviors observed during the lessons. After you have listed the effective aspects of the teaching and suggestions for improvement for each lesson, compare the lessons taught by the inexperienced and experienced teachers.

4. Choose the science subject that you are most comfortable in teaching to a class of middle or high school students. Then, make an arrangement to teach a science lesson in a public or private school. Ask the cooperating teacher to use the feedback and evaluation form, which you designed or the one in this chapter, to record observations and to identify effective aspects of your teaching as well as suggestions for improvement. Spend some time discussing the instrument with the cooperating teacher in order for him or her to understand the purpose of this exercise and how to assess it.

Remember to do the following in preparation for your teaching: (a) determine what the cooperating teacher would want you to teach; (b) find out the number of students in the class, the arrangement of the classroom, and the characteristics of the students; (c) prepare a long-form, detailed lesson plan and share it with the cooperating teacher for his/her suggestions; (d) gather all materials needed for the lesson well in advance of the session; and (e) practice the lesson before you deliver it.

After the lesson, discuss the teaching with the cooperating teacher. Several days after the lesson, reflect on your instruction and write a few paragraphs highlighting the effective aspects of your teaching as well as those that need more work.

Developmental Considerations

5. Find one or more books or papers that address teaching effectiveness research. Summarize for your professional files teaching behaviors and strategies that might be useful to you in becoming a successful science teacher.

RESOURCES TO EXAMINE

Qualities of Effective Teachers. 2002. Alexandria, Virginia: Association for Supervision and Curriculum Development, Alexandria Virginia.

This short paperback by James Stronge addresses many aspects of effective teaching. The chapter on "The Teacher as a Person" discusses the personal aspects of a teacher that influence teaching and learning. The book gives many bulleted tips on the teaching skills and instructional strategies discussed in this chapter on teaching science. It also gives a long list of the research studies that support the ideas put forth in this paperback.

Classroom Instruction That Works: Research-Based Strategies for Increasing Student Achievement. 2001. Alexandria, Virginia: Association for Supervision and Curriculum Development, Alexandria Virginia.

This is a valuable resource for teachers and educators. The book describes many of the instructional strategies and learning techniques that have been successful in promoting learning, such as cooperative learning, reinforcement, homework, practice, cues, questions, and advanced organizers. Further, the instructional effect of each factor on learning is given.

Universal Teaching Strategies. 2005. Boston: Allyn and Bacon.

This book by Jerome Freiberg and Amy Driscoll goes into depth in discussing many instructional strategies and management strategies. It describes the strategies and offers examples on how to implement them in the classroom. The chapters often provide some historical research background of effective teaching.

"An Illumination of the Role of Hands-on Activities, Discussion, Text Reading and Writing in Constructing Biology Knowledge in Seventh Grade." 2004. *School Science and Mathematics, 104*(2), 70–77.

Carolyn Wallace's study highlights the efficacy of engaging students in expressing their thoughts in writing when learning science. The research study shows that the students who used the techniques called Science Writing Heuristic did better on a conceptual test than those students who did not benefit from this aid to their learning. Reading, writing, and discourse should be implemented more frequently in the science classroom.

REFERENCES

Brophy, J. E. (1983). Classroom organization and management. *The Elementary School Journal, 83*(4), 265–285.

Good, T. L., & Brophy, J. E. (2000). *Looking into classrooms.* New York: Longman.

Marzano, R. J., Pickering, D. J., & Pollock, J. E. (2001). *Classroom instruction that works: Research-based strategies for increasing student achievement.* Alexandria, VA: Association for Supervision and Curriculum Development.

National Research Council (NRC). (1996). *National science education standards.* Washington, DC: National Academy Press.

Rogers, C., & Freiberg, H. J. (1994). *Freedom to learn.* Upper Saddle River, NJ: Merrill/Prentice Hall.

Rosenshine, B. (2002). Converging findings on classroom instruction. In A. Molnar (Ed.), *School reform proposals: The research evidence* (pp. 175–196). Tempe, AZ: Arizona State University, College of Education, Educational Policy Research Unit.

Wallace, C. S. (2004). An illumination of the role of hands-on activities, discussion, text reading and writing in constructing biology knowledge in seventh grade. *School Science and Mathematics, 104*(2), 70–77.

Managing the Science Learning Environment

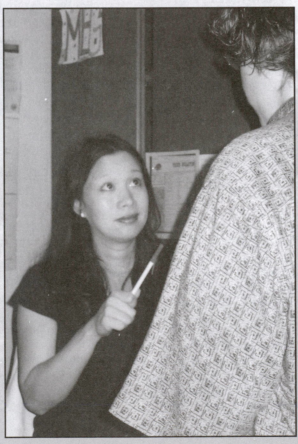

Effective classroom managers emphasize student self-regulation and responsibility over student obedience.

*L*et's look again into the classroom of Ms. Melissa Longorio, the physical science teacher you first met in Chapter 1. Today, Melissa is teaching a follow-up lesson to her introduction on acids and bases. She has invited Mrs. Reed, her mentor, to observe her lesson and asked her to provide specific feedback on her classroom management. Melissa confided in Mrs. Reed that the students in this class have become harder to handle, and she is not sure what to do next.

Today's warm-up questions and homework assignment were projected on the whiteboard at the front of the classroom as students filed in. This was Ms. Longorio's way of telling students to find their seats, copy down their homework assignment, and begin to answer the questions. As her mentor had suggested, this routine allowed Melissa time to check attendance and complete other routine chores, which today included entering into the school's computer grading system the test scores for two students who had recently taken a make-up test.

Ten minutes after the bell sounded, Melissa moved from her desk to the overhead projector located on a rolling cart in the front of the room.

MS. LONGORIO: Today, we're going to do a lab on pH, which is what we talked about yesterday. Your task will be to determine the pH of six unknown liquids using both pH test paper and a pH meter, and then order the unknowns from lowest to highest along the pH scale. I'd like you to work in your four-person lab groups. The materials you need, including the lab instructions, are at the lab stations. Any questions?

JULIO: I have a question, Ms. Longorio. Do we have to write anything down?

MS. LONGORIO: Of course you have to record your results. Just read the directions that are at the lab stations. The directions tell you

what data to record. Ok, if there are no more questions, please go to your assigned lab stations, and don't forget to wear your safety goggles and don't taste anything.

Five minutes later, the murmur of student groupwork was broken by shouts coming from the lab station in the right rear corner of the room. Ms. Longorio looked up to see two girls shoving each other and walked quickly to where the girls were standing.

TAMIKA: This girl isn't supposed to be here. She's not in our lab group. She needs to go somewhere else.

TAMIKA'S LAB PARTNERS, IN UNISON: That's right, she needs to go.

MS. LONGORIO: Ok, students. That's enough. Katie, right? Is this your lab group?

KATIE: I don't know. I wasn't here the day you assigned lab groups, so I just thought I'd join this one. I didn't think it would be a big deal.

MS. LONGORIO: Alright Katie, come with me, and we'll look at the lab assignment sheet to determine which group you were assigned to. Tamika, are you able to work with the other members of your group without causing another disturbance?

TAMIKA: Yeah, now that she's gone!

As Ms. Longorio was searching her desk computer to find the class lab group assignments and to identify the group to which Katie had been assigned, other things were happening in the lab. Eric and Clyde mixed their group's unknowns, even though the lab sheet had given no such instructions; two other groups were engaged in a paperwad basketball game, using the lab station sinks as goals; and Jong-jin walked from one lab station to another with his goggles pushed up on his forehead.

After directing Katie to her assigned lab group, Ms. Longorio scanned the classroom. She noticed that the students were tightly packed *around the lab benches and that bookbags lay on the floor around students' feet. Before she could begin to circulate, Ms. Longorio heard Lillie's call for help from the closest lab station.*

LILLIE: *Ms. Longorio, my group is lost. We still don't understand this pH stuff. Why don't our readings using the pH meter match those we got using the pH test paper? Shouldn't they be about the same since they are just different ways of collecting the same data?*

MS. LONGORIO: *Yes, your pH readings using the two data collection methods should be similar. Did you use the pH test paper that I set out at your lab station, and did someone in your group calibrate the pH meter before starting?*

RAUL: *Yes, Ms. Longorio, we used the test paper that was here, and we calibrated the pH meter. Just look at our data table.*

MS. LONGORIO: *Well, I see a pattern in your data based on my knowledge of the unknowns I gave you to test. The pattern suggests to me that you may not have rinsed the pH meter electrode in distilled water before testing each new solution. Did you read the directions?*

RAUL: *Brandon, you read the lab directions. Were we supposed to do that?*

BRANDON: *I don't know. Ms. Longorio, you didn't say to rinse the electrode.*

MS. LONGORIO: *Students, I think you need to collect new data, but you can't use the unknowns here at your station because now they're contaminated. I bet that you were not the only group who didn't read the lab instructions.*

BRANDON: *This was a waste of time! We didn't learn a thing! Why didn't you tell us what to do? You're the teacher, aren't you?*

With 20 minutes left in the class period, Ms. Longorio instructed the class to clean up their lab stations and return to their desks. She was frustrated. The laboratory activity that she thought would be very simple seemed to confuse the students and took almost the whole period to complete. She feared that most of the students had made data collection errors because they had not read the lab instructions. Even the questions that she had planned to ask as the students' "ticket out the door" now seemed to be inappropriate. Rather than discussing the lab as she had planned, Ms. Longorio allowed the class to work on their homework assignment until the bell rang. Some chose to take advantage of this time, while others talked, did homework for other classes, and requested hall passes to visit the restroom.

AIMS OF THE CHAPTER

Use the questions that follow to guide your thinking and learning about some fundamental aspects of managing the science learning environment:

- What should science teachers know about the first days of school?

- What are some causes of middle and high school students' inappropriate behavior?

- What can science teachers do to build positive relationships between themselves and students and among students in their classes?

- What organizational and management strategies can science teachers use to develop productive learning habits and on-task behaviors among their students?

- What can teachers do to motivate and enable their students to be engaged science learners?

Classroom management is much more than responding to student misbehavior. It "encompasses all that teachers do to encourage learning in their classrooms, including creating an environment that supports instruction to promote and maintain student learning and engagement" (Evertson & Harris, 2000, p. 61). This holistic definition of classroom management reflects a significant shift in thinking about the teacher's role as classroom leader and the relationship between teacher and student and among students. The shift is from a paradigm of *obedience,* where the teacher uses her power to compel students to comply, to a paradigm that emphasizes *responsibility,* where the teacher helps students to develop inner self-guidance (Brophy, 2000). Important changes reflective of this paradigm shift are presented in Table 5.1.

TABLE 5.1   Changing Emphasis in Classroom Management

Less Emphasis On	More Emphasis On
• Management as a bag of tricks and recipes to be followed	• Management as thoughtful decision making
• Student obedience	• Student self-regulation and responsibility
• Teaching rules	• Developing trust and caring
• Short-term responses to misbehavior	• Long-term solutions to personal and classroom problems
• Work-oriented classrooms	• Learning-oriented classrooms
• Adopting a behavioral management program	• Developing a personalized classroom management plan
• Professional development that involves learning from an expert during a workshop	• Professional development that is ongoing, reflective, and collaborative

Based on information from "Reflections on Best Practice and Promising Programs" by C. S. Weinstein, 2000, in H. J. Freiberg (Ed.), *Beyond Behaviorism: Changing the Classroom Management Paradigm* (pp. 147–163), Boston: Allyn & Bacon.

From the perspective highlighted in this paradigm shift, disciplining students becomes something done when classroom management is not successful. The major focus of the teacher's work as a classroom manager becomes developing and implementing a systematic plan that encourages appropriate student behavior rather than figuring out how to deal with behavior problems once they have erupted. This plan must be consistent with the educational aims of the classroom as well as considerate of students' personal and educational needs. An effective plan will lead to the creation and maintenance of a learning environment that supports student academic success and well-being.

THE FIRST DAYS OF SCHOOL

The first days of school are critically important, particularly so for the beginning science teacher. The year's success or failure is largely determined by what the teacher says and does during the first days of school (Evertson & Emmer, 1982; Sanford & Evertson, 1981). By and large, beginning science teachers will not have experienced the excitement and stress associated with starting the school year, at least not from the teacher's side of the desk.

Your memories of the first days of school as a middle or high school student probably include visiting with friends, scoping out the new kids, and meeting your teachers. You may recall how your new teachers introduced themselves and explained their expectations. Your first impressions of those teachers likely told you a great deal about how the class would operate, what you would learn, and what would be expected of you throughout the year.

Today is the first day of school, and as a beginning biology teacher Jennifer Kilborn wants to get off to a good start. She arrives in her classroom at 7:45 A.M. to make sure that everything is ready. After straightening the rows of student desks and hanging the large poster of Dian Fossey and her gorillas on the wall, Jennifer sits nervously at her desk watching the clock in anticipation of the first-period bell. As she watches the clock's secondhand sweep around the dial, her mind is filled with the stories told by two veteran teachers she met during the district's preplanning days. Her thoughts keep returning to the teachers' parting words: "Start out the year by showing them who is boss," "As a young teacher, you'll need to be extra tough," and "Don't even think about smiling until Christmas." Jennifer is very anxious. She knows she is not a mean person by nature and does not want to appear mean spirited to her students, but she feels that she must be extremely stern with her students during the first days of school to avoid the many problems that often befall beginning teachers. What advice would you give Jennifer to help her resolve her dilemma?

The learning environments initiated by beginning science teachers during the first days of school will vary considerably. Some may be academically oriented and stress the socialization of students into a learning community, while others may discourage students from asking questions, emphasize grades over learning, and foster argumentation rather than cooperation. Helen Patrick and her colleagues (2003) provide insights into the messages conveyed by teachers during the first days of school. The instructional practices used by teachers who cultivate a supportive learning environment are summarized in Table 5.2. It is these instructional practices associated with a supportive learning environment that enable students to achieve academically.

TABLE 5.2   Instructional Practices of Teachers in Supportive Environments During the First Days of School

Tasks, Learning, and Expectations for Students	Relationships Between Teacher and Students	Relationships Among Students	Rules and Management Strategies
• Express enthusiasm for the curriculum and learning • Discuss the empowering nature of learning • Present learning as an incremental process • Portray learning as enjoyable, valuable, and worthwhile • Exude confidence in their abilities to teach and help students learn	• Introduce themselves in personal and caring ways • Share some information about themselves and families • Use humor that is developmentally appropriate • Convey a sensitivity to students' needs and willingness to help • Show genuine respect for students	• Promote an atmosphere of community • Discuss the importance of respect among students • Encourage thoughtfulness of others and consideration for the feelings of all students • Encourage inclusive rather than exclusive behaviors	• Identify classroom rules and explain the reasons for them • Emphasize fairness • Give clear examples of appropriate and inappropriate behaviors • Stress students behaving responsibly and with self-control • Share expectations that students will behave and show respect to others • Enforce expectations in instances of student misbehavior

Based on information from "How Teachers Establish Psychological Environments During the First Days of School: Associations with Avoidance in Mathematics," by H. Patrick, J. C. Turner, D. K. Meyer, and C. Midgley, 2003. *Teachers College Record, 105*(8), 1521–1569.

MRS. REED: You know, Melissa, a lot of what we know about starting the school year and teacher practices that contribute to a supportive learning environment is a result of the teacher effectiveness research that was conducted during the 1970s, 1980s, and 1990s. People[1] who synthesized all of this research are very clear in their affirmation of three sets of teacher behaviors that influence students' behavior and academic success. The first of these sets of behaviors centers on the *interpersonal relationships* that teachers develop with their students and that teachers foster among students in their classes. The second set of behaviors focuses on the teacher's ability to *organize and manage* learning activities. The third set highlights teacher behaviors associated with *lesson design and teaching* that lead to heightened student motivation and content mastery.

MS. LONGORIO: Wow, I never thought about classroom management in terms of these categories of teacher behaviors.

MRS. REED: No doubt about it, engagement in these sets of behaviors is what distinguishes informed beginning teachers from uninformed beginning teachers during the first days of school and throughout the school year.

MS. LONGORIO: As my mentor, perhaps it would be a good idea for you to help me focus of these three sets of behaviors.

MRS. REED: Sure, Melissa, I'm very willing to help.

Stop and Reflect!

■ Based on the information presented in Table 5.2, what advice would you give to Jennifer regarding how to begin the school year? What advice would you give Melissa that might help her reestablish a positive learning environment in her physical science class?

■ What would you likely say or do during your first days of school to promote a supportive and responsibility-oriented environment in your classroom?

---

[1] These behaviors are described in Jones, V., & Jones, L. (2004). *Comprehensive classroom management: Creating communities of support and solving problems.* Boston: Allyn and Bacon.

Determining the Causes for Student Misbehavior

Before focusing on the actions of teachers that lessen the likelihood of student misbehavior and foster a supportive learning environment, it is important to consider the causes of student misbehavior. Misbehavior observed in students can usually be attributed to underlying conditions that may not be obvious. A teacher should try to identify the deeper problems causing the misbehavior before attempting to deal with it. Treating the symptoms without knowing the conditions causing them could result in more undesirable behaviors that may be more problematic than the behavior first observed.

The forces and pressures that students encounter in and out of school can generate many of the misbehaviors exhibited in the classroom. Common causes of student misbehavior include family pressures and expectations, students' academic abilities and motivation toward schoolwork, involvement in after-school activities, as well as health and personality factors. In addition, the school administration and the science teacher may unwittingly contribute to student misbehavior.

A useful tool for understanding the motives behind student misbehavior is Abraham Maslow's (1968) theory of a hierarchy of human needs. According to Maslow, humans are motivated by unsatisfied needs, and certain lower needs must be satisfied before higher needs can be considered. His hierarchy includes four general types of needs—physiological, safety, love and belonging, and esteem—that must be satisfied before a person can address his or her need for self-actualization. The need for self-actualization is the desire to be all you can be and is often fulfilled through learning (Maslow, 1968). Thus, middle and high school students' basic physiological needs, along with their needs for safety, love and belonging, and esteem must often be met in order for them to be engaged science learners. As a teacher, there is much that you can do to enable students to meet many of the needs that will allow them to be engaged learners. The information presented in Figure 5.1 may help you think about misbehavior as a student's response to the frustrations associated with being in a learning environment in which his or her basic needs are not being met. The questions in Figure 5.1 may help you consider the actions that you can take as a teacher to help students become self-actualized learners.

As a student in science methods class, Melissa Longorio also was introduced to Maslow's theory. She remembered discussing the different types of needs with her instructor and classmates, but she never really thought about the theory's applicability to her own teaching until she began to discuss her classroom management concerns with Mrs. Reed. Let's listen in on their discussion about Melissa's lesson on the pH of acids and bases presented at the beginning of this chapter.

 Mrs. Reed: It seems that you recall a good bit about Maslow's theory. So, let's consider how Maslow's hierarchy can help you understand and address Tamika's misbehavior. What unsatisfied need do you think Tamika might have been responding to in her altercation with Katie this morning?

Ms. Longorio: Well, it doesn't seem to be personal safety. She was the aggressor. And I don't think she was expressing a need for belonging, at least not in my class, because she seems to be well accepted by members of her group. In fact, Tamika and the other members of her group asked to work together.

Mrs. Reed: I agree with your thinking so far. So, what need might be prompting Tamika's misbehavior? Surely, it would have been easy for her to allow Katie to join the group, just for today's lab. What likely prompted her aggression toward Katie?

Ms. Longorio: I won't know for certain until I talk with Tamika one-on-one, but I think that she may have been trying to show off. You know, by confronting Katie, Tamika was hoping to gain respect from her group. Through her aggression toward Katie, Tamika may have been hoping to become more powerful among her friends.

Mrs. Reed: I hear you saying that Tamika's misbehavior was likely an attempt to address her need for attention and recognition from her peers. In the lingo of Maslow's theory, she is fulfilling her need for esteem.

Ms. Longorio: Ok, this helps me think about Tamika's needs and about how I might help her address them in ways that don't lead to class disruptions. Let me think. . . . I could recognize and praise Tamika's accomplishments in class. I could point out her accomplishments to others in her group and encourage them to seek Tamika's help. I might even appoint Tamika to take on a leadership role in the class—one that I know she can successfully accomplish.

Mrs. Reed: Melissa, I think you are well on your way to understanding Tamika and her behavior. Thinking about her needs seemed to be a big help to you. Next time we get together, I would like us to discuss Jong-jin. What unmet needs might be prompting his misbehavior of walking around the room during the lab?

FIGURE 5.1   Questions to aid the teacher in addressing students' unmet needs.

Esteem Needs

Self-esteem may be met through achieving capability or proficiency regarding an assignment or piece of work. Esteem coming from others in the form of recognition or admiration may fulfill a student's craving for power and might.

- Do I provide opportunities for students to show competence and mastery of learning tasks?
- Do all my students participate in group activities and class discussions?
- Do I listen to my students' suggestions for improving my teaching?
- Do I praise my students' accomplishments and encourage their classmates to do the same?

Love and Belonging Needs

Needs for love and belonging may be met through group membership and by being accepted and appreciated by peers and adults.

- Do my students know that I like them?
- Do my students know that I am accepting of them as individuals regardless of their personalities and backgrounds?
- Is my class organized to encourage camaraderie and teamwork?
- Do I take time to talk with my students about their out-of-class activities?

Safety Needs

Safety needs may be met by providing for a stable and consistent learning environment. School administrators and counselors should be informed of students' safety needs that extend beyond the purview of the classroom.

- Are students free from teasing or bullying in my classroom?
- Am I equitable in my enforcement of school and classroom rules?
- Are my assignments and tests fair?
- Do students feel free to express their feelings about my teaching?
- Can my students trust that I will not divulge information shared in confidence?
- Can my students get help from me when they need it?

Physiological Needs

Unmet needs for water, food, sleep, and the like can make learning impossible. Some physiological needs of students' are under the direct control of the teacher, while others are better addressed by parents or guardians.

- Are my students seated in the classroom where they can hear me and see the whiteboard or TV monitor?
- Is the temperature of my classroom too hot or too cold?
- Is my classroom well lit and free of unnecessary distractions?
- Do I provide sufficient time for students to complete tests and class assignments?

A teacher's knowledge of the possible causes of student misbehavior in addition to an understanding of unmet personal needs that may prompt episodes of misbehavior can be of tremendous help in managing the classroom. Viewing misbehavior as a student's response to the vexation associated with being in an environment where his or her basic needs are not being met may enable a teacher to think about long-lasting solutions to behavior problems rather than just short-term ones.

Stop and Reflect!

Jong-jin Kim moved with his family to the United States from South Korea and speaks little English. He was enrolled in high school by his father and joined Melissa's physical science class 2 weeks before the pH laboratory lesson. How would you respond to the question asked of Melissa by Mrs. Reed: "What unmet needs might be prompting his misbehavior of walking around the room during the lab?"

CREATING POSITIVE SCIENCE LEARNING COMMUNITIES

A learning community in which students' personal needs are met is one in which the relationships between the teacher and students and among students are positive. The relationships that teachers build with their students are ones that encourage students to feel significant and take responsibility for their own actions. In building a learning community, the teacher also has the responsibility of creating positive relationships among students. Teachers must help students get to know one another and develop a sense of group identity that leads to cordial interactions and friendship. The time spent developing positive teacher–student and peer relationships is indeed a worthwhile investment. The research clearly shows that the quality of these relationships has a significant influence on student behavior and academic success (Good & Brophy, 2000; Marzano, 2003; Purkey & Novak, 1996; Schmuck & Schmuck, 2001).

Teacher–Student Relationships

The foundation for positive teacher–student relationships is teachers communicating to students that they are interested in them and have concerns for them as persons and learners. Learning students' names is the way to initiate positive relationships because it communicates the teacher's interest in them. However, it is not easy to learn 30 or 40 names in a hurry, and if a science teacher has five classes, then he or she must learn 150 or more names. Seating charts and digital photographs of classes are helpful in learning names quickly and in associating names with individuals.

In addition to learning names, it is important to learn something about students' interests, aspirations, and academic backgrounds. This is particularly true for students whose cultural backgrounds are different from that of the teacher. It may be helpful to learn more about their family structure, ideas about discipline and punctuality, food preferences, and thoughts about science activities or topics that may be in conflict with religious beliefs (Jones & Jones, 2004). These "getting to know you" conversations may occur during individual conferences or while eating lunch with a small group of students in the school cafeteria. Teachers sharing information about their own families and hobbies, inviting students to place their ideas about the classroom in a suggestion box, and sending letters and memos to students that include information about what they will learn in class are all great ways to initiate open, professionally appropriate dialog with students.

Building positive teacher–student relationships also has a lot to do with expectations. Middle and high school students may well expect their science teacher to control the classroom, provide challenging assignments, and be firm, compassionate, and interesting. And, of course, teachers have expectations for their students that are associated with academic achievement, good manners, and personal growth. Students in Steve Thompson's chemistry and physics classes at Meadowcreek High School in Gwinnett County, Georgia, are reminded each day about expectations. Posted on the wall of his classroom are two charts that detail the expectations he holds for himself and his students. According to Mr. Thompson:

My job as a teacher is to . . .
- present information in an enthusiastic and organized manner
- return all graded activities in 1 day
- help students become problem solvers at home and at school
- give no busy work
- hold students responsible for their actions and inactions

Your job as a student is to . . .
- be present in school and on time for class
- be in charge of your learning and growth
- complete all work to the best of your ability
- recognize that performance counts
- be successful, which requires consistent and dedicated work

Teachers, like Steve Thompson, who are explicit about their expectations, communicate to students that they are interested in them and have concerns for them as persons and learners.

Positive teacher–student relationships also develop when teachers give encouragement and praise and when they project personality and enthusiasm. It is important for a teacher to acknowledge that a class has performed well on an assignment, a student has done outstanding work on a project or homework, or a class is well behaved when a substitute teacher is in charge. The acknowledgments should be made as frequently as the opportunities arise, and students should understand that they are given with sincerity.

Teachers also can strive to build positive teacher–student relationships in other ways. They can listen carefully to what students have to say about themselves and the class. Listening carefully shows respect and caring and provides students with the opportunity to share their thoughts with an adult. A teacher's listening and careful questioning may enable students to clarify problems and arrive at productive solutions. Teachers should also strive to be positive in their interactions with students and give meaningful feedback. Students, like all people, are more apt to respond positively when they are requested to do something in a pleasant and courteous manner.

Similarly, students respond more favorably to teacher verbal and nonverbal behaviors that they perceive as inviting, such as when they are told they are valued members of the class and are given responsibility for deciding how they should tackle a laboratory task or when an assignment is due. The feedback that science teachers provide should be specific rather than general and focus on aspects of learning that students are able to control. It is helpful for teachers to reinforce through their feedback that science achievement and success in science class have more to do with effort than with luck or innate ability.

Student–Student Relationships

Peer relationships can make a classroom a comfortable and exciting place where students want to be or an uninviting environment where students feel unsafe, insignificant, and disrespected. It is the job of the science teacher to ensure that peer relationships are positive and contribute to a supportive, interactive, and friendly learning environment. This job starts with understanding how classroom groups are formed and how functioning classroom groups can lead to positive peer relationships.

It is unrealistic to expect middle and high school students to start the school year with a sense of group cohesiveness. They will need to get to know one another and understand each other's strengths and limitations before they can be expected to develop a class identity or work effectively as learning teams. To help students move toward developing a class identity, some science teachers work with students to adopt a class motto. "Work Hard, Play Hard" is the motto adopted by an advanced-placement physics class whose teacher rewards students for their hard work with a 30-minute game of Ultimate Frisbee once a month. Other teachers incorporate acquaintance activities into their lessons at the beginning of the school year. For example, a biology teacher may ask students to find their "genetic twins" in the class based on observable hereditary traits such as tongue-rolling, free earlobe, widow's peak, and mid-digital hair. Common hereditary traits can be the starting point for conversations between students that might otherwise not speak to each other. This acquaintance activity can also serve as an advance organizer for studying human genetics later in the year.

Science classes provide numerous opportunities for group work. Students of diverse backgrounds and abilities can be assigned to study groups responsible for checking each other's homework and making sure that assignments are understood. In addition, students will work in laboratory groups where they may be assigned different tasks that support the group's overall efforts. By involving students in collaborative learning activities throughout the year, group cohesiveness can be further enhanced. Group cohesiveness is likely to foster peer-helping relationships, even among students who might not ordinarily be friends, and improve the quality of the learning environment. Group cohesiveness among a class of students is also likely to enable the teacher to work more effectively with parents and other family members. Parents who understand from their children that good things are happening in a teacher's class are more receptive to meeting with the teacher and providing support when needed to encourage appropriate behavior.

Stop and Reflect!

- What strategies might a teacher implement to develop positive relationships with students in his or her classes?
- What strategies might a teacher implement to develop positive relationships among students in his or her classes?

ORGANIZING AND MANAGING SCIENCE LEARNING ACTIVITIES

There are patterns of organization and behavior that are characteristic of successful learning environments. As Brophy (2000) described, the classroom is arranged to facilitate defined learning activities and to store needed equipment and supplies in easy reach of students. Movement of students around the classroom is orchestrated by a set of routines that require only minimal directions from the teacher. Students are engaged in lessons with an understanding of what they are doing and what materials are needed to achieve the intended learning goals. By attending to the classroom setting, classroom rules, and classroom procedures and routines the informed beginning teacher is able to manage the classroom in ways that facilitate these patterns of organization and behavior and, in doing so, increases the time students spend actively engaged in science learning.

Classroom Setting

Elements to consider within the learning space include the dimensions of the classroom as well as the position of laboratory workstations, storage closets and shelves, fixed safety equipment, and access routes to points beyond the classroom. Within this physical space, the teacher can position the active elements of the environment to make them responsive to the learning needs of students. For example, students' desks can be positioned in a circle to facilitate a class discussion, or they can be arranged so that all students can see the teacher and chalkboard or overhead projector screen without twisting and turning during whole-class instruction. The teacher's strategic arrangement of the physical environment is of great importance because it communicates to students how materials are to be used and what is expected of them as learners.

The physical learning environment is an important consideration in all aspects of science teaching, but especially when engaging students in laboratory work. Laboratory work may be done in the same classroom space used for other purposes, in a special area within the classroom, or in a separate laboratory room. Conducting labs in the same classroom space used for general instruction requires attention to special details. Furniture needs to be moved to accommodate the demands of space and student movement that accompany most laboratory activities. Since desks or chairs must often be moved within a single class period, students must be instructed in how to arrange the room for laboratory work. The placement and use of laboratory materials and equipment must be considered. Frequently used materials such as thermometers, rulers, small beakers, test tubes, and graph paper should be readily accessible, while often-used equipment such as electronic balances and microscopes should be kept in a location easy for students to reach. Answers to the following questions can help the teacher plan for the spatial organization of the laboratory work area, the arrangement of materials, and other aspects of the physical environment:

- How many students will be at the laboratory station at one time?
- Will students sit, stand, or move about?
- Will they talk, work cooperatively, or work independently?
- Will they use gas and electrical outlets?
- How will students gather materials, moving from one location to another?
- How will chemicals and laboratory materials be set out for students to use?
- How should students exit the laboratory work area in case of emergency?

Classroom Rules

Just as highway safety is based on drivers understanding and obeying traffic laws, an effective learning environment involves students understanding and following a planned system of classroom rules. Rules communicate

a teacher's expectations and should be introduced to students on the first or second day of school (Wong & Wong, 2001).

Establishing rules for the sake of rules is a poor practice, but those rules that create a classroom environment that supports learning and minimizes classroom disturbances are desirable. Rules should be kept as simple as possible, direct, realistic, understandable, and enforced once established. They should be few in number and stated in a positive fashion rather than as what *not* to do. Emmer and his colleagues (1994, pp. 22–23) listed a set of classroom rules, similar in many ways to the expectations for students that Steve Thompson has posted in his classroom, that may serve as a starting point for beginning teachers:

- Bring all needed materials to class.
- Be in your seat and ready to work when the bell rings.
- Respect and be polite to all people.
- Listen and stay seated when someone else is talking.
- Respect other people's property.
- Obey all school rules.

Consistent with the shift from management for student obedience to management for student self-regulation, more and more teachers are involving their students in helping to set class rules. This practice is encouraged because it allows students to take ownership of the rules and know the reasons for having them (Kohn, 1996).

Procedures and Routines

According to Wong and Wong (2001, p. 167), "The number one problem in the classroom is not discipline; it is the lack of procedures and routines." Activities such as passing out papers, organizing students into groups, and assigning student tasks are routines that can create problems unless they are handled efficiently. Teachers who spend unnecessary amounts of time passing out papers and collecting them create situations in which students keep themselves occupied by talking loudly and engaging in play. Many routine situations can cause a great deal of confusion unless simple procedures are established beforehand. Simple procedures that communicate the teacher's expectations for starting and ending class, whole-group instruction, grading, and laboratory work can prevent unnecessary misbehavior.

Most teachers believe that how they start class sets the tone for the entire class period. For this reason, many teachers insist that students are in their seats and prepared to learn when the bell rings. However, starting class at the sound of the bell is not usually possible due to the administrative duties that must be performed by the teacher, such as checking attendance. Informed beginning teachers plan activities that engage students as soon as the bell rings, allowing time to deal with the necessary administrative tasks. They also favor the practice of dismissing students themselves rather than allowing students to leave the room when the bell rings. When students are dismissed by the teacher, final instructions regarding homework, classroom cleanup, or tomorrow's test can be given with the assurance that all students have received the information.

With science classes exceeding 25 students in most public schools, teachers need to establish procedures for ensuring that large-group instruction goes smoothly. Students will want to know when and how the teacher will call on them to respond to questions. They will want to know when talking among students is permitted. Students also will want to know under what conditions they may leave their seats to sharpen pencils, collect papers, and go to the restroom.

Consideration also should be given to procedures related to grading. Students will want to know how their work will be graded. The informed teacher will be prepared to discuss personal grading practices with students. A gradebook, perhaps on computer, will need to be established and a system developed for recording daily grades, scores for major tests and projects, and student absences and tardies. A decision will also need to be made regarding how different assignments and tests will be weighted. Finally, it is important to explain major class assignments and grading practices to parents. This information will enable parents to better monitor their children's progress and to assist with learning problems that may arise.

In the laboratory, students will encounter many practices that are new to them. It is for this reason that science teachers need to attend to procedures related to appropriate dress, disposal of chemicals and specimens, keeping a notebook, and laboratory cleanup. Standards established by the National Science Teachers Association (NSTA) and the Occupational Safety and Health Administration (OSHA) provide guidance for many aspects of laboratory work. Teachers should use these standards in formulating their laboratory procedures including those regarding appropriate dress and the disposal of chemicals and used laboratory specimens.

To be sure, classroom procedures and routines are important elements of the science learning environment. According to Wong and Wong (2001, p. 194), the teacher who is successful in establishing and managing a positive learning environment:

1. Has well-thought-out and structured procedures for every activity
2. Teaches the procedures for each activity (to students) early in the year
3. Rehearses the class so that the procedures become class routines
4. Reteaches a procedure when necessary and praises to reinforce when appropriate

Stop and Reflect!

- Reread the vignette at the beginning of this chapter. Develop a list of rules or expectations for Ms. Longorio and her students that you would recommend posting on the classroom wall.
- Identify one problem in Ms. Longorio's classroom that you believe is due to the lack of classroom procedures. Describe the procedures that you believe will eliminate the problem.

Designing Lessons and Teaching to Motivate and Engage Students

Productive student behavior can often be traced to a teacher's success in planning science lessons and teaching in ways that enhance student motivation and engagement. Student motivation and engagement are influenced by the teacher's instructional practices, the curriculum, and other factors that are related to a student's self-esteem. These factors include students' confidence in their abilities to succeed, the value they find in the work to be done, and their feelings of safety and support (Jones & Jones, 2004).

Instructional Practices

Beginning teachers must enter the classroom with the confidence of knowing what is to be done during each minute of the teaching day. Overplanning lessons can provide the comfort and ease needed to enter the classroom with confidence. It is good practice to always plan more activities than can possibly be done by the students during a single class period. It is also good practice to have an alternative plan available in case of emergency. Poor planning is often cited as the number one cause of students becoming disinterested and uninvolved in a lesson, which in turn leads to student inattention, increased talking, and class disruption. However, teachers who communicate organization and confidence as a result of their planning can avoid many behavioral problems.

Additionally, teachers must consider in their planning how to begin and end learning activities, how to transition from one learning activity to another, and how to begin and end the class period. One way to think about organizing instructional activities is to break the class period into smaller segments and plan for each. The class period might begin with students doing a warm-up activity that may consist of copying the day's objectives and agenda while the teacher takes attendance and deals with other administrative tasks. Next, the student's initial work could be quickly checked before beginning the lesson. The lesson may consist of one or more activities. Finally, the period is closed with the teacher giving students homework instructions, reviewing the day's lesson, and presenting an overview of the lessons for the next several days.

Two critical times during group instruction are when transitioning from one activity to the next and when communicating directions and information (Emmer et al., 1994). To prevent misbehavior and wasted time, transitions should be planned to be smooth and brief. Informed beginning teachers establish procedures for students to follow during transitions. For example, when moving from desks to lab stations, students know to go directly to their lab stations without visiting with friends. Smooth transitions also are more likely to occur when planning has taken place to ensure that materials and equipment needed for the next activity are at hand. The possibility of student misbehavior is further reduced when planning has occurred to ensure that lesson objectives are clearly communicated, activity directions are presented in an orderly sequence, and students understand the purpose of the lesson (Emmer et al. 1994).

Curriculum

The curriculum, or what students are asked to learn, is a central element of the science learning environment. Good classroom managers recognize this fact and use their knowledge of students to make sure the curriculum matches their abilities and interests. When the curriculum is too difficult, too easy, or perceived as boring by students, they give up on learning and find something else to do in class. Often the "something else" is considered to be misbehavior by the teacher.

Making changes to the curriculum is often no simple matter. Today, state legislatures, school boards, and administrators have as much to say about what is taught in science classes as do teachers. Nevertheless, teachers must consider the relationship between the curriculum and student behavior. Minor adjustments to the curriculum can mean the difference between having to constantly reprimand students for being off-task and inattentive and having a lively discussion among a class of enthusiastic adolescents. The importance of the curriculum to a well-managed classroom cannot be overstated. According to Kohn (1996, p. 21), "How students act in class is so intertwined with curricular content that it may be folly even to talk about classroom management or discipline as a field unto itself."

Student Readiness to Learn

Students' motivation and engagement in science class has as much to do with their readiness to learn and their feelings of comfort as the teacher's instructional practices and the curriculum. It is a fact that far too many students in middle and high school today are unable to succeed because they lack the basic skills necessary to do so (Cummings, 2000). These students need to be taught basic study skills such as how to take notes, or-

ganize a notebook, and keep up with assignments and graded papers. They also need help in learning how to manage their time and work, how to prepare for different kinds of tests and alternative assessment tasks, and how to engage in academic reading. In addition, many middle and high school science teachers find that some of their students do not have the mathematical skills to do even the simplest calculations.

If teachers see their job as helping all students succeed, they will do all that they can to ensure students develop these skills as they learn science content. For example, many middle school teachers require their students to keep assignment books in which homework and due dates are recorded on a daily basis. To help students prepare for tests, some teachers reserve 15 minutes of class time every Friday to review sample test items and discuss test-taking strategies with their students. Other teachers teach multiplication, ratio-and-proportion, and algebra when understanding science concepts requires these mathematical skills. Still other teachers, in an attempt to improve academic reading proficiency, teach students to read textbook chapter headings, photograph captions, and summaries for contextual clues before reading a chapter page for page.

While helping students develop these necessary skills, the science teacher must also convey to students that they are capable of performing at high levels (Jones & Jones, 2004). By breaking learning tasks into smaller steps and providing feedback on students' learning, teachers can help students experience success and at the same time teach them strategies that will enable them to achieve success again and again. Especially for students with special learning needs, experiencing success is important because these students may have fewer opportunities to experience success in school compared to higher-ability students. Modifications to instruction and assessment activities can be especially helpful to them. Feelings of success also are associated with working in groups, especially for African American, Hispanic, and Native American students (Banks & McGee Banks, 1993; Freeman & Freeman, 2003). Thus, science teachers should consider using cooperative learning in their classrooms and laboratories to enhance the learning experience. There is no doubt that teaching students who are motivated by their own successes is far more pleasant than dealing with the disruptive behavior of students who are frustrated by their inability to cope with the demands of learning.

Students are also more likely to value their science learning experiences when they see the content as personally relevant. When introducing course content during the first days of school, informed teachers will ask students what they want to learn about the different course topics. They will then construct their lessons to take advantage of students' interests. Students also attach greater value to science class when they have choices about their learning.

Project-work, problem-based activities, and guided inquiries are among the many science learning opportunities where, once provided with the learning goals, students are allowed to decide what methods and materials to use and how much time is needed in achieving the goals. Compared to students given cookbook directions for a lab activity to be completed in a single period, students allowed to design and carry out their own laboratory experiments over several class periods are likely to exhibit greater interest and stay on-task longer.

The value that students place on science learning is also associated with their understanding of the learning goals. Teachers can help students understand the goals of science learning by explaining the purpose of instructional activities in language that is easily understood and in ways that are meaningful to them. As discussed in Chapter 2, the goals of science learning encompass personal and societal needs, career education, and academic preparation. An informed teacher knows that science course learning goals emphasizing only academic preparation will not be valued by most of today's students. Teachers can help students understand the purpose of instruction by telling them what they need to accomplish and why it is important to them as adolescents and as future adults.

When students feel safe and supported, they also are motivated to focus on the tasks of learning. Central to student safety and its implications for motivation are problems that may arise from bullying or teasing of students by other students. The psychological trauma associated with bullying and teasing can be debilitating for some students. Teachers may be unaware of the bullying going on among students they teach (Barone, 1997), making it important to help "students develop empathy for their peers and improved skills in interacting with others" (Jones & Jones, 2004, p. 151).

DEALING WITH STUDENT MISBEHAVIOR

Even under the best classroom conditions, student misbehavior will occur. When student misbehavior disrupts the learning environment, then it is time to use disciplinary interventions. *Disciplinary interventions* are "actions taken by the teacher to bring about changes in the behavior of students who do not conform to class or school expectations" (Brophy, 1996, p. 5).

Student behaviors that warrant disciplinary actions include:

- Continually horsing around and disrupting classroom routines and procedures
- Repeatedly preventing other students from conducting normal classroom activities

- Cheating on tests
- Swearing
- Being disrespectful to the teacher
- Deliberately destroying or damaging laboratory equipment, school property, or the property of other's
- Endangering the safety of the teacher or fellow students

Of course, some of the misbehaviors listed are more serious than others, but they all must be dealt with in one way or another. The teacher can deal with most misbehavior in the normal course of daily activity, while the more serious ones that violate the school's code of conduct are handled by the school administration. In cases where student misbehavior involves the violation of law, school administrators will request the assistance of law enforcement officials to deal with the problem.

A sequential list of disciplinary interventions that range from preventive to remedial is set out in Shrigley's (1979, 1985) list of coping skills. Presented in Figure 5.2, this list is a valuable guide for beginning teachers when attempting to curb student misbehavior in the science classroom. Research indicates that 40% of 523 classroom disruptions investigated were curbed when teachers used the first four coping skills—ignoring behavior, signals, proximity control, and touch control (Shrigley, 1985). Teachers considering the use of Shrigley's coping skills should also heed his warning, "The teacher majoring in coping skills and minoring in excellent teaching will wind up constantly reacting, constantly putting out brush fires. Coping skills serve to rescue the teaching act, and they usually focus on the symptoms. They may do little to answer the deep-seated problems of disruptive individuals" (Shrigley, 1979, p. 3).

Teachers should determine the causes of student inattentiveness and misbehavior.

FIGURE 5.2   Shrigley's coping skills useful for curbing student misbehavior.

1. *Ignore behavior.* An annoying behavior will often subside if ignored by the teacher.
2. *Signal interference.* Body language, such as a stare, can indicate that a behavior is unacceptable.
3. *Proximity control.* The teacher stands near a misbehaving student to provide the adult support needed to diffuse a disruption.
4. *Touch control.* By placing a hand on the shoulder of a student, the teacher can relieve tension and anger. Discretion must be used when applying this coping skill.
5. *Gordon's active listening.* The teacher listens carefully to the student's description of the problem and acknowledges the student's concern and frustration.
6. *Gordon's I-messages.* An I-message reveals the problem and the teacher's feelings and is best used when rapport has been established between teacher and student. "When students play around Bunsen burners in lab (behavior), I am afraid (feelings) that someone will get burned (effect)."
7. *Speak to the situation.* The teacher describes the problem but does not directly address the students. "Shoving discs into the CD player can break the machine."
8. *Direct appeal.* Often in the form of a question, the statement attempts to appeal to the student's sense of logic and fairness. Two examples are, "John, do you know you're disturbing others with your singing and drumming?" and "Is it fair to disrupt others because you want to sing and drum on your book?"
9. *Interrogative.* A question can be used to indicate that the student has a choice regarding his or her behavior. "Will you please return to your seat?"
10. *Glasser's questions.* "What are you doing? What should you be doing?" When used in combination, these questions help students analyze their behavior and take corrective action.
11. *Logical consequences.* The teacher responds directly and logically to the student misbehavior. If two students make a mess of the classroom by throwing paper, then a logical consequence would be to have them clean up the paper from the classroom floor.
12. *Contrived consequences.* This teacher response to student misbehavior is punitive. If two students make a mess of the classroom by throwing paper, then a contrived consequence would be for the students to stay after school for a week.
13. *Canter's broken record.* The teacher repeats an assertive command two or three times rather than arguing or trying to reason with the student. "Michael, put down the thermometer and return to your seat . . . put down the thermometer and return to your seat."
14. *Compliance or Penalty.* "Michael, put down the thermometer and return to your seat or go to the office . . . Michael, if you don't put down the thermometer and return to your seat, I'll call for Mr. Big who will help me escort you to the office." The student is given the choice to comply with the teacher's request or pay the price.

Based on "Strategies in Classroom Management", by R. L. Shrigley, 1979, NASSP Bulletin, 63(428), 1–9; and "Curbing Student Disruptive Behavior in the Classroom–Teachers Need Intervention Skills", by R. L. Shrigley, 1985, NASSP Bulletin, 69(479), 26–32.

As Shrigley suggests, it also is desirable at times to ask students who continuously misbehave to remain after class or appear after school to discuss the reasons for their persistent disruptions. Individual conferences are often very desirable to avoid student embarrassment and even teacher–student confrontations during class. Students will regard the situation seriously when the teacher asks for a private conference to discuss persistent misbehavior. Conferences are particularly effective to handle problems that cannot be settled quickly and reasonably when they occur. During the conference, both the teacher and student can discuss the situation amicably and reasonably to correct the behavior. Under certain circumstances, conferences are more effective when school administrators and parents are involved. Some students require this type of conference to realize the seriousness of the situation.

Punishment is a special type of disciplinary intervention that is perceived as adverse by students. Punishment should only be considered when all other disciplinary interventions have failed. If it is decided that punishment must be used, Shrigley (1979, p. 6) recommends that it be legal, infrequent, prompt, appropriate, impersonal, private, just, and mild. Punishment can have unexpected negative side effects. When students are unable to see the relationship between their misbehavior and the punishment, hostility and aggression toward the teacher may result.

Of course, there are a host of disciplinary interventions besides those mentioned that can be used to curb students' misbehavior. Others that have been used successfully by experienced teachers include changing seating assignments, removing seductive objects, and sending a note to parents. Regardless of the interventions used, Brophy's (1996, p. 21) general principles for effectively handling student misbehavior may prove to be a helpful source of guidance:

■ Minimize power struggles and face-saving gestures by discussing the incident with the student in private rather than in front of the class

■ Question the student to determine his or her awareness of the behavior and explanation for it

■ Make sure that the student understands why the behavior is inappropriate and cannot be tolerated

■ Seek to get the student to accept responsibility for the behavior and to make a commitment to change

■ Provide any needed modeling or instruction in better ways of coping

■ Work with the student to develop a mutually agreeable plan for solving the problem

■ Concentrate on developing self-regulation capabilities through positive socialization and instruction rather than controlling behavior through power assertion

■ Emphasize that the student can achieve desirable outcomes and avoid negative consequences by choosing to act responsibly

Most uninformed beginning teachers view classroom management as a bag of tricks and recipes that, when followed, will ensure student obedience. In believing that classroom management requires enforcing rules of discipline, they fail to recognize that classroom management involves making thoughtful decisions, developing trusting and caring relationships, and sharing responsibility with students. The outcomes often associated with the obedience-oriented classrooms directed by too many uninformed beginning teachers are teacher frustration, rampant student misbehavior, ineffective instruction, and less well-educated students. We believe it is important for beginning teachers to attend to the sets of teacher behaviors that promote a positive, responsibility-oriented learning environment. Teachers that strive to develop interpersonal relationships, organize and manage learning activities, and design lessons and teach in ways that enhance student motivation and learning will increase the occurrence of appropriate student behavior.

ASSESSING AND REVIEWING

Analysis and Synthesis

1. Prepare a list of strategies that you would implement during the first days of school to build rapport with your middle or high school science students. Share your list with classmates and discuss the strategies about which you disagree.

2. Read the following vignette. Then, work with a partner to construct a list of classroom rules and procedures that you believe would help Mr. Hirshhorn more effectively end the lesson.

Five minutes before the bell rang to dismiss the class, Mr. Hirshhorn told the students to stop their work, return the microscopes to the storage cabinet, and clean up their work areas. The students rushed to the storage cabinet to see who could get their microscopes put away first. A few students neglected to remove the microscope slides from the stage of the microscope. Others did not lower the body of the microscope completely so that the eyepiece struck the lower part of the shelf above, possibly doing damage to the microscope. As students were about to return the slides to the box

on the teacher's lab desk, the bell rang. As a result, some students returned the slides in a disorderly fashion, and many simply left the slides at their worktables. Mr. Hirshhorn also attempted to announce the next day's assignment, but half the class had already left the room.

3. Examine Steve Thompson's lists of teacher and student expectations presented in this chapter. How would you modify his lists before posting them in your classroom?

Practical Considerations

4. Draw a floor plan for a middle school or high school classroom that would facilitate quality science instruction and reduce the probability of student misbehavior. On the floor plan, show the location of students' and teacher's desk, student laboratory stations, safety equipment (e.g., first aid kit, fire blanket, safety shower, etc.), materials and equipment storage, chalkboard or overhead projector and screen, and doorways. Also draw lines to represent student traffic patterns.

5. Observe a science class taught by a veteran teacher and pay particular attention to how he or she addresses the areas of classroom management discussed in this chapter: interpersonal relationships, organization and management, and lesson design and teaching. Arrange to meet with the teacher after the class to discuss your observations, and ask the teacher to talk about his or her reasons for the management decisions and strategies you observed.

6. Talk with a school principal or the assistant principal in charge of discipline. Ask about the school's disciplinary procedures and under what conditions it is considered appropriate for teachers to send students to the school office for discipline.

Developmental Considerations

7. Select a concept or topic from a middle or high school science course that you believe students will find boring. Develop a plan to teach the concept or topic in a way that will motivate students to be engaged science learners.

8. Read about different models of classroom management that teachers can use to guide their actions to effectively manage the science learning environment.

RESOURCES TO EXAMINE

The First Days of School.   2001. Sunnyvale, CA: Harry Wong Publications.

   Address for ordering: 1030 W. Maude Ave., Suite, Sunnyvale, CA 94086.

   Authored by Harry and Rosemary Wong, this book should be required reading for beginning teachers. It is full of illustrations and pithy advice about how to become an effective instructional planner, teacher, and classroom manager. Inspiring students to want to learn is a central theme of this book.

Connecting with Students.   2001. Alexandria, VA: Association for Supervision and Curriculum Development.

   Address for ordering: 1250 N. Pitt Street, Alexandria, VA 22314

   In this short book, acclaimed author Allen Mendler discusses numerous strategies for identifying disconnected students and connecting with all students. Strategies highlighted include those for developing personal, academic, and social connections with students.

Classroom Management That Works: Research-Based Strategies for Every Teacher.   2003. Alexandria, VA: Association for Supervision and Curriculum Development.

   Address for ordering: 1250 N. Pitt Street, Alexandria, VA 22314

   Robert Marzano's book addressed the major areas of classroom management discussed in this chapter. In addition, it highlights the research and theory that supports many practical recommendations for classroom rules and procedures, teacher–student relationships, students' management responsibilities, and disciplinary interventions.

Comprehensive Classroom Management: Creating Communities of Support and Solving Problems. 2004. Boston, MA: Allyn & Bacon.

   Address for ordering: 75 Arlington Street, Boston, MA 02116

   This is a 10-chapter volume on classroom management by Vern Jones and Louise Jones. Creating positive interpersonal relationships, increasing student motivation, minimizing disruptive student behavior, and altering unproductive student behavior are among the topics addressed. Cartoons and questions to prompt reader reflection are found in every chapter.

REFERENCES

Banks, J., & McGee Banks, C., (1993). *Multicultural education: Issues and perspectives* (2nd ed.). Boston: Allyn & Bacon.

Barone, F. (1997). Bullying in the classroom: It doesn't have to happen. *Phi Delta Kappan, 79,* 80–82.

Brophy, J. (1996). *Teaching problem students.* New York: Guilford Press.

Brophy, J. (2000). Perspectives of classroom management: Yesterday, today, and tomorrow. In H. J. Freiberg (Ed.), *Beyond behaviorism: Changing the classroom management paradigm* (pp. 43–56). Boston: Allyn & Bacon.

Brophy, J. (1996). *Teaching problem students*. New York: Guilford Press.

Cummings, C. (2000). *Winning strategies for classroom management*. Alexandria, VA: Association for Supervision and Curriculum Development.

Emmer, E. T., Everston, C. M., Clements, B. S., & Worsham, M. E. (1994). *Classroom management for secondary teachers*. Boston: Allyn & Bacon.

Evertson, C. M., & Emmer, E. (1982). Preventive classroom management. In D. Duke (Ed.), *Helping teachers manage classrooms* (pp. 2–31). Alexandria, VA: Association for Supervision and Curriculum Development.

Evertson, C. M., & Harris, A. H. (2000). Support for managing learning-centered classrooms: The classroom organization and management program. In H. J. Freiberg (Ed.), *Beyond behaviorism: Changing the classroom management paradigm* (pp. 59–74). Boston: Allyn & Bacon.

Freeman, Y., & Freeman, D. (2003). *Closing the achievement gap: How to reach limited-formal-schooling and long-term English learners*. Portsmouth, NH: Heinemann.

Good, T., & Brophy, J. (2000). *Looking into classrooms* (8th ed.). New York: Longman.

Jones, V., & Jones, L. (2004). *Comprehensive classroom management: Creating communities of support and solving problems*. Boston: Allyn & Bacon.

Kohn, A. (1996). *Beyond discipline*. Alexandria, VA: Association for Supervision and Curriculum Development.

Marzano, R. J. (2003). *Classroom management that works: Research-based strategies for every teacher*. Alexandria, VA: Association for Supervision and Curriculum Development.

Maslow, A. (1968). *Toward a psychology of being*. New York: D. Van Nostrand.

Patrick, H., Turner, J. C., Meyer, D. K., & Midgley, C. (2003). How teachers establish psychological environments during the first days of school: Association with avoidance in mathematics. *Teachers College Record, 105*(8), 1521–1569.

Purkey, W., & Novak, J. (1996). *Inviting school success: A self-concept approach to teaching, learning, and democratic practice* (3rd ed.). Belmont, CA: Wadsworth.

Sanford, J. P., & Evertson, C. M. (1981). Classroom management in a low SES junior high: Three case studies. *Journal of Teacher Education, 32*(1), 34–38.

Schmuck, R., & Schmuck, P. (2001). *Group processes in the classroom* (8th ed.). Boston: McGraw-Hill.

Shrigley, R. L. (1979). Strategies in classroom management. *NASSP Bulletin, 63*(428), 1–9.

Shrigley, R. L. (1985). Curbing student disruption in the classroom—teachers need intervention skills. *NASSP Bulletin, 69*(479), 26–32.

Wong, H. K., & Wong, R. T. (2001). *The first days of school*. Sunnyvale, CA: Harry Wang Publications.

6

Assessing Science Lessons

*Planning instruction should
begin with the end in mind.*

Within hours of graduating from college with a degree in chemical engineering, Howard Seung was commissioned as a 2nd Lieutenant in the U.S. Army. Howard's Reserve Officer Training Corp experiences prepared him well for entry into the military. He didn't mind the rigorous physical training of infantry service and enjoyed the responsibilities of commanding troops, many of whom entered the army right out of high school. After 20 years of service, Colonel Howard Seung decided to retire. Prodding from his wife and teenage children led Howard to consider science teaching as a second career. The Troops-To-Teachers program at the local university enabled Howard to secure a high school chemistry teaching position as he earned teacher certification credentials.

This logo appears throughout the chapter to indicate where vignettes are integrated with chapter content.

On the day that Howard was hired to teach at Grande Hills High School, only 2 days before the start of the school year, he was given the state standards for high school chemistry and the teacher's edition of the textbook adopted by the district. Howard was told to organize his chemistry course around the state standards, but to make sure that he covered Chapters 1–10 from the textbook before the Christmas break. One week into the school year, Howard is teaching a lesson on physical and chemical change that is part of a unit on Matter, Change, and Energy. Let's listen in on his class, paying particular attention to how Howard assesses student learning.

MR. SEUNG: Good morning, students. Let's get started. Today, we are going to be learning about chemical and physical changes of matter. The state standard for our topic is written on the board.

STANDARD 6A: Understand the nature of matter and how matter is classified.

Does anyone have any questions about what is expected?

JERRY: Mr. Seung, I have a question. What will you hold us responsible for from today's lesson?

MR. SEUNG: It's stated in the standard that I wrote on the board. If no one else has questions, please focus your attention on the demonstration table.

At the demonstration table, Mr. Seung had set out materials to show physical and chemical changes. He presented cutting paper and chewing food as examples of physical changes and burning a candle, digesting food, and burning paper as examples of chemical changes. In addition, he identified distinct signs of chemical change, including the formation of a gas or precipitate, an odor, a color change, and a change in temperature.

After about 10 minutes of showing and discussion about the various examples, Howard held up a stick of melting butter. He asked the students to close their eyes and to:

- Hold up one finger if you think melting butter is a physical change
- Hold up two fingers if you think melting butter is a chemical change
- Hold up three fingers if you are not sure

Howard was delighted to see that all the students were holding up one finger.

Next, Howard showed the students a sample of spoiling meat and offered assurances that it was not from the school's cafeteria. He then asked the students to perform the same finger exercise for the spoiling meat. The results showed that of the 26 students in the class, 7 thought it was a chemical change, 14 thought it was a physical change, and 5 were not sure.

MR. SEUNG: You may open your eyes now, students. Your fingers tell me we need to talk about chemical change a little more.

Will someone tell us how they voted and explain why they voted that way?

CONRAD: *I held up one finger. It didn't seem to have any of the signs of chemical change that we talked about. Nothing was burning!*

MR. SEUNG: *Your right, Conrad. Nothing was burning, but keep in mind that burning is only one of many signs that a chemical change is taking place. Can you remind everyone of other signs of chemical change?*

CONRAD: *I wrote in my notes that they are the formation of a gas, color change, precipitate, which I don't really understand, and change in temperature.*

LORI: *Mr. Seung, Mr. Seung. I raised two fingers for chemical change because I could smell the rotten odor from the meat. Maybe Conrad couldn't smell it at his seat in the back of the room.*

CONRAD: *She's right, Mr. Seung. I didn't smell anything back here.*

MR. SEUNG: *Ok, everyone check your notes to make sure that you have odor as one sign of chemical change. Let me pass around the spoiling meat. Let's also clarify what a precipitate is.*

After having students respond with their fingers to a few more examples of physical and chemical change and explaining what is meant by precipitate, Howard instructed the students to collect a handout for the laboratory activity he had planned and to get into lab groups. He also told them that the materials they would need were at the lab stations, and not to forget to wear their safety goggles.

The lab handout that Howard prepared for his students provided them with background about the lab and introduced the materials to be used. The lab procedures on the handout instructed them to:

- Mix two solids—sodium bicarbonate and calcium chloride—in a ziplock bag
- Mix two liquids—universal indicator and water—in a film canister
- Combine the two mixed liquids and two mixed solids by opening the film canister inside the sealed ziplock bag.

As the students followed the lab instructions on the handout, Howard walked among the lab groups asking questions and observing the students' work. He systematically recorded his observations on a checklist that he had constructed with other beginning teachers also enrolled in the alternative certification program. The checklist included categories for working collaboratively, following procedures, recording results, and engaging in safe lab practices. The questions he asked probed students' understanding of the procedures and their interpretation of what they had observed when mixing the different substances.

MR. SEUNG: *Merri, when I observed that you and Juanita tipped over the film canister inside the ziplock bag to mix the liquid and dry chemicals, I noticed that you did not have your ziplock bag completely sealed. How might this affect the mass of your bag? More importantly, what will the mass of the bag tell you about whether you are observing a chemical or physical change?*

MERRI: *I'm not sure what you are asking, Mr. Seung.*

MR. SEUNG: *Well, you determined the mass of the chemicals and the bag, including the film canister, before mixing them, right?*

MERRI: *Yea, we determined that the mass was 145.6 g.*

MR. SEUNG: *That sounds good, but why . . .*

The crackle of the intercom with the morning announcements let everyone know that only 5 minutes remained before the end of the class period. Unable to speak over the voice of the principal, Howard signaled students to clean up their lab work, and he wrote on the board:

Hold on to your lab handouts. We will finish this tomorrow.

———————————————■———————————————

AIMS OF THE CHAPTER

Use the questions that follow to guide your thinking and learning about some of the fundamental aspects of science lesson assessment:

- Why is it important to build aligned assessments?

- What is the purpose of national and state standards in assessing lesson effectiveness and student learning?

- How are instructional objectives useful in specifying learning outcomes based on state standards?

- How can teachers monitor student learning during a lesson?

- How can teachers assess student learning at the end of a lesson?

- Can you assess your own lesson assessment practices?

FEATURES OF A LESSON ASSESSMENT SYSTEM

Assessment is more than testing and calculating grades. It is the guiding force for what and how teachers teach and students learn. Teachers organize lessons to ensure that students do well on high-stakes tests. Students tend to be more focused during lessons when they know when and how they will be assessed on the material taught. National and state standards provide direction for what should be taught and assessed by specifying the core content for audiences of learners. It is this critical relationship between assessment, teaching, learning, and standards that has led many science teachers to think about assessment differently, particularly when viewed in the context of a single science lesson.

The important idea that we want you to grasp from this chapter is that assessment is not an isolated event that occurs at the end of a unit of instruction. Rather, it is a central element to be considered in planning and teaching science lessons. Your consideration of assessment as applied to a science lesson should include four components.

1. **General Learning Goals**   The general learning goals that a teacher may consult when preparing to teach a lesson could be national standards or the standards documents developed by the state or school district.
2. **Instructional Objectives**   Instructional objectives are constructed by the teacher and are

Assessment should involve many ways of measuring student learning.

based on the general learning goals. Instructional objectives operationalize the general learning goals and are linked to assessment activities by indicating specifically what students should know or be able to do at the end of the lesson.
3. **During-Lesson Monitoring**   Assessment need not wait until the end of the lesson, but can be embedded in instruction. Much information about student learning and the quality of instruction can be gathered during a lesson.
4. **End-of-Lesson Assessment**   Before a class is adjourned, it is important to determine what students have learned from the lesson. End-of-lesson assessment can take many forms and may be graded or used only for diagnostic purposes.

These four components comprise the essential features of a lesson assessment system, as shown in Figure 6.1. No one component is more or less important than the others. Planning lessons with assessment in mind will contribute to your success as an instructional leader and to the success of your students as science learners. Let's now look at each of these four components of a lesson assessment system in turn, using the chapter's opening vignette to contextualize our discussion.

FIGURE 6.1 Essential features of a lesson assessment system.

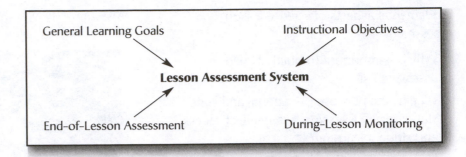

GENERAL LEARNING GOALS

When you are asked to teach a science lesson, your first thoughts will undoubtedly be of the lesson topic and the content to be addressed. For example, the person with a strong biology background who is asked to teach a lesson on genetics may well begin to think about Mendel's experiments, the principles of segregation and independent assortment, or the Punnett square. This line of thinking is very natural, since you have spent many years learning science content.

After considering the topic of the lesson, your thoughts will likely turn to activities that you have experienced or read about that you believe may do a good job of helping students learn the important understandings associated with the topic. This, too, is a natural progression of thought given that you want to provide the students in your class with an enjoyable as well as meaningful learning experience.

So, you have tentatively identified the concepts to be addressed and the activities that will be used to engage the students. You are ready to plan for the lesson. But, what about the general learning goals for your course, the so-called standards? Where do they fit into the picture? And, why are they important to consider in terms of assessment?

Science standards tend to be the product of months or years of work involving stakeholders from many groups concerned about science education, including science teachers, scientists, parents, business leaders, and many others. The *National Science Education Standards* (NRC, 1996), as well as the standards developed at the state- and school-district levels, present what students should know and be able to do as a result of science instruction, based on the thinking of the group who developed them. Most state- and district-level science standards are based on national standards that emphasize the development of a scientifically literate citizenry. When considering the standards in your planning, you can be certain that you are addressing the core understandings that your students will be held accountable for on high-stakes tests.

Most likely, you have been given or soon will be given the standards that you should use to guide your instruction. If you have not heard anyone talk about standards, ask about them and where they can be found. As a result of local decisions, you may be required to follow national, state, or district standards. The *National Science Education Standards* are available on-line at http:/www.nsta.org/standards. State standards documents can most often be found at the state's department of education Web site. For example, the Georgia standards can be found at http://www.doe.k12.ga.us, and the Texas standards can be found at http://www.tea.state.tx.us. In addition, district standards are often presented at the school district Web site or available in paper copy.

After examining the standards for your course, you may find that your ideas for the lesson that includes your favorite activity may or may not be a good match with the core content identified in the standards. If you feel that your lesson will not help students achieve the standards, then you will want to make modifications to your lesson, which may mean dropping your favorite activity and developing or choosing other ones.

Returning to the vignette at the beginning of this chapter, you will recall that Howard Seung took into consideration the standard most applicable to the core content he was teaching. Prior to teaching the lesson it is likely that he went back and forth between the standards related to the topic of matter and his lesson plan, honing his ideas to ensure that his lesson matched Standard 6A as closely as possible. He wrote the standard on the board to inform his students how the day's lesson is related to the prescribed course of study.

You also will recall that Howard's students had questions about Standard 6A. In particular, Jerry asked, "What will you hold us responsible for from today's lesson?" This question brings to the forefront an important consideration for teachers. Standards tend to be broad statements of learning goals that are extremely helpful for providing guidance and direction. However, they do not indicate specifically what students should know and be able to do at the end of a lesson. This lack of specificity often leads to confusion about lesson purpose and teachers disregarding standards in their instructional planning, particularly when assessment is considered. For this reason, it is important that science teachers clarify the standards for the courses they teach through developing lesson assessments and matching instructional objectives. It is these topics that we will address next.

Stop and Reflect!

- Examine a standards document that is used to guide the teaching of a science course that interests you. What are some of the core content understandings specified in the standards for a particular science course?

- How might you use the standards to guide your teaching and assessment of student learning?

INSTRUCTIONAL OBJECTIVES

In Chapter 3, you learned about writing instructional objectives. The power of instructional objectives lies in their link to both standards and lesson assessment. When constructing an instructional objective, you are operationalizing the standards for your students by de-

scribing for them what they should know or be able to do at the end of a lesson.

We have found that writing instructional objectives for a lesson is a much easier task once you have constructed your lesson assessment. That's right, we recommend that you construct your lesson assessment first, before writing your instructional objectives and selecting your instructional activities. Through the process of developing your assessment, you will make explicit what students should know or be able to do at the end of the lesson, the conditions under which they will be assessed, and the criterion for success. In essence, we are encouraging you to plan your lesson with the end in mind (Tileston, 2004; Wiggins & McTighe, 1998).

Let's see how this might work using a few examples. Presented in Table 6.1 are some typically stated science content standards. The standards differ in their level of content specificity, as is often the case in actual state and district standards documents. Lesson assessments are shown that address the standards. As you can well imagine, it is a harder task to develop an assessment that stays true to the developers' intention when a standard addresses a broad content area or is vaguely worded. A number of standards documents include more precisely worded benchmarks along with the content standards. These benchmarks help to explain the content standards and to guide teachers' decisions about what students should learn.

TABLE 6.1   Content Standards and Lesson Assessments

Example 1—Cell Organelles
  Standard: Students will understand the role of cell organelles in eukaryotes in maintaining homeostasis and cell reproduction

Possible Lesson Assessments:
  - Students are given 5 minutes to write an answer for the following question: How does the cell membrane work to maintain homeostasis?
  - Students are directed to make a rough drawing of an animal cell and label two cell organelles that play a role in cell reproduction.

Example 2—Magnetism and Electricity
  Standard: Students will understand the relationship between magnetism and electricity

Possible Lesson Assessments:
  - Students are asked to make a sketch that shows the magnetic field created by a straight wire carrying a current.
  - Students are shown a photograph of a powerful electromagnet lifting large chunks of metal and asked to briefly explain how the electromagnet works.

Example 3—Periodic Table
  Standard: Students will investigate the arrangement of the periodic table

Possible Lesson Assessments:
  - Students are given an incomplete concept map and told to complete the map using the following terms: periods, groups, alkali metals, noble gases, and halogens.
  - With a periodic table in front of them, students are asked to predict the expected electron configuration of a yet-to-be-discovered element, such as element 114.

More will be said later in this section about the standards development process and how to increase the likelihood that lesson assessments do, in fact, reflect the intentions of those who developed the standards. For now, feel confident that by constructing lesson assessments that are aligned with standards or their more precisely worded benchmarks and by writing instructional objectives that match your lesson assessments, you are doing a lot to help your students be successful science learners.

If you look back at the chapter's opening vignette, you will notice that Howard Seung did not share an instructional objective with his students. Thus, it was unclear to the students what Howard expected them to learn from the lesson and how their learning would be assessed. It is possible that Howard himself was not clear on what he expected his students to know or do as a result of his instruction.

Let's say that Howard had planned his lesson with the end in mind. He may have decided to use the last 5 minutes of class to show his students a small sample of gallium metal that melts in his hands and also to heat a mixture of iron filings and sulfur as they watch. After a few minutes of silent observation, the students could have been asked to write on a half-sheet of paper whether each example was a physical change or chemical change and to list the observations supporting their choices.

Had he decided on this assessment for the lesson, his instructional objectives could have been written as:

> When presented with unknown materials undergoing a change, state if the materials show a physical change or chemical change, and list one observation that supports your choice.

This instructional objective includes the three components found in a clearly stated instructional objective: *performance* (*state* if the materials show a physical change or chemical change), *condition* (when presented with unknown materials undergoing a change), and *criterion* (one observation that supports your choice). It could have been easily constructed by Howard based on the simple lesson assessment described and presented to his students at the beginning of the lesson. Had Howard written this objective on the board, it is likely that Jerry's question, "What will you hold us responsible for from today's lesson?" would not have been asked.

The idea of planning with the end in mind also has implications for instruction. Determining what you want students to know or be able to do at the end of your lesson provides guidance for the selection of instructional activities. Table 6.2 presents two different descriptions of assessments, instructional objectives, and instructional activities that could be derived from what Howard Seung wrote on the board:

TABLE 6.2   Assessments, Instructional Objectives, and Instructional Activities

Condition 1

Assessment: Students will perform the operations described here and then indicate if each operation is an example of a physical or chemical change and provide at least one reason for each answer.

- mix salt, sand, and water
- mix sodium hydrogen carbonate and hydrochloric acid

Instructional Objective: After mixing given materials, state if the mixtures show a physical or chemical change and give at least one reason that supports your choices.

Instruction: Students should be provided with guidance and practice in carrying out laboratory procedures that lead to chemical and physical changes. They must also be provided with opportunities to observe the physical properties of matter that allow them to determine if a physical or chemical change has occurred, such as physical state, color, odor, solubility in water, and the effect of magnetism. In addition, students must practice constructing criteria based on their observations that will enable them to distinguish between a physical change and a chemical change. Finally, the students must be reminded of safety precautions for laboratory work.

Condition 2

Assessment: Students will be asked to write definitions for physical change and chemical change and give two examples of each type of change.

Instructional Objective: After listening to a lecture on changes of matter, write definitions for physical change and chemical change and describe two examples of each type of change in one or two sentences.

Instruction: This assessment calls for students to restate memorized definitions of physical change and chemical change, so the students would need to be provided with and memorize accurate definitions. Examples of physical and chemical changes also should be described for students, and they should be provided with opportunities to generate their own examples. The teacher could check the examples generated by students.

Based on information from *Test Better, Teach Better: The Instructional Role of Assessment*, by W. J. Popham, 2003, Alexandria, VA: ASCD.

Standard 6A: Understand the nature of matter and how matter is classified.

The two assessments place different expectations on students. The level of intellectual activity required of students is much greater for condition 1 than for condition 2. This difference in cognitive demand also is reflected in the instruction for the two conditions. The understanding that you should take from examining Table 6.2 is that aligning lesson assessment with instructional objectives and instructional activities is critical to the success of your lesson and student learning. Failure to consider these three elements in your planning will increase the likelihood that your assessment won't match your instructional activities.

Stop and Reflect!

- Describe an assessment for a lesson in a content area that interests you. Next, construct an instructional objective that is aligned with the lesson assessment. Finally, describe one or more instructional activities that will help students perform well on your assessment.

- Share your lesson assessment, instructional objective, and activities with a classmate. Have the classmate comment about the alignment between them.

The sequence of constructing assessments, then writing instructional objectives, and finally selecting or developing instructional activities is not as linear as it might first appear. As you engage in this process, you will undoubtedly find yourself tweaking your assessments and instructional objectives to ensure alignment with your instructional activities. You might find an activity or hear of a different way of helping students learn the lesson content that may be more interesting or make greater or lesser cognitive demands on them than your initially proposed assessment. It is perfectly fine to make adjustments to your assessments and instructional objectives. In fact, it is very much a part of the lesson planning process.

Our discussion about instructional objectives and planning with the end in mind would be incomplete without saying a little more about the relationship between standards and instructional objectives. Careful thinking about the assessments described in Table 6.2 will likely lead you to the conclusion that it is impossible to effectively teach to the many content standards and their related benchmarks written for the science course or courses that you will likely teach. Every teacher could interpret each content standard or benchmark differently and thus develop different instruc-

tional objectives, assessments, and instructional activities. The result would be teachers developing different assessments and instruction based on their interpretations of the content standards. In fact, this is exactly what happens!

Most teachers realize that there are far too many content standards and benchmarks for most middle and high school science courses. The state- and district-level standards development process tends to bring together content experts who have a hard time discarding any of the curricular aims that they associate with a high-quality biology, physics, chemistry, or other science courses. Many teachers cope with this dilemma of too many content standards by deciding on their own which standards and benchmarks are most important, probably between one-third and one-half of all those listed, and teaching to these. These individual decisions about what content standards and benchmarks to emphasize are often based on the teacher's knowledge of the course content or rumors about what might be included on the applicable high-stakes test.

An alternative coping strategy recommended by W. James Popham (2003) is to work with other science teachers at your school or across your school district to prioritize the many content standards and benchmarks for the science courses you teach. Next, develop appropriate assessments and instructional objectives for each of the high-priority items as a group. Again, those selected as high priority might be between one-third and one-half of all the content standards and benchmarks listed. Then, work collaboratively to develop instructional options. The selection of agreed upon high-priority standards and benchmarks, more robust lesson assessments, and properly worded instructional objectives are just some of the benefits associated with working with others teachers to accomplish the important task of operationalizing the content standards. It also is likely that the decisions of the group, more so than the decisions of one teacher, may influence what is included on the high-stakes tests, particularly if the tests are developed at the school-district level.

As a beginning teacher, you may find that the task of prioritizing content standards has already been accomplished by other science teachers in your school or school district. Ask other teachers to find out if this has been done. You also may learn that lesson assessments and instructional objectives have been developed for the courses you have been assigned to teach. Regardless of the situation in which you find yourself, remember that lesson assessments are operationlized versions of the content standards and that instructional objectives mirror lesson assessments and inform students about what is expected of them. Instruction that flows from well-conceived lesson assessments will enable you to help students master important science understandings.

DURING-LESSON MONITORING

You have thought about your lesson with the end in mind; you know what you expect your students to learn from your lesson, having designed a lesson assessment; and you are prepared to tell your students of your expectations through the instructional objectives that you constructed. You are ready to engage your students in instructional activities and assess their learning. However, do you need to wait until the end of your lesson to find out if students are learning? Certainly not. There is much information about student learning and the quality of instruction that a teacher can gather during the lesson.

In our chapter's opening vignette, Howard Seung did not wait until the end of his lesson to find out about his students' learning. You will recall that after he showed and discussed with his students several examples of physical change and chemical change, Howard checked for student understanding. He simply presented them with two additional examples, a melting stick of butter and a sample of spoiling meat. But this time, he asked his students to close their eyes and hold up one, two, or three fingers. We can speculate that Howard asked his students to close their eyes so that each student's response would not be biased by the responses of their classmates.

The students' responses told Howard that the entire class grasped the concept of physical change, but a majority of the class did not have a good grasp of the concept of chemical change. Howard's request for students to explain their votes brought a response from Conrad that provided insight into the signs of chemical change that the students were cueing on when raising their fingers. This information, along with Conrad's admission that he didn't understand the meaning of the word *precipitate,* enabled Mr. Seung to make adjustments to his lesson—adjustments intended to enhance student learning.

Howard also monitored his students' learning in other ways during the lesson. As he walked around to the lab groups, Howard questioned students about what they were doing and thinking. He also kept track of student work using a checklist with multiple data-entry categories. We can surmise that the information gathered by these means was used by Howard to help students construct meaning about the physical and chemical changes of matter.

It probably comes as no surprise to you that teacher questioning is a central feature of monitoring student learning during a lesson. Student responses to teacher questions tell a lot about what understandings they are constructing from the lesson. Incorrect responses and responses of "I don't know" tell the teacher that students are not learning what is intended. Incorrect or incomplete responses to a question suggest that re-teaching a

Stop and Reflect!

- If you were an observer in Howard Seung's class on the day recounted in the chapter's opening vignette, what would you say about his efforts to monitor student learning during the lesson?

- What strategies, in addition to those used by Howard Seung, might a teacher consider to monitor student learning during a science lesson?

part of the lesson may be necessary, particularly if these types of responses come from many students.

To gather the most useful information about lesson success and student learning, it is important for you to prepare the questions to be used to monitor student learning in advance of the lesson. It is much easier to generate high-quality questions when planning the lesson than when teaching it. Having questions before you, perhaps written on a note card, will remind you to check for student understanding at certain points during the lesson and will make asking follow-up questions that much easier. In a later chapter of this textbook, you will learn more about different types of questions and questioning strategies. For now, think about how you can ask questions during a lesson that will enable you to monitor student understanding.

You will find that it is not always necessary to ask questions of students to gauge their learning and the success of your lesson. Students will often tell you that they don't understand something that was taught, request assistance to complete an assignment, or ask for further clarification if a concept is unclear to them. Additionally, student inattentiveness or off-task behavior can be a clue that the lesson is perceived as boring or that the learning task is too easy or too difficult. You will need to be attentive to such signals and be prepared to modify your instruction, if not on the spot at least during the next lesson.

Assessing student learning should be an integral part of teaching a lesson. It does no good to press through a lesson if students are not learning. By monitoring student learning during the lesson, you are telling your students that you value them as individuals and want them to experience success. You also are helping yourself be an effective teacher by modifying your lesson to address the needs of your students.

END-OF-LESSON ASSESSMENT

An excellent way to bring closure to any lesson is to allow your students to show what they have learned. This can easily be done during the last 5 minutes of the class period. However, assessing student learning at the end of a lesson is not something you can do on-the-fly.

Preparing for an end-of-lesson assessment is an important part of the lesson planning process. As has already been discussed, when planning with the end in mind, your end-of-lesson assessment will serve to guide the construction of your instructional objectives and selection of lesson activities.

As you think again about the opening vignette, you will recall that Howard Seung did not provide his students with an opportunity to show what they had learned at the end of the lesson. He found himself in a situation that happens all to often in middle school and high school science classes—the bell or administrative interruption, rather than the teacher, brings the lesson to a close. We can only image what Howard might have discovered about his teaching and his students' learning had he engaged his students in a few minutes of reflective thinking about the understandings they constructed during the class period.

Given that Howard did not share the instructional objective for his lesson, we speculated earlier in the chapter about the nature of the end-of-lesson assessment that he might have used. Recall that we suggested a possible assessment for closing Howard's lesson that would involve:

> Howard showing his students a small sample of gallium metal that melts in his hands and also heating a mixture of iron filings and sulfur as they watched. After a few minutes of silent observation, the students could be asked to write on a half-sheet of paper whether each example was a physical change or chemical change and to list the observations supporting their choices.

This assessment is only one of many that could have been used to gather information about Howard's teaching and his students' learning. In fact, end-of-lesson assessments can take many forms. Your imagination is the only factor limiting your choice of end-of-lesson assessments, but what you choose must be something that students can do quickly. For example, you can present your students with one or two questions designed to reveal their understanding of the lesson's content. The questions may be ones that students can answer with a word, a short phrase, or a sentence or two. Some teachers like to use questions similar to these to gauge student learning at the end of a lesson:

- What have you learned today?
- What about today's lesson was confusing or unclear to you?
- What could I do as the teacher to better help you understand the content of today's lesson?

You also can ask students to develop visual representations of their learning. Sketches and drawings can easily be created in a matter of minutes as long as limits are applied to the level of detail. Another end-of-lesson assessment option is to have your students demonstrate

their learning by filling in blank spaces in a simple concept map using vocabulary words from the lesson. Assuming that students have constructed concept maps before, they should be able to complete an assessment of this type in short order.

Stop and Reflect!

- What other assessment formats, besides those mentioned, might be used as end-of-lesson assessments?
- Using one of the assessment formats you identified, construct an alternative end-of-lesson assessment for Howard Seung's lesson on physical and chemical changes. Then, construct an instructional objective that is aligned with your new assessment.

Just like the end-of-lesson assessments themselves, the students' science understandings captured by end-of-lesson assessments take many forms, including written answers, sketches, concept maps, and much more. These understandings can function as data to answer questions about your teaching and your students' learning, making them very important. By examining the data generated from end-of-lesson assessments, you can determine what students are learning from your teaching and what kinds of learning difficulties students might be encountering. You also can tell if the majority or only a few of your students have grasped a concept and if identifiable learning difficulties are common among students. From this information, you can decide if re-teaching an entire lesson is necessary or if working with individual students to address particular learning needs is in order. In essence, an end-of-lesson assessment can provide you with evidence of your teaching effectiveness.

The data captured by end-of-lesson assessments can also be used to give constructive feedback to the entire class or individual students. Feedback to the entire class will likely entail oral instructions or an explanation from which all students can benefit. Feedback to individual students will be more personal and may range from a check mark that indicates a satisfactory response to a numeric score that highlights correct answers to written remarks of encouragement or praise.

Regardless of the type of feedback that you prefer to give to students, keep it straightforward and simple. We recommend that you structure your end-of-lesson assessments so that you spend about 10 minutes per class examining them and providing individual student feedback. Spending more time than this on a daily basis will likely lead to end-of-lesson assessments becoming a burden for you.

TABLE 6.3   Assessing Your Own Lesson Assessment Practices

Lesson Planning	Not Done	Adequate	Well Done
I identified a science lesson topic and content to be addressed in my lesson.			
I identified instructional activities and teaching strategies that I can use to help students learn the content of my lesson.			
I examined the content standards for the science course I am teaching and clarified the relationship between the standards and the content of my lesson.			
I developed an end-of-lesson assessment that shows what students know or can do relative to the content standard [or benchmark] for the my lesson.			
I wrote an instructional objective that is aligned with my end-of-lesson assessment.			
I planned for ways to monitor student learning during the lesson.			
I checked the alignment between the standard [or benchmark], lesson assessment, instructional objective, and lesson content.			
Evidence that supports your rating: _____ _____ _____ _____			
Lesson Teaching	**Not Done**	**Adequate**	**Well Done**
I shared my instructional objective with the students near the beginning of my lesson.			
I monitored students' learning during the lesson.			
I used student feedback to make instructional changes during the lesson to improve student learning.			
I assessed students' learning toward the end of the lesson.			
Evidence that supports your rating: _____ _____ _____ _____			
Teaching Debriefing	**Not Done**	**Adequate**	**Well Done**
I examined the information generated by students' during the end-of-lesson assessment.			
I considered how to use the data provided by the end-of-lesson assessment to inform my future lesson planning and teaching.			
Evidence that supports your rating: _____ _____ _____ _____			

While the primary purpose of end-of-lesson assessment is to provide constructive feedback to students about their learning and to you about your teaching effectiveness, it is possible to use scores from end-of-lesson assessments to generate daily grades. Some teachers believe that end-of-lesson assessments should be used to generate grades because the grades provide added incentives for student engagement and on-task behavior. Other teachers believe that nongraded assessments are good for students, affording opportunities for risk taking and divergent thinking. There is no right or wrong answer to the question about using end-of-lesson assessments to generate grades. It is a question that you will likely wrestle with as you contemplate the logistics of student assessment. More information about assessment and grading is presented in Chapter 16 on long-term planning and assessment.

Another question to consider when using end-of-lesson assessments centers on the kinds of knowledge that is actually assessed. In 5 minutes at the end of a class, it is likely that you will only assess students' knowledge of science facts and formulas—their declarative knowledge. Harder to assess with short end-of-lesson assessments will be your students' procedural knowledge, the understandings that require them to use their declarative knowledge to answer questions and solve problems. Planning is the key to ensure that your end-of-lesson assessments tap students' procedural knowledge in addition to their declarative knowledge. The questions that follow should help you distinguish between end-of-lesson assessments that target these two types of knowledge:

Examples of Declarative Knowledge Assessment
- What are the three alleles that code for human blood type?
- Of the three alleles that code for human blood type, which are co-dominant?

Examples of Procedural Knowledge Assessment
- What blood phenotypes are possible from two parents who both have blood type AB?
- In a case of disputed paternity, the child has blood type O and the mother has blood type A. Could the father have blood type AB? Why or why not?

The real benefit of end-of-lesson assessments comes from regular use and student awareness of their alignment with instructional objectives and comprehensive assessments. Regular use of end-of-lesson assessment provides you and your students with immediate information about your teaching and their learning. No one will be surprised at the time of end-of-unit or end-of-course tests. Additionally, when students know that end-of-lesson assessments are aligned with instructional objectives and that end-of-lesson assessments are similar in many ways to what will be included on end-of-unit or end-of-course assessments, students can use end-of-lesson assessments to monitor their own learning.

HONING YOUR LESSON ASSESSMENT SKILLS

In this chapter, we have emphasized the central role of assessment in planning and teaching a science lesson. In formulating this position, we introduced the idea of lesson planning with the end in mind and discussed four components that should be addressed in science lesson assessment: general learning goals, instructional objectives, during-lesson monitoring, and end-of-lesson assessment. We now challenge you to assess your own lesson assessment practices using the checklist presented in Table 6.3. It is our hope that through the use of this checklist you will be able to hone your lesson assessment skills.

ASSESSING AND REVIEWING

Analysis and Synthesis

1. Describe in your own words the relationships among the four features of a lesson assessment system: general learning goals, instructional objectives, during-lesson monitoring, and end-of-lesson assessment.

2. Examine the *National Science Education Standards* and your state's science standards. How do the two standards documents compare? What information do the documents provide about how to assess students' learning from a science lesson?

3. Construct a lesson assessment that is aligned with a content standard or benchmark for a science course that you would like to teach. Then, write an instructional objective that is aligned with your lesson assessment.

4. Suppose a teacher told you that she does not have time for end-of-lesson assessment in her science classes. What would you say to try to convince her to make end-of-lesson assessment a part of her teaching practice?

5. Think of a science lesson in which you participated as a learner. How did the teacher monitor your learning during the lesson? If invited by the teacher to offer suggestions for improving this aspect of the lesson, what would you say?

6. Write three questions that could be used to monitor students' learning during a science lesson. What information would you likely obtain from students' responses to these questions that would cause you to modify your lesson?

7. Reread the information for the two conditions presented in Table 6.2. Then, write another assessment, instructional objective, and instructional description that could be included as a third condition in this table.

Practical Considerations

8. Develop a lesson plan for a science topic that interests you. Check your lesson plan against the statements in the Lesson Planning section of Table 6.3. Make improvements to your lesson plan to ensure that the elements listed in the Lesson Planning section of Table 6.3 are adequately addressed.

9. Interview two science teachers at different schools about their lesson assessment practices. Ask about alignment among standards, assessments, and instructional objectives.

10. Ask a veteran science teacher to assess her own lesson assessment practices using the checklist presented in Table 6.3. Discuss with her your own thoughts about lesson assessment and determine what changes she would suggest to improve the checklist and your own thinking about lesson assessment.

Developmental Considerations

11. Share your students' end-of-lesson assessment data with a trusted science teacher colleague. Ask the colleague to offer suggestions based on the data to improve your teaching and your students' learning. Implement one or two of your colleague's suggestions and see what happens.

12. Read an article from *Science Scope* or *The Science Teacher* that focuses on lesson assessment. Discuss the article with others interested in science assessment. Devise a plan to implement a suggestion from the article in your lesson planning and teaching.

RESOURCES TO EXAMINE

Assessing Student Understanding in Science.   2001. Thousand Oaks, CA: Corwin Press.

Address for ordering: 2455 Teller Road, Thousand Oaks, CA 91320.

This book by Sandra Enger and Robert Yager includes a wealth of information about assessment in science applicable to middle and secondary school classes. Topics addressed in chapters for grades 5 through 12 include group performance tasks, standardized testing, and students' views of the scientific process.

Testing Better, Teaching Better: The Instructional Role of Assessment.   2003. Alexandria, VA: Association of Supervision and Curriculum Development.

James Popham highlights the relationship between assessment, instruction, and standards. In addition, he discusses the strengths and limitations of different types of assessments, the importance of affective assessment, and appropriate uses of standardized test.

Classroom Assessment and the National Science Education Standards.   2001. Washington, DC: National Academy Press.

A supplement to the *National Science Education Standards,* this book makes a case for strengthening assessment in the science classroom. It contains sections on summative and formative assessment, school-system-level support for assessment, and teacher professional development for improving science classroom assessment.

What Every Teacher Should Know About Student Assessment.   2004. Thousand Oaks, CA: Corwin Press.

Address for ordering: 2455 Teller Road, Thousand Oaks, CA 91320.

Chapter 7 of this book by Donna Tileston provides detailed instructions for building aligned assessments. The instructions are presented as six steps for teachers to follow. Other chapters address teacher-made tests, performance tasks, and state and national assessments.

REFERENCES

National Research Council. (1996). *National science education standards.* Washington, DC: National Academy Press.

Popham, W. J. (2003). *Test better, teach better: The instructional role of assessment.* Alexandria, VA: ASCD.

Tileston, D. W. (2004). *What every teacher should know about student assessment.* Thousand Oaks, CA: Corwin Press.

Wiggins, G. & McTighe, J. (1998) *Understanding by design.* Alexandria, VA: ASCD.

Part Two

BACKGROUND FOR SCIENCE TEACHING

7

The Nature of Science

*Role playing a famous scientist can stimulate
students' interest in science.*

Science instruction must reflect valid views of the nature of science. Teachers' lectures, classroom discussions, laboratory activities, assigned readings, long-term investigations, and examination questions should correspond to what are generally accepted as science content and process. Erroneous beliefs about how scientists go about their work must be eliminated, as must highly simplistic approaches to problem solving and overly simplistic examples of concepts, laws, and principles that distort this scientific knowledge. Science teachers, curriculum developers, and science educators must possess a broad understanding of the nature of science so that they make accurate interpretations and presentations of this discipline. Further, their understanding must lead to helping students appreciate the worth of science and how it directly benefits their lives. Science teaching must be in line with relevant and authentic science information in order to improve the scientific literacy of all people.

Aims of the Chapter

Use the questions that follow to expand your understanding about the nature of science:

- Why is it important for science teachers to understand the nature of science?

- Can you give a concise definition of science?

- How well can you explain the scientific enterprise by describing what scientists do in their work?

- How well can you explain the myths of science that are held by people in society that would indicate that you hold a more authentic view of science than the general public?

- How familiar are you with the nature of science put forth in some of the science education reform documents?

- To what extent can you discuss four facets or themes of scientific literacy that science teachers can use to provide a more balanced treatment of important aspects of science and technology in planning and teaching science?

Before you begin reading this chapter, please engage in a pre-assessment to determine your understanding of the nature of science. Figure 7.1 lists 12 statements, some of which are considered myths of science. Respond to the true/false quiz; then write a paragraph to support your response to each item. When you have completed the quiz and written explanations, read the chapter to see how well you understand the nature of science and the beliefs or myths of science that are held by many individuals.

What Is Science?

Science is a particular way of knowing about the world. In science, explanations are limited to those based on observations and experiments that can be substantiated by other scientists. Explanations that cannot be based on empirical evidence are not part of science. (The National Academy of Sciences, 1999, p. 1)

Toward a Definition of Science

Science is a broad-based human enterprise that is defined differently depending on the individual. The layperson might define science as a body of scientific information; the scientist might view it as a set of procedures by which hypotheses are tested; and a philosopher might regard science as a way of questioning the truthfulness of what we know. Prospective science teachers might put forth the following statements when asked for a definition of science:

Discovering nature
Organizing facts into theories
A method of discovery
A body of organized knowledge
Problem solving
A process of finding out
Logical reasoning

Myths of Science Quiz

Directions: Each statement that follows is about science. Some statements are true
and some are false. On the line in front of each statement, write a "T" if it is true
and an "F" if it is false. Then support your response to each statement with at least
one paragraph on a separate sheet of paper.

_____   1. Science is a system of beliefs.

_____   2. Most scientists are men because males are better at scientific thinking.

_____   3. Scientists rely heavily on imagination to carry out their work.

_____   4. Scientists are totally objective in their work.

_____   5. The scientific method is the accepted guide for conducting research.

_____   6. Experiments are carried out to prove cause-and-effect relationships.

_____   7. All scientific ideas are discovered and tested by controlled experiments.

_____   8. A hypothesis is an educated guess.

_____   9. When a theory has been supported by a great deal of scientific evidence, it becomes a law.

_____ 10. Scientific ideas are tentative and can be modified or disproved, but never proved.

_____ 11. Technology preceded science in the history of civilization.

_____ 12. In time, science can solve most of society's problems.

From "Myths of Science Quiz," by E. Chiapetta and T. Koballa, 2004, The Science Teacher, p. 59.

A study of the universe
The search for truth
Observing and describing reality

All of these views have some connection with science, but each is limited. Only collectively do they begin to portray science.

Science is the study of nature in an attempt to understand it and to form an organized body of knowledge that has predictive power and application in society. This definition parallels a statement by Edward Teller (1991), an eminent nuclear physicist: "A scientist has three responsibilities: one is to _understand,_ two is to _explain_ that understanding and three is to _apply_ the results of that understanding" (pp. 1, 15). Further, science is based on observation, experimentation, and reason. The key terms—understand, explain, and apply, along with observation, experimentation, and reasoning—can be used to form a useful explanation of science. They can be used to guide the planning and teaching of science where students are expected to understand science concepts, to explain them in writing and orally, and to apply them in the laboratory and in everyday life through an active learning process that mirrors authentic science.

The assertion that scientists try to understand, explain, and apply offers science teachers a simple and clear idea of the scientific enterprise. Scientists strive to understand the phenomena that make up the universe—from the beating of our hearts to the migration of birds to the explosion of stars. Their aim is to describe the internal and external structure of objects, the mechanism of forces, and the occurrence of events to the point where their ideas can be used to predict future events with great precision. Scientific understanding goes beyond description to the deeper level of explanation, which combines many observations, facts, laws, and generalizations into coherent theories that connect ideas with reality, not only specifying what is occurring, but how and why it is occurring. Scientific inquiry aims at determining cause-and-effect relationships, as well as all that occurs in between.

The Scientific Enterprise

Scientists go about their work in many ways, creating methods and techniques to study those aspects of the universe that interest them. Further, some scientists are more theoretical, others are more experimental, and still others are more technologically minded. When envisioning how new knowledge is created by science, one could say that scientists decide on what they are looking for and do not merely pursue ideas casually. Scientists make *careful observations,* collecting information they hope will support their beliefs. They *design experiments* and *ingenious ways* to answer their questions. Scientists rely heavily on *empirical data* to settle claims about nature. They use *logic and reasoning* to form conclusions.

Scientists *make public* their understanding through carefully written papers. Their manuscripts are presented at professional meetings and often submitted for publication in professional journals. In both instances, especially the latter, the work is carefully reviewed by colleagues who make critical comments and suggestions, thereby recommending the work for publication or rejection. Published works are open to *additional examination* by the scientific community, whereby the logic and reasoning can be evaluated and procedures and results can be tested by additional observation and experimentation. Further, the work is open to scrutiny by colleagues in order to determine if *ethical principles* have been violated, such as presenting erroneous data or taking credit for discoveries that others have claimed.

Scientific claims must be articulated in a manner that permits other scientists to *confirm* or *disprove* these assertions and translate them into useful products. At any time during the journey to understand nature, the most cherished ideas can be *disproved, falsified,* or *modified.* Scientists must remain open-minded and willing to change their ideas based on new data and compelling arguments that maintain the tentative nature of science claim.

In addition to understanding and explaining phenomena, scientists strive to apply the knowledge that they construct about the world. Many scientists, along with engineers and technologists, spend much of their time designing and producing *useful products* for society. Most of these products hold the potential to improve the quality of life, such as manufactured drugs, genetically engineered hormones, electronic communications, superconducting materials, and so on. It's impossible to calculate the number of ways in which science and engineering have added to our quality of life, but the fact that they have done so has earned them high esteem in our society. Unfortunately, the products of science and engineering can be misused, such as drug abuse and weapons used to kill innocent people.

In some instances, determining what something "is not" helps to better understand what that something "is." At first thought, this idea appears quite useful and simple for distinguishing science from nonscience. For example, would not most scientists be quick to say that astronomy and psychology are different from astrology or parapsychology? Identifying a single criterion (or several for that matter) to distinguish science from mythology or popular misconceptions, however, is a

formidable exercise. Most criteria proposed have met with criticism from philosophers of science.

Morris (1991) presents the example of distinguishing between superstring theory and the claims given by astrologers. He points out that if subjecting one's theory to empirical testing is used as the criterion for being scientific, then astrologers fare even better than the superstring theorists. Most physicists would agree that it is virtually impossible to observe a superstring, because this fundamental entity is hypothesized to be many millions of times smaller than a quark, for whose existence superstrings are theoretically responsible. On the other hand, one can set up tests to determine the apparent influences that heavenly bodies exert on human affairs, even if the results may provide little data to confirm these relationships. Morris points out that both scientific and nonscientific theories seem to be the result of thought, imagination, speculation, and problem solving. Both enterprises put forth bizarre ideas. In the final analysis, however, scientific theories generally offer clear, logical, and simple explanations of phenomena that provide useful insights into nature.

To say that science is a way of knowing implies that science is only one of many ways to establish knowledge about the world and that it competes with other ways humankind establishes knowledge. We must be mindful that other cultures—African, Asian, Hispanic, and Native American—have their particular worldviews that differ from the Western view of science (Stanley & Brickhouse, 1994). Among these cultures there may be alternative views, say of medicine, that have value. To many people, these alternative views and practices do not seem to offer a serious challenge to the contemporary scientific establishment when it comes to understanding and explaining nature (Loving, 1995). However, we do not want to assert that science can solve all problems, because many societal problems are political in nature and difficult to resolve.

Sometimes teachers and science textbooks portray science and the work of scientists in a manner that is misleading and distorts science. They incline toward giving a popularized history of science that "romanticizes scientists, inflate[s] the drama of their discoveries, and cast[s] scientists and the process of science in monumental proportions" (Allchin, 2003, p. 329). Allchin gives us the story of Alexander Fleming, who is often credited with the discovery of penicillin. While Fleming did stumble on to the effects of penicillin on the growth of bacteria, he did little to take that finding to the production of a drug that has been used to save tens of millions of lives. It was actually Howard Florey and Ernst Chain at Oxford University, with the help of many technicians, who worked out the production of penicillin for commercial use.

Many stories about the advancement of science in textbooks center on male scientists, giving the impression that this type of work is best carried out by men. However, many females have contributed significantly to the advancement of science, such as Marie Curie, Rosalind Franklin, Barbara McClintock, and Lisa Meitner. Textbooks must include the achievements of women and many others who are underrepresented in science in order to present a more valid view of the nature of science.

THE NATURE OF SCIENCE AND NATIONAL STANDARDS

> Science distinguishes itself from other ways of knowing and from other bodies of knowledge through the use of empirical standards, logical arguments, and skepticism, as scientists strive for the best possible explanations about the natural world. (National Research Council, 1996, p. 201)

The quote from the *National Science Education Standards* (National Research Council [NRC], 1996) indicates that science is a way of coming to understand the world in which we live. Although there are other ways of knowing, science is unique in that it has standards and practices that generate ideas to explain phenomena and to predict outcomes. Regardless of their durability and utility, scientific theories can be rejected with new findings.

The *Standards* (NRC, 1996) remind us that scientific explanations must meet certain criteria, which distinguish science from myth, personal belief, religious values, mystical belief, superstition, and authority. Scientific explanations must accurately reflect empirical observations and experimental results. The knowledge generated also must be formed from logical reasoning that conforms to rules of evidence. Further, the knowledge is made public so that it can be scrutinized and challenged, resulting in a continual process of confirmation, modification, or rejection.

The national reform document *Science for All Americans* (American Association for the Advancement of Science [AAAS], 1990) places great emphasis on the importance of understanding the nature of science. This document reinforces the NRC quote that science employs certain ways of finding out, as evidenced by the ways in which it gathers data and puts forth logical arguments to explain ideas while reserving the right to reject any of its theories or principles.

THEMES OF SCIENCE AND SCIENCE LITERACY

Sometimes reading about the philosophy of science can become confusing and leave one with the impression that science is not much different than mysticism or religion. Further, this literature presents many discussions on what science is not, obscuring the intent of science education, which is to promote an appreciation for science and help people to learn more about this enterprise. Fortunately, there are dimensions of science that scientists and science educators readily recognize and accept as useful. These dimensions or themes can be used to plan, carry out, and analyze science instruction.

We will refer to these dimensions or facets as *themes of scientific literacy* and state them as follows: (1) science as a way of thinking, (2) science as a way of investigating, (3) science as a body of knowledge, and (4) science and its interactions with technology and society. These major areas of science can be used to analyze what is being emphasized in a teaching session, laboratory exercise, textbook chapter, and so on. Their presentation in Figure 7.2 emphasizes that science content is often given more consideration than the other dimensions.

Before reading further, recall your experiences as a student in a college science class. What stands out in your mind regarding these experiences? Did the instructors get you to think about the topic under discussion? Did they spend time explaining to you how ideas were invented and their related phenomena discovered? Were major investigations or experiments discussed, illustrating how they contributed to the establishment of the laws and theories under study? Was lecture time spent on the applications of the subject matter or their relevance to society? Did a particularly interesting demonstration illuminate the lecture material? The chances are high that many of the science classes in which you enrolled in college or took in high school were comprised mostly of lectures that presented a large body of information.

FIGURE 7.2   Four themes or dimensions of science that should be evident in science instruction to various degrees.

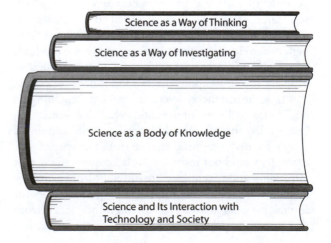

Science as a Way of Thinking

Science as a Way of Investigating

Science as a Body of Knowledge

Science and Its Interaction with Technology and Society

We believe strongly that science lectures at the middle school, high school, and college levels must go beyond the presentation of technical information. These sessions should be more balanced, showing how scientists go about their work and how their results impact the work of other scientists, as well as society. Science textbooks must also convey a more balanced view of science than they have in the past. If the presentation of science content comprises 80% or 85% of a given textbook, little text is left to help students understand how ideas were formed (Lumpe & Beck, 1996). The four themes we will discuss here—thinking, investigation, knowledge, and science/technology/society—can help science teachers to become more sensitive to the importance of balance in the curriculum (Chiappetta, Sethna, & Fillman, 1991).

Science as a Way of Thinking

"The whole of science is nothing more than a refinement of everyday thinking."

(Einstein, 1954, p. 283)

Beliefs

Scientists are passionate about their ideas regarding phenomena that make up the natural world. They often hold strong beliefs as to the mechanism of events and the structure of objects in the universe. Although many scientists would reject the idea of absolute truth, they seek what they believe to be true about the world. While some would like to think that scientific beliefs are special in that they are based on evidence, this is not always the case. The history of science includes theories that had little empirical support, yet were believed to be true for centuries. For example, the belief that the earth was the center of the universe was dominant for thousands of years. Even Copernicus believed that the earth's orbit around the sun was circular rather than elliptical.

Not everyone agrees that belief is a part of science or that scientists should even hold beliefs in the body of knowledge that forms this discipline. Some define belief as faith, asserting that religious belief is different from scientific belief. Others suggest that scientists should be "forbidden to express belief in the absolute truth of any of the scientific observation statements that make up the body of science. There is always the possibility, no matter how small it may be that a scientific statement will be shown to be false" (Strahler, 1992, p. 22).

Scientists are humans, and they do believe in their ideas. Even particle physicists, who theorize about realms of reality smaller in scale than a proton, believe they are getting to the bottom of it all. Steven Weinberg, a Nobel laureate in physics says: "What drives us onward in the work of science is precisely the sense that there are truths out there to be discovered, truths that once discovered will form a permanent part of human knowledge" (Weinberg, 1998, p. 7). Therefore, science teachers should bring out the beliefs of scientists in order to illustrate how they view the world and what underlies their attitudes and curiosity. However, the body of scientific knowledge that becomes durable is based more so on compelling evidence than on the beliefs of individual scientists.

Curiosity

Scientists as a group seem to be uncontrollably curious. They constantly explore their environment and frequently ask the question, Why? This curiosity is often manifested in their having many interests, even beyond that of unraveling the mysteries of natural phenomena. Nicholas Copernicus (1472–1543), for instance, who caused a scientific revolution by placing the sun at the center of our solar system, pursued many vocations. "Copernicus was a churchman, a painter, a poet, a physician, an economist, a statesmen, a soldier, and a scientist" (Hummel, 1986, p. 55). Benjamin Franklin (1706–1790) likewise demonstrated his many interests as a printer, writer, publisher, inventor, statesman, and scientist. Jean Henrie Fabre (1823–1915) began his insatiable fascination with insects at a young age in the French countryside. His studies remained within the enormous field of insects where he produced volumes describing the anatomy and behavior of many insects including bees, wasps, gnats, dung beetles, spiders, and scorpions. Leonardo da Vinci (1452–1519) epitomizes the curiosity and creativity of the human mind. Not only was da Vinci regarded as a great artist, but his accomplishments extended into science and technology. From his sketch books, we observe the study of gears, hydraulic jacks, flying machines, parachutes, cranes, pulley systems, drilling machines, underwater breathing apparatus, and so forth.

"Scientists—that is, creative scientists—spend their lives trying to guess right" (Polanyi, 1958, p. 143) because they are motivated to get to the truth. For them, the truth is a deeper understanding of the world. This is a creative process that is fueled by personal passion to find out. Scientists are so driven by their curiosity to explain their ideas that they often risk ridicule, discrimination, and persecution to continue their work.

Imagination

In addition to being curious, scientists rely heavily on imagination. Albert Einstein reminds us that "imagination is more important than knowledge." He evidences his thinking in many ways, especially when he put forth his theory of special relativity. Einstein imagined himself riding on a beam of light while holding a mirror in front of him, reasoning how long it would take a light beam to register his image back to him and to a stationary observer. The early Greek philosophers and scientists tried to visualize a harmonious universe with heavenly bodies moving in a particular manner. James Clerk Maxwell formed mental pictures of the abstract problems that he attempted to solve, especially electromagnetic fields. Many in a college organic chemistry course have listened to the story of how August Kekule came to visualize the benzene ring during a dream:

> The atoms flitted before my eyes. Long rows, variously, more closely, united; all in movement wriggling and turning like snakes. And see, what was that? One of the snakes seized its own tail and the image whirled scornfully before my eyes. (Cited in Beveridge, 1957, p. 76).

In the development of the atomic model, J. J. Thomson put forth the "raisins in a bun" model. His conception shows a ball of positively charged matter with negatively charged electrons embedded in it, similar to raisins in a bun. Although this model did not last very long, it was a useful way to explain the charged nature of the atom. A great deal of scientific and technological knowledge is based on models of phenomena generated by imaginative thinking on the part of scientists and engineers.

Reasoning

Associated with imagination is reasoning. The history of science provides many examples of how those who participate in the scientific enterprise study phenomena with considerable reliance on their own thinking as well as that of others. According to Albert Einstein, science is a refinement of everyday thinking. This belief becomes evident when one studies the work of scientists in their attempt to construct ideas that explain how nature works. Science teaching can benefit greatly from the inclusion of narratives about the development of the major theories of the natural and physical world, illustrating how these explanations evolved and changed over time (Duschl, 1990). Examples of science courses that focus on the nature of scientific thinking can be found among the national curriculum projects produced during the 1960s. Harvard Project Physics, in particular, centered its textbook and supplemental reading on historical accounts of how scientific principles and theories were put forth by various individuals. A classic example of how a scientist used a thought experiment to illustrate correct and incorrect reasoning about the motion of celestial bodies is given in Galileo's *Two New Sciences*, where he presents a conversation between three characters: Simplicio, who represents the Aristotelian view of mechanics; Salviati, who represents the

new view of Galileo; and Sagredo, who represents a man with an open mind and eagerness to learn. Such literary constructions were a necessary and clever way to put forth one's reasoning regarding a belief that was offensive to the current political and religious powers of the period (Project Physics Course, 1975).

If educators turn to the history of science, they will find many examples of thought experiments that illustrate creativity, imagination, and reasoning. The writings of Ernst Mach contain numerous examples of puzzles that were contrived to cause one to think deeply about physical phenomena. Mach (1838–1916), a great scientist and philosopher, presented thought experiments for his readers to perform in each edition of his *Zeitschrift*. One such mind teaser asks, "What happens when a stoppered bottle with a fly on its base is in equilibrium on a balance and the fly takes off" (cited in Matthews, 1991, p. 15). Einstein formulated his theories of relativity following concepts he conceived during his thought experiments.

Scientists engage in a variety of reasoning behaviors to elucidate patterns in nature. Sometimes they use inductive thinking; at other times they use deductive thinking. Through inductive reasoning, one arrives at explanations and theories by piecing together facts and principles. Although Sir Francis Bacon did not originate the inductive method, he did a great deal to promote this approach. Bacon argued strongly that the laws of science are formed from data collected through observation and experimentation (Bruno, 1989). In doing so, he stressed empiricism over deductive logic. Nevertheless, deductive thinking is no less important in the thinking process.

Deductive thinking involves the application of general principles to other instances. The deductive process makes inferences about specific situations from known or tentative generalizations. This form of reasoning is often used to test hypotheses, either confirming or disproving them. Deduction is frequently used in astronomy to predict events from existing theories. It also has been used extensively in the area of theoretical physics to predict the existence of certain subatomic particles, many of which have been discovered years after their announcements. The hypothetical–deductive approach is also a suggested strategy to use for instructing students in biological sciences to help them better understand these disciplines (Moore, 1984).

Cause-and-Effect Relationships

Scientists often seek to establish cause-and-effect relationships to advance their understanding of the world. The search for cause and effect is central to experimentation and to modern science. Further, this conceptual relationship helps to explain the mechanism by which cause produces effect. Many events can stimulate cause-

and-effect reasoning, from the very common to less frequent, such as:

- Why do cats give birth only to kittens?
- Why do some people who smoke develop lung cancer?
- Why do tornadoes form?
- Why do comets reappear every so many years?

In concept, the logic of the cause-and-effect relationship is simple: here A is shown to cause B. A common example of this simple relationship can be observed by plucking a guitar string. If you shorten the string and pluck it, the string produces a higher-pitched sound. Consider human respiration. If you cut off all oxygen to the human body, the person will die. Cells need oxygen to carry out important processes, which, in humans, enters the body by way of the lungs. Thus the phrase: Oxygen supports life.

The cause of an event must provide the antecedent conditions that are necessary and sufficient for the event to occur. For example, we often hear the comment that cigarette smoking causes lung cancer. Some scientists, as well as tobacco company representatives, object to that statement. Not every person who smokes gets lung cancer. Some people smoke for 50, 60, 70, or 80 years and never contract lung cancer. Smoking may more correctly be termed a risk factor for lung cancer, because we cannot say that tobacco is the sole agent for causing this disease or that smoking tobacco will always result in lung cancer.

With living organisms, cause-and-effect relationships are very difficult to establish. The problems involved in the search for causes in living organisms are formidable. Ernst Mayr (1961) posits the cause for a single bird's migration from New Hampshire in late August:

> There is an immediate set of causes for the migration, consisting of the physiological conditions of the bird interacting with the photoperiodicity and drop in temperature. We might call these the proximate causes of migration. The other two causes, the lack of food during the winter and the genetic disposition of the bird, are the ultimate causes. . . . There is always a proximate set of causes and an ultimate set of causes; both have to be explained and interpreted for a complete understanding of the given phenomenon. (p. 1503)

Do not assume that physical scientists have an easier task determining causation than biological scientists. Consider investigations into the nature of subatomic particles. Physicists have turned to probability and complex mathematical formulas to explain the behavior of electrons and dozens of other subatomic particles, rather than determining the exact nature of a given particle. The Heisenberg uncertainty principle limits the extent of our knowledge regarding the position and momentum of a particle along any axis. Further, those in the historical sciences (evolutionary biology and geology) are very hard pressed to establish cause-and-effect relationships in their work.

Self-Examination and Skepticism

Scientific thinking is more than an effort to understand nature. For centuries, philosophers of science have examined the ways in which scientists have arrived at their conclusions about nature. To paraphrase Poincare (1854–1912) the French mathematician, an intelligent person cannot believe everything or believe nothing. What then can intelligent persons believe, what must they reject, and what can they accept with varying degrees of reservation?

Scientists have always concerned themselves with these questions; indeed, physics was once called "natural philosophy." But never have scientists spent more effort than today in examining their processes of reasoning. Investigations into the particulate nature of matter, quantum mechanics, and acceptance of the principle of indeterminacy have undermined our earlier notions of the predictability and well-behaved order of nature that once were never questioned. Even the more reluctant scientists have been forced to look closely at their ways of thinking.

Along with self-examination, skepticism is a healthy disposition that every citizen should possess, not only the scientist. Everyone should be skeptical about the many claims made about products, events, and phenomena we hear and read about. We should question advertisements and commercials offering herbs and pills that will cause weight loss or cure cancer. We should question claims from those who say they can detect your thoughts. We should also observe how the scientific community reacts to claims, such as those reporting energy from cold fusion, a human clone, or a perpetual motion machine.

When a claim is made about a *too good to be true* product or event, a skeptical reaction should be in order as well as a call for the evidence to support the claim. Michael Shermer, the founder of the Skeptic Society and editor-in-chief of the *Skeptic Magazine,* offers the general public, especially science teachers, a great deal of literature to assist in understanding normal science, nonscience, and the fringes of science. Shermer (2001, pp. 18–22) posits 10 questions that one might ask with regard to a claim:

1. How reliable is the source of the claim?
2. Does this source often make similar claims?
3. Have the claims been verified by another source?
4. How does this fit with what we know about the world and how it works?
5. Has anyone, including and especially the claimant, gone out of his or her way to disprove the claim, or has only confirmation evidence been sought?

6. In the absence of clearly defined proof, does the preponderance of evidence converge to the claimant's conclusion or a different one?

7. Is the claimant employing the accepted rules of reason and tools of research, or have these been abandoned in favor of others that lead to the desired conclusion?

8. Has the claimant provided a different explanation for the observed phenomena, or is it strictly a process of denying the existing explanation?

9. If the claimant has proffered a new explanation, does it account for as many phenomena as the old explanation?

10. Do the claimant's personal beliefs and biases drive the conclusions, or vice versa?

Objectivity and Open-Mindedness

Many more characteristics than those mentioned can be assigned to scientific thinking. For example, objectivity and open-mindedness are often ascribed to the scientific attitude. Although these images of scientists are put forth in textbooks, they may not necessarily represent the manner in which all scientists conduct their work. Scientists are not more dispassionate about their life's work than are other people. Holton (1952) reminds us about the distinction between public and private science that challenges the empiricist stereotype of the detached, objective researcher, whom the public sees in the final edited version of the scientist's work. Gauld (1982) cautions science educators about their beliefs regarding the empiricist conception of the scientific attitude and suggests perhaps eliminating it from science education. "Teaching that scientists possess these characteristics is bad enough but it is abhorrent that science educators should actually attempt to mold children in the same false image" (Gauld, 1982, p. 118).

If scientists do not have great conviction in the ideas they are pursuing, they would lack the drive necessary to carry out their research. Scientists must believe in the theories that guide their research agenda for which they have a strong allegiance (Kuhn, 1962). However, some of their scientific beliefs create personal biases that interfere with their progress, because their interpretation of data and reasoning causes them to view the phenomenon under study less objectively. While complete objectivity by individual scientists is not possible, it is this personal view of the world that makes science productive, especially when it is mixed in with the views of other scientists working on the same problems. Polanyi (1958, p. 18) states the notion of scientific objectivity as follows in his book *Personal Knowledge:* "The purpose of this book is to show that complete objectivity as usually attributed to the exact science is a delusion and is in fact a false idea. But I shall not try to repudiate strict objectivity as an idea without offering a substitute, which I have called 'personal knowledge'."

Science as a Way of Investigating

"The" Scientific Method expressed in that way haunts the introductions of textbooks, lab report guidelines and science fair standards. Yet we consider it a poor model for learning about method in science. (Wivagg & Allchin, 2002, p. 2)

The preceding quote highlights what Wivagg and Allchin (2002) call "The" Dogma of The Scientific Method. These writers, as well as others who have studied the history and philosophy of science, point out a myth in science education that continues in spite of the historical record of how science actually takes place. You can still find in science classrooms a poster that lists the five or six steps of The Scientific Method. Although scientific reports follow a format similar to the steps listed in The Scientific Method, this procedure is a standardized way of preparing scientific papers for publication. The actual research took a very different path than what appears in print.

The work of Karl Pearson (1937) and others, who believed that they could capture the scientific method in the five steps that follow, is still taught in some science courses and it sometimes appears in the introductory chapter of many elementary, middle, and senior high school science textbooks:

1. Observing
2. Collecting data
3. Developing a hypothesis
4. Experimenting
5. Concluding

Science as a way of investigating utilizes many approaches to constructing knowledge. Science has many methods, which demonstrates humankind's inventiveness for seeking solutions to problems. Some of the approaches used by scientists rely heavily on observation and prediction, as in astronomy and ecology. Other approaches rely on laboratory experiments that focus on cause-and-effect relationships such as those used in microbiology. Percy Bridgman's (1950) comment reinforces this idea: "The scientific method, as far as it is a method, is nothing more than doing one's damndest with one's mind, no holds barred." Alan Chalmers (1982, p. 169) stresses that "there is no timeless and universal conception of science or scientific method" that can distinguish science from other forms of knowing or make science superior to other human enterprises. Some scientists are experimenters who do the investigating, while others are theorizers who attempt to explain data and pose interesting questions to guide inquiry. Among the many processes often associated with science and inquiry are observing, inferring, hypothesizing, predicting, measuring, manipulating variables, experimenting, and calculating. While these are useful skills to possess, a more realistic view of investigative science might be in these ideas offered by Franz (1990):

experimentation	strategy
reason	intuition
chance	overcoming difficulties
observation	serendipity
hypotheses	

In spite of what is often reported about scientific investigations, especially in science textbooks, the inquiry process is rather idiosyncratic. Furthermore, because there is no "scientific method," the current science education reform documents avoid using the term "the scientific method," instead using the terms *scientific methods* and *scientific methods of inquiry* (AAAS, 1990, p.1). The *Standards* (NRC, 1996) state:

> The importance of inquiry does not imply that all teachers should pursue a single approach to teaching science. Just as inquiry has many different facets, so teachers need to use many different strategies to develop the understandings and abilities described in the *Standards*. (p. 2)

James Conant, chemist and president of Harvard University, asserted: "There is no such thing as *the scientific method*. If there were, surely an examination of the history of physics, chemistry, and biology would reveal it" (1951, p. 45). The Harvard historian of science Gerald Holton supports this sentiment as follows:

> All too often the suggestion has been made that the successes of science are the results of applying "the scientific method." But if by "scientific method" we mean the sequence of and rule by which scientists now and in the past have actually done their work, then two things soon become obvious. First, as for every task, there are here not one but many methods and unaccountable variants, and second, even these different methods are usually read into the story after the work has been completed, and so reflect the actual working procedures only in a rather artificial and debatable way. The ever-present longing to discover *one* master procedure or set of rules underlying all scientific work is understandable, for such a discovery might enormously benefit all fields of scholarship; but like the search for the philosopher's stone, this hope had to be abandoned. (Holton & Roller, 1958, p. 216)

Among the contemporary philosophers of science in the 20th century, Paul Feyerabend has voiced perhaps the most vehement position against a scientific method. His sentiments are expressed in a notable book titled *Against Method* (Feyerabend, 1993). Feyerabend goes so far as to say there is not one science, but many sciences, which proceed in radically different ways. In fact, we might think of this enterprise as many different science projects. Feyerabend proclaims "there is no common structure to the events, procedures and results that constitute science" (1993, p. 1). Therefore, one cannot explain progress in science in a simple, one-method manner.

Hypothesis

A hypothesis is an investigative tool that helps the inquirer to clarify ideas and state relationships so they can be tested. It is an untested condition to be examined. A hypothesis is a concise statement that attempts to explain a pattern or predict an outcome. Hypotheses stem from questions that a scientist asks concerning a problem under study. A hypothesis is a generalization to be tested by additional observation, experimentation, or prediction. It is tentative and therefore can be rejected or modified. Hypotheses set the stage for challenging an idea in order to determine if it merits at least a temporary place in the fabric of scientific knowledge.

Even though a situation can be set up that could disprove a hypothesis, contrary evidence may not necessarily lead to the complete rejection of a hypothesis. Revision of the hypothesis rather than rejection may be appropriate.

> If the generalization has any reasonable body of supporting data, the finding of new facts which do not fit usually leads to the refinement or elaboration of the original hypothesis. ... On the other hand, if the original basis for the hypothesis was slender, the unfavorable instances may so outweigh the favorable ones as to make it reasonable to believe that the earlier agreement was a matter of pure chance. Also, a new hypothesis may be developed which fits the original data as well. (Wilson, 1952, p. 28)

People who engage in experimentation probably do so from a more optimistic point of view than attempting to discredit their ideas, as suggested by Popper (1963). In reality, they are betting on their hypotheses, hoping their experiments will confirm their predictions. What generally occurs is an unexpected result, however, which can be difficult to explain. Chamberlin (1965) urges researchers to propose not just one hypothesis but as many as the mind can invent, thus freeing the mind from bias that might result from excessive love of one's intellectual child. With many hypotheses, the researcher can be somewhat more objective and increase the probability for identifying several causes, knowing that some of the hypotheses will not survive. Nature is complex; attempting to explain it by limiting ourselves to one hypothesis is too narrow and self-defeating.

The term *hypothesis* poses a problem in science education, because it is used widely and often misunderstood.

For example, consider science fair competitions where the term *hypothesis* usually appears in the project report as one of the steps of the scientific method. Many of these student-generated hypotheses are poorly understood. A better choice to guide these investigations would be a set of questions. With many science fair projects, it is doubtful that students create statements that apply to a general class of objects and events to be tested. This shortcoming is evident by sampling what took place as well as their lack of understanding of how the sample fits with the population of objects or events under study.

Some science educators object to defining a hypothesis as an "educated guess," a term often expressed by pre-service and in-service science teachers. They realize that scientists carefully study phenomena and problems before they launch their research projects. Why would a scientist devote a great deal of energy and money pursuing a guess? Galus (2003, p. 10) states: "In the scientific world, the hypothesis is formulated only after hours of observation, days of calculating and studying, and sometimes years of research into the phenomena of interest."

Observation

Observation is certainly one cornerstone of science. Although most observations are carried out through the sense of sight, other senses like hearing, feeling, smelling, and tasting can also be part of the observation process. Through observation, data and information are gathered and organized in order to make sense out of reality. This is how facts are established so that hypotheses can be tested to support theories. The body of knowledge formed by scientists is the result of extensive observations that eventually coalesce into concepts, principles, and theories.

The list of individuals who have made significant contributions to science as the result of their keen observations is long. Among those worth mentioning is Tycho Brahe, who amassed the most important early observations regarding the motion of stars and planets during the Middle Ages. These observations, in turn, were used by Kepler to produce the now-accepted idea that planets move in elliptical orbits around the sun. Tycho used his eyes as well as a few simple devices to study the movement of celestial bodies. Tycho made his observations with scrupulous regularity, repeating them, combining them, and trying to allow for the imperfection of his instruments. As a result, he reduced his margin of error to a fraction of a minute of an arc and provided the sharpest precision achieved by anyone before the telescope (Boorstin, 1985, p. 307).

Although observation plays a central role in scientific investigation, this skill is tied closely to the knowledge, thinking, and motivation of the observer. As Goethe said, "We see only what we know." Thus, the scientist as well as the layperson sees with the mind. Beveridge (1957) points out that what people observe in a situation depends upon their interests. Furthermore, he claims that false observations occur when the senses provide the wrong information to the mind or when the mind plays tricks on the observer by filling in information from past experiences. Often, the observer focuses attention on what is expected, thus missing unexpected occurrences and valuable facts. Although observation is one of the most fundamental inquiry skills, it is a complex activity that merits careful study in and of itself. Further, science observation is guided by theory.

Experimentation

Along with observation, experimentation is central to the scientific enterprise and the development of modern science. Through experimentation, ideas can be confirmed or supported and erroneous beliefs that have been passed down by authority can be discarded. Experimentation permits us to probe nature's secrets, which seem to be tightly guarded and often disguised. The controlled experiment offers the scientist an opportunity to test ideas and determine cause-and-effect relationships. Experimental activities range from using a match to burn a peanut to using a particle accelerator to smash a proton.

Modern science came into being in the 16th century when individuals like Galileo and Copernicus turned away from Greek science, which was dominated by philosophers who distrusted experimentation. Greek philosophers relied primarily on reasoning to develop their ideas. Some of these individuals placed little value upon practical activities that could reveal the obvious. They shunned the technologies of the craftsman, such as mechanical and optical devices that could provide accurate observations (Aicken, 1984).

When one experiments, events are introduced producing relationships that can be studied carefully. The conditions of these interventions are known and controlled. In this manner, the procedure is documented and thus can be reproduced by others. The controlled experiment is often used to test a hypothesis concerning cause-and-effect relationships. Condition *A,* for example, is altered to determine its effects on condition *B.* The situation that is manipulated by the researcher is called the *independent variable,* and the resultant variable is called the *dependent variable.* Other variables are held constant and their conditions noted. In situations where living organisms are under study, randomization of organisms or subjects into experimental and control groups is most desirable.

We must guard against placing ultimate trust in experimentation for evidence. Beveridge (1957) warns not to put excessive faith in experimentation because the possibility of error in technique always exists, which can result in misleading outcomes. It is not at all rare for scientists in different parts of the world to obtain contradictory results with similar biological material. Sometimes these can be traced to unsuspected factors; for instance, a great difference in the reactions of guinea pigs to diphtheria toxin was traced to a difference in diets of the animals. In other instances, it has not been possible to discover the cause of the disagreement despite a thorough investigation (p. 34).

Mathematics

Roger Bacon expressed it well when he said, "Mathematics is the door and the key to science." His quote suggests that mathematics is necessary to the understanding of nature's clockworks and without it we cannot get inside to find out what is taking place. The formulas and symbols assist us to identify relationships that represent laws and patterns in nature. At a very deep level, mathematics helps us to express models of situations that we cannot possibly observe. The atom, for example, is so small that we cannot see it or the electrons and protons that form its structure. The simple planetary models that we often see in textbooks or the packet-of-pulsating wave models may be inaccurate visualizations of the atom. According to scientists who study atoms and subatomic particles, the atom may be an entity that we cannot visualize. Nevertheless, mathematical models have been devised that predict with great accuracy the behavior of groups of atoms and subatomic particles. Mathematics has been used successfully to provide useful representations of nature for objects and phenomena that are out of our direct perceptual reach.

The power of numbers and the intimate association between mathematics and the evolution of science is evident throughout recorded history (de Santillana, 1961). For example, Pythagoras, in his studies of nature, mingled astronomy, geometry, music, and arithmetic. He indicated that numbers are special and that the universe produces melody and is put together with harmony. He described the motion of the stars in terms of rhythm and melody. Pythagoras's one physical discovery had to do with the patterns of sound produced by changing the length of a plucked string. He noted that moving a bridge to different locations or intervals on the string changed the sound. The ratios 1:2, 4:3, and 3:4 were important numerical relationships that resulted in distinct sounds. He further discovered that the numbers 1, 2, 3, and 4, which formed these ratios, added up to 10, the "perfect number."

Galileo, it is often said, made significant contributions to modern science because he attempted to explain phenomena with evidence, using mathematical relationships. Many connect Galileo with the falling stone controversy. Those who subscribed to Aristotle's notion of falling bodies believed that a heavier object falls at a faster rate than a lighter object. Galileo probably said, "Wait a minute." If you try this out, you will find that they both fall at the same rate, provided that air resistance is ignored. His work on this problem resulted in the celebrated formula,

$$s = 16t^2$$

which states that a falling body has traveled a certain distance, *s,* after falling *t* seconds. Galileo also showed that the trajectory of a ball thrown in the air follows the parabolic path.

Science as a Body of Knowledge

The body of knowledge produced from many scientific fields represents the creative products of human invention that have occurred over the centuries. The enormous collection of ideas pertaining to the natural and physical world is organized into astronomy, biology, chemistry, geology, physics, and at the interface of these disciplines. The result is a compilation of carefully catalogued information, containing many types of knowledge, each of which makes its own unique contribution to science. The facts, concepts, principles, laws, hypotheses, theories, and models form the content of science. These ideas possess their own specific meaning, which cannot be understood apart from the processes of inquiry that produced them. Therefore, the content and methods of science are tied together, and teaching one without the other distorts the learner's conception and appreciation for the nature of science.

Facts

The facts of science serve as the foundation for concepts, principles, and theories. A fact is often thought of as truth and the state of things. Facts represent what we can perceive through our senses, and they are usually regarded as reliable data. Often, two criteria are used to identify a scientific fact: (1) it is directly observable and (2) it can be demonstrated at any time. Consequently, facts are open to all who wish to observe them. We must remember, however, that these criteria do not always hold, because factual information regarding a one-time event, such as a volcanic eruption, may not be repeatable. In addition, uncertainty and limitation are inherent in measurement that accompanies facts. Therefore, data can never be considered absolutely pure and unequivocally true, because they contain a probability of error.

The presentation of facts alone in a science course is not enough, because the receiver of the information should know how the facts were established. For example, it is widely known that food can spoil in the presence of microorganisms, causing whoever eats it to become very sick or die. This fact becomes intelligible and meaningful when students learn how various types of food poisoning have been established. For example, one of the most deadly food poisonings is botulism, which is caused by the anaerobic bacteria *Clostridium botulinum*. A tiny amount of toxin produced by this organism is deadly. A lethal dose of the *botulinum* toxin is approximately .0000001—one ten-millionth of a gram (Black, 1994). Therefore, one gram of this compound is enough to kill about 10,000,000 people. The toxin acts by paralyzing muscles, blocking the neurotransmitter acetylcholine, thus stopping breathing. Canned foods, such as beans, corn, and beets, must be heat-treated to prevent this bacterium from multiplying while in an airtight container.

The historical accounts of food poisoning from bacteria and fungi are numerous. Microbial contamination of milk, cereal, and bread, for example, provide a meaningful context for explaining the mechanisms that have established the causal factors of food poisoning. Therefore, it is a fact that microorganisms can impart toxins to food, causing sickness or death. Perhaps not all of the facts given in a science course can be taught within a context of how they were arrived at, but many can and should be.

Concepts

Facts have little meaning by themselves. They are raw material, in a sense, and must be examined to form meaningful ideas and relationships. Thinking and reasoning are required to identify patterns and make connections between the data, thus forming relationships we call concepts. A concept is an abstraction of events, objects, or phenomena that seem to have certain properties or attributes in common. Fish, for example, possess certain characteristics that set them apart from reptiles and mammals. Most bony fish have scales, fins, and gills. According to Bruner, Goodnow, and Austin (1956), a concept has five important elements: (1) name, (2) definition, (3) attributes, (4) values, and (5) examples. The process of concept formation and attainment is an active process and requires more than simply conveying these elements to the learner. The students must establish some of the attributes and discover some of the patterns between data if the concepts are to become linked to other meaningful ideas in their minds. In addition, concepts can be affective as well as cognitive.

Many of the terms associated with scientific fields represent concepts. They are ideas used to form categories. In biology, for example, tree, grass, insect, ape, gene, and enzyme each represent a class of entities that share common characteristics. In chemistry, element, molecule, compound, mixture, acid, base, and isotope can be considered concepts. There are physics concepts, such as electron, proton, neutron, wave, solid, and x-ray. Concepts become meaningful to learners when they

have had many opportunities to experience examples or instances of them. For example, we form the class of animals called fish by observing a variety of fish and noting that they live in water, take in water through their mouths, have fins, and so on. Categorizing phenomena aids scientists and the public at large to form knowledge about the world in which we live.

Laws and Principles

Laws and principles also fall into the general category of a concept. Although they can be considered broader than a simple concept, principles and laws are often used synonymously. These higher-order ideas are used to *describe* phenomena and patterns in nature. Laws and principles state that which exists. They are often accepted as facts; nevertheless, their distinction and empirical basis must be remembered. Laws and principles are composed of concepts and facts. They are more general than facts, but they are subject to limiting conditions and are related to observable phenomena. For example, gas laws and laws of motion specify what can be observed under certain conditions. The principles that regulate growth and reproduction provide reliable information regarding changes that take place in living systems.

Theories

Science goes beyond the classification and description of phenomena to the level of explanation. Scientists use theories to *explain* underlying patterns and forces. Theories are ambitious intellectual endeavors, because they deal with the complexities of reality—that which is obscure and hidden from direct observation. Theories deal with magnitudes of time, distance, and size that defy ordinary perception. Consider the theory of the atom, which states that all matter is made up of tiny particles called atoms, many millions of which would be required to cover the period at the end of this sentence. This visual conception becomes even harder to grasp when we consider the aspect of the theory that suggests an atom is mostly empty space with a small, dense, positively charged center with a cloud of negatively charged particles moving in certain regions of space far out from the center.

Theories have a different purpose than to organize facts, concepts, and laws. They incorporate this type of knowledge into explanations of why phenomena occur as they do. Theories are of a different nature; they never become fact or law, but remain tentative until disproved or revised.

> Any physical theory is always provisional, in the sense that it is only a hypothesis: you can never prove it. No matter how many times the results of experiments agree with some theory, you can never be sure that the next time the results will not contradict the theory. On the other hand, you

can disprove a theory by finding even a single observation that disagrees with the predictions of the theory. As philosopher of science Karl Popper has emphasized, a good theory is characterized by the fact that it makes a number of predictions that could be disproved or falsified by observation. Each time new experiments are observed to agree with the predictions the theory survives, and our confidence in it is increased; but if ever new observation is found to disagree, we have to abandon or modify the theory. At least that is what is supposed to happen, but you can always question the competence of the person who carried out the observation. (Hawking, 1988, p. 10)

Theories are of great importance to science. They represent some of the most monumental and creative works of humankind, which is evident in the theories of the atom, special and general relativity, plate tectonics, and natural selection, to name a few. These inventions of the mind incorporate a great deal of thinking, imagination, writing, and modeling. Consider natural selection, for example. Darwin used domestic breeding as a model for selection and used Malthus's notion of struggle for existence for survival of the fittest (Harre, 1970). Recall the four postulates of natural selection: (1) all organisms produce more offspring than can survive, (2) overproduction occurs that leads to a struggle for survival, (3) individuals within a species vary, and (4) those organisms best adapted tend to survive. Overproduction, competition, variation, mutation, struggle for existence, and adaptation are just some of the concepts and principles that are used in Darwin's theory for explaining the evolution of life on this planet, which has been changing for some three billion years. Science educators have the responsibility to help others to comprehend the nature of theories by showing how they attempt to explain complex phenomena that cannot be observed directly.

Models

The term *model* is often used in the scientific literature. A scientific model is a *representation* of phenomenon that we cannot see or observe directly. These models become mental images or constructs that are used to explain abstract ideas. They include the most salient features of an idea or theory that the scientist is attempting to make comprehensible. While not a replica of reality, a scientific model can be in the form of a concrete structure as well as a mathematical formula. The Bohr model of the atom, the planetary model of the solar system, the wave and particle models of light, and the double helix model of DNA have all been represented in material and visual forms as well as in mathematical expression.

Generally, models are deduced from abstract ideas, and sometimes there are no sharp distinctions between models, hypotheses, and theories. Textbooks are the major referent for most of our notions about scientific models. They are useful in helping us to become familiar with important ideas. Unfortunately, many people come to believe that the models presented in science textbooks are the real thing, forgetting that they are used only to help the learner conceptualize the salient features of a principle or theory, and that the mental picture is not what exists in reality. McComas (2000) goes so far as to assert that scientific models do not represent reality. Models are more useful than exact representations of phenomena. This view is correct if one interprets "represent" to mean identical copy.

Remember that because models are not perfect, they are problematic in teaching science. Too often, the model becomes the reality that is under study. Students rarely see the limitations of these analogies, which result in a highly simplistic representation of a phenomenon. Amdahl (1991, p. 18) advises that when devising a concrete model of the universe, for example: "Don't mistake your watermelon for the universe."

In closing this section on science as a body of knowledge, science educators should be alerted to the problems associated with the categorization and definitions of science content. There is no standardized or universally accepted definition for the terms scientific fact, concept, law, principle, theory, and model. Often, these conceptions are used interchangeably and poorly defined. After an analysis of 12 introductory college biology textbooks, Kugler (2002) points out how many biologists/authors disagree on the definitions of these content terms and how they provide examples that are inconsistent with their own definitions. Therefore, when teaching science, we must strive to define terms carefully and to use them in a consistent manner.

Science and Its Interactions with Technology and Society

Science is often portrayed as the individual scientist, working by herself, in pursuit of an important discovery. Unfortunately, the characterization of science as an individual activity is misleading. A great deal of scientific work is carried out collaboratively by many individuals working as a team. Further, scientific progress is influenced by society and the availability of technology to support data collection and analysis.

Today, science is intimately related to technology and society. Each influences the other, causing them to advance or make little progress. Basic science could not advance without the use of highly sophisticated equipment, such as particle accelerators, chromatographs, spectroscopes, electron beam microscopes, space telescopes, electrophoresis apparatus, spaceships, and integrated circuits. These and thousands of other technological products help us to answer questions about nature's deeply held secrets. Questions posed about nature give rise to the necessity for developing equipment that can help to answer these inquiries. For example, there have been great advances in the sophistication of chromatographic instruments over the past half-century to determine the composition of complex substances. Computer software programs have been developed to advance understanding of protein synthesis, weather patterns, and changes in the oceans' floor.

Society also plays a key role in the progress of science and technology. Society, through governmental organizations such as the National Science Foundation and the National Institutes of Health, exerts a large influence on the funding that takes place in science, engineering, medicine, agriculture, and mathematics. Business and industry carry out research and development programs that expend billions of dollars each year to improve on their products, employing many scientists, engineers, and technicians.

Technology

Technology advances when both science and society have needs to fulfill and problems to solve. For example, the desire to travel long distances in a short period of time, to process enormous amounts of data, and to build light-weight structures have stimulated the creation of products that are very advanced technologically from those built only 50 years ago. The production of jumbo jets can carry thousands of people daily across continents and the oceans. Small personal computers are becoming common in society, because they can be used for tasks from computing to word-processing. Pipes, wallboard, and ceiling materials made from polymers have replaced steel, copper, wood,

and cement as building materials that have exceptional properties. Technology has been around longer that science. It began when people fashioned tools to carry out everyday tasks, such as cooking, hunting, and making shelters.

Society

Just as scientific knowledge impacts society, society impacts science. Most scientific work is funded through governmental grants and private business. The money is generally targeted for projects that study important societal problems, such as cardiovascular disease, cancer, and weapon systems. The Manhattan Project, which produced the first atomic bomb, serves as an example of how national security stimulated scientific and technological advances in capturing the power of the atom. Today's research is carried out by teams of scientists working cooperatively to solve societal problems. These efforts require large amounts of money to support every phase of the projects, from writing grant proposals to conducting research to communicating results. Politics play an important part in determining which research is needed and how much funding will be provided. Politicians are interested most in research and technology that can solve problems of high public interest rather than basic research that appeals to few people. Recall that the government stopped work on the large Superconducting Super Collider Project in Texas that could have advanced particle physics. Most people would rather see their tax dollars go into cancer and cardiovascular research than the more theoretical exploration of tiny particles that constitute the atom. More than ever before, science is rooted in society and connected with technology. This topic will be taken up in greater detail in the Chapter 12.

ASSESSING AND REVIEWING

Analysis and Synthesis

1. How did you score on the true/false quiz (Figure 7.1) with regard to identifying some myths of science? Compare your true/false answers with this key: 1-F, 2-F, 3-T, 4-F, 5-F, 6-F, 7-F, 8-F, 9-F,10-T, 11-T, 12-F. In order to better understand the 12 statements, go back through the chapter and look for discussions of the nature of science that pertain to each quiz item. The 12 statements parallel the development of the chapter from beginning to end.

2. Present a definition of science. How does science differ from other ways of knowing such as myth and religion?

Practical Considerations

3. Let's assess a science teacher's approach to experimentation in order to determine the extent to which it reflects authentic science to the students.

TEACHER: Today, class, you are going to conduct an investigation to determine how many paper clips you can hang on the end of a magnet before the force gives way and the clips fall off. I want you to follow the scientific method that we use to guide our laboratory work. Remember the steps of this method listed on the poster.

The Scientific Method

1. Problem
2. Hypothesis
3. Procedure
4. Results
5. Conclusion

a. Evaluate this approach to teaching science by writing one sentence indicating the extent to which it reflects the way scientists go about their work.

b. In one or two paragraphs, substantiate your evaluation of this teaching episode from what you read in this chapter.

5. Analyze a teaching situation or instruction materials to determine which dimension(s) or theme(s) of science discussed in this chapter is(are) emphasized. Make an outline of the major terms associated with: (1) science as a way of thinking, (2) science as a way of investigating, (3) science as a body of knowledge, and (4) science and its interactions with technology and society. Use these categories to determine the science curricular emphasis in the following paragraphs that you might find in a science textbook:

a. Bones are a complex tissue. The outer covering is composed of a tough membrane called the periosteum, which aids in nourishing the bone. The periosteum contains a rich supply of blood and is where muscles are attached to the bone. Beneath the periosteum is a bony layer that contains mineral matter. This layer can range from very hard to spongy material. The bony layer is penetrated by many channels, called the Haversian canals, that carry nourishment to the living cells of the bone.

b. There is a global debate taking place concerning the rain forests that are being cut down in South America. The people of that region believe it is their right to clear the trees so that they can cultivate the land and grow crops to feed themselves. People in other parts of the world are distressed to learn of the rain forest destruction; they want the trees to take in carbon dioxide from the atmosphere and give off oxygen. Further, they fear that many species of plants and insects will become extinct with the disappearance of the rain forest habitat.

6. Identify the ideas that you will use in planning and teaching science to help students understand and appreciate this enterprise. Construct a visual representation of major terms that presents your conception of science. You might begin by placing "The Nature of Science" at or near the center of your graphic organizer and connecting it with lines to the key terms.

Developmental Considerations

7. Begin or add to your professional library, with paperback books on the nature of science. These can be purchased from the Internet at bookseller sites and in local bookstores. In some cities, there are half-priced bookstores where science and nature of science books can be purchased for very little money.

RESOURCES TO EXAMINE

Science for All Americans. 1990. New York: Oxford University Press.

Read the first chapter, "The Nature of Science." This important document by the American Association for the Advancement of Science gives a presentation on what is science. All science teachers should have a copy of this book in their professional library and refer to it for guiding their understanding of science teaching.

"Elements of The Nature of Science: Dispelling The Myths." 2000. In *The Nature of Science in Science Education: Rationales and Strategies* (pp. 53–70). Dordrecht: Kluwer.

William McComas presents his 15 myths of science with discussion about these established ideas of science. He provides excellent insight into the nature of science distilled from a scholarly examination of the history, philosophy, and sociology of science. McComas's writing is clear and informative and will enlighten those who have not read widely about the nature of science in scholarly literature.

"The Dogma of The Scientific Method." Nov./Dec., 2002. *American Biology Teacher.*

The authors, Wivagg and Allchin, write a clear, crisp, two-page article about the naïve ideas of a scientific method. The article should convince most readers that science is a creative enterprise and scientists use many tools in their quest to understand nature. The authors also point out that scientific papers, although appearing to follow the scientific method, are written to fit a standard publication format.

On Being a Scientist: Responsible Conduct in Research. 1999. Washington, DC: National Academy Press.

The National Academy of Science produced this excellent 30-page booklet that presents many aspect of science with examples from the work of scientists. The booklet addresses the social foundations of science, experimental techniques, values in science, publications and openness, error and negligence, ethical standards, and scientists in society. These topics are accompanied with case studies to give them more meaning.

Skeptic Magazine. Skeptic at P.O. Box 338, Altadena, CA; Phone: 626-794-3119; Fax: 626-794-1301; E-mail: skepticmag@aol.com

The *Skeptic Magazine* offers science educators and the general public many resources for better understanding science, pseudoscience, and non-science. The magazine's articles address many topics, such as science and religion, creationism and evolution, fad diets, paranormal claims, astrology, alien abductions, and so on. In addition, many resources are listed in the magazine that readers can obtain, such as the Skeptics' Lecture Series at Caltech, *Skeptic Magazine* back issues, The Skeptic's Book Club, and *The Skeptic Encyclopedia of Pseudoscience.*

REFERENCES

Aicken, F. (1984). *The nature of science.* London: Heinemann Educational Books.

Allchin, D. (2003). Scientific myth-conceptions. *Science Education, 87,* 329–351.

Amdahl, K. (1991). *There are no electrons.* Arvada, CO: Clearwater Publishing Co.

American Association for the Advancement of Science (AAAS). (1990). *Science for all Americans.* New York: Oxford University Press.

American Association for the Advancement of Science. (1993).*Benchmarks for science literacy.* New York: Oxford University Press.

Beveridge, W. I. B. (1957). *The art of scientific investigation.* New York: Vintage Books.

Black, H. (1994, December). Poison that heals. *Chem Matters,* 7–9.

Boorstin, D. J. (1985). *The discoverers.* New York: Vintage Books.

Bridgman, P. W. (1950). *The reflections of a physicist.* New York: Philosophical Library.

Bruner, J. S., Goodnow, J. J., & Austin, G. A. (1956). *A study of thinking.* New York: John Wiley.

Bruno, L. C. (1989). *The landmarks of science.* New York: Facts on File.

Chalmers, A. F. (1982). *What is this thing called science?* Portland, OR: International Specialized Book Service.

Chamberlin, T. C. (1965). The method of multiple working hypotheses. *Science, 148,* 754.

Chiappetta, E. L., Sethna, G. H., & Fillman, D. A. (1991). A quantitative analysis of high school chemistry textbooks for scientific literacy themes and expository learning aids. *Journal of Research in Science Teaching, 28,* 939–951.

Conant, J. B. (1951). *On understanding science.* New York: A New Mentor Book.

de Santillana, G. (1961). *The origins of scientific thought.* New York: New American Library of World Literature.

Duschl, R. A. (1990). *Restructuring science education.* New York: Teachers College Press.

Einstein, A. (1954). *Ideas and opinions.* New York: Dell.

Feyerabend, P. (1993). *Against method.* London: Verso.

Franz, J. E. (1990). The art of research. *ChemTech, 20*(3), 133–135.

Galus, P. J. (2003, May). A testable prediction. *The Science Teacher,* p. 10.

Gauld, C. (1982). The scientific attitude and science education: A critical reappraisal. *Science Education, 66,* 109–121.

Harre, R. (1970). *The principles of scientific thinking.* Chicago: University of Chicago Press.

Hawking, S. W. (1988). *A brief history of time.* New York: Bantam Books.

Holton, G. (1952). *Introduction to concepts and theories in physical science.* Reading, MA: Addison-Wesley.

Holton, G., & Roller, D. H. D. (1958). *Foundations of modern physical science.* Reading, MA: Addison-Wesley.

Hummel, C. E. (1986). *The Galileo connection.* Downers Grove, IL: InterVarsity Press.

Kugler, C. (2002, May). Darwin's theory, Mendel's laws: Labels and the teaching of science. *The American Biology Teacher,* 341–351.

Kuhn, T. S. (1962). *The structure of scientific revolutions.* Chicago: University of Chicago Press.

Loving, C. C. (1995). Comments on multiculturalism, universalism, and science education. *Journal of Research in Science Teaching, 79,* 341–348.

Lumpe, A. T., & Beck, J. (1996). A profile of high school biology textbooks using scientific literacy recommendations. *The American Biology Teacher, 58,* 147–153.

Matthews, M. R. (1991). Ernst Mach and contemporary science education reforms. In M. R. Mathews (Ed.), *History, Philosophy, and Science Teaching* (pp. 9–18). New York: Teachers College Press.

Mayr, E. (1961). Cause and effect in biology. *Science, 134,* 1503.

McComas, W. F. (2000). Elements of the nature of science: Dispelling the myths. In W. F. McComas (Ed.), *The nature of science in science education: Rationales and strategies* (pp. 53–70). Dordrecht: Kluwer.

Moore, J. A. (1984). Science as a way of knowing. *American Zoologist, 24,* 467–534.

Morris, R. (1991). How to tell what is science from what isn't. In J. Brockman (Ed.), *Doing science.* New York: Prentice Hall.

National Academy of Sciences. (1999). *Science and creationism: A view from the National Academy of Sciences.* Washington, DC: National Academy Press.

National Research Council (NRC). (1996). *National science education standards.* Washington, DC: National Academy Press.

Pearson, K. (1937). *The grammar of science.* London: Dutton.

Polanyi, M. (1958). *Personal knowledge.* Chicago: University of Chicago Press.

Popper, K. (1963). *Conjectures and refutation: The growth of scientific knowledge.* New York: Harper & Row.

Project Physics Course. (1975). *Project physics.* New York: Holt, Rinehart and Winston.

Shermer, M. (2001). *The borderlands of science.* New York: Oxford Press.

Stanley, W. B., & Brickhouse, N. W. (1994). Multiculturalism, universalism, and science education. *Journal of Research in Science Teaching, 78,* 387–398.

Strahler, A. N. (1992). *Understanding science.* Buffalo, NY: Prometheus Books.

Teller, E. (1991, March 12). Teller talks. *The Daily Cougar, 57*(83), pp. 1, 15.

Weinberg, S. (1998, Oct. 8). The revolution that didn't happen. *New York Review of Books.* [On-line]. Available: http://w.w.w.nybooks.com/nyrev/.

Wilson, E. B., Jr. (1952). *An introduction to scientific research.* New York: McGraw-Hill.

Wivagg, D., & Allchin, D. (2002, Nov./Dec.). The dogma of the scientific method. *American Biology Teacher,* 484–485.

chapter

8

Diverse Adolescent Learners and Their Schools

*Teachers need to make a special effort in order
to interest all students in science.*

The American educational system is facing a great challenge today to provide an equitable education for all students. The diverse student population in schools is causing science teachers to rethink how they teach and what they teach. To meet the challenge before them, teachers must consider cultural background, ethnicity, gender, disabilities, and adolescent development in their decisions about the science education of today's students. Schools are also changing to prepare this new generation of learners for the societal demands that lie ahead of them. So it is that science education occurs in a context that is bound by the nature of the learners and their schools. An understanding of adolescent learners and their schools is needed to meet the demands of science teaching.

AIMS OF THE CHAPTER

Use the questions that follow to guide your thinking and learning about important understandings regarding adolescent learners and their schools:

- What are the demographics of today's middle and secondary school population?

- What is multicultural science education? How is multicultural science education different from the universalist tradition of science education?

- What can teachers do to provide all students, regardless of cultural background, ethnicity, gender, or special needs, with the opportunity to learn quality science?

- What are salient features of today's middle and secondary schools?

STUDENT DIVERSITY

As educational leaders search for new ways to enhance excellence in science teaching and learning, the middle and secondary student population is becoming more diverse. The increasing population diversity often leads to challenges for science teachers as they strive to provide learning experiences that meet the needs of all their students. Factors responsible for the growing diversity of the student population include rising immigration, higher birthrates among some ethnic groups, and the inclusion of students with special learning needs into regular school classes.

Demographics

The specifics of these changes are described in reports released by the U.S. Department of Education's National Center for Educational Statistics (2002a, 2003, 2004). In 2003, the White K–12 school-age population was estimated at about 31 million students. While this number seems large, it reflects nearly an 18% decrease from 1973. During this same 30-year period, the population of African- American students increased from 14.7 to nearly 17%. This increase brings the total school-age population of African Americans to more than 8 million. Also increasing in number was the population of other groups, mostly Asian Americans but also Native Americans, to more than 2 million or about 5.5% of the total school-age population. The largest increase was witnessed in the Hispanic population. From 1973 to 2003, the Hispanic K–12 school-age population has increased from 5.7% to greater than 17%. Hispanics are the fastest growing segment of the school-age population and now number more than 8 million. These demographic shifts are most pronounced in many cities and non-metropolitan areas in the southern and western regions of the United States, where African American and Hispanic students, traditionally underrepresented in science, are the majority of the public school population (U.S. Department of Education, National Center for Educational Statistics, 2002a).

Another U.S. Department of Education (2002b) report revealed that about 6 million students, or more than 11% of the school-age population, are served under the Individuals with Disabilities in Education Act (IDEA). Student disabilities covered by IDEA range from specific learning disabilities, emotional disturbance, and attention deficit disorder to orthopedic, hearing, and visual impairments. In recent years, the greatest growth in disability services has occurred among students between 12 and 17 years of age. Students with disabilities are found among all demographic groups, adding to the diversity of middle school and high school science classes.

Factors Affecting Success in Science

Diversity by itself does not affect students' success in science, but factors often related to diversity do. For instance, socioeconomic status is viewed as the "single most powerful factor" that affects science performance and motivation (Lynch et al., 1996, p. 13). Students from poor families who attend schools that are inadequately funded do not do as well in science as their contemporaries (Kozol, 1991). A disproportionate number of African Americans, Hispanics, and Native Americans are poor and attend poor schools. There is little doubt that poverty contributes to the poor science performance and lack of motivation among students from these ethnic groups. Children of the poor lack many of the experiences that help other students succeed in school, and inadequately funded schools are ill prepared to help these children catch up. Many Asian Americans seem to have escaped the conditions of poverty through their educational achievements, but among recent Asian American immigrants, particularly those from Southeast Asia, the problems of poverty are very evident (United States Commission on Civil Rights, 1992).

Many recent immigrants, particularly young Asians and Hispanics, come from homes in which English is not spoken (U.S. Department of Education, 2003). This places excessive demands on a student to learn English while at the same time trying to learn science. Poor science performance among these students is due to the high vocabulary demands and the abstract understandings associated with science learning (Lee, Fradd, & Sutman, 1995). Some Asian Americans seem to compensate for their limited English proficiency by excelling in school subjects that make low demands on their language skills (Lynch et al., 1996). Students from rural areas, regardless of ethnicity, also are disadvantaged when their science experiences and curricular choices are compared with those of students at schools in larger communities. The lack of opportunity negatively impacts the science performance of these students.

The factors of socioeconomic status, immigration status, English language proficiency, and geographic location are among those used to identify at-risk students. At-risk students are those students that past trends indicate have a greater-than-average chance of not succeeding in school and dropping out before graduating from high school. U.S. Department of Education statistics reveal that most at-risk students have one or more of the following risk factors (2002a):

- Changed schools multiple times before completing eighth grade
- Live in families with incomes below the poverty level
- Have average grades of C or lower during middle school
- Are from single-parent families
- Have siblings who dropped out of high school
- Are limited in English proficiency

But, as Muth and Alvermann (1999, p. 49) acknowledge, socioeconomic status "is not the sole determinant of who will succeed in school and who will drop out." Students from all population groups drop out when they become disillusioned with the school experience. Science classes can either contribute to feelings of disillusionment or make school an exciting and enjoyable place to be. It is the responsibility of the teacher to take into account the diversity of the student population in terms of background, knowledge, motivation, and language in order to provide an equitable and high-quality science experience for all.

Stop and Reflect!

Before reading further, do the following:

- Write a description for a class of students that you think reflects the diversity of today's middle school and high school population. Then, pick one student from the class description. What factors are likely to affect this student's success in science?

- Read the entries from Ms. Kendal's journal in Box 8.1. What ideas do you have for enhancing the likelihood that Ms. Kendal will be successful in helping all her students do well in physical science? How could you prepare yourself to meet the science learning needs of a diverse student population?

EQUITY IN SCIENCE EDUCATION

Equity in science education means that all students, regardless of cultural background, ethnicity, gender, or special needs, have the same opportunity to learn quality science (Atwater, Crockett, & Kilpatrick, 1996). The outcome of this quality science experience is citizens able to make use of science in their daily lives and to pursue science and science-related jobs of the highest caliber. There is much that science teachers can do to help realize this goal.

Lynch and her colleagues (1996) offer two compelling reasons for advancing equity in science education. The first is economic. Equity in science education will result in a workforce better prepared for the science- and technology-related jobs that are increasing in number. This highly skilled workforce will benefit the nation's economy as "high-tech" jobs are filled by United States citizens and not lost overseas. The second is based in social justice. We have the

Classroom Snapshot 8.1

Ms. Kendal's Journal

Ms. Kendal is starting her first year of teaching at Riverview High School. She was an excellent student and decided to pursue a teaching career during her junior year in college. While feeling quite comfortable with the concepts addressed in the chemistry and physical science courses she was assigned to teach, she is not sure that she is ready for dealing with the diverse needs of the students in her classes. Here are some excerpts from her weekly journal.

Pre-Planning

My teaching schedule was changed from what I was told when I was hired in June. I'm now assigned to teach three sections of physical science this semester. Mr. Schultz, my principal, said that I should expect to teach only chemistry classes in the spring. I think he said this to appease me. The names that appear on my class roles suggest that many different cultural backgrounds will be represented in my classes. There are many students with Hispanic surnames. The "ESOL" [English for Speakers of Other Languages] designation next to 11 of the names means that these students will also be trying to learn English as they learn physical science. In addition, I have five students who require IEPs [Individualized Education Plans], suggesting that they have some kind of disability. I sure hope that I can meet their learning needs.

Week 1

I feel that I got off to a good start with my classes. I was firm and took time to work with my students to establish our class rules and expectations. I met with Mr. Sanchez, our school's lead ESOL teacher, and discussed ideas about how to best help the ESOL students. His suggestions were consistent with what I learned in my college classes, but making time to plan for all the students' needs is my real challenge. It was also good to learn from Mr. Sanchez that students will not be pulled out of my physical science classes for special ESOL sessions, but that Ms. Birdwell, an ESOL teacher, will periodically attend my classes and will be available to help me plan for the special learning needs of these students during my planning period on Wednesday. The best thing that happened this week is that I met Ms. Jameson. We have the same lunch schedule. She is a very nice person and has taught physics and physical science at Riverview for the past 9 years. She offered to help me develop lesson plans and to share her teaching materials. I'm hoping that she will be able to suggest ways to engage Josh and a couple of other students who seem disillusioned with school.

Week 5

A new student joined my first period physical science class this week. She came from Pakistan and speaks no English other than "Hello, My name is Nazmoon." Her father is a chemical consultant and will be working at the nearby chemical plant for the next year. Since there are no Punjabi-speaking students in my classes, I'm unable to assign a buddy to help her understand what I am saying, like I have done with several of my Spanish-speaking students. I'm very fortunate to have some wonderful bilingual students in my classes who are willing to translate my instructions for Spanish-speaking students who are just learning English. I was pleased to receive compliments from both Ms. Jameson and Ms. Birdwell for my use of hands-on learning experiences and demonstrations to help all my students learn. Ms. Jameson said that the lesson she observed engaged students with limited English proficiency along with Josh and his friends. This was a great way to end to the week.

Week 10

Eight students withdrew from my physical science classes this week. Their parents are migrant farm laborers. The students told me that they would return to the Riverview community in the spring when their parents are hired to plant next year's crop. The students were unsure about the schools they would attend in the locations where their families will live in the coming months. I learned from Ms. Birdwell that ESOL students' withdrawing from school is something that happens each year at about this time. I feel sorry for these students. They seem to be making such good progress in learning both physical science and learning English.

obligation to prepare all students to function in our modern science-based society. Additionally, these authors advance the argument that equity in science education should be about educating students in the culture of power that permits access to scientific knowledge. Central to this argument is the idea that the more you know, the more powerful you are. And as our previous discussion of demographics clearly indicates, science knowledge is not equally distributed among all groups in American society. According to Atwater et al. (1996), teachers maintain power in science classrooms through their selective silence and by the ways in which they present information and interact with students. Empowered science classrooms, where teachers and students function as a community of learners, are the desirable state.

Culturally Based Deficiencies

Schools must respond to the needs of today's diverse student population by addressing the issue of equity. But how should this occur? In the past, it was believed that equity in science education could be achieved by overcoming the deficiencies that are brought to school by diverse students. The lack of success had by these students was assumed to be due to their home life or cultural background being less advanced than that of students from the cultural mainstream. Remediation designed to compensate for their lack of knowledge, skills, and attitudes in science was considered the solution to increasing science participation and performance in school, and ultimately, the number of culturally diverse persons who pursued science and technical careers.

Today, most people reject this deficit model. Instead, the focus is on the incompatibilities between the students' background and special needs and the expectations of the science classroom. As a microcosm of the school culture, science classes tend to promote the values ascribed to by the mainstream White, male-dominated, middle-class culture (Hodson, 1993; Stanley & Brickhouse, 1994). Competition, fast work, and respect for the teacher are valued; rigid time schedules are followed; and students are expected to graduate from high school and go to college or seek work. In attempting to achieve equity in science education, teachers must recognize that these values are not shared by all cultures and that the related goals are not achievable by all students. Fairness and impartiality on the part of the science teacher are key to an equitable science education for all.

Multicultural Science Education

An alternative to the notion of cultural assimilation in science is multicultural science education. Nested within the larger framework of multicultural education, it is a concept not without ambiguity. Multicultural science education "can mean many things to many people" (Hodson, 1993, p. 688). According to Ogawa (1995), "Awareness of cultural diversity in science education seems to be at the crux of multicultural science education" (p. 584). Extending the work of James Banks, Atwater and Riley define cultural diversity in science education as "a construct, a process, and an educational reform movement with the goal of providing equitable opportunities for culturally diverse student populations to learn quality science in schools, colleges, and universities" (1993, p. 664). Hodson (1993) warns about defining multicultural education too narrowly and contends that what constitutes multicultural science education will vary depending on the region, community, school, and classroom in which it is practiced. And, that which constitutes multicultural science education in a class of mostly African American or Hispanic students will be different than in a class of mostly White students (Hodson, 1993).

Before addressing ways in which school science can be presented to make it attractive and accessible to all students, we will first turn our attention to the nature of science and how science is perceived from the perspective of different cultures. In Chapter 7, you learned about science as a way of knowing and the need to be mindful of the worldview of other peoples. In the next section, that discussion will be extended with attention given to a debate that has influenced the current thinking about multicultural science education. The central tension of this debate is whether or not multiculturalism is at odds with a universalistic view of science.

Multiculturalism and Universalism in Science Education

Some people who write about the nature of science claim that science is universal. What is meant by this claim is that science, as a human construction, is a universal form of knowledge that transcends cultural interpretations (Matthews, 1994). That is to say that scientific knowledge has no national, political, or cultural boundaries. "Pure universalist science educators question the multiethnicity of atoms, quasars and quarks, while voicing a concern over the inaccuracies inherent in attempting to paint a social picture of science" (Weld, 1997, p. 265). An important tenant of the universalist tradition is that the efficacy of humans' explanations of the natural world are grounded in reality. An example may help clarify this idea. Consider a violent thunderstorm. People outdoors during the storm will likely get wet or even struck by lightning. According to the universalist position, it is the character of the storm, not the meteorologists' culturally based rules of evidence and justification, that ultimately judges the efficacy of the science of meteorology (Matthews, 1994).

Students' cultural backgrounds affect how and what they learn in science classes.

The universalist position has been challenged by multiculturalists on the grounds that it presents a biased interpretation of the nature of science. The universalist position is considered biased primarily because it fails to consider knowledge systems developed by non-Western and ancient cultures as science (Luft, 1998). Multiculturalists claim that the universalist position is only one among many possible scientific frameworks for investigating the natural world (Loving, 1995). By considering modern Western science as the only knowledge system, Stanley and Brickhouse (1994) warn that we run the risk of limiting our ability to generate new knowledge by destroying knowledge systems viewed as inferior. The consideration of non-Western science has recently spawned interest in the indigenous knowledge of science and technology held by Native Americans and other peoples in Africa, New Zealand and the Philippines.

Siegel's (1997) examination of the universalist and multiculturalist perspectives on both epistemological and moral grounds has brought some clarity to the debate. Siding with Matthews (1994), his position is that multicultural science education cannot be justified from an epistemological basis because different knowledge systems are not equally valid. As Matthews (1994) points out, "no ethnic science is going to adequately explain how radios work, why the moon stays in orbit, why hundreds of thousands of Africans are dying of AIDS and so on. Mainstream science may not give us complete answers, but my claim is that it gives better answers than others" (p. 193).

However, Siegel argues in defense of multicultural science education from a moral stance. He urges that all students and the scientific ideas that reflect their cultures be treated with justice and respect in science classes. Referencing the work of Hodson (1993), Siegel goes on to remind the reader that Western science conceptions, including those of objectivity and rationality, are not shared by all peoples and that teachers need to be sensitive to this, but that exposure of all students, regardless of their cultural background, to Western science seems to be exactly what science education should be about (Siegel, 1997, p. 102). The study of Western science affords students the opportunity to investigate ideas that are unfamiliar to them and learn from their experiences. Siegel's position is that multiculturalism is very compatible with a universalistic view of science.

It is likely that the debate between multiculturalists and universalists will continue for some time. But despite their differences, there are some points on which the two sides agree. One is that not all knowledge systems developed by different cultures, and called science, are equally sound. A second is that students in the United States must come to understand modern Western science. The final point is that multicultural science education is a moral imperative, an imperative that has significant implications for the science classroom.

Teaching Science to All Students

Suggestions are plentiful about how to alter science curriculum and instruction to make them better reflect the vision of multicultural science education. Textbook publishers are very cognizant of the need to provide teachers with information about the contributions of other cultures, men and women, and persons with disabilities to modern science as well as ideas for addressing the needs of culturally diverse students, students of both genders, and those students with special learning needs. Nevertheless, most science teachers may still need help regarding how to augment their classroom practice. What can you do to make your science classroom a better place for all students? In the next sections of this chapter, we try to help you answer this question by presenting research-based recommendations about how to address the science learning needs of culturally and linguistically diverse students, female students, and exceptional students, including those that have disabilities and those that have special gifts and talents.

CULTURAL AND LINGUISTIC DIVERSITY

Science education researchers describe three approaches for promoting meaningful science learning among culturally and linguistically diverse students. Each approach has a different emphasis for addressing the needs of these students. Many of the instructional strategies associated with each approach are applicable to all students, regardless of cultural and linguistic diversity, in promoting meaningful science learning.

Content Integration

Incorporating examples and content from different cultures into lessons enhances their excitement and relevance and promotes science learning as students connect lessons to their personal lives (Atwater et al. 1996). Baptiste and Key (1996) describe three levels of content integration.

Levels one and two focus on multicultural awareness and integrating the contributions of many cultures and peoples into the curriculum. Mentioning the scientific accomplishments of African Americans such as Charles Drew (blood groups) and Percy Julian (isolating sterols from soybeans) on their birthdays is an example of level one integration. An example of level two is the culminating experience in the *ChemCom* (American Chemical Society, 2000) unit "Understanding Food." The culminating experience for this unit asks students to compare the nutritional value of meals from several cultures, including Mexico and Japan, in terms of food energy, protein, iron, and vitamin B_1.

Level three requires making cultural and social issues the centerpiece of the curriculum. Farming practices, medicines used to treat diseases and other ailments, tools for making calculations, and chemical dyes are just a few examples of topics that provide ideas for science curricula that integrate information about ancient and modern cultures and may lead students to take socially responsible actions. According to Atwater and her colleagues (1996), teachers function as social activists at Baptiste's third level. "They help their science students promote equitable opportunities, have respect for those who are members of oppressed groups, and practice power equity in the school and community. Furthermore, they help students to use their science knowledge to change the world around them" (Atwater, et al., 1996, p. 170).

It is not always easy to develop lessons and units that integrate content that reflect different cultural perspectives. The good news is that more and more textbook publishers are including suggestions for multicultural connections in the teacher edition of their texts and developing student reading and activity books and supporting Web sites that highlight the scientific contributions of individuals and cultural groups. Information useful for developing science learning experiences that reflect Baptiste's upper levels can be found in such books and Web sites as:

- The Faces of Science: African Americans in the Sciences (http://www.princeton.edu/~mcbrown/display/faces.html)
- Multicultural Education Internet Resource Guide (http://jan.ucc.nau.edu/~jar/Multi.html)
- *Science Across Cultures: An Annotated Bibliography of Books on Non-Western Science, Technology, and Medicine,* by Helaine Selin (1992)
- *Multicultural Science Education: Theory, Practice, and Promise,* edited by Maxwell Hines (2003)

Cultural Harmony

For many culturally diverse students, particularly those who are recent immigrants, the culture of the science classroom is an unfamiliar one. For these students to be successful, school science must be related to their home culture and language. In *Science in the Multicultural Classroom* (1998), Roberta Barba writes about "culturally harmonious variables as those culture-of-origin beliefs, attitudes, and practices which influence (both positively and negatively, functionally and dysfunctional) the teaching/learning process" (p. 14). These variables, Barba notes, affect students' interactions with teachers and classmates and how they go about constructing knowledge in the science classroom. Culturally diverse students develop meaningful science understandings when they see their culture and language facilitating learning rather than acting as an impediment to it.

Six culturally harmonious variables described by Barba (1998, pp. 14–20) that affect science learning are: (1) format of print materials, (2) instructional language, (3) level of peer interactivity, (4) role models, (5) elaboration of context, and (6) interactivity with manipulative materials. Ways in which these harmonious variables can be addressed in science classes to promote meaningful learning among culturally diverse students, especially those who are learning English, include:

- Use printed materials that are highly visual and tell a story, much like a comic book. Students can construct meaning from following along with the pictures or by reading with assistance.

- Reduce the cognitive demand associated with science vocabulary by having students construct picture dictionaries of essential terms.
- Have students draw and label laboratory equipment that will soon be used. Label the laboratory equipment using English and the languages of students in the class whose home language is not English.
- Introduce science concepts through laboratories or demonstrations, follow these initial learning experiences with discussion that highlights essential vocabulary, and culminate with textbook reading.
- When naming objects or materials that students are to use, hold them up for all to see or pass them around the room for all to examine.
- Demonstrate procedures that students should follow multiple times and involve students in role-playing to clarify directions.
- Engage students in learning experiences that involve working in collaborative groups. Encourage discussion among group members to develop understandings.
- Organize learning groups to enable limited-English-proficient and bilingual students to work together. Choose bilingual students who are highly motivated science learners and have a good command of English and the home language they share with the limited-English-proficient students.
- Select instructional materials that present culturally familiar role models. The role models may range from famous scientists like Luis Alverez to high school graduates who tell about their first semester of college.
- Couple the presentation of new science content with culturally familiar objects, examples, and analogies.
- Talk to parents to learn more about your students' science backgrounds and to determine if they are able to reinforce classroom instruction in their home after school. (Barba, 1998; Simich-Dudgeon & Egbert, 2000; Sutman, Guzman, & Schwartz, 1993; Watson, 2004)

The results of work by Aikenhead (1998) also suggest that the notion of "border crossings" is an appropriate way to frame the science experiences of most culturally diverse students, particularly for those students whose home language is not English. These students have greater difficulty than their mainstream counterparts crossing the cultural boundaries between their everyday world and the world of science because the differences are greater. For example, culturally diverse students may not construct arguments based on logic, tolerate ambiguity, feel comfortable presenting evidence rather than deferring to authority, or hold other attitudes and values typically associated with Western science. For this reason, it is important for science teachers to learn about their students' home languages and cultural experiences in order to develop shared understandings and ways of communicating with them about science topics.

Countering Racism and Stereotyping

Multicultural content reviewers check textbooks published today to ensure that racist language and stereotyping are not present and that photographs reflect the diversity of the student population. In addition, teachers must be careful of their language so as not to offend or make any student feel uncomfortable.

Addressing racism and stereotyping in science classes also means establishing more democratic procedures (Hodson, 1993). While it is essential that the teacher be the classroom leader, it is equally important that students be able to make some decisions about their own learning. Making allowance for students' preferred learning styles is one way to incorporate the ideas of democracy into the science classroom. It is well documented that many culturally diverse students tend to possess the characteristics of field-sensitive learners. These students prefer collaborative work and working one-on-one with teachers. They also like to interact with teachers on a personal basis, desire careful explanations of all assignments and learning expectations, and are more highly motivated when science concepts are related to their personal lives (Atwater et al., 1996). Designing lessons that address different learning styles sends the message that all students are valued and respected.

GENDER-INCLUSIVENESS

Equity in science education certainly extends to issues of gender. Viewing knowledge from the perspective of women is helpful to an understanding of girls' beliefs and decisions regarding science. Belenky, Clinchy, Goldberger, and Tarule (1986) group women's ways of knowing into five stages that can be viewed as a developmental pathway beginning with silence and leading to constructed knower (Figure 8.1). The challenge for science teachers is to help girls move along this pathway.

Connected Teaching

This challenge can be met, according to Belenky and her colleagues, by engaging in connected teaching. Connected teaching in the science classroom involves helping students realize that science is a human construction, that all that is written in textbooks and recorded on CDs and DVDs is not to be accepted at face value, and that conversations in science classes are usually not about facts but about models and theories. In

FIGURE 8.1 Stages of women's ways of knowing.
From Women's Ways of Knowing (p. 15), by M. F. Belenky, B. M. Clinchy, N. R. Goldberger, and J. M. Tarule, 1986, Basic Books, New York.

Silence →	**Received Knower** →
No voice in what constitutes knowledge and subject to the whims of outside authority	Recipient of knowledge, but incapable of creating knowledge

the connected classroom, students are comfortable with uncertainty and knowledge is constructed through consensus building. The connected teacher is not the voice of scientific authority, but one who, much like the students, struggles to make sense of the world. Belenky et al. (1986) clarify the teacher's role in a connected classroom by comparing the metaphors of teacher as midwife and teacher as banker. "While the bankers deposit knowledge in the learner's head, the midwives draw it out. They assist the students by giving birth to their own ideas, in making their own tacit knowledge explicit and elaborating on it" (p. 217). It is this connected learning experience that most female students prefer.

Feminist Science Education

If credence is given to women's ways of knowing, then changes can be made to make science classes more inviting to girls. Bentley and Watts (1986) offer three approaches to consider: girl-friendly science, feminine science, and feminist science.

1. Girl-friendly science advocates making traditional science more attractive to girls by changing the image of science presented in classes. Challenging stereotypes, emphasizing the aesthetic appeal of science, and framing science curricula in a social context are all examples of ways to make science girl-friendly.
2. Feminine science emphasizes changing the atmosphere of science classes to better suit girls. Changes to foster feminine science include attending to the social and moral issues of science and emphasizing cooperation and caring rather than competition in all school science activities.
3. Feminist science steps beyond the other two approaches to challenge the universalist assumptions about the nature of science mentioned earlier in this chapter on moral grounds. Feminist science, according to Bentley and Watts (1986), is based on a philosophy of wisdom rather than knowledge. This philosophy of wisdom takes into account the personal, social, and creative aims of the individual and is reflected in investigative approaches that embrace subjectivity. A science class based on this feminist approach would allow for considerable learner autonomy, explore multiple views of science, and emphasize personal feelings and intuition as important to developing science understandings.

Rennie (2001) advocates adding a social-critical dimension to feminist science. With the addition of a social critical perspective, attention is also given to how women have been actively excluded from science. Justification for this added attention is based on the view that science content and practices are biased in ways that favor men over women.

To overcome the inequities associated with science and the science curriculum, Rennie (2001) advocates that teachers must teach both male and female students to recognize the sexism inherent in science and science education and help students to reconstruct their understanding of who participates in science and what being proficient at science means. It is the feminist science approach aided by the use of a social-critical lens that most closely aligns with the connected learning experience suggested by Belenky and her colleagues.

Teachers concerned with gender-inclusiveness in science education should, according to Reiss (1993), view these three approaches as different answers to the question: What should science education for girls be like? While feminist science with emphasis on the sociocultural context of science might be the final answer, feminine science is seen as an acceptable answer, and girl-friendly science is better than doing nothing at all.

There are many strategies a teacher can use to move along the continuum from doing nothing to a feminist school science. Following are several suggestions by Bentley and Watts (1986), Kahle (1996), Parkinson (1994), and Rennie (2001) for doing so. The list is not unlike excellent teaching strategies intended to ensure the inclusion of all students in science:

- Choose science materials, such as case studies and life histories, to portray science as the subjective and passionate study of the natural world.
- Involve students in activities that focus on visual–spatial skills, such as constructing molecular models, graphing data, making mobiles, and working with tangram puzzles.
- Engage students in learning experiences that examine myths and stereotypes about science and the people who do science.

Subjective Knower	→	**Procedural Knower**	→	**Constructed Knower**
Creator of knowledge by objective, systematic analysis		Creator of personal knowledge perceived as intuitive and subjective		Creator of contextualized knowledge through the use of both subjective and objective procedures

- Be on the lookout for unintended biases in your classroom, such as calling on boys more than girls and allowing boys to dominate discussions and laboratory groups.
- Teach the skills of listening, supporting, and negotiating along with the more traditional skills of science.
- Use gender-sensitive language and encourage your students to do so.
- Invite women scientists and girls studying science in college to visit your classroom.
- Celebrate the contributions of women in science and other human endeavors.
- Assess student progress in science often, using a variety of assessment forms.

As powerful as these suggestions are, Tobin (1996) points out that teachers are unlikely to be successful in achieving gender-inclusiveness in the classroom without the direct involvement of students. He recommends that students be taught to recognize gender inequities in the science classroom and empowered to create learning opportunities that benefit all.

Stop and Reflect!

Before going on, do the following:

- Think of a personal science learning experience that you believe is a good illustration of compatibility between students' background or culture and the expectations of the science classroom. What characteristics of the science learning environment discussed in the sections on cultural and linguistic diversity and gender-inclusiveness might you associate with this science learning experience?
- Suppose that you questioned a student whose science grades and interest were declining. In response to your questioning, the student told you "Science is for White males, not for me. So, why should I try?" What is one thing that you would recommend to this student's science teacher that might show her and other students who may have the same thoughts that science is socially constructed, subjective, and equally accessible to all?

EXCEPTIONALITIES

Although all students should be considered exceptional, there are some students who perform much differently than typical. They deserve the same opportunities afforded all other students to learn quality science. For these students, equity in science education requires accommodating their exceptionalities.

The list of special needs is extensive, and therefore our focus will be on those students with special needs who are often found in general education science classes. These include students with learning disabilities and behavioral disorders, the physically disabled, and the gifted and talented. Special education or resource teachers are sometimes assigned to help the science teacher address the special needs of these students. Four federal laws directly impact the teaching of students with special needs in science classes.

Inclusion and the Law

The first law passed by Congress in 1975 is Public Law 94–142, the Education for All Handicapped Children Act. This law, reauthorized as the Individuals with Disabilities Education Act (IDEA) in 1990 and amended in 1997, requires that all schools must place students who have mental or physical disabilities in the "least restrictive environment." Least restrictive environment is often interpreted to mean the general education classroom. Two other laws are Section 504 of the Rehabilitation Act of 1973 and the Americans with Disabilities Act, signed by President George H. W. Bush in 1990. These two laws assure the full civil rights of all persons with disabilities and have a broader interpretation of disabilities than does the IDEA. This broader interpretation provides students with learning disabilities, but who are not eligible for special education services, with access to "virtually anything that they could receive under the IDEA" (Bateman, 1996, p. 183). The most recently passed law that impacts the teaching of special needs students is the No Child Left Behind Act of 2001 (NCLB) that was signed by President George W. Bush on January 8, 2002. NCLB, an extension and revision of the Elementary and Secondary Education Act, reinforces the goals of the other laws by directing additional funds to school programs that serve special needs students, but with the additional burden of demonstrating annual increases in students' test performance.

Practically speaking, these laws have resulted in the inclusion of students with special learning needs in all school programs. Thus, the likelihood is great that students who require instructional and assessment accommodations will be found in most science classes. Addressing the learning needs of these students presents the science teacher with unique challenges. What should you do when called upon to make provisions for the special needs student in the regular classroom? Where can you obtain information about the instructional needs of such a student?

According to the IDEA, an Individualized Education Program (IEP) must be written for every special needs student, regardless of disability, who is placed in a general education classroom. A team of individuals is called upon to develop the IEP. The team typically includes the student's parents or guardians, educational specialists, teachers, and school administrators. In many cases, the adolescent student also participates as a member of the IEP development team. The parents or guardians of the student as well as appropriate school personnel must approve the IEP before it can be enacted. The IEP for each student includes goals, instructional activities, and evaluation procedures that can guide the teachers as well as the student. Any information may be included with the IEP that will assist teachers, including records relating to past performance and areas of needed focus and service. The Americans with Disabilities Act guarantees that the IEP and other records be maintained in confidence and be available to parents or guardians at their request. It also gives parents or guardians the right to challenge the IEP and to bring counsel, legal or otherwise, to meetings where the IEP is developed and discussed.

Once approved by appropriate parties, the IEP becomes mandatory and must be followed as closely as possible. An IEP may include information such as:

1. The results of an assessment battery given to the student
2. The interpersonal relationships of the student with special needs with other students
3. Behavioral problems and recommendations as to how to handle the problems
4. The goals that have been set for the student
5. The services that should be provided to help the student achieve his or her educational goals
6. Procedures for evaluating goals and the timetable for evaluating them
7. A statement regarding the general health of the student as well as the disability or disabilities exhibited by the student
8. Recommended instructional activities for various subject areas
9. When working with students 14 years of age and older, transition activities intended to help them prepare for personal independence and employment or post-secondary education

When dealing with students with special needs in the general education classroom, teachers should refer to IEPs for assistance. The IEP is the best source to obtain direction and guidance for instructing and assessing the student with special needs. It is also important for teachers to know that under a special regulation of the Family Educational Rights and Privacy Act (1974), they may obtain access to a student's IEP without written permission from the student's parents or guardians. Access under these conditions is possible if it is determined by school authorities that the information in the IEP may help the teacher address the student's learning needs (Bateman, 1996).

Learning Disabilities and Behavioral Disorders

The term *learning disabilities* is used to describe students of average or above-average intelligence with learning difficulties that result from some type of brain or central nervous system dysfunction. The dysfunction affects the person's ability to take in information and make use of it and is often manifested in difficulties with reading and written language in addition to skills associated with mathematics, studying, and social interaction. In contrast, students with *behavioral disorders* are those that engage in disruptive or inappropriate behaviors that interfere with learning and relationships with other people (Smith, 1998). Characteristics of students with behavioral disorders include inability to concentrate, lack of motivation, aggression, and chronic disobedience. Contributing to behavioral disorders are biological influences as well as influences from home, community, and school.

Attention deficit disorder (ADD) and attention deficit hyperactive disorder (ADHD) are special categories of disabilities whose manifestations are similar in many ways to those associated with learning disabilities and behavioral disorders. Inattentiveness and distractibility are major characteristics associated with these disorders, with the addition of impulsive behavior and incessant restlessness for students affected by ADHD (Keller, 2003). Students with these disorders may be taking prescriptive medication like Ritalin to help them function in regular classes.

It is very likely that one or more students with these disabilities or disorders will be found in most science classes. As a teacher of these students, there are a few things to consider. First, it is important to learn as much as possible about the students' abilities and disabilities. But rather than trying to accommodate a student's needs based solely on your own course work and reading or past experiences, ask the student for help to devise individual learning accommodations. Students with these disabilities and disorders are perhaps the best sources of information about their learning challenges and should be consulted regularly about what they can and cannot do (Hofman, 1994). Second, discrimination is too often associated with students who face these learning challenges. Too many teachers and counselors hold low expectations for students with learning disabilities or disorders and discourage them from enrolling in advanced science classes and pursuing science careers. The consequences of pullout programs and ability grouping can be particularly devastating to these students. Pullout programs, where students with learning disabilities and disorders engage in special learning activities away from the general education classroom, often deprive these students of science learning opportunities, and low expectations are likely to become self-fulfilling prophecies when these students' access to challenging science experiences is limited by placement in general education courses. Third, science instructional strategies that work well with students with learning disabilities and disorders are generally the same ones that work well with all types of students. This enables students with learning disabilities and disorders to participate in most general education classroom activities.

To address the special learning needs of students with learning disabilities and disorders in middle school and high school science classes, teachers often must modify or retool their regular lessons. According to Finson and his colleagues (1997), lesson retooling for these students often involves pre-lesson preparation and modifications to verbal directions and written materials. Pre-lesson preparation includes considering learner prerequisites and deciding on the most appropriate instructional approaches and assessment methods. Modifications to verbal directions should include gaining and holding the student's attention and removing possible distractions from the work area. Providing straightforward directions and reducing the cognitive demand associated with reading text are two suggestions for making written materials more accessible.

In addition, the following list includes examples of instructional modifications and accommodations recommended by Mastropieri and Scruggs (1995), Keller (2003) and Patton (1995) for teaching science to students with learning disabilities, behavioral disorders, or ADD/ADHD:

- Choose approaches to teaching and learning that are activity-oriented
- Emphasize structure, clarity, redundancy, enthusiasm, appropriate pace, and maximum engagement in teaching strategies
- Partner regular students with students who have learning disabilities and disorders
- Help students with learning disabilities and disorders to monitor their own behavior by using checklists
- Adapt science activities by reducing the level of abstraction or breaking them into smaller parts

- Use performance assessment to assess science understandings
- Be flexible in deciding how students with learning disabilities and disorders are allowed to demonstrate their mastery of course content and skills

Physical Disabilities

Students who have physical disabilities are being aggressively integrated into regular science classes. These students may lack the science experiences and understandings common to non-disabled students, because science has traditionally not been a part of the early schooling provided these students (Keller, 1994). If this is found to be the case, opportunities to involve students in these missed learning experiences will need to be built into the curriculum. Engaging students in activity-oriented science and using role models to inform students with disabilities that they are capable of performing well in science are important first steps in any accommodation efforts (Lang, 1994; Scruggs, Mastropieri, & Boon, 1998). When making curricular accommodations, the teacher must develop an understanding of the student's disability and the implications of the disability for science instruction. More importantly, the teacher must actively solicit from the student with a physical disability ways to address his or her special needs.

It is becoming commonplace to find students with visual, hearing, orthopedic, and health impairments in regular science classes. There are many accommodation and inclusion strategies appropriate for addressing the special learning needs of students with these physical disabilities. Table 8.1 describes some characteristics associated with these disabilities and presents a number of strategies for working effectively with these students based on the writings of Anderson (1982), Keller (1994), Kucera (1993), Mertens (1991), Scruggs and Mastropieri (1993), Smith (1998), Watson and Johnson (2004), and Weigerber (1993).

Gifted and Talented Students

Often overlooked in science classes are the special needs of bright and highly motivated students. These so-called gifted students are not only the high academic achievers but also those who exhibit high levels of creativity and substantial task commitment (Renzulli & Reis, 1997). The abilities and special talents of these young people are often first noticed in the area of oral and written language, mathematics, music, and problem solving. But they are also evident in psychomotor ability and leadership.

Of course, no individual may be outstanding in all these areas. Youth who tend to exhibit any combination of special talents will need the curricular and instructional

TABLE 8.1 Physical Disabilities and Accommodations

Students with Visual Impairments

Some individuals are totally blind, whereas others can see outlines of objects to various degrees. Some individuals can see only objects and print that are within a few inches or feet of their eyes and then only with corrective aids. And some individuals are limited to a narrow field of vision of 20 degrees or less, as opposed to the 180 degrees that individuals with normal vision experience.

Instructional Accommodations
- Use explicit language when providing verbal descriptions or directions. For example, say "arm and wrist" rather than "those body parts" and "from pH 4.3 to pH 7.1" not "from this pH to that."
- Make use of tactile experiences, such as 3–D models.
- Use Braille or audio recordings of text materials for blind students and enlarge copies of textbook pages for low-vision students.
- Ensure that low-vision students have good overhead lighting, a seating position that allows for maximum visibility of the whiteboard and demonstration areas, enlarged printed materials, and extra time for reading and viewing.
- Orient students with visual impairments to the classroom layout, especially the location of exits, fire extinguishers, and other safety equipment.
- Remind the classmates of visually impaired students to keep pathways clear of bookbags and other obstructions.
- In the laboratory, supply chemicals in small quantities in plastic containers and label equipment with Braille and/or with large letters.
- Insist that visually impaired students wear rubber gloves, in addition to aprons and goggles, when using chemicals.

Students with Hearing Impairments

Deaf people are disabled to the extent that they cannot understand speech through their ears, with or without the use of a hearing aid. People who are hard-of-hearing are disabled to the extent that they have difficulty understanding speech with or without a hearing aid. Because students with hearing impairments struggle with communication and reading in their early years, some may not be as advanced as their classmates (Mertens, 1991).

Instructional Accommodations
- Request that a sign language interpreter join the class, particularly on days when much information will be communicated orally.
- To benefit the hard-of-hearing student, consider wearing a frequency-modulated (FM) transmission device that will enable the student to hear over classroom background noise.
- During lectures and discussions, repeat questions asked by other students, and summarize class discussions. Also, use visual aids, including diagrams, models, and pictures to augment presentations.
- Make provisions for closed-captioning of videos shown in class.
- Arrange for the student to get class notes from other students, since watching the teacher or interpreter and taking notes at the same time is difficult for a person who is hearing impaired.
- Write new scientific terms on the whiteboard during class or provide them to the student in advance.
- Engage students in writing–to–learn experiences that involve writing predictions about an experiment, creating science–based imaginative stories, and reflecting on what was learned from a lesson.

Students with Orthopedic and Health Impairments

The range of conditions that represent students with orthopedic and health impairments is enormous. These conditions affect the spinal column (spina bifida), brain functioning (epilepsy), muscular system (muscular dystrophy), limbs (amputation), joints (arthritis), respiratory system (asthma), heart (heart disease), blood (sickle cell anemia), and the immune system (HIV). These students have special needs according to their health, mobility, communication ability, and social and cognitive status (Keller, 1994). The students' impairments may cause them to miss class unexpectedly and for prolonged periods of time.

Instructional Accommodations
- Make the classroom accessible for a wheelchair and other orthopedic aids.
- Recognize that it may take the mobility-impaired student longer to move between classes, set up lab equipment, take notes, and complete tests.
- Provide alternative assessment options, if requested.
- Allow the student to audio- or videotape class sessions.
- Pair the impaired student with a buddy who can assist him/her during class.
- In the lab, place equipment and materials in accessible locations.
- Prepare a detailed syllabus that includes such information as reading assignments, test dates, and dates when projects are due. Post the syllabus on a Web site to allow access away from school.
- Build opportunities in the curriculum to allow the student to access science experiences that were not part of his/her earlier schooling.
- Contact administrators and counselors regarding specialized adaptive equipment needed by the student. Specialized equipment may include a lowered lab table, platform and ramp to accommodate a wheelchair, or a modified computer.

flexibility to demonstrate their unique skills. However, special attention to developing the talents of gifted students has waned in recent years due to the stigmas associated with gifted education, including that it is elitist, contributes to educational inequity, reduces the overall quality of general education, and represents a legal form of tracking (Smith, 1998).

These and other criticisms have led to a broader, more inclusive focus for gifted education that is reflected in the theme of *talent development*. According to Treffinger and Feldhusen (1996), the goal of talent development is to help able youth develop their abilities in all dimensions of human activity, not just intellectual and academic achievement. Coupled with this more inclusive focus for gifted education are broadened eligibility criteria for gifted programs. For example, in a number of states, measures of creativity and motivation are used in addition to measures of mental ability and academic achievement for determining who should receive differentiated educational experiences and/or services beyond those normally provided by the general school program. The use of multiple measures, particularly ones that are sensitive to cultural and linguistic differences, has helped ensure that students from diverse populations are not overlooked when decisions are made about students' needs for certain levels and types of programs and services (Frasier, 1997). Thus, students selected to receive special programs or services will not only be those who have obtained high scores on tests of intelligence but also those who demonstrate potential to benefit from enhanced educational opportunities.

Once identified as able to benefit from special programs and services, Feldhusen (1997) recommends that adolescents work with school counselors, teachers, and parents or guardians to develop personalized, long-range talent development plans. Each student's plan is a way to focus more attention on talent development and may include information about the student's interests, prior experiences in gifted programs, standardized test scores, and current courses, as well as personal goals and recommendations for classes to be taken at school and extracurricular activities.

A number of programs, services, and opportunities that enable these bright and able students to carry out their development plans are provided in middle and secondary schools. Most involve some form of acceleration or enrichment. According to Schiever and Maker (1997), acceleration may take the form of service delivery or curriculum delivery. An example of acceleration as service delivery in middle school might involve a sixth grader joining a seventh-grade class for science instruction. In high school it might involve a student passing a science course by examination or taking a science course on a part-time basis at a local college or university. In contrast, an accelerated curriculum is one in which students move through the same subject mat-

ter as their peers but at a faster pace. When this type of acceleration occurs in a general education science class, it almost always adds to the teacher's workload because of the need to provide differentiated instruction for the special students. Acceleration is sometimes scorned for interfering with students' social development; however, research indicates that acceleration does not impede social development. Acceleration does provide achievement gains beyond those possible when no special provisions are made for gifted students and tends to improve their motivation and confidence (Schiever & Maker, 1997; Van Tassel-Baska, 1986).

Enriched curriculum or special enrichment programs permit gifted and talented students to have new experiences in addition to what other students are experiencing. Enrichment can be provided by modifying or adding to the curriculum through activities such as field trips and WebQuests. Science bowls, academic decathlons, Saturday and summer mini-courses, and mentor or apprenticeship programs, where students spend time working with scientists in the field or their laboratories, are other forms of enrichment. Science enrichment experiences are designed to develop students' thinking skills, expand their content knowledge, or lead to the development of a product, such as a science fair exhibit or invention, that demonstrates creativity and cognitive growth (Schiever & Maker, 1997). Advanced placement (AP) courses, which allow students to study college-level content while still in high school, provide both acceleration and enrichment and exemplify the complementary nature of these two strategies to meet the needs of gifted students.

In heterogeneous classes, students of above-average intelligence and with special talents should carry out the regular class work as well as special assignments. They can participate in introductory phases of units, fieldwork, and group work. Gifted students particularly benefit from student-centered instruction and the opportunity to investigate real problems.

The greatest help that can be given to gifted students is the opportunity to do original research. They prefer to investigate problems that have undisclosed outcomes. Their investigations may begin as an outgrowth of regular class work, but they should be encouraged to carry out their investigations in and out of school.

Stop and Reflect!

Before reading further, consider the following questions:

- What purpose is served by an IEP? What information included in an IEP would be of use to a science teacher?

■ What adaptations would make a science learning experience more suitable for a visually impaired student? For a student with ADHD?

■ Distinguish between accelerated and enrichment experiences for gifted and talented students. How might each experience type contribute to the cognitive development of these students?

Adolescents' School Science Experiences

Science museums, nature centers, zoos, wilderness areas, mechanic shops, and our homes provide for many science learning opportunities. However, it is in schools where most people learn about science as a way of thinking and investigating, science as a body of knowledge, and how science interacts with technology and society. Schools attended by adolescents in the United States today have an interesting history and are constantly changing to meet the learning needs of the diverse student population.

Secondary schools grew out of the tradition of the 19th-century academy, with its dual purposes of educating students for life and preparing students for college. A school that includes grades 7 through 12 in any combination has traditionally been called a secondary school. Today, however, a distinction is made between the high school and schools intended for young adolescents—middle schools and junior high schools.

High schools generally house students in grades 10 through 12, with some also including grade 9 students. Most high schools are described as comprehensive in that they are intended to provide a general education for all, special vocational and college preparation programs, and enrichment experiences (e.g., band, sports, and so on). High school science class offerings include biology, chemistry, physics, and numerous applied, special interest, and advanced placement (AP) courses. The diversity of the class offerings is largely dependent on teacher expertise, the size of the student population, and the distance learning capabilities available at the school. The science teacher at a large high school may have only one preparation, whereas a teacher at a small high school may have three or more. In most high schools, science teachers are organized as a content area department, with one teacher serving as the department head.

Junior high schools developed in the first half of the 20th century in response to recognition of the different educational needs of the young adolescent. Students in grades 7, 8, and 9 are typically taught in these schools. Junior high schools were intended to provide young adolescents with a general education by making use of curricula particularly suited to their interests, needs, and abilities. But, as Tanner and Tanner (1975) make clear, this focus was lost during the 1950s and 1960s as academic preparation for high school and beyond took precedence. The result was that the junior high school became a high school, but for young adolescents.

The initial intention of the junior high school was resurrected in the middle school movement of the 1960s and 1970s. Most middle schools include grades 6, 7, and 8, and some also incorporate grade 5. The differences between today's junior high school and middle school are quite profound. Jones, DeLucia, and Davis (1993) describe some of the differences with respect to science instruction. First, middle school science teachers participate as interdisciplinary team members, rather than as members of a science department. The instruction provided by these teachers is student-centered, not science-centered, and often makes use of flexible block scheduling. Rather than separate content courses, the curriculum is organized into theme-based interdisciplinary units that emphasize science in addition to reading, writing, mathematics, social studies, and fine arts. Middle school science teachers represent a mix of certification levels, including secondary science, middle grades, and elementary. By comparison, most junior high and high school teachers hold secondary science (grades 7–12) certification.

In general, middle schools are viewed as providers of educational experiences better suited to the needs of young adolescents. But as Jones and her colleagues (1993) point out, interdisciplinary teams are no substitute for a strong science department when it comes to leadership for science instruction at the school level. Middle school science teachers need to compensate for the missing departmental structure by meeting regularly to discuss issues such as science clubs and fairs, equipment purchase and inventory, and science professional development opportunities.

Assessing and Reviewing

Analysis and Synthesis

1. In 2061, Haley's Comet will again be visible from the earth, and science education will be radically different than it is today; so say the framers of the Project 2061 *Benchmarks*. Given what you know about today's school-age population, what do you think will be the nature of this population in 2061? Will the factors that affect student success

in science in 2061 likely be the same as they are today? Explain.

2. A common medical practice today is for a physician to prescribe a calcium supplement for a new mother to replenish the calcium lost during childbirth. In China, new mothers have traditionally been fed a thick broth, high in calcium ions, prepared by boiling pig's feet in vinegar. Even today, many Asian American mothers eat dishes of sweet and sour pork in the weeks following childbirth. (based on a description by Barba, 1998, pp. 61–62). How could a science teacher utilize the information about this Chinese practice to formulate a multicultural science learning experience for students?

Practical Consideration

3. Use the Internet to locate student demographics for a school system in which you would like to teach. How do the student demographics for the school system compare with the demographics of the national school-age population presented in this chapter? What factors likely contribute to the demographics of the school system?

4. Interview two teachers whose classes include students ranging from the learning disabled to the gifted and talented. Question the teachers about how they address the special learning needs of the

students in their classes. As a result of the interview, describe at least three learning strategies that you would consider using in your own teaching. Share your learning strategies with classmates.

5. Observe a science class that includes students who are English language learners. While observing, note the accommodations that the teacher makes to address the learning needs of these students. Talk with the teacher after the lesson in order to learn more about the accommodations you observed and the teacher's assessment of the success associated with each accommodation.

Developmental Consideration

6. Start a collection of newspaper clippings, magazine articles, and Internet sites that present information about equity in science teaching and learning.

7. Attend a regional or national conference of the National Science Teachers Association (NSTA). Participate in sessions that address issues of multicultural science education.

8. Search out funding agencies that support initiatives that focus on the science learning needs of at-risk students. Work with colleagues to develop a proposal to support the implementation of your initiative.

RESOURCES TO EXAMINE

Better IEPs: How to Develop Legally Correct and Educationally Useful Programs.   1996. Longmont, Co: Sopris West.

Address for ordering: 1140 Boston Avenue, Longmont, Colorado 80501.

Barbara Bateman, educator and attorney, takes the perspective that the IEP process should be child-centered and individualized. Using the law as the starting point for IEP development, she discusses IEP team composition and functioning, what an IEP must contain, and when an IEP is inappropriate. Excerpts based on the IEPs of real students are included to illustrate various points.

Inclusion in Science Education for Students with Disabilities.   [On-line.] Available: http://www.as.wvu.edu/~scidis (August 21, 2004).

This Web site is a comprehensive resource for teachers seeking suggestions for accommodating the science learning needs of disabled students. The

site is organized into sections for easy access of information. One section provided over 800 teaching strategies for students with learning disabilities and physical impairments. Other sections present suggestions for developing IEPs and general information about learning disabilities and physical impairments.

Multicultural Science Education: Theory, Practice, and Promise.   2003. New York: Peter Lang Publishing.

Address for ordering: 275 7th Avenue, 28th Floor, New York, New York 10001

This book includes contributions from science teachers, scientists, and anthropologists that provide different perspectives on multicultural science education. Culturally relevant science, how the discourse of power and good intentions undermines the *National Science Education Standards,* and Native American science are among the topics addressed.

"Teaching Science to Newcomers." 2004, February. *The Science Teacher*, pp. 27–31.

> George Hademenos, Nancy Heires, and Rose Young, teachers at Richardson High School in Texas, describe how they provide authentic science experiences for English for Speakers of Other Languages (ESOL) students. Their strategy involves combining classes of ESOL students and students who are native English speakers and having the students work together to design and conduct experiments and present their results. The teachers describe the advantages of the strategy for both ESOL and advanced physics students.

Gifted and Talented Education. [On-line.] Available: http://gt.dpsk12.org/resources.html (August 21, 2004).

> Hosted by the Denver Public Schools, this Web site provides resources useful for science teachers of gifted and talented students. Presented at the site are books, professional associations for teachers of the gifted and talented, and organizations that support and study gifted and talented students.

REFERENCES

Aikenhead, G. S. (1998). Border crossings: Culture, school science and assimilation of students. In D. A. Roberts & L. Ostman (Eds.) *Problems of meaning in science curriculum* (pp. 86–100). New York: Teachers College Press, Columbia University.

American Chemical Society. (2000). *Chemistry in the community* (*Chem Com*). New York: W. H. Freeman and Company.

Americans with Disabilities Act, 42 U.S.C. section 121101 (1990).

Anderson, J. L. (1982). Chemical instrumentation for the visually handicapped. *Journal of Chemical Education, 59*, 871–872.

Atwater, M. M., Crockett, D., & Kilpatrick, W. J. (1996). Constructing multicultural science classrooms: Quality science for all students. In J. Rhoton & P. Bowers (Eds.), *Issues in science education* (pp. 167–176). Washington, DC: National Science Teachers Association.

Atwater, M. M., & Riley, J. P. (1993). Multicultural science education: Perspectives, definitions, and research agenda. *Science Education, 77*, 661–668.

Baptiste, H. P., & Key, S. G. (1996). Cultural inclusion: Where does your program stand? *The Science Teacher, 63*(2), 32–35.

Barba, R. (1998). *Science in the multicultural classroom.* Boston: Allyn & Bacon.

Bateman, B. D. (1996). *Better IEPs: How to develop legally correct and educationally useful programs.* Longmont, CO: Sopris West.

Belenky, M. F., Clinchy, B. M., Goldberger, N. R., & Tarule, J. M. (1986). *Women's ways of knowing.* New York: Basic Books.

Bentley, D., & Watts, D. M. (1986). Courting the positive virtues: A case for feminist science. *European Journal of Science Education, 8*, 121–134.

Education for All Handicapped Children Act, Public Law 94–142 (1975).

Family Educational Rights and Privacy Act (FERPA), 20 U.S.C. section 1232 (1974).

Feldhusen, J. (1997). Secondary services, opportunities, and activities for talented youth. In N. Colangelo & G. A. Davis (Eds.), *Handbook of gifted education* (pp. 189–197). Boston: Allyn & Bacon.

Finson, K. D., Ormsbee, C. K., Jensen, M., & Donald T. Powers. (1997). Science in the mainstream: Retooling science activities. *Journal of Science Teacher Education, 8*, 219–232.

Frasier, M. (1997). Gifted minority students: Reframing approaches to their identification and education. In N. Colangelo & G. A. Davis (Eds.), *Handbook of gifted education* (pp. 498–515). Boston: Allyn & Bacon.

Hodson, D. (1993). In search of a rationale for multicultural science education. *Science Education, 77*, 685–711.

Hofman, H. M. (1994). Learning disabilities. In J. Egelston-Dodd (Ed.), *Proceedings of a working conference on science for persons with disabilities* (pp. 71–87). Cedar Falls, IA: University of Northern Iowa.

Individuals with Disabilities Education Act (IDEA), PL 101–476 (1990).

Jones, G., DeLucia, S., & Davis, J. (1993). From junior high to middle school: How science instruction is affected. *NASSP Bulletin, 77*, 89–96.

Kahle, J. B. (1996). Equitable science education: A discrepancy model. In L. H. Parker, L. J. Rennie, & B. J. Fraser (Eds.), *Gender, science and mathematics: Shortening the shadow* (pp. 129–139). Dordrecht: Kluwer Academic Publishers.

Keller, E. C., Jr. (1994). Science education for the motor/orthopedically-impaired students. In J. Egelston-Dodd (Ed.), *Proceedings of a working conference on science for persons with disabilities* (pp. 1–39). Cedar Falls, IA: University of Northern Iowa.

Keller, E. C. (2003). Inclusion in science education for students with disabilities. [On-line.] Available: http://www.as.wvu.edu/~scidis (August 21, 2004).

Kozol, J. (1991). *Savage inequities.* New York: Crown Publishers.

Kucera, T. J. (Ed.) (1993). *Teaching chemistry to students with disabilities.* Washington, DC: American Chemical Society. (ERIC Document Reproduction No. ED383131)

Lang, H. G. (1994). Science for deaf students: Looking into the next millennium. In J. Egelston-Dodd (Ed.), *Proceedings of a working conference on science for persons with disabilities* (pp. 97–109). Cedar Falls, IA: University of Northern Iowa.

Lee, O., Fradd, S. H., & Sutman, F. X. (1995). Science knowledge and cognitive strategy use among culturally and linguistically diverse students. *Journal of Research in Science Teaching, 32,* 797–816.

Loving, C. C. (1995). Comments on "Multiculturalism, universalism, and science education." *Science Education, 79,* 341–348.

Luft, J. (1998). Multicultural science education: An overview. *Journal of Science Teacher Education, 9,* 103–122.

Lynch, S., Atwater, M., Cawley, J., Eccles, J., Lee, O., Marrett, C., Rojas-Medlin, D., Secada, W., Stefanich, G., & Willetto, A. (1996). *An equity blueprint for Project 2061, 2nd draft.* Washington, DC: American Association for the Advancement of Science.

Mastropieri, M. A., & Scruggs, T. E. (1995). Teaching science to students with disabilities. *Teaching Exceptional Children,* Summer, 10–13.

Matthews, M. (1994). *Science teaching: The role of history and philosophy of science.* New York: Routledge.

Mertens, D. M. (1991). Instructional factors related to hearing impaired adolescents' interest in science. *Science Education, 75,* 429–441.

Muth, K. D., & Alvermann, D. E. (1999). *Teaching and learning in the middle grades.* Boston: Allyn & Bacon.

No Child Left Behind Act of 2001. (P.L. 107–110)

Ogawa, M. (1995). Science education in a multiscience perspective. *Science Education, 79,* 583–593.

Parkinson, J. (1994). *The effective teaching of secondary science.* London: Longman.

Patton, J. R. (1995). Teaching science to students with special needs. *Teaching Exceptional Children,* Summer, 4–6.

Rehabilitation Act Section 504, 19 U.S.C. section 794 (1973).

Reiss, M. J. (1993). *Science education for a pluralist society.* Buckingham, England: Open University Press.

Rennie, L. J. (2001). Gender equity in science teacher preparation. In D. R. Lavoie & W-M. Roth (Eds.) *Models for science teacher preparation: Theory into practice* (pp. 127–147). Dordrecht: Kluwer Academic Publishers.

Renzulli, J. S., & Reis, S. M. (1997). The schoolwide enrichment model: New directions for developing high-end learning. In N. Colangelo & G. A. Davis (Eds.), *Handbook of gifted education* (pp. 136–154). Boston: Allyn & Bacon.

Schiever, S. W., & Maker, C. J. (1997). Enrichment and acceleration: An overview and new directions. In N. Colangelo & G. A. Davis (Eds.), *Handbook of gifted education* (pp. 113–125). Boston: Allyn & Bacon.

Scruggs, T. E., & Mastropieri, M. A. (1993). Current approaches to science education: Implications for mainstream instruction of students with disabilities. *Remedial and Special Education, 14*(1), 15–24.

Scruggs, T. E., Mastropieri, M. A., & Boon, R. (1998). Science education for students with disabilities: A review of recent research. *Studies in Science Education, 32,* 21–44.

Siegel, H. (1997). Science education: Multicultural and universal. *Interchange, 28,* 97–108.

Simich-Dudgeon, C., & Egbert, J. (2000). Science as a second language. *The Science Teacher,* March, 28–32.

Smith, D. D. (1998). *Introduction to special education: Teaching in an age of challenge.* Boston: Allyn & Bacon.

Stanley, W. B., & Brickhouse, N. W. (1994). Multiculturalism, universalism, and science education. *Science Education, 78,* 387–398.

Sutman, F. X., Guzman, A., & Schwartz, W. (1993). *Teaching science effectively to limited English proficient students.* (ERIC Reproduction No. ED 357113)

Tanner, D., & Tanner, L. (1975). *Curriculum development.* Upper Saddle River, NJ: Merrill/Prentice Hall.

Tobin, K. (1996). Gender equity and the enacted science curriculum. In L. H. Parker, L. J. Rennie, & B. J. Fraser (Eds.), *Gender, science and mathematics: Shortening the shadow* (pp. 119–127). Dordrecht, Kluwer Academic Publishers.

Treffinger, D. J., & Feldhusen, J. F. (1996). Talent recognition and development: Successor to gifted education. *Journal of Education of the Gifted, 19,* 181–193.

United States Commission on Civil Rights. (1992). *Civil rights issues facing Asian Americans in the 1990s.* Washington, DC: U.S. Government Printing Office.

U.S. Department of Education, National Center for Education Statistics. (2002a). *The condition of education 2002,* NCES 2002–025. Washington, DC: U.S. Government Printing Office.

U.S. Department of Education. (2002b). *Twenty-fourth annual report to congress on the implementation of the Individuals with Disabilities Act.* Washington, DC: U.S. Government Printing Office. Available: http://www.ed.gov/about/reports/annual/osep/2002/index.html (August 9, 2004).

U.S. Department of Education, National Center for Education Statistics. (2003). *The condition of education 2003,* NCES 2003–067. Washington, DC: U.S. Government Printing Office.

U.S. Department of Education, National Center for Education Statistics. (2004). *The condition of education 2004,* NCES 2002–077. Washington, DC: U.S. Government Printing Office.

Van Tassel-Baska, J. (1986). Acceleration. In C. J. Maker (Ed.), *Critical issues in gifted education. Defensible programs for the gifted* (pp. 179–196). Austin, TX: Pro-Ed.

Watson, S. (2004). Opening the science doorway. *The Science Teacher,* February, 32–35.

Watson, S., & Johnston, L. (2004). Teaching science to the visually impaired. *The Science Teacher,* July, 30–35.

Weigerber, R. A. (1993). *Science success for students with disabilities.* Menlo Park, CA: Addison-Wesley.

Weld, J. (1997). Viewpoints: Universalism and multiculturalism in science education. The *American Biology Teacher, 59,* 264–267.

Learning in Middle Grades and Secondary Schools

Students should be encouraged to represent their knowledge in many ways.

Often, beginning as well as experienced science teachers plan their instruction by identifying the knowledge and skills they want students to learn. They select the science facts, principles, and process skills they desire to focus on during instruction. Usually, however, these teachers spend very little time considering what students know, the misconceptions they possess, and how students feel about science. Without more attention to what students are thinking, very little learning may occur. There is more to effective teaching than focusing on the subject matter in the curriculum. One must know a great deal about student learning and attempt to ascertain what students know when they enter the classroom door. In addition, science teachers must be sensitive to students' attitudes toward science and how their interests can aid or interfere with learning science.

AIMS OF THE CHAPTER

Use the questions that follow to guide your thinking about student learning and how you can advance it during instruction:

- How would you distinguish cognitive psychology from behavioral psychology with regard to learning science subject matter?

- How do attitudes, motivation, and alternative conceptions affect students learning science?

- How would you describe instructional practices that use the following techniques to improve student learning: prior knowledge, contradictions of beliefs, analogies, models, and concept maps?

INTRODUCTION

The work of cognitive psychologists, learning theorists, and science educational researchers can help sci-

ence teachers to actively engage students in learning. One of the recommendations from cognitive psychologists is to view learning as an *active process* of student engagement with instruction, rather than a process whereby students take in information in a passive manner. Also, they remind us that learning begins with what the student *knows*, which is the foundation of the learning process as well as the starting point. It follows then that students' ideas should be *modified* during instruction and become more complex and differentiated, building gradually over time through a series of small steps.

Importantly, students must find the content and instruction *meaningful* in order for them to pursue learning with interest. Students must be encouraged to *represent their ideas*. This view of learning is in contrast to one that considers learning as the acquisition of knowledge, mostly through the transmission of ideas that have been organized by the teacher or the textbook, ready-made for internalization and retention for future use.

Today, many science educators believe constructivism is a good guide for teaching and learning science. They have adopted the recommendations from cognitive psychologists to focus on students' ideas. Thus, science teachers are advised to incorporate into their instruction contradictions that puzzle students in order to cause them to modify their thinking. Teachers are advised to engage students in a conceptual change process in order for them to gain new science concepts. The conceptual mapping of key ideas to be learned is also a recommended technique for promoting the meaningful organization of science content. Further, images, analogies, and models also can help students connect what they know with abstract concepts to be learned.

Cognitive psychologists, science educators, and experienced science teachers have come to realize that learning science and becoming scientifically literate is a complex, slow process. These professionals have observed how difficult it is for students to learn many of the most fundamental principles of biology, chemistry, and physics, noting that these ideas are formed over time through considerable experience both inside and outside of school. Further, many students have not mastered the simplest science process skills, such as making accurate observations, graphing data, and designing investigations. Because of the difficulty students have in learning science, science teachers need to understand and use many strategies and techniques to guide them in planning and teaching.

Although constructivism is popular, behavioral principles and theories of learning also have importance in education. Science teachers should use many of the ideas learned from behavioral psychologists to complement what is now popular in cognitive psychology (Duit & Treagust, 1998). An earlier chapter of this textbook focused on teaching science and discussed teaching skills, instructional strategies, and learning techniques. In this chapter, we will build on techniques for improving learning.

COGNITIVE APPROACHES AND STRATEGIES FOR TEACHING SCIENCE IN A CONSTRUCTIVE MANNER

Pupils come to science lessons with ideas about the natural world. Effective science teaching takes account of these ideas and provides activities which enable pupils to make the journey from their current understanding to a more scientific view. (Driver, Squires, Rushworth, & Wood-Robinson, 1994, p. xii)

At present, constructivism is a movement associated with teaching and learning science. This notion is used to explain learning, guide instructional practices, and conduct research. The central thesis is that humans construct knowledge as opposed to knowledge being transmitted into their minds. Constructivism stresses the importance of considering what is already in the learner's mind as a place to initiate instruction. Learning is regarded as an active process whereby students construct personal meaning of the subject matter through their interactions with the physical and social world. It is the student who must make sense out of experiences. Knowledge is not just out there in textbooks and in teachers' heads, ready to be transferred into the minds of students. Instead, "out there" is where one finds information and experiences that are incorporated into existing knowledge structures, which in turn are modified.

A skilled teacher, who engages students in thinking, asking questions, testing ideas, representing thoughts, and explaining phenomena, can facilitate the learning process. As stated in the quote from Driver et al., effective science teaching must take into account what students know, then modify this knowledge so that it reflects scientific views.

The theory that the mind constructs useful ideas of reality has implications for instruction. If people have to conceptualize reality, they need to process, organize, and reflect upon it. Thus, learning becomes an active process that builds upon prior knowledge. What learners know becomes as important as what we want them to know.

Teaching and learning must be an interactive process that engages learners in constructing knowledge. Negotiation takes place between the teacher and students, whereby the teacher moves students toward greater understanding of reality. Often, these interactions take time, requiring many small steps toward reforming and building new ideas (Driver, Asoko, Leach, Mortimer, & Scott, 1994). Through this approach, students' ideas become more differentiated and more closely resemble scientific conception.

There are at least two sources for constructing knowledge—personal experience with the physical world and interaction with the social world. Jean Piaget, Lev Vygotsky, and David Ausubel made significant contributions to these learning perspectives. During the last half of the 20th century, Piaget's work on cognitive development has provided educators with one foundation for constructivism. His theory of mental structures and logical-mathematical operations has given us greater insight into development and learning. Importantly, the work underscores the significance of experience in developing cognitive structures. The interaction with objects and events stimulates the construction of knowledge, as opposed to passive listening. For Piaget, it is the learner who brings to bear mental operations in reaction to the environment, engaging learning and furthering cognitive development. In translating this theory into practice, science teaching has promoted more experiences with concrete materials, emphasizing manipulation of objects, testing ideas, and organizing data. More emphasis has been placed on the use of contradictions and discrepant events to cause cognitive dissonance, motivating students to "wonder why and find out how." Piaget's theory of equilibration has given teachers a strategy to help students assimilate information and to modify thinking.

Another dimension of learning and development is the role of others—peers and adults—in facilitating the construction of knowledge. Whereas Piaget focused some of his attention on physical interaction, Vygotsky focused much of his attention on social interaction. He believed that peers and adults greatly influence learning and the acquisition of science concepts. The organization of ideas by others has enormous influence on what people learn. Although Vygotsky believed as Piaget that knowledge is constructed and developed over time, he stressed that the major contribution to cognition is social interaction. He used the idea of a zone of proximal development to focus attention on the potential (Sternberg, 1995) for learning and development via adult interaction. The zone of proximal (or potential) development is a range of possible development between what learners can do by themselves and what they can do with assistance from others who are at a more advanced level of thinking or possess more knowledge (Vygotsky, 1978).

For Vygotsky, direct instruction had a more influential role on the assimilation of ideas than for Piaget. Further, he stressed the importance of language in the mediation of ideas, which advances learning and development. Vygotsky emphasized that students learn about science from others. Similarly, scientists learn about their enterprise by interacting with other scientists and examining the ideas that they have contributed to the discipline. Thus, knowledge is a product of culture that has been constructed over time, growing and changing as the result of human interaction with ideas that have been socially constructed.

David Ausubel also promoted a cognitive approach to learning, except he focused on the conceptual rather than the operative forms of knowledge that were stressed by Piaget. He advocated that reception learning is directed toward discipline-based concepts that can be learned by students, and, in fact most of what is learned, both in and out of school, is acquired through the transmission of ideas rather than through discovering them. Ausubel, however, advised that reception learning must be meaningful in order for it to be effective. He cautioned educators that discovery as well as reception learning can be rote, and that they must avoid this situation and take every measure to make learning meaningful. However, he pointed out that students must relate the material under study to their existing cognitive structures of organized information (Ausubel, 1963). When students learn in a meaningful manner, they form mental connections between new ideas and the relevant elements within their existing cognitive structures. Ausebel's work has stressed the importance of logical organization of science content and the use of concept maps.

Today, constructivism has taken on a different meaning for many educators from the one widely used during the 1960s, 1970s, and 1980s. In the past, the Piagetian stage theory and his generalizable thinking skills dominated a great deal of teaching and learning in science education. The theory that developmental reasoning sets limits on what students can learn was central to the stage theory. As a result, considerable emphasis was placed on general reasoning ability with much less emphasis on learning specific concepts. This movement is evidenced by the importance placed on learning science process skills, which has been observed in science education over the past 40 years. For some science educators, this stance to separating content and process de-emphasizes the importance of subject matter content and elevates the importance of science process skills. As a result of the stress placed upon general reasoning skills and problem solving associated with the Piagetian psychology, neo-Piagetian researchers suggest that we modify our views regarding learning science and that we place more emphasis on the acquisition of subject matter content and science concepts.

Affective Learning

If teachers want to help students construct their own science understandings, they must be cognizant of the attitudes and values that students bring with them to science class. Students' attitudes and values should not be discounted as unimportant, nor should attempts be made to override them in the context of science instruction. The attitudes and values that students bring with them to science class are aspects of the affective domain, and as such they are critical indicators of the worth students place on science and how they view the scientific enterprise.

Not only should students' attitudes and values be considered as factors that affect science knowledge construction, they should also be regarded as outcomes of science instruction. There is much that teachers can do to help students develop favorable feelings toward science, scientists, and science learning and strengthen commitment to certain science-related ideas and actions. Students should be engaged in instructional activities specifically designed to achieve affective outcomes. It should not be assumed that favorable feelings and strong commitments will likely develop as students learn more science content.

Affective Concepts

Attitude has long been one of the most important affective concepts in science education. Attitude represents a favorable or unfavorable feeling toward something (Koballa & Warden, 1992); therefore, *attitude* is primarily an affective concept that centers upon the evaluation of an idea. The word *attitude* is often confused with belief, value, interest, and opinion, which, although related, are somewhat different. *Beliefs* are the cognitive bases for attitudes and are the more informational and factual. In recent years, as the disciplines of social psychology and educational psychology have become more cognitively oriented, belief has replaced attitude as the most studied affective concept in science education. *Values* relate to moral and ethical issues of right and wrong and are much broader than either attitudes or beliefs. Although the term *interest* is thought of as synonymous with attitude, it has a slightly different meaning and has been addressed in a different line of research. Interest addresses someone's willingness to respond to something and explains some aspects of motivation. *Opinion* is often used interchangeably with attitude and interest, but it is seldom used as the focus of inquiry in affective studies in science education.

Affect and Action

Affective variables are important because of their links to behavior. By knowing about a student's science-related attitudes, beliefs, or values, a teacher is provided with some insight into the student's science-related actions. Whereas the correspondence between a student's

FIGURE 9.1 Azjen's planned behavior model.

Adapted from Understanding Attitudes and Predicting Social Behavior *(p. 71), by I. Ajzen and M. Fishbein, 1980, Englewood Cliffs, NJ: Prentice-Hall.*

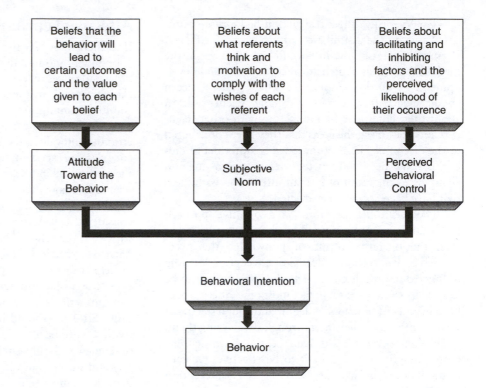

attitude toward science and his or her decision to engage in a science activity when other options are available is not absolute, the links between affective variables and behavior are considered strong enough to warrant instructional efforts that target affective variables. By systematically targeting affective variables in science instruction, students are likely to develop dispositions to think and act in responsible ways toward science learning and the scientific enterprise.

One model that illuminates various links between affective variables and behavior is Ajzen's (1989) model of planned behavior, shown in Figure 9.1. According to the model, the best predictor of behavior is one's intention to engage in the behavior. This means that if a person intends to attend a science club meeting, barring unforeseen circumstances, he or she will be there. Affective variables that are considered antecedents of intention include attitude toward the behavior, subjective norm, and perceived behavioral control. Attitude is concerned with personal feelings about engaging in the behavior, and subjective norm is concerned with impressions about the support coming from significant referents. Perceived behavioral control addresses the perceived barriers and facilitating factors that may make engaging in the behavior difficult or easy. For any given behavior, the three variables may contribute equally to an individual's motivation to engage in the behavior, or one variable may contribute more than the other two. The following questions capture the essence of these three antecedents:

1. Attitude: What is in it for me?
2. Subjective norm: Who wants me to do it?

3. Perceived behavioral control: What factors may make it easy or difficult for me to do it?

Attitude, subjective norm, and perceived behavioral control also have antecedents, according to the model. The antecedents are based on the expectancy-value formulation of attitude proposed by Fishbein (1963) to show the link between attitude and belief. Consistent with the expectancy-value theorem, a student's attitude toward engaging in a behavior is the product of two forces, the beliefs that the student holds about engaging in the behavior and the value that he gives to the outcome associated with each belief. Likewise, subjective norm is the product of the student's beliefs about what people think she should do and her motivation to comply with their desires, and perceived behavioral control is the product of beliefs about factors that will facilitate or inhibit her action and the likely occurrence of these factors. These expectancy-value linkages reflect the cognitive processing that takes place prior to decision making and action, according to Crawley and Koballa (1994), and provide a means to target affective variables in science instruction and promote reflection and affective change.

Motivation

Motivation is a central element of instruction to achieve both affective and cognitive objectives. According to Brophy (1988, p. 205), a student's tendency to find schoolwork meaningful and worthwhile and to try to benefit from it is the essence of motivation to learn. In science, students are motivated to engage in activities for the personal satisfaction gained from them and for the rewards or punishment that may be linked to them. Motivation that comes from personal satisfaction, interest, or curiosity is called intrinsic motivation. Motivation that has little to do with the activity itself but rather with the associated rewards or punishment is called extrinsic motivation. One of the important jobs of teachers is to encourage students to engage in activities for the intrinsic benefits derived from them.

By observing a student's behavior, it is impossible to determine if the motivation for engaging in an activity is intrinsic or extrinsic. Only by understanding the student's reasons for his or her action can it be determined whether the action is prompted by personal satisfaction, interest or curiosity, or by rewards or punishment. In some cases, teachers can develop intrinsic motivation in students by stimulating their interest in a topic or by gradually increasing the difficulty level of lessons to ensure continued success. For example, biology teachers are often successful in creating intrinsic motivation among their students to learn genetics by having them develop family pedigrees. It is also true that at times teachers must rely on rewards and external inducements to achieve their instructional objectives, such as when a reminder about slipping grades is used to encourage a student to work harder. However, teachers should always be looking for ways to help students shift the emphasis from extrinsic incentive to intrinsic satisfaction.

According to Woolfolk (1995, p. 349), intrinsic motivation is only one attribute that contributes to student motivation to learn. Four others are challenging learning goals, involvement in the learning task, achievement based on mastery learning, and feelings of control over effort and ability. All five attributes of motivation should be considered when planning instruction to achieve both affective and cognitive objectives.

In summary, the affective domain is an important dimension of science learning. Students need to leave science classes not only with science understandings, but with favorable feelings toward science learning and the scientific enterprise and with commitment to some science-related ideas and actions. Motivation to learn is an important affective concept because of its role in mediating the achievement of both affective and cognitive objectives. It serves science teachers well to be familiar with aspects of the affective domain in order to better address this dimension of learning in the science classroom.

Equilibration and Contradictions

Knowledge is not a copy of reality. To know an object, to know an event, is not simply to look at it and make a mental copy or image of it. To know an object is to act on it. To know is to modify, to transform the object, and to understand the process of this transformation, and as a consequence to understand the way the object is constructed. An operation is the essence of knowledge; it is an interiorized action which modifies the object of the knowledge. (Piaget, 1964)

This quote by Piaget underscores a central theme in cognitive psychology: Learning is an active process. It is not a transmission process whereby knowledge is photocopied by the nervous system, but an interactive process whereby mental actions lead toward the understanding of objects and events that make up our world. The growth of knowledge is tied to internal mechanisms and cognitive organization. What implications do these views have for teaching science? What can science teachers do to encourage students to think deeply in order to construct a body of knowledge that they can understand and use?

Piaget used the concept of *equilibration* to explain learning and cognitive development (Piaget, 1971). His conception of equilibration is that of a dynamic, continuous process that controls intelligence and learning (Furth, 1969). This process coordinates what infants, children, adolescents, and adults do when interacting with the world around them. It regulates their thinking and intellectual responses and does so by affecting what individuals can react to and how they respond. Piaget used the terms *assimilation* and *accommodation* to explain equilibration, suggesting how learning and development progress.

When an individual takes in information from objects and events, he or she *assimilates* it into existing cognitive structures. The cognitive organism perceives (assimilates) only what it can "fit into" the structures it already has (von Glasersfeld, 1995). Note that this notion is central to constructivist psychology, which stresses the belief that new knowledge builds upon prior knowledge. Constructivistic thinking would question the value of a learning situation where the ideas to learn have no connection with existing ideas in the mind of the learner. For example, if a person were in a cafeteria line and saw a vegetable that she enjoyed eating, she would recognize it and perhaps take it. This individual would assimilate the idea right into her organization of foods. If she did not recognize a particular food, however, the chances are high that she would not place it on her tray. We would question a science teacher's effectiveness in trying to explain Einstein's theory of gravitation to a group of middle school students who have no sense or knowledge of space-time curvature. Where is the foundation for the geometry of curved space in the cognitive structures of these students? The presence of already-existing knowledge increases the possibility for learners to fit external ideas into their thinking, assimilate them into their schemata, and therefore find these ideas meaningful.

Along with assimilation, *accommodation* occurs (Piaget, 1971). When one assimilates information and events, he or she must also accommodate to it. Accommodation is the modification of existing cognitive structures to fit the ideas that one is internalizing. The degree to which individuals have to modify their existing beliefs and ideas depends upon the situation. Again, consider the cafeteria line. When people select a food that they eat regularly and place it on their tray, they accommodate the selection process with relative ease. However, if a friend suggests that you try an unknown vegetable, because it is a delicious food, you may try it. As you reach for the dish, you will be convincing yourself that this vegetable is going to suit your taste. Regardless of how the vegetable tastes, you will have learned something new about this food as well as the trust you place in the friend. Now, you have accommodated by modifying your knowledge about eating this food.

The continuous equilibration process of assimilation and accommodation is one way to envision the growth and differentiation of knowledge and is a mechanism for learning science. Now, how does this theory assist us to teach science in a manner that will help students better understand important abstract ideas? Piaget and others (Fosnot, 1996; Lawson, 1994) recommend the use of *contradictions* to stimulate assimilation and especially accommodation. Situations that contradict what students think or believe may cause them to alter their thinking and to find out about the situation at hand. External events that challenge what people know or believe and create puzzlement or surprise motivate them to think more deeply and to alter their worldview (Kasschau, 1986). Even discussing ideas can cause cognitive perturbations, creating cognitive disequilibrium.

Discrepant events are used by science teachers to challenge students to think and encourage them to focus on a concept, law, or principle under study. For example, Bernoulli's principle is used to explain a phenomenon that many find difficult to comprehend. Demonstrations centering around this principle present contradictions to what people believe, thus putting them into a state of mental disequilibrium (Lawson, 1994). Note the demonstration setup in Figure 9.2 in which a sheet of paper is supported by two thick textbooks. Pose the question: What will happen to the paper when I blow hard between the tabletop and the paper? Many students will respond that the paper will fly off the books or move upward. Place the responses of the students on the board and take a count of those who hold certain ideas regarding what will occur.

FIGURE 9.2   A discrepant event can be demonstrated by blowing under a sheet of paper supported by two books.

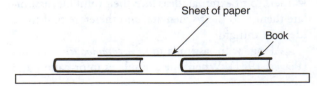

Demonstrate what happens when you blow vigorously beneath the paper. Ask a few students to come forward and do the same. Note the surprise and discrepancy between what most of the class believed would occur and what actually did occur. Now, how do you explain these results? Through a series of questions, develop a description of this event and an explanation of the principle involved. Many in the class will still be hooked to their beliefs with regard to the effects of rapidly moving air pushing directly on the paper. Write a scientific explanation on the chalkboard of what happened, then call on a few more participants to test the principle. Ask some individuals to blow under the paper and some to blow over the paper. Perhaps some participants will begin to incorporate a different view of a stream of air moving across an object.

Do not believe that this one demonstration will produce enough conceptual change for students to reach a level of equilibrium that solidifies scientific understanding of Bernoulli's principle. The task of the effective science teacher is to present many discrepant situations that produce disequilibrium, causing students to make many cognitive connections to accommodate to the events and information. For example, another demonstration that can be conducted in order to study Bernoulli's principle is to drop playing cards into a box. You can demonstrate this card drop one or two times and then call on some members of the class to try it. There is a certain way to hold the cards so that they fall into the box. Most students will not know this technique, so the cards they drop will fall away from the box when released. This activity generates cognitive dissonance, and the participants will need to examine what they know about air pressure to figure this out. Examine and try the several discrepant event demonstrations on Bernoulli's principle in Appendix A that are written up for use with in-service and pre-service science teachers.

Alternative Conceptions and Conceptual Change

A critical aspect of scientific literacy is to develop students' understanding of science concepts in order for them to comprehend the biological and physical world in which they live. Even though most students will not become experts in a particular scientific field, we do expect them to learn a core of concepts from the major fields of science that represents the most basic ideas of science (AAAS, 1993). By the time students complete their high school education, they should be able to provide correct explanations for these core concepts. All of this sounds so simple, but in reality it is difficult to achieve. The journey from where most students are to where we want them to be is far more difficult than most educators realize. A major hurdle is changing what students believe and think to what we would like them to believe and think.

Central to the problem of learning science appears to be what students *know* when they come to science class. All students have preformed conceptions about phenomena. Their minds are not empty, ready to be filled with a body of scientific knowledge. They already possess many ideas. Unfortunately, what students know frequently does not correspond well with scientific knowledge. Some researchers view students' ideas as primitive or naïve or as misconceptions (errors in what has been learned). Others refer to students' knowledge as *alternative conceptions*, different from accepted beliefs, but nevertheless very important. Wandersee, Mintzes, and Novak (1994) provide science educators with an extensive review of alternative conceptions research in which they present a useful synthesis of eight knowledge claims (Figure 9.3). A brief discussion of these claims highlights important findings regarding students' scientific conceptions.

There is a strong consensus that students possess alternative conceptions about the natural world before, during, and after school science instruction (claim 1). For this reason, students' conceptions must become a focus of instruction and their ideas the starting point for instruction. The task of science teachers is to *change* students' ideas that are not in line with science, ideas that will be prevalent among many students of different ages, abilities, genders, and cultures (claim 2). Even the most capable students hold ideas about basic science that are not correct. We simply cannot cover up these alternative conceptions by piling on new information, nor can we erase them by logical presentation. For some of the most important concepts, alternative conceptions persist beyond formal instruction. Yes, these alternative conceptions "hang on" even after science course participation (claim 3). With certain natural phenomena, alternative conceptions parallel the growth of that knowledge as evidenced by explanations put forth by scientists and philosophers in earlier times (claim 4). This is especially evident when students are attempting to learn about force and motion.

Where do these alternative conceptions originate? In our diverse multicultural society, students from many different backgrounds arrive at the classroom. Their perceptions and beliefs vary widely (claim 5). Consider, for example, students' views of modern medicine. Those from families of means may hold the belief that going to the doctor for treatment of an illness is beneficial and, thus, is a common practice. Some students from poor immigrant families may hold the belief that doctors are to be avoided, and only in a life-and-death situation do they go to a doctor or hospital. Students from these different backgrounds and belief systems will interact with instruction on disease and medicine in different ways. Not only is family background a source for alternative conceptions, but textbooks, personal experiences, and teachers also contribute. Yes, science teachers often possess the same alternative conceptions as their students (claim 6).

The distressing fact is that students' alternative conceptions interact with the conceptions presented in

---

Knowledge Claims About Alternative Conceptions

Claim 1:   Learners come to formal science instruction with a diverse set of alternative conceptions about natural objects and events.

Claim 2:   The alternative conceptions that learners bring to formal science instruction cut across age, ability, gender, and cultural boundaries.

Claim 3:   Alternative conceptions are tenacious and resistant to extinction by conventional teaching strategies.

Claim 4:   Alternative conceptions often parallel explanations of natural phenomena offered by previous generations of scientists and philosophers.

Claim 5:   Alternative conceptions have their origins in diverse sets of personal experiences including direct observations and perceptions, peer culture and language, and in teachers' explanations and instructional materials.

Claim 6:   Teachers often subscribe to the same alternative conceptions as their students.

Claim 7:   Learners' prior knowledge interacts with knowledge presented in formal instruction, resulting in a diverse set of unintended learning outcomes.

Claim 8:   Instructional approaches that facilitate conceptual change can be effective classroom tools.

FIGURE 9.3   This set of knowledge claims derived from the research literature on alternative conceptions can be used to guide teaching and learning science.

From "Research on Alternative Conceptions in Science," by J. H. Wandersee, J. J. Mintzes, and J. D. Novak, in D. L. Gabel (Ed.), Handbook of Research on Science Teaching (p. 195) 1994, Upper Saddle River, NJ: Merrill/Prentice Hall.

school science, resulting in varied learning outcomes, some of which are not desired (claim 7). Today, researchers are coming to accept the idea that learning science is not a matter of simply adding information or replacing existing information. After many days and even weeks of instruction, students fail to walk away with certain facts and beliefs because they are still grounded in what they knew prior to instruction. Further, that which takes place during science instruction sometimes merely serves to reinforce what some students believe. Attempting to teach evolution of animal species from simple life forms to humans is a good example of how personal belief in special creation is very resistant to change. However, for many science topics, there are change strategies that seem promising in moving students toward more scientifically accepted ideas (claim 8).

How do science teachers help students to understand and explain major science concepts? A teaching strategy recommended by Driver (1988) to facilitate conceptual change, from a constructivist point of view, is shown in Figure 9.4. In the teaching sequence presented in the figure, the teacher begins with a brief *orientation,* which introduces students to what they will be studying. This is followed by the *elicitation* phase in which students are asked to present their ideas. This activity is effective when conducted in small groups, because all students can participate and put forth their conceptions. Each group can present its descriptions and explanations, placing them on large sheets of paper for the entire class to view and discuss, which helps to *clarify* student understanding. Similarities and differences among the ideas are noted. Here is where students' prior knowledge is made explicit and clear. This information is important because it is the knowledge base that must be restructured during the unit of study.

A powerful step in this sequence is the introduction of *conflict.* When students experience events that are contrary to what they believe or think, they take note. This can cause students to reconsider their ideas about phenomena.

The *construction* phase is where students engage in a variety of learning activities to attain the desired conceptions. It is essential that students verbalize their knowledge using proper terms. They also can test ideas and compare and contrast the results with others in the class. Students can design experiments and engage in problem solving.

The teacher should *evaluate* students' understanding after the construction phase. How well have students learned the intended concepts or principles? Probably at this point, it will be determined that some reteaching needs to occur.

When most of the students have mastered the new content, they are ready to *apply* that knowledge to new situations. This step can lend greater meaning to the concepts, principles, and theories under study and help to form richer cognitive connections in the mind of the learner.

Finally, the teaching experience will end with a *review* of what was to be learned, permitting students to compare what they first thought regarding the concepts under study with what they learned from many instructional experiences.

The constructivist/conceptual change approach aims toward teaching a smaller number of science con-

FIGURE 9.4 An instructional sequence to facilitate conceptual change of abstract science concepts.

From "Theory into Practice II: A Constructivist Approach to *Curriculum Development,*" by R. Driver, 1988, in P. Fensham (Ed.), Development of Dilemmas in Science Education (p. 141), *Philadelphia:* Falmer Press.

Conceptual Change Instructional Sequence

Orientation:	Begin the instruction with a focus on what is to be learned.
Elicitation:	Call on students to explain their ideas of the concept under study.
Clarification:	Probe students to clarify their understanding.
Conflict:	Create discrepant events that cause the learners to see that their conceptions are incorrect.
Construction:	Help students view their ideas differently and to provide more correct explanations.
Evaluation:	Assess students' understandings of the concepts under study.
Application:	Provide instances to apply what has been learned, especially to everyday life.
Review:	Ask each student to describe how his/her conceptions have changed from the beginning of the instructional sequence to the present.

cepts, placing greater emphasis upon understanding. The teacher begins with students' prior knowledge, urging them to reflect on the ideas and beliefs they possess regarding a particular science concept or principle. Many opportunities are provided for students to find personal meaning from interacting with objects, events, and people. In addition, there is a deliberate attempt to utilize relevant contexts with which students can identify. Finally, there is a realization by the teacher that student misconceptions and naïve ideas may continue after the completion of the unit of study.

Students come to science class with a "commonsense view of phenomena, which they have constructed through personal experiences and social interactions with others" (Driver, Squires, et al., 1994). These commonsense views differ from scientific views and do not provide a coherent, accurate picture of the world. Nevertheless, these ideas serve the learner in everyday life and are difficult to replace. Science teachers can help students to acquire scientific conceptions with instruction that promotes both personal and social construction of knowledge through concrete experiences and teacher intervention. It is the teacher's role to introduce students to the culture of the scientific community, which cannot be discovered by students. The skillful teacher "introduces new ideas or cultural tools where necessary and provides the support and guidance for students to make sense of these for themselves" (Driver, Squires, et al., 1994, p. 11).

Strike and Posner (1992) indicate that many factors are related to changing students' conceptions so that they more accurately reflect science. For example, students' motivation to learn, their ability to represent what they know, and the complexity of the concepts under study are among many factors that affect learning science. Osborne and Wittrock (1983) point out other factors that we should note in our attempts to implement a new way of teaching when using conceptual change strategies. They remind us that many students do not have the desire to alter what they believe. Most students are satisfied with interpreting science terms to fit what they know, rather than modifying what they think. Students make only some of the connections that science teachers want them to make. Often, students form isolated branches of knowledge that they use only in science class. Further, many students are either incapable of or unwilling to restructure their knowledge to coincide with that of science. This takes a great deal of mental effort. Nevertheless, science teachers should consider the following four conditions in order to improve the possibilities for students to acquire scientific concepts (Posner, Strike, Hewson, & Gertkzog, 1982):

1. Students must be *dissatisfied* with their ideas in order to consider changing them.
2. Students must believe that they can *comprehend* the conceptions.

3. Students must perceive that the concepts are *plausible*.
4. Students must feel that they can *find out* about the idea.

Stop and Reflect!

The section on alternative conceptions and conceptual change should impress upon you the significance of a psychologically based body of knowledge that relates to science teaching. Before rushing on to the next section in this chapter, do the following:

■ Make a list of important assumptions regarding the alternative conceptions that you should consider when teaching science.

■ Form a list of strategies and techniques that you will use to help students alter their conceptions of scientific ideas.

■ Identify a science principle, law, or theory, and design a sequence of instructions that will help a given age group of students to change their ideas and guide them toward more correct scientific understanding. A beneficial approach to this activity might be to work with a partner or group of peers.

Meaningful Learning and Concept Mapping

Joseph Novak has translated and extended Ausubel's cognitive learning theories for teaching and learning science. He stresses the importance of meaningful learning and believes that effective learning occurs when the learner "constructs new and more powerful meaning" from educational experiences (Novak & Gowin, 1984, p. xi). Novak and many other researchers have focused on meaningful learning. Their psychologically based view of science teaching is that of the social constructivist who stresses the importance of learning scientific concepts from others who understand them. They believe that there is a body of scientific knowledge that can be learned by individuals. More importantly, this knowledge is most efficiently learned under the guidance of an experienced mentor. Therefore, one of the tasks of science teachers is to help students acquire a body of scientific knowledge in a meaningful way and to form correct explanations for these abstract ideas.

One technique to encourage students to construct relationships between ideas is called *concept mapping*. This approach to learning science began in the 1980s. The technique helps students to visually represent meaningful relationships between science concepts (Novak & Gowin, 1984). In Figure 9.5, a concept map

FIGURE 9.5 A concept map for learning about water.

From Learning How to Learn, (p.16) by J. D. Novak and D. B. Gowin, 1984, New York: Cambridge University Press. Reprinted with the permission of Cambridge University Press.

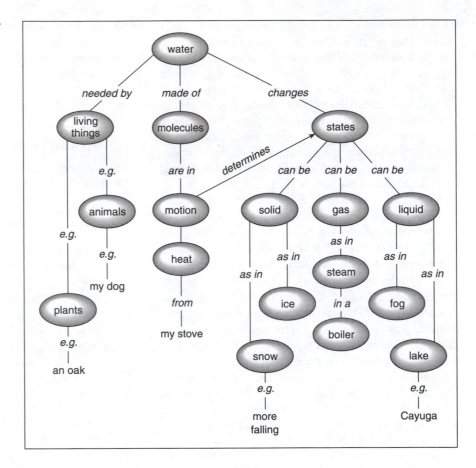

for water is presented. The key concepts are shown in ovals, and words linking these ideas are placed along the lines connecting them. The picture presents the superordinate–subordinate relationships of the topic under study. It graphically places the knowledge structure of water into a hierarchy, with broad general concepts at the top and the more specific concepts at the lower levels.

A variety of spatial organizations can be formed for the same topic, depending on the nature of the learning outcomes and students. The concept map shown for water is probably appropriate for a middle school science course. A concept map for water in a high school chemistry class during the study of solutions would be much different because of the emphasis on solubility, ionization, and polarity.

Novak (1995) recommends the following suggestions to science teachers who desire to incorporate concept mapping in their instruction:

- Begin with a content or subject area that students are familiar with.
- Identify the key ideas or propositions that form the concept under study.
- Rank-order the ideas from the most general to the most specific.
- Construct a preliminary concept map using ovals or boxes.

- Identify and label the linking lines between concepts that serve to form propositions that relate ideas.
- Make cross-link connections between different domains of knowledge.
- Do not construct sentences in the boxed or closed-in areas of the map.
- Continually revise maps and consider them never final.

Novak and Gowin indicate that concept mapping promotes meaning through active learning, because each student must make connections between the ideas in the picture and those in his or her mind. They emphasize that students must participate in the creation of the concept map. Consequently, the new knowledge the students gain is constructed, not discovered. These researchers state that "knowledge is not discovered like gold or oil, but rather it is constructed like cars or pyramids" (Novak & Gowin, 1984, p. 4).

Novak and Gowin (1984) indicate that concept maps can be used to:

1. Determine pathways for organizing meanings
2. Negotiate meaning with students
3. Point out misconceptions
4. Promote higher-level thinking (p. 23)

Concept mapping is used in other fields besides science instruction. For example, it is used under the name *semantic mapping* for language arts instruction.

Concept mapping is an effective way to engage students in finding meaning in the ideas that are under study in science courses. This tool encourages social thinking among students and between teacher and students (Roth, 1994). Concept mapping can be used in a variety of ways and at many points during the study of a unit. Students can be asked to construct concept maps on their own and place them into their science notebooks. They can be asked to construct them with other students in collaborative learning groups. Students can be asked to construct a map at the beginning of an instructional sequence in order to determine their entry level of knowledge. Further, this map will identify alternative conceptions that they hold. During the instructional sequence, the students can be asked to revise their concept maps, which will permit them to externalize their thinking and illustrate the conceptual change that is taking place. At the end of the instruction for a given unit, concept mapping can be used as a review.

Images, Analogies, and Models

Images

The study of imagery has been part of the history of psychology from the time of the early philosophers who attempted to describe the mind to the present (Kosslyn, 1980). Images can be thought of as thinking aids that help to transfer information. They are one way of representing objects that constitute the perceptible and imperceptible aspects of reality. The ability to produce images in the mind offers the possibility for humans to construct meaningful connections with ideas. The representation of phenomena and concepts are important to comprehending science.

Many scientific conceptions are very abstract, and therefore, difficult to imagine and represent pictorially. Nevertheless, these ideas are central to learning science and necessary for students to understand and explain. Science textbooks and teachers often present ideas with which students are familiar in order to make the unfamiliar comprehensible. You probably have heard the phrase, "now picture this in your mind," used to encourage students to imagine what they are about to learn. This prompt requests students to represent in their minds relationships that will transfer knowledge from one domain to another. Analogical reasoning encourages students to construct cognitive connections between the familiar and the unfamiliar. It facilitates meaningful learning of abstract subject matter by helping students to integrate new information with existing knowledge, thus forming new conceptions.

Pictures and diagrams are used frequently during science instruction to represent concepts and principles. Science textbooks are filled with these teaching aids. Teachers use them in their lectures. Visualization provides students with cognitive aids that make abstract ideas more comprehensible. Because we cannot observe directly the movement of electrons or ions, for example, we must find ways to illustrate these concepts. Abstract ideas must be made accessible by visual representation through diagrams or other means. You can find experienced chemistry teachers who weave diagrams into their presentations to help students conceptualize concepts like pH. Some teachers use a diagram similar to the one shown in Figure 9.6 to illustrate how the acidity and basidity of a solution changes as the relative concentrations of hydrogen ions (H^+) and hydroxide ions (OH^-) change.

FIGURE 9.6 A visual representation of the pH scale showing the relative concentrations of hydrogen and hydroxide ions.

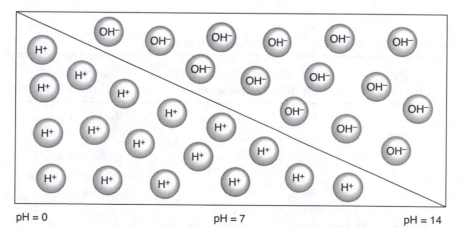

pH = 0 pH = 7 pH = 14

Teachers can reinforce science understandings through active learning experiences.

Analogies

The use of diagrams for instruction can further be enhanced by interactive techniques such as analogical reasoning. *Analogies* are one tool for getting students to make connections between what they know and what we want them to know. In some research studies, they have been reported to further students' comprehension of scientific concepts and to help them to construct meaning (Dagher, 1995; Duit, 1991; Glynn, Duit, & Thiele, 1995). An analogy forms a relationship between what the learners are familiar with and what they are expected to learn (the unfamiliar).

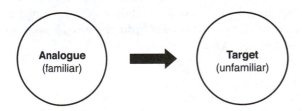

The familiar is referred to as the *analogue* and the unfamiliar the *target*. For example, science teachers have used the analogy of water flowing through a pipe (analogue) to help students comprehend electrical current (target).

Ausubel (1963) recommended the use of advanced organizers to facilitate the acquisition of knowledge. His idea of the comparative organizer serves to illustrate how we can show similarities and differences between what the students know and what they are expected to learn. This approach uses analogies to facilitate assimilation of new material into existing cognitive structures. Examine the analogy in Table 9.1 that a life science teacher might use to help students learn about the structure of the cell from their knowledge of a car. We will examine six operations for teaching analogies, developed by Glynn (1995, p. 27) for his teaching-with-analogies model, to guide our discussion regarding this instructional strategy:

1. Introduce the target concept
2. Review the analogue concept
3. Identify the features of the target and analogue
4. Map the similarities
5. Indicate where the analogy breaks down
6. Draw conclusions

For the comparison given in Table 9.1 and the six operations just stated, let's examine a car analogy instructionally. A science teacher might begin by introducing the purpose of the exercise. This statement can be accompanied by listing the structures of the cell (target) on the chalkboard (operation 1). Information can be given regarding the structure and function of cellular parts, similar to those shown in the left-hand column of the table. The teacher can pose a question to prompt students to search for an analogy in everyday life that is similar to the workings of a biological cell. Students may or may not come up with the car as an analogy. They may provide an example that is more relevant to them than an automo-

TABLE 9.1   An Analogy Between a Car and a Biological Cell

Structure or Function of the Concept to Be Learned	Structure of the Car Cell (familiar analogue)	Structure of the Biological Cell (unfamiliar target)
Outer structure	Body	Wall and membrane
Inner part	Interior	Cytoplasm
Control center	Driver	Nucleus
Communication	Electrical system	Endoplasmic reticulum
Energy	Engine	Mitochondria
Waste removal	Exhaust system	Vacuole

bile, which would certainly be an important path to pursue. In any event, if the students do not offer the car as a comparison, the teacher can present it (operation 2). Given the interest that adolescents show in driving automobiles, the car is likely to be familiar to them and a relevant analogue concept. The features of a car and a biological cell can be discussed (operation 3). A diagram of a cell can be constructed, and a discussion of how its structures are related to a car can take place. In this manner, a comparison of key features of the analogue and target are mapped by bridging similar features (operation 4).

Many analogies can be discussed to help students widen their understanding of a living cell. For example, some life science teachers have used a house or a factory to provide an analogy for a living cell. Then, after students have had a variety of instructional experiences with cell analogies, using automobiles, houses, factories, and so on, the salient features of these objects should be critically analyzed to point out their limitations in representing a biological structure (operation 5). Finally, the teacher should draw conclusions about the cell that highlight the important functions carried out by this fundamental biological entity (operation 6).

The use of analogies is widespread in science lectures and textbooks. In some instances, these examples are beneficial to students; in others, they are less than effective. Glynn et al. (1995) have analyzed many textbooks for examples of analogies as well as gathered analogies used by science teachers in their classrooms. These researchers report that textbooks and teachers who were judged to be effective with analogies used the six operations of the teaching-with-analogies model. Further, these authors and teachers carefully relate the familiar with the unfamiliar so that erroneous ideas do not come into their comparisons. Glynn et al. (1995) point out that Paul Hewitt's *Conceptual Physics* textbook contains many excellent analogies.

The idea of teaching abstract concepts and principles using analogies has great instructional appeal. Nevertheless, this approach is not always effective. Students can and often do miss the connection between the analogue and the target concept (Glynn et al., 1995). Pedagogical skill is needed to map the important features of analogical comparisons in order for conceptual bridges to be established by the learner. Remember, the key connections must be made by the student. Further, teachers must be on guard so that students do not form misconceptions (Thagard, 1992). For example, when using the flow of water through a pipe to illustrate electrical current, students as well as many elementary and middle school science teachers have formed the idea that electrons "zip" through a wire, similar to water shooting through a pipe. With direct electrical current, electrons move very fast in the spaces between atoms, but their net movement in the direction of the positive terminal is relatively slow. Many misconceptions have been found in textbooks and among teachers attempting to use analogical reasoning to explain concepts and phenomena whose features cannot be perceived directly.

Models

Scientists frequently use physical and mathematical models to represent phenomena. These representations, especially the physical models, provide concrete means to view reality and give science teachers and students a visual image to facilitate learning. Some common models are diagrams of the atom, the solar system, the cell, the DNA double helix, the water cycle, the Krebs cycle, structural chemical formulas, and the movement of electrical impulses along nerve cells. These and many other scientific models play an important role in conveying fundamental ideas to students. Without scientific models, teachers would experience much difficulty initiating student learning.

When using models to teach students about a theory or principle, we must remember that the model is a representation of a phenomenon, which is referred to as the target. The target is the object, phenomenon, or system in nature. Because the target cannot be observed directly and photographed, it must be represented diagramatically. Therefore, a scale model of a bridge or car, for example, would not be considered a scientific model. Scientific models cannot be considered exact replicas of reality, but working ideas that facilitate communication and guide research.

Science teachers must realize that although models appear simple and concrete, students do not readily learn them. Students need to construct a mental model of the scientific model under study, a process that is incremental and takes considerable instructional time. Consider the following when teaching students about a model (Greca & Moreira, 2000):

- Students do not have the same background knowledge as the teacher; therefore, students do not visualize and understand a scientific model as readily as the teacher might expect.
- Students conceptualization of a model is often incomplete, unstable, simplified, and unscientific.
- Mental modeling on the part of students is a very complex process and takes place over time through a series of small steps.
- Mental models are personal constructions for students as well as scientists.
- The acquisition of a mental model requires new language and involves a conceptual change process.

ASSESSING AND REVIEWING

Analysis and Synthesis

1. What have you learned from this chapter about cognitive psychology as it pertains to teaching and learning science?
   a. Without referring to the chapter, write a paragraph presenting the major ideas associated with constructivism.
   b. Compare and contrast a constructivist approach to learning science with a traditional approach.
2. How would you use the Piagetian ideas of equilibration and contradiction to engage learning? In brief form, outline an activity to teach a science concept, principle, or law using:
   a. A discrepant event situation with concrete materials
   b. A verbal or written statement that contradicts the beliefs of many people
   Share these examples with others so that everyone expands their knowledge of how to stimulate learning in the science classroom.
3. Compare the conceptual change instructional sequence with the 5E Instructional Model presented in Chapter 10, Figure 10.3." How might each of these teaching sequences aid students to restructure their ideas about abstract science concepts and laws?
4. Construct a concept map to represent the major ideas presented in this chapter on learning.
5. Develop an analogy that you might use to teach a concept to either a middle or senior high school group of students. Refer to the teaching-with-analogies model discussed in the chapter. Present the analogy to a group of peers and get their feedback regarding the effectiveness of the instruction. Pay special attention to the potential for introducing misconceptions or incorrect notions about the target concept.

Practical Considerations

6. Find a teacher-developed or commercial instructional unit for a middle or high school science course. Examine the activities to determine the potential the unit holds for promoting conceptual change among the students who will participate in it. For this exercise, consider the conceptual change model discussed in this chapter. Focus on:
   a. Eliciting ideas
   b. Clarifying knowledge
   c. Examining conflicting views
   d. Constructing new ideas
   e. Applying new knowledge
   f. Reviewing the knowledge restructuring that might take place
7. Construct an observational checklist for studying the extent to which conceptual change might be taking place among the students in a science classroom. Then, identify a middle or high school science teacher to observe. Take notes on the instruction and determine the potential for producing student understanding of the topic under study. More than one observational session will be necessary in order to make a valid assessment of the type of teaching (constructivist/conceptual change or traditional) and learning taking place.

Developmental Considerations

8. Obtain some textbooks and paperback books that discuss behavioral and cognitive principles of learning. Summarize the descriptions of these approaches and techniques for incorporating them into your teaching. Focus on strategies and techniques that you intend to use.

RESOURCES TO EXAMINE

Learning Science and the Science of Learning.   2002. Arlington, VA: National Science Teachers Association (NSTA) Press.

This paperback edited by Roger Bybee provides short, easy-to-read descriptions of learning strategies and techniques for science teachers. It addresses many topics, such as how students learn, inquiry and learning science, making connections,

learner-centered teaching, assessment and student learning, selecting curriculum materials, etc.

Making Sense of Secondary Science.   1994. New York: Routledge.

Rosalind Driver, Ann Squires, Peter Rushworth, and Valerie Wood-Robinson have assembled a compendium of research on students' ideas of science. They discuss the construction of knowledge through conceptual change. The book gives many illuminating examples of the growth of concepts related to the major areas of science. Among the concepts described are nutrition, microbes, solids, air, particles, electricity, light, and sound.

"Conceptual Bridges." 1995, December. *The Science Teacher*, pp. 25–27.

Shawn Glynn provides a good explanation of how to use analogies to help students understand scientific concepts. He presents his teaching-with-analogies model and illustrates how the elements of this model have been used by scientists and effective teachers to further scientific understanding.

Science Teaching and the Development of Thinking. 1995. Belmont, CA: Wadsworth.

Anton Lawson gives a psychological basis for learning science. He emphasizes the importance of students testing their ideas in authentic learning situations. Lawson gives many examples of how to involve students in science activities to promote active learning and develop thinking.

Teaching Science for Understanding: A Human Constructivist View. 1999. New York: Academic Press.

Joel Mintzes, James Wandersee, and Joseph Novak edited a large compendium of articles by science educational researchers on many topics related to teaching and learning science. These articles go into greater depth than the topics discussed in this chapter. Some of the areas are: human constructivism, conceptual change, metacognition, concept maps, development, cognitive analysis of content, analogies and models, computer assisted instruction, simulations, scaffolding, and verbal interactions.

"Investigating a Grade 11 Student's Evolving Conceptions of Heat and Temperature." 1999. *Journal of Research in Science Teaching, 36,* 55–87.

This is an award-winning research study that illustrates the difficulty students have in learning some of the most fundamental concepts in physics. It centers on the thinking and learning of a small number of students and how their ideas evolve over many weeks of instruction. The article provides the reader with many ways to view the learning from a conceptual change point of view.

References

Ajzen, I. (1989). Attitude structure and behavior. In A. R. Pratkanis, S. J. Breckler, & A. G. Beckman (Eds.), *Attitude structure and function* (pp. 241–274). Hillsdale, NJ: Erlbaum.

American Association for the Advancement of Science (AAAS). (1993). *Benchmarks for science literacy.* New York: Oxford University Press.

Ausubel, D. P. (1963). *The psychology of meaningful verbal learning.* New York: Grune & Stratton.

Brophy, J. (1988). *On motivating students.* In D. Berliner & B. Rosenshine (Eds.), *Talks to teachers* (pp. 201–245). New York: Random House.

Crawley, F. E., & Koballa, T. R. (1994). Attitude research in science education: Contemporary models and methods. *Science Education, 78,* 35–55.

Dagher, Z. R. (1995). Analysis of analogies used by science teachers. *Journal of Research in Science Teaching, 32,* 259–270.

Driver, R. (1988). Theory into practice II: A constructivist approach to curriculum development. In P. Fensham (Ed.), *Development and dilemmas in science education* (pp. 133–149). Philadelphia: Falmer Press.

Driver, R., Asoko, H., Leach, J., Mortimer, E., & Scott, P. (1994). Constructing scientific knowledge in the classroom. *Educational Researcher, 23*(7), 5–12.

Driver, R., Squires, A., Rushworth, P., & Wood-Robinson, V. (1994). *Making sense of secondary science.* New York: Routledge.

Duit, R. (1991). On the role of analogies and metaphors in learning science. *Science Education, 75,* 649–672.

Duit, R., & Treagust, D. F. (1998). Learning science—from behaviorism towards social constructivism and beyond. In B. J. Fraser & K. G. Tobin (Eds.), *International Handbook of Science Education, Part One* (pp. 3–26). A. A. Dordrecht, The Netherlands: Kluwer.

Fishbein, M. (1963). An investigation of the relationship between beliefs about an object and attitude toward the object. *Human Relations, 16,* 233–240.

Fosnot, C. T. (1996). *Constructivism: Theory, perspectives, and practice.* New York: Teachers College, Columbia University.

Furth, H. G. (1969). *Piaget and knowledge.* Englewood Cliffs, NJ: Prentice-Hall.

Glynn, S. (1995). Conceptual bridges. *The Science Teacher, 62*(9), 25–27.

Glynn, S. M., Duit, R., & Thiele, R. B. (1995). Teaching science with analogies: A strategy for constructing knowledge. In S. M. Glynn & R. Duit (Eds.), *Learning science in the schools: Research reforming practices.* Mahwah, NJ: Erlbaum.

Greca, I. M., & Moreira, M. A. (2000), Mental models, conceptual models, and modeling. *International Journal of Science Education, 22*(1), 1–11.

Kasschau, R. (1986). A model for teaching critical thinking in psychology. In J. Halonen (Ed.), *Teaching critical thinking in psychology*. Milwaukee, WI: Alverno College Institute.

Koballa, T. R., & Warden, M. A. (1992). Changing and measuring attitudes in the science classroom. In F. Lawrenz, K. Cochran, & J. Krajcik (Eds.), *Research matters . . . to the science teacher* (pp. 75–83). Manhattan, KS: National Association for Research in Science Teaching.

Kosslyn, S. M. (1980). *Image and mind*. Cambridge: Harvard University Press.

Lawson, A. E. (1994). Research on the acquisition of science knowledge: Epistemological foundations of cognition. In D. L. Gabel (Ed.), *Handbook of research on science teaching and learning*. Upper Saddle River, NJ: Merrill/Prentice Hall.

Novak, J. D. (1995). Concept mapping: A strategy for organizing knowledge. In S. M. Glynn & R. Duit (Eds.), *Learning science in the schools*. Mahwah, NJ: Erlbaum.

Novak, J. D., & Gowin, D. B. (1984). *Learning how to learn*. New York: Cambridge University Press.

Osborne, R., & Wittrock, M. (1983). Learning science: A generative process. *Science Education, 67,* 489–508.

Piaget, J. (1964). Cognitive development in children: Development and learning. *Journal of Research in Science Teaching, 2,* 176–186.

Piaget, J. (1971). *Biology and knowledge*. Chicago: University of Chicago Press.

Posner, G. J., Strike, K. A., Hewson, P. W., & Gertkzog, W. A. (1982). Accommodation of a scientific conception: Toward a theory of conceptual change. *Science Education, 66,* 211–228.

Roth, W. M. (1994). Student views of collaborative concept mapping: An emancipatory research project. *Science Education, 78,* 1–34.

Sternberg, R. (1995). *In search of the human mind*. New York: Harcourt Brace College Publishers.

Strike, K. A., & Posner, G. J. (1992). A revisionist theory of conceptual change. In R. A. Duschl & R. J. Hamilton (Eds.), *Philosophy of science, cognitive psychology, and educational theory and practice* (pp. 147–176). Albany: State University of New York Press.

Thagard, P. (1992). Analogy, explanation, and education. *Journal of Research in Science Teaching, 29,* 537–544.

von Glasersfeld, E. (1995). *Radical constructivism: A way of knowing and learning*. London: Falmen Press.

Vygotsky, L. S. (1978). *Mind in society: The development of higher psychological processes*. Cambridge: Harvard University Press.

Wandersee, J. H., Mintzes, J. J., & Novak, J. D. (1994). Research on alternative conceptions in science. In D. L. Gabel (Ed.), *Handbook of research on science teaching*. Upper Saddle River, NJ: Merrill/Prentice Hall.

Woolfolk, A. E. (1995). *Educational psychology*, (6th ed.). Needham Heights, MA: Allyn and Bacon.

Part Three

STRATEGIES FOR SCIENCE TEACHING

10

Inquiry and Teaching Science

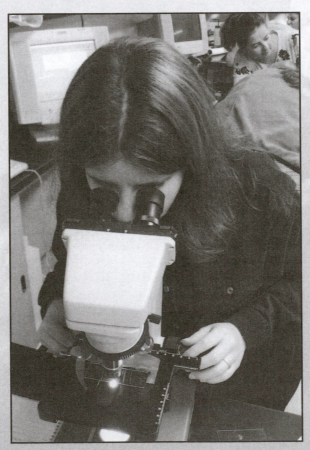

*We must remember that inquiry takes many
forms and goes beyond laboratory work.*

All students should be given the opportunity to explore the natural world in order to learn about the wonders of nature. Most middle and senior high school science students become excited when they are placed in situations where they can study patterns and processes inherent among physical and biological phenomena. In order for these experiences to be authentic and productive, they must reflect the nature of science and how new knowledge is acquired through investigation. Textbooks and other instructional materials must also present the thinking and investigative activities in which scientists and engineers engage as well as the knowledge and products they produce. Therefore, science courses should include teaching practices that reflect how individuals who construct knowledge and invent products go about their work. The two terms that seem to capture the nature of finding out, which can serve as a philosophy and a guide for teaching and learning science, are *inquiry* and *inquiry-based instruction*.

AIMS OF THE CHAPTER

Use the questions that follow to guide your thinking and learning about inquiry-based science instruction and how you can be successful in implementing it:

- How would you explain the difference between traditional science instruction and inquiry-based instruction?

- How would you distinguish between everyday inquiry conducted by laypeople and scientific inquiry conducted by scientists?

- Which of the following instructional approaches is recommended by many of the national science education reform documents, teaching science *by* inquiry or teaching science *as* inquiry, and how would you explain these conceptions?

- What are the potential learning outcomes likely to occur when each of the following are emphasized: content, content with process, process with content, and process?

- How would you describe eight strategies and techniques to initiate and sustain inquiry-based science?

- What would your teaching plan look like if you intended to demonstrate a certain instructional strategy or technique to engage students in finding out about a given phenomenon?

- What problems and concerns can you cite that are associated with science teachers' attempts to implement inquiry-based science programs?

WHAT IS INQUIRY?

Scientific inquiry refers to the diverse ways in which scientists study the natural world and propose explanations based on the evidence derived from their work. (National Research Council, 1996, p. 23)

Teaching science must be consistent with the nature of science in order for course content and methods to reflect how scientific knowledge is constructed and established. Science is generally characterized as an active process whereby men and women, curious about nature, contribute to humankind's understanding of objects and events that surround them. Inquiry is a word that has been used over and over in the science education literature to characterize the active processes involved in scientific thinking, investigation, and the construction of knowledge. Consequently, inquiry has been used as a guide for establishing goals and objectives, selecting instructional strategies and teaching techniques, and developing assessment procedures. For the past 40 years, the term *inquiry* has been used frequently in national, state, and local science curriculum guidelines, as well as course materials, and it is still being used for these purposes.

The recommendations of national committees concerning the school science reform that is taking place across the nation stress the inclusion of inquiry in the curriculum. Project 2061 of the American Association for the Advancement of Science (AAAS, 1990) reminds us that teaching science should be consistent with the nature of scientific inquiry. Its publication *Science for All Americans* urges science teachers to begin with questions about nature, actively engage students, concentrate on the collection and use of evidence, provide a historical perspective, insist on clear expression, use a team approach, do not separate knowledge from finding out, and de-emphasize the memorization of technical vocabulary. Further, the difficulty in describing scientific inquiry apart from the content of a particular investigation and that there is no set of procedures followed by scientists is pointed out in *Benchmarks for Science Literacy* (AAAS, 1993. p. 9): "Scientific inquiry is far more flexible than the rigid sequence of steps commonly depicted in textbooks as 'the scientific method'."

In the *National Science Education Standards* from the National Research Council (NRC, 1996), the term *science as inquiry* appears frequently throughout the publication. "The *Standards* call for more 'science as process' in which students learn such skills as observing, inferring, and experimenting. Inquiry is central to science learning" (p. 2). Science teachers must engage students in inquiry so that they ask questions, describe objects and events, test their ideas with what is known, and communicate what they are learning.

In general, inquiry is finding out about something. It centers around the desire to answer a question or to know more about a situation. Humans have always been inquirers, searching for food and places to live. People from all walks of life inquire on a routine basis. Parents search for the best bargains when purchasing food and clothing for their families; businesspeople look for customers who need their products and services. Journalists seek out people who can provide them with information to produce a good story, and detectives look for clues to the causes of accidents and homicides. Teenagers try to find friends with whom they like to associate. Inquiry, in general, is being used by people around us all the time.

Scientific inquiry also takes place in our society, but it has a specialized focus and is conducted by a group of people called scientists. As stated often in this textbook, scientific inquiry centers upon natural phenomena and is an attempt to understand nature by explaining it and applying that knowledge. However, the knowledge has to be more than personally satisfying; it has to pass the scrutiny of other scientists through verification. Scientists take many paths in their quest to answer questions. Thus, scientific inquiry is a creative process that is fueled by curiosity and hard work, often resulting in frustration and sometimes leading to useful knowledge. Scientific inquiry has at least two critical aspects, the process of finding out and the product of the search.

A great deal of the science teaching that takes place in middle and senior high schools, as well as at the collegiate level, can be characterized as teaching the products of science. This mode of teaching is designed to present a body of information that has been organized by the teacher or the textbook. Unfortunately, this approach often omits the thinking that was used and the paths that were taken to form the knowledge. The approach also minimizes the firsthand and minds-on experiences that students should be provided. Teaching science as a body of knowledge results in conveying the abstracted and distilled, polished, and pristine outcomes of the learning process that others have gone through to construct new knowledge. As a consequence, this approach often conveys ideas that have little meaning to students, resulting in the memorization of ideas that are learned poorly. Content with little or no process is not recommended for science education.

One other distinction of terms is important to note. The term *discovery* is often used synonymously with inquiry. However, these two concepts have a different meaning. Discovery is more limited in scope than inquiry, and it pertains to the act of figuring out something for one's self—"Aha, I've got it." Science as inquiry contains many elements, some of which do not involve discovering something for one's self. Scientists often call upon others for information to assist them in solving a problem. They read professional journals to gather information in order to gain insights into their problem solving. Although scientists are engaged in a constant state of inquiry, they do not often make discoveries.

Given the importance of inquiry, all science teachers must understand this idea in order to advance scientific literacy. Unfortunately, inquiry is often misunderstood and thus leads to unintended outcomes. Before we provide many examples of how to use this idea for teaching science, it is necessary to describe and analyze inquiry as it pertains to science teaching.

CONTENT AND PROCESS AS THEY RELATE TO INQUIRY AND DISCOVERY LEARNING

The purpose of scientific inquiry is to understand nature and to apply that understanding in society. As was discussed in Chapter 7 on the nature of science earlier in this textbook, science is a broad-based discipline that has many facets. Similarly, inquiry is a multifaceted activity and therefore we must be cautious not to define inquiry too narrowly by aligning it only with knowledge or only with investigation. Natural phenomena and ideas about them are central to inquiry, and the pursuit of these ideas is driven by interest and fascination that scientists have for understanding

FIGURE 10.1 Four ways to view inquiry and science instruction.

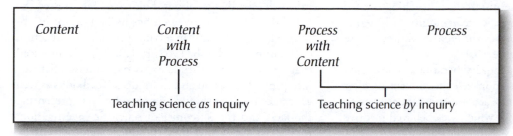

nature. Scientific inquiry, in its simplest form, is about the *what* and the *how* of understanding the world in which we live. One way to conceptualize inquiry as it relates to teaching science is to analyze it by using the terms *content* (what) and *process* (how). Figure 10.1 shows four conceptualizations of science teaching: (a) content, (b) content with process, (c) process with content, and (d) process.

Content is the body of knowledge that results from scientific activity as well as the ideas upon which knowledge is built. It consists of facts, concepts, laws, principles, and theories that are used to explain objects and events. Knowledge and understanding about the world is the major goal of scientific inquiry. The knowledge forms the major truths upon which science builds and progresses. However, a major problem arises when science is presented as a body of knowledge that is lacking in how scientific ideas were arrived at during human history. The reasoning, methods, techniques, experiments, and so on are all important for understanding scientific knowledge. Further, it is necessary for students to engage in active learning in order for them to reconstruct scientific knowledge and to find meaning in it, which requires them to go through a rather lengthy conceptual change process in order to form correct ideas about nature.

Content with process is another way to view science teaching (Figure 10.1). This conception brings into science teaching the process of finding out about something, and thus reflects an important way to teach science as inquiry. Again, the goal is to learn about phenomena by bringing into instruction the ways and means that are used to arrive at various understandings. The methods, techniques, and apparatus are all important aspects of the scientific process. The paths scientists have taken to discover objects and events, and the explanations they have created, can be taught in many ways: lecture, discussion, role-playing, films, readings, and simulations. However, the instruction must go further; students must be involved in the processes of finding out about the subject under study. They must engage in laboratory and firsthand investigations of ideas, sometimes replicating the activities scientists use to study nature and sometimes designing investigations

to answer questions that have not been answered by others but are of special interest to them.

Process with content is a third way to view science teaching (Figure 10.1). Its main focus is to engage students in finding out about many phenomena and events. The purpose is to promote active student engagement and to teach students how to inquire. The curriculum includes a variety of content that supports student investigation. The content serves as the context for the investigation. Hands-on activities are the focus, along with some student understanding of the content. This approach is found in elementary and some middle school science classrooms. However, it must be evaluated because students can be busy while learning very little content. Science process skills and scientific reasoning are best learned within a context of important science content. Further, there must be a focus on the ideas that form our knowledge about nature, which are the critical issues that scientists think about.

A *process* approach has been used in science teaching to promote inquiry and discovery learning. Its main intent is to teach students investigative skills purported to be used by scientists. Among the science process skills that serve as the main focus of process-based science programs are observing, inferring, measuring, using numbers, hypothesizing, experimenting, interpreting data, and so forth. This type of curriculum can be found in the elementary school and in certain aspects of middle school science programs. The process approach omits or deemphasizes critical science content. Such programs are *not* aligned with the national standards that view content knowledge as an essential learning outcome of school science. Further, it is not supported by decades of research in cognitive science, which indicates students learn important skills in the context of learning about something. This is not to say that science teachers should avoid all instruction unless it is aimed at teaching content. There is a place for special emphasis on process skill instruction, for example, to help students practice graphing, designing experiments, and identifying variables. However, a heavy emphasis on process without content is not a defensible position for science teaching at any level of schooling.

Two phrases that have been used in science teaching can help educators to understand better the purpose and history of the content/process dichotomy associated with inquiry. These phrases are "teaching science *by* inquiry" and "teaching science *as* inquiry." The terms *by* and *as* connote important differences between these phrases, as shown in Figure 10.1.

Teaching science *by* inquiry became a phrase used during the science education reform movement after *Sputnik* in 1957. The phrase accompanied the attempt to emphasize active learning, which was believed to drive inquiry and to de-emphasize the rote learning of content, especially in the elementary and junior high schools. Educators and learning psychologists wanted students to experience the excitement of finding out and not to be turned off to science by having to memorize large numbers of terms and vocabulary words. They wanted students to develop scientific attitudes and skills. The aim was to promote learning *by* discovery or teaching science *through* inquiry whereby students would learn how to learn and discover answers to questions for themselves. Thus, teaching science *by* inquiry is associated with process and process with content (see Figure 10.1).

Jerome Bruner, an eminent learning psychologist, helped to galvanize the inquiry and discovery movement by extolling the virtues of finding out by doing, which was often referred to as learning by discovery. He claimed that students who practiced discovery learning would obtain efficient strategies for acquiring, transforming, organizing, storing, and using information that is essential in problem solving (Bruner, 1961). The reasoning behind this hypothesis began with the recognition that much information comes to the learner before the problem is solved. Success and efficiency in problem solving, therefore, depends upon the learner's ability to manipulate the information according to how it might have to be used. Bruner assumed that practice with discovery learning would develop efficient and powerful ways to manipulate information, which can be used not only in discovery learning but in other forms of learning as well. Bruner admitted that it is very difficult to describe the heuristics of inquiry. Nevertheless, he believed that the modes of discovery can be acquired only through the practice of discovery. There is no question that Bruner's work did a great deal to promote active learning.

During the post-*Sputnik* era of science education reform, some learning psychologists and science educators promoted science process skill instruction to the neglect of science content. However, there also existed those who promoted an alternative view of content and process. Joseph Schwab, a curriculum theorist at the University of Chicago, exerted enormous influence on teaching science *as* inquiry. As a member of the Biological Sciences Curriculum Study (BSCS) Committee in the late 1950s and early 1960s, he discussed the "enquiry approach" (the term he used for inquiry) and how to use it in the classroom. At the time, Schwab urged science educators to take a different approach to science

teaching and to adopt one that better reflects the ways in which scientists go about their work. He stressed the belief that "scientific research has its origin, not in objective facts alone, but in a conception, a construction of the mind" (Schwab, 1962, p. 12). Schwab proposed that we should help students to realize how scientists interpret information and form ideas. Textbooks as well as science teachers should go beyond merely presenting the facts and the outcomes of scientific investigation; they must show how these products were derived by scientists—how a body of knowledge grows and how new conceptions come about. Schwab felt that to teach science *as* inquiry would show students:

1. How knowledge arises from interpretation of data
2. That the interpretation of data—indeed, even the search for data—proceeds on the basis of concepts and assumptions that change as our knowledge grows
3. That because these principles and concepts change, knowledge also changes
4. That though knowledge changes, it changes for good reason—because we know better and know more than we knew before (BSCS, 1978, p. 306)

Examination of these recommendations shows clearly that Schwab believed that the aim of science is to produce content, but that it can only be understood by examining the process of that evolution. Schwab (BSCS, 1978) went further in his recommendations to stress the importance of student-conducted research to further their understanding of science and the development of skills and habits of an inquiring mind. The spirit and the phrase teaching science *as* inquiry can be found today in the *National Science Education Standards* (NRC, 1996).

Stop and Reflect!

Before going further, respond to the following statements and questions:

- Describe four conceptions of science teaching and their purpose: (a) content, (b) content with process, (c) process with content, and (d) process.

- Why do you think that teaching science *as* inquiry is recommended by the science education reform movement?

- Recall the four themes of scientific literacy presented in the chapter on the nature of science: (a) science as a way of thinking, (b) science as a way of investigating, (c) science as a body of knowledge, and (d) science and its interactions with technology and society. Describe each theme, using content and process as they were discussed here.

STRATEGIES AND TECHNIQUES FOR CONDUCTING INQUIRY–BASED INSTRUCTION

Science teachers have many pedagogical strategies and techniques available to help them plan and conduct inquiry-oriented science. These pedagogical tools have been used successfully by many science teachers to initiate student thinking and sustain their interest during instruction. You should master these approaches and use them to support the content/process focus that you believe appropriate for a given group of students. For the beginning science teacher, the following is a list of strategies and techniques to begin to master:

Asking questions	Deductive activities
Discrepant events	Gathering information
Science process skills	Solving problems
Inductive activities	Science fair projects

Asking Questions

Questions are fundamental to scientific inquiry as well as to science instruction. Asking the right question is critical in investigative work. Questions can engage thinking and orient mental activity toward meaningful ends. For instructional purposes, questions can be clas-sified in many ways. For example, there are the *what, where, which, when,* and *why* types of questions. The questions can be phrased to match Bloom's taxonomy—knowledge, comprehension, application, analysis, synthesis, and evaluation. Questions also can be asked to direct student thinking along the lines of the science process skills such as observing, inferring, hypothesizing, experimenting, and so on. These questioning techniques are discussed later in this textbook.

One questioning technique that some science teachers use is to write questions on the board for the students to answer. These questions, generally small in number, can guide the instruction toward the intended learning outcomes. Examine the questioning techniques used by Ms. Sanchez in Box 10.1.

Science teachers who encourage students to state what they think, test out their ideas, and explain their findings are using pedagogy that reflects scientific inquiry and strategies recommended by cognitive psychologists. Let's continue by examining other inquiry strategies that can be used to promote learning through the use of questioning.

Yes/No Questioning Technique

Richard Suchman (1966), who created the Inquiry Development Program in the 1960s for the middle school, offers many suggestions to teachers who want to implement in-

---

Classroom Snapshot 10.1

A Questioning Technique

Ms. Sanchez placed a small transparent container filled with water before the class. She held up a paper clip and directed students' attention to a question on the chalkboard.

What Will Happen When I Place This Paper Clip on the Water?

The class was silent for a short time, then one hand went up. When the student was given permission to answer, she indicated that the paper clip would drop to the bottom of the pan. The rest of the class seemed to support this prediction. With that, the teacher asked all of the students to write their prediction in their notebook. Then she requested every student to go back to the laboratory tables to test their prediction. She provided each student with a small container of water and three different sizes of paper clips. At first, all of the paper clips were sinking to the bottom of the container when the students placed their clips on the water. With some guidance, most students were able to float the small paper clip on the water.

When most of the students were successful in floating the paper clip, Ms. Sanchez directed student attention to another question that she had written on the board.

What Variables Are Related to Your Success in Floating a Paper Clip on the Water?

Answering this question caused students to think hard because they had three paper clips to work with and their manual dexterity to consider as variables. When the hands-on part of the activity concluded, the teacher discussed the properties of water and surface tension as she guided students' explanations regarding the flotation of a metal paper clip more dense than water. Then the discussion was directed toward the scientific reasoning students used to determine how to float a paper clip.

quiry in their classrooms. His six rules for inquiry sessions reflect the openness and freedom that he believed students should be given in order to develop their inquiry skills.

Rule One: Encourage students to ask questions that the teacher can answer with a "yes" or "no" response.

Rule Two: Permit students to ask as many questions as they wish when they initiate their question asking.

Rule Three: Avoid evaluating the worth or accuracy of students' explanations.

Rule Four: Allow students to test out their own ideas at any time.

Rule Five: Encourage interaction and discussion among students.

Rule Six: Permit students to "mess around" with lots of materials connected with a given inquiry session.

Suchman's suggestions provide us with one way to promote inquiry in the science classroom. This approach places the learner in the position of having to find out and explain how, shifting the responsibility for learning away from the teacher to the student. Perhaps this is a questioning technique to practice and use for certain inquiry sessions.

Science Process Skills

One way to actively engage students and to help them become more proficient in representing the world around them is to focus instruction on science process skills. A process skill approach stresses the acquisition of investigative skills that are often associated with scientific inquiry. These skills are called observing, classifying, inferring, measuring, using numbers, predicting, defining operationally, forming models, controlling variables, interpreting data, hypothesizing, and conducting experiments. Many educators hold the belief that the acquisition of these skills will better enable students to solve problems, learn on their own, and appreciate science. Table 10.1 presents a list of many commonly used science process skills in science programs.

TABLE 10.1 Basic and Integrated Science Process Skills

Process Skill	Definition
Basic Skills	
Observing	Noting the properties of objects and situations using the five senses
Classifying	Relating objects and events according to their properties or attributes (This involves classifying places, objects, ideas, or events into categories based on their similarities.)
Space/time relations	Visualizing and manipulating objects and events, dealing with shapes, time, distance, and speed
Using numbers	Using quantitative relationships, for example, scientific notation, error, significant numbers, precision, ratios, and proportions
Measuring	Expressing the amount of an object or substance in quantitative terms, such as meters, liters, grams, and newtons
Inferring	Giving an explanation for a particular object or event
Predicting	Forecasting a future occurrence based on past observation or the extension of data
Integrated Skills	
Defining operationally	Developing statements that present a concrete description of an object or event by telling one what to do or observe
Formulating models	Constructing images, objects, or mathematical formulas to explain ideas
Controlling variables	Manipulating and controlling properties that relate to situations or events for the purpose of determining causation
Interpreting data	Arriving at explanations, inferences, or hypotheses from data that have been graphed or placed in a table (this frequently involves concepts such as mean, mode, median, range, frequency distribution, t-test, and chi-square test)
Hypothesizing	Stating a tentative generalization of observations or inferences that may be used to explain a relatively larger number of events but that is subject to immediate or eventual testing by one or more experiments
Experimenting	Testing a hypothesis through the manipulation and control of independent variables and noting the effects on a dependent variable; interpreting and presenting results in the form of a report that others can follow to replicate the experiment

Data compiled from *Science: A Process Approach, Commentary for Teachers,* by the American Association for the Advancement of Science, 1965, Washington, DC.

Many middle school science programs place heavy emphasis on science process skill development. These curricula use process skills as one of the primary learning goals along with science concepts. Some school districts devote 4 to 6 weeks to science skills at the beginning of the school year. These programs use a variety of content and contexts within which students practice scientific skills during hands-on instruction.

Scientifically literate students must be competent in using science process skills. For example, graphing is an essential skill for all students to develop. Graphs organize information in an efficient manner. Graphing is a communication skill that is used throughout school science, from elementary school through college. It also is used in the business world to convey information in a concise manner. Middle school science programs must ensure that all students are proficient in graphing before they enter high school. Some of the graphing subskills are:

- Identifying the appropriate type of graph—bar or line—to represent data
- Providing a useful title for a graph and correctly labeling the x and y axes
- Constructing a bar or line graph when given a data table
- Interpreting a graph by communicating its significance
- Interpolating and extrapolating information from a line graph

At first thought, graphing seems so simple to the college science major who is preparing to become a science teacher. This is deceiving because graphing is tied closely to the context in which it is used. Change the context or content, and many students seem lost and unable to demonstrate this skill. Examine the table and axes for a graph provided in Figure 10.2. Fill in the missing data on the table, and construct a graph to represent the information, complete with a title and labels for the axes. While this mental activity may appear simple for an adult teacher who has majored in science, it is not so easy for many middle and high school students to perform, especially those students who are learning English as a second language.

In addition to the basic science process skills, inquiry is carried out using integrated process skills or more advanced reasoning skills. Let's read about the process/content emphasis used by Mr. Roosevelt, a middle school science teacher who wants students to better understand how to manipulate and control variables (see Box 10.2).

Analyze Mr. Roosevelt's use of the string telephone laboratory. Identify which of the four perspectives of teaching science and inquiry that was discussed at the beginning of this chapter Mr. Roosevelt is using: content, content with process, process with content, or process. Explain your answer and whether you feel the

FIGURE 10.2 The data table shows the relationship between the volume of a piece of iron and its mass, which can be used to construct a graph to represent the information.

Volume of iron (milliliters) x	Mass of iron (grams) y
1	2
2	4
3	8
4	16
5	—
6	64

Title of graph:

teacher is using an appropriate instructional approach with his middle school students.

Discrepant Events

An attention-getting, thought-provoking approach to initiate inquiry is through the use of discrepant events. A discrepant event puzzles the observer, causing him or her to wonder why the event occurred as it did (see Box 10.1). These situations leave the observer at a loss to explain what has taken place. Discrepant events influence equilibration and the self-regulatory process, according to the Piagetian theory of intellectual development. Situations that are contrary to what a person expects cause him or her to wonder what is taking place, resulting in cognitive disequilibrium. With proper guidance, the individual will attempt to figure out the discrepancy and search for a suitable explanation for the situation. When a person arrives at a plausible explanation for a discrepant event, he or she will establish cognitive equilibrium at a new level. The individual is now better equipped mentally to approach new situations that cause curiosity and puzzlement (Piaget, 1971).

Classroom Snapshot 10.2

Manipulating Variables

Mr. Roosevelt engages his middle school students in an extensive laboratory investigation with the "string telephone." Mr. Roosevelt initiates this activity by demonstrating how two metal soup cans connected with a wire transmit voice sounds between two people. He challenges the students to construct many different phones to determine which pair will transmit the clearest voice messages. He also asks them to predict which phones will work best and to explain why. Working in groups, the students bring to class many cans and containers of various sizes and composition—from small metal cans to large coffee cans, from small paper cups to giant soft drink containers, and from Styrofoam cups to plastic dairy food containers. The students also bring to class a variety of lines to connect the phones, such as thread, string, monofilament fishing line, and wire.

After the students have tested many combinations of phones and lines, they select a set of phones that produces very clear voice sounds. For example, a pair of paper cups connected by carpet thread produces amazing results. Mr. Roosevelt asks his students to identify the variables that seem to produce good sounds through these simple devices. He guides students' thinking so that they realize they were conducting an experiment and controlling variables. The students come to realize not only that the size and composition of the phones are important but also that these variables affect the vibration of the transmitting material. Even though the students lack the scientific terminology to explain the effects of elasticity on vibration, they feel good about conducting an investigation that seems scientific. Mr. Roosevelt continues the discussion of vibration and sound quality by asking students to demonstrate pleasing sounds and music with musical instruments they play, such as guitars, pianos, and drums.

An inquiry session initiated with a discrepant event can begin with a demonstration or film, preceded by directions to focus students' attention on what they are about to observe. Discrepant-event demonstrations of the laws of motion, center of gravity, Pascal's principle, density, and vacuum, to mention just a few, can be used to initiate inquiry sessions. The discrepant-event approach receives support from the cognitive psychologists because of its potential impact on learning.

Here is a discrepant event you can try right now. Go to the kitchen and cut a piece of wax paper approximately 4 inches by 4 inches square. Place a drop of water in the center of the wax paper. Tilt the wax paper until the drop of water moves down the paper. Continue to tilt the wax paper so that the bead of water can move down its surface. Observe carefully the downward movement of the drop. Question:

Does the drop of water roll or slide down the wax paper?

After you have committed yourself to an answer, try to support your inference with an explanation. When you have "experimented" with this little puzzle and are confident that you can describe and explain the movement of the drop of water, go to Appendix A and read about "A Drop of Water" in the Section titled "Little Science Puzzlers." Then, present the problem to a group of adults or middle or high school students and determine the extent to which this activity is a discrepant event for them and how well they can explain the movement of the drop of water across the wax paper.

Inductive Activities

The inductive approach provides students with learning situations in which they can *discover* a concept or principle through experiences in the laboratory, field, or classroom. With this approach, the attributes and instances of an idea are encountered first by the learner, followed by naming and discussing the idea under study. The inductive approach provides students with concrete experience whereby they obtain data from objects and events, which in turn gives them a foundation upon which to anchor information and build new knowledge. Inductive activities can be thought of as an experience-before-vocabulary approach to learning. Note the sequence of this instructional format in Box 10.3.

The inductive approach was formalized into a teaching cycle called the Learning Cycle [Science Curriculum Improvement Study (SCIS), 1974], originally intended for use in elementary school science instruction. The method has been used and researched at many levels, including the middle, high school, and college level. Results have shown that the Learning Cycle promotes inquiry and perhaps intellectual development (Fuller, 1980; Renner et al., 1985). The Learning Cycle has three phases: exploration, invention, and application. As you read the

Classroom Snapshot 10.3

An Inductive Activity

Mrs. Talbert often initiates the study of a topic with an inductive activity in order to stimulate student thinking and to establish a concrete reference for understanding the principle under study. For example, she begins the study of ocean currents with a laboratory exercise that has students examine the movement of colored solutions, each with a different density, as they mix with tap water. Mrs. Talbert gives each lab group a set of the following solutions:

1. A blue solution of tap water
2. A green solution that is partially saturated with salt
3. A red solution that is saturated with salt

Mrs. Talbert directs her students to carefully pour each of the colored solutions into a separate beaker of clear tap water and observe the movement of the solutions as they mix. She does not tell students that the colored solutions are of different densities. After the students have made their observations and attempted to explain how the colored solutions mix with the tap water, the teacher initiates a discussion about ocean currents and the density of salt water. She places key terms on the board, calling students' attention to the science behind the differential mixing of solutions. This is followed by sending the students back to the lab tables to prepare salt solutions of different densities, adding food coloring and observing what occurs when they are poured into plain water. In addition, Mrs. Talbert asks students to indicate where in the science classroom the air-conditioned cold air moves when it is forced out of the ventilation ducts located near the ceiling. Then, the class discusses the density of cold and warm air masses and how it relates to weather conditions.

explanation for these phases, locate their use by Mrs. Talbert in the vignette given in Box 10.3.

Exploration

The exploration phase allows students to experience objects and events in order to stimulate their thinking about a concept or principle; students are engaged in activities that permit them to discover patterns and relationships. During this phase, students are given some guidance to keep them focused on the learning task. Questions are posed and cues are given to channel thinking. However, students are not given answers or labels.

Invention

The invention phase allows students to determine relationships between objects and events that they have experienced. Initially, the teacher serves as a guide to channel thinking, encouraging students to construct appropriate labels for the relationships they have just discovered. Then, the teacher provides key terms to explain the concept under study.

Application

The application phase allows students to apply their knowledge of a given concept or principle. The teacher encourages the students to find (discover or inquire into) examples to illustrate the concept they have just experienced. In addition, the ideas are discussed as to

their application in everyday life. This phase permits students to generalize their learning, thus reinforcing newly acquired knowledge.

The three-phase learning cycle has been expanded to a five-phase approach to science inquiry, called the 5E Instructional Model (Trowbridge & Bybee, 1996). This strategy incorporates more instruction than the learning cycle; therefore, it engages students in more learning opportunities. Study Figure 10.3 for a summary of the 5E Instructional Model's phases, which are: engagement, exploration, explanation, elaboration, and evaluation.

Deductive Activities

In contrast to the inductive approach, the deductive approach is used often in science courses. It is the traditional lecture/laboratory sequence with which most science majors are familiar. This strategy is commonly observed in middle school through college science teaching. With the deductive strategy, a concept or principle is defined and discussed using appropriate labels and terms, followed by experiences to illustrate the idea. The deductive approach is a vocabulary-before-experience model of teaching where lecture and discussion precede firsthand or concrete experiences. It can also involve hypothetical-deductive thinking, whereby the learner generates ideas to be tested or discovered or the teacher makes explicit what it is the students should be looking for in the laboratory or field.

FIGURE 10.3   The 5E Instructional Model for engaging students in inquiry-based instruction.

Engagement

Introduce students to the concept or topic under study. Pique their interest. Determine what the students know about the topic and motivate them to learn more about it. Give the learners a good sense for what they will be studying without telling them too much about the ideas or subject matter to be learned. Stimulate interest to the point that students might say: "I would like to find out more."

Exploration

Design an instructional event that gives students concrete experiences with the key concepts or principles of the topic. Guide their thinking toward the attributes and patterns of the phenomenon, which should be evident from their firsthand experiences. Ask students to carefully record what they see and to organize their data/information.

Explanation

Call on students to describe their experiences and findings. Ask for deep reasoning by encouraging them to explain what they have found. Provide plenty of time for discussion before presenting the scientific labels and terms for the ideas under study. Build from students' findings toward defining, describing, and explaining the concepts that are the focus of the investigation.

Elaboration

Give students more instruction so that they might form rich connections with what they know and what they are expected to learn. Implement many instructional strategies and learning techniques to expand and reinforce learning. In addition, show applications of the concepts and principles, especially as they pertain to everyday living.

Evaluation

Assess what students are learning at many points during the instruction to determine how well they are grasping main ideas. Solicit oral and written responses to gauge learning. Conclude the five-phase instructional cycle with an assessment to measure how well students have mastered the instructional objectives of the mini-unit or major unit of study.

Consider the intent to teach part of an acid-base unit using the deductive approach. The instruction might begin with a discussion of acids and a bases—their properties, occurrence in everyday life, pH, and indicators. This might be followed by a laboratory activity to classify solutions as either acid or base, and to order them according to their pH. This deductive activity would conclude with a postlaboratory discussion of students' findings and their comprehension of the content under study.

Gathering Information

Scientific inquiry includes more than constructing knowledge through hands-on activities. Laboratory work and hands-on activities are not the only ways in which scientists and others expand their knowledge. A great deal of the inquiry that scientists and engineers carry out involves reading and conversing with others. Many of these professionals probably spend more time gathering ideas and information from literature sources and other people than they spend in their laboratory.

Science teachers must encourage students at many points during the inquiry process to obtain information from a variety of sources. Information gathering can occur during the application phase of the learning cycle, for example, when students are assigned to read about a topic. Reading articles and reading the textbook may be appropriate at this point because the students have had firsthand experiences from which to relate. In other instances, the teacher may ask students to bring in newspaper clippings on a topic or to search the Internet for information.

Reading Printed Material

Newspapers and magazines are rich sources of information for students to improve their scientific knowledge. A science course requirement might require students to cut out or photocopy articles and organize them into a notebook. Another technique to improve knowledge and understanding of a given topic is to require a short written report. These reports can be compiled from a single source or a few sources. When long reports are desired, students should be required to use a variety of sources for their write-up, such as newspapers, textbooks, magazines, encyclopedias, journals, and the Internet. Students can research information in their home, the school library, and the public library. They should be taught how to cite information sources in their reports. Effective science teachers require information gathering throughout the school year, but they are careful not to burden students with this type of work.

Assignments of this nature are not always successful because of lack of student motivation and competence. Therefore, some science teachers identify topics they are familiar with before giving the assignment to students. They arrange topics on 3-by-5-inch index cards, and along with a topic title, they list appropriate literature sources that are readily available to the students. Also, there may be duplicate index cards with the same topic title, because there may exist a limited number of topics that can be researched on a given subject for a class of 30 students. Using this approach, students are guided during their information-gathering experiences. However, as students gain more experience and competence with this procedure, they require less direction and guidance.

Seeking Information from Individuals

People are a rich source of information and ideas. They can explain concepts to teenagers and improve their understanding of these ideas, often better than a textbook or science classroom explanation can. Older siblings, parents, aunts, uncles, pharmacists, lawyers, nurses, doctors, firefighters, engineers, construction workers, electricians, bakers, mechanics, coaches, musicians, and florists are among those with whom science students can interact to learn more about a topic. These people are often willing to spend time with young people to explain how something works or to clarify ideas and concepts.

Inquiry techniques that engage students in gathering the opinions of others are an excellent way for students to find out what others believe about issues and problems. This approach also can teach students how to develop questionnaires and survey instruments. Furthermore, this is an excellent way to make science relevant and to illustrate its relationship to society.

Accessing Information from the Internet

The Internet is one of the great human inventions of the 20th century. This electronic network is an almost infinite source of information that is at the fingertips of anyone using a personal computer. The Internet consists of massive quantities of information available electronically from locations across the globe. It also provides access to people through e-mail and chat rooms. This gigantic electronic network is giving information a new meaning. Most university scientists and science departments are on the Internet, as are exploratoriums, museums, planetariums, zoos, and government research facilities. Many people and sites will respond to inquiries pertaining to science. In addition, these facilities offer instructional materials that can be downloaded to personal computers. Many well-known Web site address are given at the end of this chapter in the Resources to Examine section.

Problem Solving

The problem-solving approach to science instruction has the potential to engage students in authentic investigations, develop their inquiry skills, and lead to a firmer understanding of the content under study. This strategy can give students a feeling for conducting scientific inquiry. Problem solving can also make science course learning more meaningful for teenagers (Box 10.4).

Problem solving is often used synonymously with inquiry and science process skill reasoning (Helgeson, 1989, 1994). As such, this concept is associated with the nature of scientific inquiry as well as instructional methodology. The problem solving that will be addressed in this section involves situations that are relevant to students' lives and raise their doubt or uncertainty (Dewey, 1938). This type of problem solving often engages students in investigations where they *raise questions, plan procedures, collect information,* and *form conclusions.* These learning experiences can be short in duration or long, taking up to several months to complete. This approach is not the sort of activity that directs students to answer questions at the end of the textbook chapter or to substitute numbers into a formula to compute an answer.

Science Projects

Science projects are learning activities that require many hours of student involvement. They take place over many weeks and even months. Some science projects reflect "true" inquiry whereby students identify a topic to study, propose questions to be answered, designate procedures for carrying out a project, gather information and data, present the results, and form the conclusions. These projects entail a great deal of effort on the part of students, as well as guidance from teachers and parents. A science project can be undertaken individually, by a pair of students, by a group of students, or by an entire class. Science projects should be a common component of all science courses, whether or not they are tied to a science fair competition. Figure 10.4 lists the titles of many science fair projects.

Classroom Snapshot 10.4

Problem Solving

Mrs. Daniel teaches seventh-grade life science in a neighborhood where many blue-collar families live. Part of the curriculum includes topics on nutrition and exercise. Mrs. Daniel begins the study of nutrition and exercise by referring to the bulletin board at the back of the room where the pictures of many teenage models, movie stars, and athletes are displayed. The students are attracted to these pictures and like to identify with the people in them. Mrs. Daniel poses the following question:

How do these people get to be where they are in life?

This question brings responses from everyone in the class. Students have many opinions regarding fame and success, and they are willing to express these ideas freely. During the discussion, invariably someone will mention diet and exercise. The teacher then probes to find out what the students believe regarding a good diet and the diet of these famous people. Mrs. Daniel asks:

Do you have the same diet as some of these famous people?

This question leads to a great deal of uncertainty and many different opinions regarding what fashion models, bodybuilders, and soccer players eat. Consequently, one of the first investigations that the students undertake is to keep a record of what they eat. They arrange this information so that the number of calories consumed and the percentages of fat, proteins, and carbohydrates in their diet are clearly displayed. A food diary is kept for at least 3 weeks by every student.

While the students are keeping their own nutritional diary, they are asked to inquire about the dietary needs and recommendations for young people, adults, and athletes. The students use the school and city library to gather this information. They also ask people in the community for information regarding the topic. Some of the students interview nurses, dietitians, physical therapists, coaches, bodybuilders, football players, and doctors. The students are required to present the information and its source. Tables and bar graphs are used in the reports.

The results are always startling to the students when they compare the nutritional balance in their diet with what professionals recommend. The students eat a great deal more carbohydrates and fats than is recommended by nutritionists. These young people find it a bit unsettling to learn that their diets are so high in sugars and fats. Many of the boys in the class are shocked to learn about the diets of bodybuilders who consume many calories, yet have very little body fat. Further, the students did not realize how many grams of protein bodybuilders consume each day. These activities lead many of the students to reconsider what they are eating and change their eating habits. As a result of these discussions, many of the food diaries of the students from this point on present a different pattern of eating than at the beginning of the unit.

FIGURE 10.4   Examples of titles for science fair projects or long-term science investigations.

The Effects of Electricity on Seed Germination	Bugs That Eat Oil
Electromagnetic Radiation and Bacterial Growth	Aerodynamics and Automobile Design
The Study of Oral Bacteria	Which Flashlight Batteries Last the Longest?
Does Music Affect Memory?	Light and Photography
Fluoride in Your Water	What Variables Contribute to the Strength of an
How Does Food Spoil?	Electromagnet?
Antioxidants and Your Health	What Does UV Radiation Do to Organic and
Pheromones and Ant Behavior	Inorganic Materials?
How Much Bacteria Is on Your Kitchen Dishrag?	Determining the Viscosity of Lubricants
The Association Between Alzheimer's Disease	How Does Acid Rain Affect the Growth of
and Aluminum	Plants?
Do We Need Food Additives?	Effects of Waves on Beaches

In many schools, students are encouraged to complete a project for a science fair. These are big events for science teachers, students, parents, and members of the community. Science fairs stimulate enormous interest in science. They provide students with incentives to study problems in depth and to communicate their findings. Further, they give students an opportunity to pursue investigations that they would not ordinarily be able to carry out during regular science class periods because of limitations on equipment, space, and time. In addition to identifying the gifted science students, these events encourage all students to get involved in inquiry and to design products. Science fairs not only display the talents and interests of students, but they also reveal the orientation of a school's science program, the type of science teaching that is occurring, and the type of students in the school.

Science fair projects can take many forms. The following are descriptions of activities that make good science projects:

1. **Hobby or pet show-and-tell:** A display of items of special interest to the student, such as arrowheads; seashells; photographs of cats, dogs, or horses; bee hives, and so on.

2. **Display of a natural phenomenon:** Pictures and descriptions of lightning, a volcano, an earthquake, a hurricane, a tornado, and so on.

3. **Model:** A three-dimensional model of a volcano, a brain, a heart, an internal combustion engine, a rocket, a space station, a 35 mm camera, the solar system, and so on.

4. **Report and poster:** Photographs and pictures of objects with explanations and information taken from literature sources on such topics as nuclear power, HIV infection, movement of the earth's continental plates, how a computer works, living in space, a rain forest habitat, a biome, and so on.

5. **Laboratory exercise:** The presentation of a laboratory exercise that illustrates a concept, principle, or law such as the frequencies of a pendulum, osmosis, crushing metal cans with air pressure, chemical and physical properties of acids and bases, behavior of light rays, determination of electrical current and resistance, and so on.

6. **Observational study:** Extensive observations of a situation or phenomenon and reporting the findings, such as bird counting, whale reporting, weather conditions and patterns, driving behavior and accidents at a busy intersection, changes in ozone levels and pollution counts in an urban area, and so on.

7. **Experimental study:** Manipulating a situation and determining the results of the intervention, such as the effects of fertilizer on plant growth, temperature on food spoiling, moisture on the amount of corrosion, and so on.

There are many types of science projects that students can complete, but not all students are capable of carrying out all of these projects. Some projects require much less imagination, intellectual ability, and adult guidance. When grading these projects for a course grade or judging them in a fair competition, it is best to form separate project categories because they should not be evaluated together. One cannot judge a model with the same criteria used to judge an experimental study. This should be evident from the following categories and points that are often used to judge experimental science projects:

- Creativity (20)
- Investigative procedure (30)
- Understanding of the topic (20)
- Quality of the display (15)
- Oral presentation (15)

Although experimental projects are a good way to promote inquiry, discretion must be used in determining what each student can accomplish, considering the resources that are available and the assistance from adults. Many at-risk students come from one-parent families with very low incomes. Generally, these students do not have the resources available to compete with students whose parents are professionals. In any case, science teachers should help students learn about the content of the investigation before they undertake setting up their experiments. Process without content can become a meaningless activity.

GROUPING AND COOPERATIVE LEARNING

Placing students in groups to work on a problem or to conduct an investigation is a practice supported by research findings as well as observations of classrooms of effective science teachers. The dynamics of group work can stimulate and sustain inquiry in many situations better than individual work. Not only can group work enhance student problem-solving ability, but it can improve concept development (Lumpe, 1995). Students find a great deal of meaning in science courses when their knowledge is constructed during productive, small, cooperative group activities.

Effective science teachers often group students and assign them tasks in order to facilitate inquiry-based learning. This approach seems to increase student involvement in the learning environment. When students have a specific task to carry out, they seem to have more direction and interest in their own learning. Grouping and role techniques are useful management strategies that change the role of the teacher from a dispenser of information to a manager of student-directed learning in which students tend to be more productive with fewer behavioral problems.

Grouping and assigning roles facilitate cooperative learning and hold the potential to result in important learning outcomes. For example, permitting students to work in groups to solve problems can promote scientific inquiry and develop in students a feeling for "doing" science. Cooperative learning can improve achievement and mastery of content (Slavin, 1989/1990). This approach also can develop team-building and a positive classroom environment (Kagan, 1989/1990), especially at the higher cognitive levels (Chang & Mao, 1999). Cooperative learning, as its name implies, gets students to work together, eliminating some of the competitiveness and isolation that can exist in most academic environments.

A variety of roles can be assigned to students working in small groups. Following is a list of roles commonly assigned by science teachers to facilitate group work:

- **Leader** who organizes and keeps the investigation moving
- **Manager** who gathers and maintains materials and equipment
- **Recorder** who records data and seeks information
- **Reporter** who prepares the written report

Cooperative instruction can take many forms with no set number of steps to follow. Nevertheless, the following steps are discussed to highlight important aspects of this strategy.

STEP 1   Organize students into groups, using criteria to make decisions regarding this process. Determine the desired cognitive and affective outcomes for the investigation, then place students into groups accordingly. For example, if you wish to assign tasks to individual students, identify students in each group who can carry out a particular task and who also work well together with others in the group.

STEP 2   Identify ideas or topics that will motivate student inquiry. Some science teachers provide a preliminary list of ideas for their students that relates to the course unit. However, this approach should also encourage brainstorming in order to identify additional ideas for student investigation. Group problem solving can focus on many ideas such as science concepts or principles, science topics, Science, Technology, Society (STS) issues and problems, products and services, and technological devices.

STEP 3   Ask each group to provide a preliminary outline of their project or study. This step immediately places students on a productive path. When you examine the outline, provide suggestions and guidance. Be sure each student in the group knows exactly what to do.

STEP 4   Monitor the investigations. You should have a good idea of where each group is while the investigations are carried out. Some inquiries and projects will be conducted during class time, making them easy to monitor. Other investigations will take place after school and on weekends. For this type of work, take some time during class to ask for information to determine how groups as well as individuals are progressing.

STEP 5   Help students to prepare their final reports so that they do well and feel good about their work. Provide guidance in organizing an outline for the reports and designate who will write certain sections of the report. The report is an opportunity for students to demonstrate their science process skill reasoning through the questions they attempt to answer, the inferences and hypotheses they form, and the tables and graphs they construct to communicate their findings. This phase of the work is ideal for helping students represent knowledge, visualize models, give explanations, and demonstrate understanding.

STEP 6   Assist each group to identify several, if not all, students to take part in presenting their report. This aspect of cooperative group work develops presentation skills and confidence in speaking before others. Try to avoid the same students making all of the presentations.

STEP 7   Evaluate the investigations and projects. This often takes the form of assigning points to groups and individual students and entering them into the grade book. Generally, students put a great deal of effort into the activities, and they should be rewarded accordingly.

Unfortunately, successful cooperative group instruction does not just happen according to the formula. The ability, maturity, and discipline of the students are big factors regarding how well the strategy will work. Therefore, you must think carefully about who is placed in each group. Since the leader is key to the productivity and success of a team, select students who can motivate and guide their peers in carrying out tasks. These individuals must have negotiating skills to keep fellow students on task and complete the project on time.

Managers should be students who like to build things and gather materials. They are individuals who enjoy being physically active and working with their hands. Many of these students will go all out to find equipment and bring it school or build projects at home. Often, these students get help from their parents. Recorders must be active in keeping track of group activities—taking notes and recording data. They must be responsible individuals who will stay focused on their group's activities. Reporters must be students who have the maturity and skills to organize and prepare most of the report. While they do not have to write all of the report, they usually do the bulk of the project presentation. These students should be able to use word processing and even PowerPoint programs.

CONCERNS ASSOCIATED WITH INQUIRY–BASED INSTRUCTION

In order for science teachers to make the transition from a traditional mode of instruction to an inquiry-based mode, they must better understand scientific inquiry and its relationship to science teaching. This understanding will permit them to construct a personal rationale to justify the inquiry approach to themselves, other science teachers, administrators, and parents. An understanding of inquiry—its conception and strategies—also is necessary so that inquiry-based science can be adapted to the large differences among students and schools. The challenge that faces science teachers is to understand the meaning of general inquiry, scientific inquiry, teaching science *by* inquiry, and teaching science *as* inquiry, and in particular the content/process emphasis most appropriate for a given group of students.

There are many concerns associated with inquiry-based science teaching. Science teachers must be aware of these concerns as they move toward teaching science and inquiry:

1. **Understanding.**   Science teachers must develop a clear conception of inquiry-based science and be able to explain it to administrators and parents. This conception should show how content and process are balanced to provide educational outcomes that support the scientific literacy goals of the school, district, state, and nation.
2. **Time.**   Investigative science instruction does require more time than teaching science solely as a body of knowledge. Inquiry-based instruction requires more time to plan and far more time to conduct than traditional instruction. Those using the inquiry approach must know how much time to invest in laboratory and field experiences to help students master critical content and to appreciate the way scientific knowledge is constructed.
3. **Materials and Equipment.**   Activity-oriented and hands-on experiences require materials and equipment. These items must be gathered together, purchased, or constructed by teachers, which requires a large commitment of time and effort as well as money. Science teachers should know how much money is allocated to their

school's science budget and become active in using the money to promote an activity-oriented science program. Further, they should try to increase the budget for science, purchasing equipment that will be used frequently to support student inquiry.

4. **Facilities.**   Teaching facilities that accommodate hands-on activities, group work, student movement, and storing projects are important to inquiry-based instruction. Many schools lack good science facilities, making it difficult to teach large classes of students in an activity-oriented mode of instruction. Teachers must employ a great deal of creativity to arrange the learning environment in order for students to become active learners.
5. **Learning Science Terms.**   Yes, science terms and vocabulary are import to all students' science education. Names give meaning to concepts and are essential for good communication. However, students do not always have to be given the terms and vocabulary words at the beginning of a teaching session. Sometimes, they can be given an exercise that provides concrete experiences using common nonscientific terms, which at a later time in the instructional sequence will make the introduction of scientific terms more meaningful. The inductive approach—experience before vocabulary—should be used, rather than the deductive approach—vocabulary before experience.
6. **Hands-on Activities.**   Hands-on activities hold the potential to actively engage students in learning science. However, these activities do not ensure that students are learning the knowledge and skills under study. While students may seem busy and engaged, their minds may be on matters other than gaining new knowledge and skills. Consequently, it is essential that the teacher make explicit, at many points during instruction, what students should be learning.
7. **Covering the Curriculum.**   Science teachers often voice concern about covering the curriculum. They indicate that the district or the state requires them to cover too much content and there is not time for inquiry instruction. Remember, there are at least four ways to view inquiry-based instruction. Two of the approaches discussed, content and content with process, focus on learning science subject matter. However, inquiry teaching is more than methods, approaches, and techniques. A major purpose is aimed at encouraging students to "wonder why" and to "want to find out more."
8. **Discipline.**   There always exists the possibility for students to misbehave when they are given

freedom to move around in a laboratory setting or to work in small groups. Considerable planning, structure, and rules must accompany investigations that permit students to get out of their seats and move around the classroom, laboratory, and areas in and around the school. Science teachers can withhold activities from students who misbehave. This often sends a message to students that they must behave in an orderly manner and that they must be productive if they desire to engage in interesting inquiry-oriented activities.

9. **Colleagues.**   Often, the biggest road blocks to inquiry-based instruction are the science teachers who primarily teach science as a body of knowledge and who have been doing this for many years. Experienced science teachers often are resistant to change. They are comfortable with lecture, one lab a week, "drill and kill" review sheets, and paper-and-pencil testing. Further, some teachers' students do very well on state and national examinations without the benefit of inquiry instruction. Why should they change to a more student-centered, minds-on approach that requires more work?

10. **Administrators.**   Many school building principals and assistant principals like to see quiet, orderly classrooms. They react negatively to noise coming from classrooms and view this situation as a lack of teacher control. In addition, many administrators are interested in how well students perform on standardized science tests and support teacher-directed methods of instruction that will improve test scores. Science teachers must discuss their teaching philosophies and classroom activities with administrators in order to determine how these educators view the goals of the curriculum and the methods of attaining these goals.

11. **Parents.**   Parents want their children to do well in school, and many desire for their children to be prepared well for college. Many of these adults identify with textbook-driven science courses and with teacher-assigned homework that can be completed by finding answers to questions stated at the end of the chapter. These parents are uncomfortable with schooling that deviates from what they were used to in their formal education.

Assessing and Reviewing

Analysis and Syntheses

1. Demonstrate your understanding of inquiry and science teaching by *explaining* the following concepts:
   a. Inquiry in general
   b. Scientific inquiry
   c. Teaching science by inquiry
   d. Teaching science as inquiry
   e. Discrepant events
   f. Science process skills
   g. Inductive activities
   h. Deductive activities
   i. Gathering information
   j. Problem solving
   k. Science fair projects

2. Reflect upon the science and nonscience courses that you have taken, the science and education courses in which you are presently enrolled, and the science courses that you may be observing in public schools. Indicate which of these courses were or are inquiry-based and which are not. Further, explain the type of instructional strategies that were used and whether the courses taught or teach science *by* inquiry and science *as* inquiry.

3. Conduct an analysis of laboratory exercises and other science instructional materials in order to determine the type of inquiry strategies emphasized and the extent to which they engage students in a given approach.

4. Organize a file of instructional activities that can be used to teach science *by* and *as* inquiry in your teaching area (i.e., life science, earth science, physics). These activities can be found in science textbooks, paperback books, and laboratory manuals. Some of the best inquiry-oriented activities will come to mind, however, when you reflect upon what takes place in your everyday surroundings.

5. Obtain your own professional library textbooks, paperback books, magazines, journals, manuals, Internet sites, and so on that they can provide ideas for inquiry sessions. These materials are good sources for discrepant events, problem solving, and inductive activities.

6. Plan and teach an inquiry lesson to your peers or to middle school or senior high school students that emphasizes one or more ways to initiate and carry out inquiry instruction: process skills,

discrepant events, inductive activities, deductive activities, and problem solving. Participate in the critique and feedback of this teaching session with others.

7. Develop an inquiry activity that uses grouping, role assignments, and cooperative learning. Try out your activity with peers or middle or high school students to determine the effectiveness of this technique.

RESOURCES TO EXAMINE

"Inquiry-Based Instruction: Understanding How Content and Process go Hand-in-Hand with School Science." February 2004. *The Science Teacher*, 46–50.

The article by Chiappetta and Adams supplements the discussion of the relationships among science content, process, and teaching science found in this chapter. However, it goes further by giving four approaches to inquiry-based instruction with different science content/process emphases— content, content with process, process with content, and process. The context for each example is the topic of browning or oxidation of fruit that has been bruised.

Inquiry and the National Science Education Standards: A Guide for Teaching and Learning. 2000. Washington, DC: National Academy Press.

This NRC paperback offers many useful examples of how to implement inquiry-based instruction in classrooms from elementary through high school. There is a useful chapter on preparing teachers for inquiry-based teaching. The chapters on frequently asked questions about inquiry and supporting inquiry-based teaching and learning also are informative.

The Current NSTA Catalog for Membership and Publications. National Science Teachers Association. 1840 Wilson Boulevard, Arlington, VA 22201-3000. Phone (800)722-NSTA. http//www.nsta.org.

This catalog contains hundreds of booklets, teaching guides, and resources for science teaching in grades K–12. These materials address the major science disciplines, providing background information as well as inquiry-oriented activities. All science teachers should possess this publication and be a member of the National Science Teachers Association.

Exploratorium: The Museum of Science, Art, and Human Perception. [On-line.] Available: http://www.exploratorium.edu.

The Exploratorium in San Francisco is an exceptional resource for science teachers and

students. It has information and interactive on-line instruction to enhance science learning. Some of the topics that can be explored are the science of music, sports science, the solar system, origin of the universe, and microorganisms. The programs pose interesting questions about science phenomena and technological devices, and then provide the learner with experiences to answer the questions.

The JASON Project. [On-line.] Available: httl://www.jasonproject.org.

The Project began with the adventures of Robert Ballard who discovered the shipwreck of the RMS *Titanic.* Today, it offers teachers and students many exciting educational programs to advance science literacy. You can go on expeditions to wetlands, rain forests, and seashore when you log on to the site. The Project offers videos, articles, research expeditions, and so on.

The Complete Handbook of Science Fair Projects. 1991. New York: Wiley Science Editions/John Wiley & Sons.

This paperback by Bochinski contains 50 award-winning projects from actual fairs. It describes in detail the projects, plus it has hundreds of other suggested topics for students to investigate. The explanations and illustrations make this a valuable and easy-to-follow resource for science teachers or their students to use.

Inquiring into Inquiry Learning and Teaching Science. 2000. Washington, DC: American Association for the Advancement of Science.

Minstrell and van Zee edited this very informative paperback book about inquiry, covering many aspects of this key reform idea. The book has 32 chapters addressing many aspects of school science and inquiry teaching and learning. The three main sections of the text are titled as follows: Why Inquiry?, What Does Inquiry Look Like?, and What Issues Arise with Inquiry Learning and Teaching? This is a resource that all science educators should have in their professional libraries.

REFERENCES

American Association for the Advancement of Science (AAAS). (1990). *Science for all Americans.* New York: Oxford University Press.

American Association for the Advancement of Science (AAAS). (1993). *Benchmarks for Science Literacy.* New York: Oxford University Press.

Biological Sciences Curriculum Study (BSCS). (1978). *Biology teacher's handbook.* New York: John Wiley & Sons.

Bruner, J. (1961). The act of discovery. *Harvard Educational Review, 31*(1), 21.

Chang, C-Y., & Mao, S-L. (1999). The effects on students' cognitive achievement when using the cooperative learning method in earth science classrooms. *School Science and Mathematics, 99,* 374–380.

Dewey, J. (1938). *Experience and education.* New York: Macmillan.

Fuller, R. G. (1980). *Piagetian problems in higher education.* Lincoln: ADAPT, University of Nebraska.

Helgeson, S. L. (1989). Problem solving in middle school science. In D. Gabel (Ed.), *What research says to the science teacher: Vol. 5. Problem solving* (pp. 13–34). Washington, DC: National Science Teachers Association.

Helgeson, S. L. (1994). Research on problem solving in middle school. In D. L. Gabel (Ed.), *Handbook of research on science teaching and learning* (pp. 248–268). Upper Saddle River, NJ: Merrill/Prentice Hall.

Kagan, S. (1989/1990). The structural approach to cooperative learning. *Educational Leadership, 47*(4), 2–16.

Lumpe, A. T. (1995). Peer interaction in science concept development and problem solving. *School Science and Mathematics, 96,* 302–309.

National Research Council (NRC). (1996). *National science education standards.* Washington, DC: National Academy Press.

Piaget, J. (1971). *Biology and knowledge.* Chicago: University of Chicago Press.

Renner, J. W., Cate, J. M., Grzybowski, E. B., Atkinson, L. J., Surber, C., & Marek, E. A. (1985). *Investigation in natural science: Biology teacher's guide.* Norman: Science Education Center, College of Education, University of Oklahoma.

Schwab, J. (1962). The te¬aching of science as enquiry. In J. Schwab & P. Brandwein (Eds.), *The teaching of science.* Cambridge: Harvard University Press.

Slavin, R. E. (1989/1990). Research on cooperative learning: Consensus and controversy. *Educational Leadership, 47*(4), 52–54.

Suchman, R. (1966). *Developing inquiry.* Chicago: Science Research Associates.

Trowbridge, L. W., & Bybee, R. W. (1996). *Teaching secondary school science.* Upper Saddle River, NJ: Merrill-Prentice Hall.

11

Discussion, Demonstration, and Lecture

Demonstrations are one of several instructional strategies that science teachers should master.

Discussion, demonstration, and lecture are methods of instruction that play an important role in middle and secondary science classrooms. These instructional strategies tend to be teacher-centered, but this does not have to be the case if they are planned with students in mind. Constructivist theory suggests that the meaning students construct from science discussions, demonstrations, and lectures is affected not only by the teacher but also by their prior knowledge and experiences and their interactions with other students and instructional materials. It also is known that unanticipated learning is likely if the students' perceptions of the purpose of the lesson and those of the teacher do not coincide. It is clear that the effectiveness of each method depends on the teacher's ability to use it appropriately and to relate it to the overall science instructional program and the needs of students.

AIMS OF THE CHAPTER

Use the questions that follow to guide your thinking and learning about important understandings related to the instructional approaches of discussion, demonstration, and lecture:

- What discussion approaches can be used to encourage students' science learning? What procedures may a science teacher use to lead meaningful discussions?

- What factors should a science teacher consider when planning and presenting demonstrations to promote student learning?

- When should a lecture be used to facilitate students' learning of science? How can a science teacher prepare for and present an effective lecture?

- How can oral questions and verbal interaction strategies be used to stimulate students' science learning during discussions, demonstrations, and lectures?

DISCUSSION

Classroom discussion is one of the most powerful strategies that a teacher can use to facilitate cognitive and affective development in students. A true discussion involves the free expression of viewpoints by the teacher and students about a topic that all are interested in and about which all possess the background knowledge needed to make contributions. Unfortunately, some science teachers may use the term *discussion* when they are engaged in almost any type of verbal interaction with their students. For example, when a teacher says, "We will now discuss the topic of population growth," she may really mean, "I am going to ask you questions about what you read in your textbook about the topic of population growth."

Two notable aspects of the work of Russian psychologist Vygotsky provide support for the use of discussion as an instructional method in science classes (Goldenberg, 1992). The first is the idea that students are most likely to benefit from participating in discussions when they are in their zone of proximal development. Students are in the "zone" when they possess a sufficient understanding of the topic to contribute meaningfully to the discussion and comprehend the contributions of others. The second is the emphasis placed on language by Vygotsky as a medium for intellectual development. The scaffolding provided by the teacher during a discussion when students are in their zone of proximal development and the reliance on oral language during a discussion serve to facilitate students' construction of science understandings.

Discussion Types

Kindsvatter, Witen, and Ishler (1996) identify two discussion types and one "quasi-discussion" type that can be used by science teachers: guided discussion, reflective discussion, and recitation. They apply the characteristics of purpose, structure, interaction pattern, and the level of student thinking to distinguish among these different types. Recitation is labeled as "quasi-discussion" because it lacks the element of group conversation that characterizes true discussion.

Recitation

A recitation has much in common with a TV quiz show (Roby, 1988). During a recitation, the teacher asks a series of questions and the students provide the answers. The questions are based on what students have read in their textbook or that which has been presented by the teacher during class. The interaction pattern of a recitation is teacher question–student answer–teacher reaction (Wilen, 1990). The purpose of a recitation is for the teacher to determine whether students have learned what was presented in the textbook, lecture, or other assigned material.

The success of recitation sessions depends to a large degree on the quality of the questions asked by the teacher. Unfortunately, the questions asked during most recitations tend to be low level. "How many chambers are there in the human heart?" and "What are three symptoms of tuberculosis?" are typical of these low-level questions. Questions asked during recitations could, but normally do not, invite students to demonstrate their understanding or ability to apply what has been learned (Kindsvatter et al., 1996, p. 239). Too often, recitation periods become sessions of review and drill in which few students participate and many sit quietly without making any contributions. For this reason, both volunteers and nonvolunteers should be questioned.

Recitations are generally fast paced and tend to require less time than most other instructional methods. To maintain the flow of a recitation, teachers should limit the active participation to one or two students at a time and should not permit questioning to drag or student answers to become too involved and lengthy. Additionally, questions should be prepared in advance and sequenced in the order in which they will be asked.

Guided Discussion

Science teachers can use guided discussion to help students construct for themselves the science knowledge that scientists have already determined and agreed upon. Important for the success of a guided discussion is that students have basic knowledge of the idea or topic to be discussed. Student preparedness to engage in a guided discussion may be determined through a recitation.

Guided discussion differs from recitation in terms of the teacher–student interaction pattern and the types of questions asked. The teacher is the interaction leader and primary questioner, but the interaction pattern is more varied and flexible than that of a recitation (Wilen, 1990). Two or more students may respond to a single question during a guided discussion, and the teacher need not react to each student's answer. In some instances, students may ask questions of the teacher or classmates to extend an explanation or clarify something that was said. The pace of a guided discussion is slower than that of a recitation, fewer questions are asked, and students are typically given time to think about questions asked and to formulate answers before responding.

The questions asked during a guided discussion aim at a higher cognitive level and are broader than those asked during a recitation. They require students to interpret, explain, apply, illustrate, generalize, and conclude (Wilen, 1990). "How does the Gram stain help a physician prescribe treatment for a bacterial infection?" and "What evidence suggests that plants evolved from green algae?" are examples of the types of questions asked during a guided discussion. Responses to questions may vary, as the students come to the discussion with their own personal theories about the idea or topic under consideration.

Reflective Discussion

The centerpiece of reflective discussion, or true discussion, is the open expression of ideas. The discussions that are featured on a number of nightly news programs have much in common with the reflective discussions that go on in science classes. If you have ever watched one of these news programs, you know that after acquainting the TV audience with the evening's topic or issue and introducing the guests, the moderator asks a question to get the discussion rolling. From that point on, he or she moderates the discussion and asks questions only when further explanation or clarification is required.

Controversial issues on which persons take a stand make excellent subjects for these news programs and for reflective discussions in science classes. In science classes, the issues may deal with matters of current interest such as evolution, AIDS, genetic engineering, nuclear testing, and others. Reflective science discussions may also center on questions that require problem-solving skills to answer. Questions such as the following may serve this purpose well: (1) Some people believe that all complex behaviors are learned, while others believe that many behaviors are inherited. Which position do you support and why? (2) Sedimentary rocks can be distinguished from other classes of rocks on the basis of bedding, color, fossils, ease of breakage, and porosity. Which do you believe are the poorest criteria to use as distinguishing characteristics and why? Excellent reflective discussions may also center on conflicting laboratory data. Topics that are concerned with indisputable facts, while stock-in-trade for recitations, are not suitable either for news programs or for reflective discussion in science classes.

In science class, the purpose of reflective discussion is to challenge students to think critically and creatively at the highest cognitive levels and to consider their personal beliefs, attitudes, and values (Kindsvatter et al., 1996; Wilen, 1990). During a reflective discussion, a science student may help resolve a problem of local water pollution or state and defend his or her position regarding euthanasia. Characteristics associated with reflective discussion include the use of complex thinking processes, students holding leadership responsibility, and belief and attitude change (Gall & Gall, 1976).

No recognizable interaction pattern is associated with the reflective discussion. The discussion is initiated by a question from the teacher who, much like the news program's moderator, functions thereafter to facilitate the discussion. The question must be carefully worded to trigger original and evaluative thinking on the part of students (Kindsvatter et al., 1996). Reflective discussion is slow paced, and student responses tend to be quite lengthy. The momentum of the discussion is not maintained by a series of teacher questions, but by students asking questions of each other and statements contributed both by the teachers and students and student questions (Dillon, 1990).

Unlike recitation and guided discussion, participation by all students is not critical to the success of a reflective discussion. Students whose thoughts on the topic or issue under consideration are not well formulated may choose just to listen. As is true for guided discussion, however, the success of the reflective discussion rests on student interest and background knowledge. If background knowledge is lacking, the discussion becomes what Roby (1988, p. 170) called a bull session, where "participants ventilate their implicitly agreed upon right opinions with a certain passion but with little purpose and no reflection."

Conducting a Successful Discussion

As a teacher intent on using the discussion method effectively with science classes, it is wise to think of a discussion as consisting of four phases: entry, clarification, investigation, and closure (Kindsvatter et al., 1996).

In the *entry* phase, the teacher identifies the discussion topic and tells the students what will be done and why. For example, a chemistry teacher might begin a recitation session on the properties of crystalline solids like this: "For the remainder of the period, I'm going to ask you some questions to find out what you have learned about the properties of crystalline solids. Your answers to my questions will let me know if you're ready for Thursday's quiz." When initiating guided or reflective discussions, many teachers also use attention grabbers to cognitively engage students and to arouse their interest. Questions, pictures, slides, personal testimonials, and role-plays can be used as attention grabbers.

During the *clarification* phase, rules for the discussion are communicated and terms or concepts important to the discussion are defined and clarified. Students need to know how they will be recognized to speak and that showing respect for the views of others is expected. They also need to know what role the teacher will play during the discussion. In an electronic discussion, students should be told whether it is acceptable to comment anonymously, how often to post comments, and if persons other than classmates and teacher will read their comments.

Depending on the purpose to be served by the discussion, the teacher may choose to function as the chairperson, directing student conversation, or simply listen. Experience suggests that the more the teacher talks, the less students will contribute to the discussion. Furthermore, when engaging in guided and reflective discussions, students also need to realize that it is acceptable and appropriate to question the teacher and other students and to ask for clarification of and evidence for statements made during the discussion. Defining difficult terms and clarifying students' understandings of complex concepts also facilitates discussion in science classes. For example, clarification may be necessary at the start of a reflective discussion on AIDS because of confusion regarding the difference between being HIV-positive and having AIDS.

The *investigation* phase is the heart of any discussion. The central elements of this phase are teacher questions and non-questioning techniques, all intended to encourage student engagement and learning. The kinds of questions asked by the teacher during recitation, guided discussion, and reflective discussion will differ. Generally, the questions asked during a recitation are less complex than those asked during either a guided or reflective discussion. Probing questions that ask for elaboration or further explanation serve to enhance reflective discussions, but too many teacher questions can quickly change a reflective discussion into a recitation.

While it is impossible to anticipate all questions that should be asked during a discussion, it is helpful for the teacher to have written out questions considered critical to the discussion. Pausing after asking a question, expressing a personal point of view, adding on to a student's contribution, and using verbal encouragement are all non-questioning techniques that can be used by a teacher to keep a discussion rolling and focused. Finally, student ability level, language skills, and home culture can affect a teacher's use of questions and non-questioning techniques. White (1990) concluded that culturally specific discussion strategies should be used when the participant structures found in the students' home community differ from those found in schools. For example, when working with native Hawaiian students, choral responses to questions and overlapping speech may be considered acceptable because they are features of indigenous Hawaiian verbal interaction (White, 1990).

Closure, the final phase of a discussion, is most critical to the success of guided and reflective discussions, but is too often bypassed due to time constraints or just poor planning. It is during this phase that ideas are summarized, synthesized, and applied to situations not directly discussed and where meaningful learning occurs (Kindsvatter et al., 1996, p. 247). Closure also occurs when the outcomes of the discussion are related to previous lessons and lessons to come. In a reflective discussion, closure may include the evaluation of decisions arrived at during the discussion. Closure in a recitation has minimal importance compared with its stature in guided or reflective discussions. In a recitation, closure involves reviewing the topic under consideration and highlighting those areas where student responses revealed knowledge gaps or misconceptions. Closure in a small-group discussion is the time when the spokespersons present the results of the groups' work to the entire class (Kindsvatter et al., 1996). With added attention given to the nature of the medium, all four phases can be incorporated into an electronic discussion with relative ease.

The teacher's role during a discussion varies depending on the discussion type. The teacher's role is directive during a recitation, less so during a guided discussion, and usually that of a moderator during a reflective discussion. To lead a good discussion, the teacher should be able to do the following:

1. Seat students in a circle or horseshoe arrangement so that they can interact easily and can observe each other's facial expressions. Participants also use facial expressions to communicate. (Of course, this is not possible in an electronic discussion.)
2. Keep the discussion moving at a reasonable pace.
3. Keep the discussion pertinent to the topic under consideration.
4. Encourage all students to participate. Do not allow two or three students to monopolize the conversation.
5. Acknowledge all contributions that the students make.
6. Reject irrelevant comments with tact.
7. Summarize always at the end of the discussion, and do so frequently or permit students to do so as often as is feasible.
8. Terminate the discussion when students begin to lose interest.

Stop and Reflect!

Read Box 11.1, "Decisions, Decisions . . . Teaching About Sexually Transmitted Diseases" and answer the following questions:

■ Suppose that at the afternoon meeting Ms. Block suggested to her colleagues that they consider using either a guided discussion or a reflective discussion to address the objective about the benefits and costs related to AIDS. Which of the two discussion approaches do you think would be more appropriate? Explain your reasons.

■ Ms. Block and her colleagues decided to use the recitation method to help students review for a test. Which of the four objectives assigned to Ms. Block would likely be targeted during the recitation? Why?

DEMONSTRATION

A demonstration is a concrete experience that can be considered an advance organizer for structuring subsequent information and activities into a meaningful, instructional framework for students. An effective demonstration can focus students' attention, motivate and interest them in a lesson or unit, illustrate key concepts and principles, help uncover misconceptions, and initiate inquiry and problem solving. Carefully planned and executed demonstrations can greatly enhance the learning environment and make special contributions to the teaching of science. Some sources of science demonstrations are presented in Table 11.1.

Planning a Demonstration

A demonstration is, in effect, a performance, and many factors must be considered before the event takes place. The first thing that a teacher should consider is whether the strategy is the best way to address a certain topic. It would be inadvisable, for instance, to use a demonstration to show students the test for the presence of starch in carbohydrates when a laboratory exercise would ensure visibility by all and be both inexpensive and very safe. A second point to consider is whether the topic lends itself to demonstration. Are there elements of surprise or suspense? Will the demonstration take place at a reasonable pace? Is there enough variety to maintain interest? Are there long periods of inactivity? Once these considerations have been satisfactorily addressed and the decision has been made to use a demonstration, other aspects of planning must be undertaken, including materials and equipment, visibility, and student attention.

Materials and Equipment

Materials and equipment for a demonstration should be planned and collected well in advance of the actual presentation. Last-minute preparation may prove frustrating and cause either a delay in the presentation or no presentation at all. For example, the teacher may find that the apparatus has been lost or damaged or that chemicals are too old, exist in the wrong concentrations, or are in short supply. In brief, potential problems should be recognized well in advance so that the demonstration can take place as planned.

Teachers or their students can construct the equipment needed for many demonstrations. When teachers construct devices for demonstrations, they are designed to illustrate and emphasize specific points and tend to be used with more frequency and with greater ease and finesse. When students construct demonstration apparatus, they benefit from the experiences of planning and building the devices and the presentation they make.

Classroom Snapshot 11.1

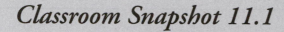

Decisions, Decisions . . . Teaching About Sexually Transmitted Diseases

Ms. Block teaches life science at a large middle school in a rural county. It's Sunday evening and she's looking over the section in her textbook on sexually transmitted diseases. The section will serve as the basis for a week-long unit on the topic. After school on Monday, Ms. Block will participate in a cooperative planning meeting with three other life science teachers. These teachers are counting on Ms. Block to bring ideas for the most appropriate teaching methods to address several of the objectives for the unit that had been agreed upon at an earlier planning meeting. The objectives that Ms. Block is responsible for are:

- Identify the ways by which HIV is transmitted
- Describe ways to reduce the risk of HIV infection
- Relate the symptoms of AIDS to HIV infection
- Evaluate the benefits of the care provided AIDS sufferers versus their cost to society

After looking over the chapter and other instructional materials, Ms. Block developed a plan to share with the other teachers. Before school on the day of the meeting Ms. Block runs into Mr. Castle, a member of the cooperative planning team, in the hall.

CASTLE: Have you given much thought to how we can address those HIV objectives?

BLOCK: I have. If you have a few minutes, I'd like to tell you what I've come up with and get your reaction.

CASTLE: Sure. Go ahead.

BLOCK: Well, there are no suitable demonstrations or lab activities that I'm aware of to address the objectives. But, I do know of a video that the district owns that would work well to address the first three. If we can get the video, working it into a lecture may be our best bet. I've written some questions that I think will engage the students and help them achieve the objectives. I'll bring them to the meeting this afternoon.

CASTLE: The students will have questions about AIDS and HIV. How can we be sure that they are addressed?

BLOCK: If we go with the video, it could be stopped periodically to give them a chance to ask questions. I have a pretty good idea what questions they will ask based on last year's experience, and the video addresses many of them.

CASTLE: Their questions would also allow us to detect their misconceptions about HIV and about the relationship between AIDS and HIV.

BLOCK: Good point.

CASTLE: I'm a little concerned about that last objective, since we didn't address it last year. How do you think we should handle having students evaluate the benefits and costs related to AIDS?

BLOCK: That's a tough one. I thought about suggesting that we try either guided discussion or reflective discussion to handle that one. How do you think Ms. Alverez and Mr. Oliver will react to this suggestion?

CASTLE: I think they'll agree with you, but will say that the students need more information than is presented in our textbook and in the video to really participate in a discussion on the topic.

BLOCK: Oh, there goes the bell. See you this afternoon in Ms. Alverez's room. Thanks for listening.

TABLE 11.1 Sources of Science Demonstrations

Science Snacks, the Exploratorium of San Francisco (http://www.exploratorium.edu/snacksinto.htlm) The demonstrations described at this Web site are miniaturized versions of some of the Exploratorium's popular exhibits.

Society for American Scientists (http://www.eskimo.com/~billb/amasci.html) This site includes numerous physics demonstrations developed by Willam J. Beaty of Seattle, Washington and links to other Internet sites that contain descriptions of additional physics demonstrations.

Chemistry Department of Elmhurst College, Illinois (http://www.elmhurst.edu/~chm/demos/) Many chemical demonstrations performed by Dr. Charles Ophardt are described by topic and presented at this site.

Science Education at the University of Nebraska-Lincoln (http://nerds.unl.edu/pages/mamres/pages/demos/demo.html) A collection of biology, chemistry, and physics demonstrations compiled by Dr. Ron Bonnstetter are presented at this site.

Hawai'i Space Grant Representatives' Space Science Activities (http://www.spacegrant.hawaii.edu/hi–nsta2001.html) This site includes more than 25 demonstrations presented at the 2001 NSTA convention. They are useful for teaching a number of space science concepts.

Chemical Demonstrations: A Handbook for Teaching Chemistry (Volumes 1–4) (http://scifun.chem.wisc.edu/) Written by Dr. Bassam Shakhashiri of the University of Wisconsin and his colleagues, this four-volume set includes descriptions of hundreds of demonstrations.

75 Easy Life Science Demonstrations and *75 Easy Earth Science Demonstrations* (http://sargentwelch.com/products.asp) Authored by Thomas Kardos, these paperback books are available from the Sargent-Welch Company, Buffalo Grove, IL.

Visibility

Simple but large-scale apparatus are best for demonstrations. But even when large equipment is used, the teacher must take care to ensure that small and important details are made visible to students. The apparatus and/or materials on the demonstration table must be arranged to avoid blind spots. Before presenting the demonstration, it is a good idea for the teacher to view the setup from various points around the classroom to determine whether there are problems in viewing. Additionally, the background behind the apparatus and proper lighting should be considered to ensure good visibility. A partially erased chalkboard makes a very unsuitable background; however, white or colored cardboard or cloth backgrounds with suitable supports provide adequate contrast for viewing. Good overhead lighting that eliminates shadows will make any demonstration easier to see.

Student Attention

Extraneous materials events not part of the demonstration or aspects of the demonstration that are particularly attention grabbing, may divert students' attention. For example, when observing the classic egg-in-the-bottle demonstration, students may fail to see it as a demonstration of the effect of changing air pressure but as a show of fire or heat. This is because they are distracted by the flaming piece of paper dropped into the bottle to heat the inside air (Shepardson, Moje, & Kennard-McClelland, 1994). See Figure 11.1 for directions for conducting the egg-in-the-bottle demonstration.

To focus student attention, some teachers begin a demonstration with a clear demonstration table and then proceed to remove the needed items from a box or other source. Items taken from a box as they are needed can introduce an element of surprise, for students will continue to wonder what will be removed next and how it will be used in the demonstration. A second way is to assemble the apparatus first, cover it with a cloth or a box before the students arrive in the room, and then unveil the setup to begin the demonstration. This technique works well when a large-scale apparatus is required for the demonstration. Another approach is to set in operation, before class begins, a scientific novelty or device that is used for the demonstration. Demonstrations that include unusual noises, lights, or motions also are useful in attracting student attention and maintaining interest.

Try Out the Demonstration Beforehand

Unexpected complexities can arise even during a simple demonstration. A damaged pulley or dead battery can sabotage an otherwise great demonstration. The only way to be certain that a demonstration will proceed smoothly is to set it up beforehand, try it out, and then use the same materials during the actual presentation. The availability of backup materials such as additional batteries, pulleys, and glassware will often allow the demonstration to proceed as planned without problems. The importance of trying out the demonstration well in advance to be certain that it will proceed smoothly when it is actually delivered cannot be overemphasized.

FIGURE 11.1 Sample demonstrations.

1. Egg-in-the-Bottle Mystery

Materials

One 1000-milliliter Erlenmeyer flask or bottle of comparable size
One peeled hard-boiled egg
One sheet of notebook paper
Matches
Water

Safety

Use caution with an open flame. Perform this demonstration on a tabletop free of objects that may catch fire. Wear safety goggles.

Procedures

1. Tear off half a sheet of notebook paper and roll it up tightly.
2. Light the rolled-up notebook paper with a match and push the burning paper into the flask.
3. Quickly set the egg on top of the flask.

Questions

1. What happens when the egg is placed on top of the flask?
2. What causes the egg to move inside the flask?
3. How can the egg be removed from the flask without damaging it?

Explanation

The fire heats the air inside the flask, causing it to expand. The expanding air causes the air pressure inside the flask to increase, which causes the egg to bounce on the lip of the flask. The bouncing egg, acting like a release valve, allows some of the hot air to escape from the flask. As the fire goes out, the air inside the flask begins to cool and contract. As the air contracts, the air pressure inside the flask is decreased, and the egg is pushed into the flask by the outside air pressure. Remove the egg by increasing the air pressure inside the flask. To do this, position the egg in the neck of the flask turned upside down and blow air into the flask.

FIGURE 11.1 *Continued.*

2. Wood Chopping by Hand

Materials

Two full sheets of newspaper
One inexpensive yardstick or a wood roofing shingle
Flat surface table large enough to cover with full sheet of newspaper

Safety

Position students to the sides of the demonstration so that no one is hit by a flying piece of wood. Wear safety goggles.

Procedures

1. Position the yardstick so that about 20 centimeters are extending beyond the edge of the table.
2. Cover the yardstick and the table surface with two sheets of newspaper, one on top of the other, and then smooth out the newspaper.
3. Slowly push down on the end of the yardstick extending beyond the table.
4. Reposition the yardstick and newspaper.
5. Hit the top of the yardstick extending beyond the table with the end of your hand in a quick karate chopping motion. (Use a hammer to strike the wooden roofing shingle.)

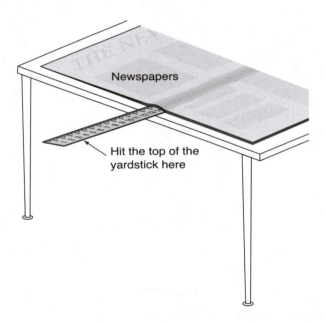

Questions

1. What will happen when the end of the stick is pushed down slowly?
2. What will happen when the end of the stick is struck with a karate chop?
3. Why did the stick break when it was hit with the karate chop?

Explanation

The paper is lifted with ease when the yardstick is pushed down slowly. This happens because air gets under the newspapers from the sides and equalizes the pressure. But when the yardstick is hit with the quick karate chopping motion, it breaks because of the tremendous force exerted by the air pressure pushing down on the newspapers.

Based on descriptions in Teaching Science to Children: An Integrated Approach, *by A. E. Friedl, 1986, New York: Random House, and* Invitations to inquiry *by T. Liem, 1987, Lexington, MA: Cinn Press.*

Presenting a Demonstration

A science demonstration can easily result in a teacher-centered instructional session, which focuses only on the "oos" and "ahs" of a neat event. However, we recommend the student-centered approach that engages all students from start to finish. This is possible by carefully selecting demonstrations, crafting questions that cause students to wonder why and to explain how, and involving students in demonstrations that have three phases: an introduction, a presentation, and a conclusion (Kindsvatter et al., 1996).

Introduction

During the introduction, the purpose for the demonstration is established and students are acquainted with the materials and procedures. Student recognition of the purpose of the demonstration is essential to assure cognitive engagement and to obtain the desired outcomes. The purposes of a demonstration should be kept simple and written on the chalkboard in short, direct statements. For example, a physical science teacher's purpose for performing a demonstration using the Van de Graaff generator may be to show students the effects of static electricity. Moreover, interesting problems for students to consider often arise from the actions of the demonstration materials themselves. The problem will often lead students to the demonstration's purpose.

Whether or not to tell the students of the outcome is a question pondered by the teacher with regard to many science demonstrations. Some teachers tell their students in advance of the demonstration what the outcome will be. This practice is not usually recommended, but it is sometimes necessary to make the outcome more meaningful. Teachers who wish to use demonstrations to initiate student inquiry say very little during this phase. They prefer to allow their students to draw conclusions based on their own observations at a later point during the demonstration.

For most demonstrations, students require help in recognizing the materials that will be used as well as in learning the function of each item in the procedure. It is wise not to assume that students are familiar with the materials that will be used during a demonstration and their functions. To ensure success, each item should be identified and its purpose made clear, preferably during the introduction of the demonstration.

Presentation

The presentation must proceed in a logical and organized manner and move along at a somewhat rapid pace. Procedures that may cause long pauses or delays should be avoided. For instance, if the demonstration requires boiling water, prepare it beforehand so that it is available at the appropriate time. A very useful tactic to hold students' attention during this phase is to create sus-

pense. Events leading to a dramatic climax such as an explosion will maintain student interest, give them a feeling of involvement, and motivate them to meet the objectives of the demonstration. Additionally, humor can be used to achieve a successful presentation. Students enjoy learning from demonstrations that end with unusual, unexpected, or humorous outcomes.

To ensure that students learn from the demonstration, there is much that the teacher can do during the presentation. One technique is to ask questions such as, "What observations have you made to this point?" or "What did I do during the last step?" When asking such questions, teachers typically do not signify approval or disapproval but proceed to ask another student the same questions. If a disagreement occurs, then it may be necessary to repeat the demonstration or step. A second technique is to conduct brief, periodic reviews. A review can be done in several parts, with one student reiterating the purpose, another describing the materials, and another describing the procedures. A third technique is to summarize what has taken place. If a demonstration consists of a number of distinct parts, interim summaries, led either by the teacher or students, are helpful. Data and charts placed on the chalkboard or overhead projector can help summarize observations or results.

Depending on the demonstration, it may be possible to have students participate physically during this phase. Students can assist the teacher in some way during most demonstrations. If a number of manipulations or parts are involved, allow one student to carry out one part and then allow other students to conduct the subsequent manipulations or parts.

Conclusion

During this phase of the demonstration, the teacher helps students construct new understandings about the concept or principle illustrated in the previous phase. One way to do this is by engaging students in a guided discussion of the application of the concept or principle to everyday life. This will make the instruction relevant to the students and make the purpose of the demonstration easier to understand. Be prepared to describe several common situations that illustrate the idea, just in case the students do not suggest any. Questions should be asked to facilitate student conversation and meaningful learning during this phase of the demonstration. Discussion that challenges students' ideas and stimulates dialogue is "necessary to promote a scientific understanding of a science demonstration" (Shepardson et al., 1994, p. 244). Too much teacher talk tends to stifle student conversation. If the demonstration is used to initiate inquiry, the questions should be carefully planned and asked to encourage intellectual speculation. Inquiry demands that teachers evaluate students' responses without being influenced by what they believe students should say or think.

TABLE 11.2   Suggestions for Effective Science Demonstrations

- Select a demonstration that clearly fits the context of the lesson or unit.
- If a series of demonstrations is to be used, make sure that the demonstrations revolve around a single concept (Shepardson et al., 1994, p. 254).
- Make sure that all materials and apparatus are available and in good working order and that proper safety precautions are planned for.
- Clear the demonstration table of extraneous and irrelevant materials and make sure that all students can see the demonstration.
- Speak at a moderate pace, loud enough to be heard by all students, and enunciate clearly.
- State the purpose of the demonstration at the beginning or end or at the appropriate time.
- Describe and simultaneously show the steps of the demonstration.
- Ask questions to stimulate student thinking, to help them draw their own conclusions, and to initiate further investigation.
- Allow sufficient time for the demonstration to achieve its expected outcomes and to maintain student attention and interest.
- Conclude the demonstration with a discussion and, if appropriate, link the demonstration to applications in everyday life.

Research indicates that the quality of science demonstrations improves as teachers grow in their science content knowledge and their understanding of science instructional practices and student characteristics (Clermont, Borko, & Krajcik, 1994). Nevertheless, there is much that beginning teachers can do to ensure the effectiveness of science demonstrations. Suggestions for making demonstrations effective science learning opportunities for students are presented in Table 11.2.

Stop and Reflect!

Before reading on, do the following:

- Work with a classmate to try out one of the demonstrations presented in Figure 11.1. Part of your work will include gathering materials.
- As you work, discuss how you could focus students' attention on the demonstration and how you could ensure that the demonstration can be seen by a class of students.

LECTURE

The lecture has certain strengths that make it useful for science instruction. A large amount of material can be covered in a short time using this teaching method. It is an effective means for introducing a unit, clarifying understandings, and defining science terms (Flowerdew, 1992; Kyle, 1972; Thompson, 1974). The lecture is an efficient way to convey information to students who

find reading textbooks a challenge. It is also an inexpensive method of instruction. A lecturer can teach many students using few materials and resources (McLeish, 1976). In general, the lecture can be as effective as other instructional methods, particularly when the purpose is immediate cognitive gains (Gage & Berliner, 1992).

Despite its usefulness, the lecture has been found to be lacking when compared with other, more "innovative" forms of science instruction. It is associated with rote learning, bored and inattentive students, and authoritative and overly structured teaching. But Ausubel (1961, p. 16) explained that the weaknesses attributed to the lecture are not due to the method itself but to the abuse of the method by teachers who use it. All too often the lecture is used inappropriately as a substitute for other forms of instruction. Teachers who substitute the lecture for laboratory work, for example, are denying students the opportunity to learn about the nature of science and preventing them from understanding the ways scientists go about their work. Additionally, adolescents are restless by nature, preoccupied with immediate problems, and often handicapped by limited vocabulary and background of experience. They also have short attention spans. The teacher must consider that lectures to such an audience will be dull and meaningless unless these factors are taken into consideration during planning.

When science teachers speak of lecture, they are most likely talking about the interactive lecture rather than a teacher monologue that resembles a Sunday sermon. Teacher and student questions and demonstrations tend to punctuate the interactive lecture. When delivering an interactive lecture, student attention span and instructional context must be considered. The increasingly common TV infomercial is a good example of the interactive lecture. The infomercial host presents information about a product to be sold. Questions about the product raised by audience members are central to the infomercial presentation. These questions and their answers, coupled with a demonstration of the product, provide consumers with information about the product needed to make an informed purchase. Similarly, the interjection of questions and demonstrations encourages students to attend to the topic or issue that is the focus of the interactive lecture. The question responses and the accompanying demonstrations should provide the arguments and evidence required by students to further develop their science understandings or change their science conceptions. Additionally, student questions about demonstrations and responses to teacher questions provide a check of student understanding.

The interactive lecture is often an underrated teaching method. But as Eick and Samford (1999) point out, it holds great promise for beginning teachers primarily for two reasons. Its use enables the beginning teacher to develop confidence in classroom management because the teacher remains the focus of classroom activity. Also, the interactive lecture can serve as a bridge for the teacher to more student-centered instruction. This bridging function is facilitated through the opportunities for student participation present in the interactive lecture.

Preparing the Lecture

Lecture preparation involves checking your understanding of the content to be presented, preparing lecture notes to guide your presentation, and organizing the lecture in a logical manner for your audience.

Checking Your Understanding

It goes without saying that teachers should be comfortable with their content knowledge in order to present a good lecture. But knowing the content is not enough. Knowing how to teach the science content knowledge you have is equally important (Gage & Berliner, 1992). This "how-to" knowledge, which Shulman (1987) called *pedagogical content knowledge* (PCK), is reflected in the teacher's ability to explain ideas in more than one way, provide persuasive examples, use helpful metaphors and analogies, and recognize where students will likely have difficulty when studying a science topic for the first time.

Teachers construct PCK as a result of a variety of experiences, including talks with other teachers, reading, science methods courses, and teaching the same content multiple times. Your own science learning experiences provide the foundation for the pedagogical content knowledge that you will use as a beginning teacher to help students construct their science understandings.

Preparing Lecture Notes

Lecture notes can be planned in prose form or they can consist of an outline of the key points that serve as a reminder of what should be presented. Some teachers feel comfortable delivering a lecture only when they have written the complete lecture in prose form. The prose form provides teachers with the security of knowing that all the information is at their fingertips should difficulty arise during the presentation. Other teachers, usually with more experience, prefer a skeleton outline that consists of a title and main headings with key terms and ideas organized under the headings. Still others feel most comfortable with an outline that provides more detail. It may consist of complete sentences of ideas and terms and be organized under specific headings.

A teacher may present a visual representation of the lecture notes to guide students through the lecture and to stimulate note taking. The visual representation may take the form of information presented on the chalkboard or screen using a projection system or provided in a handout distributed to students. Research indicates that visual representations do help students follow lectures and can improve student achievement (Hartley, 1976). Research findings related to note taking are not so clear cut. A lecturer's use of visual representations does stimulate more note taking, but student achievement may or may not be affected. Gage and Berliner (1992) report that note taking helps students remember the material when the notes are studied in preparation for a test, but that note taking by itself does not aid student comprehension of the material. This suggests that it is important for students to listen carefully to a lecture and that teachers may wish to distribute handouts that highlight important information. If handouts are not provided, then teachers may wish to cue students to the important points of their lectures.

Organizing the Lecture

A lecture that is organized around a few major ideas or concepts and presented in a logical sequence has been found to be effective with adolescent students. The effective lecture has an introduction, a main body, summaries within the presentation, and a conclusion. The *introduction* can serve to motivate students to attend to the lecture and cues them to what will be presented and emphasized. Explaining how the lecture topic is related to the students' personal lives is one way to heighten motivation. Teachers often use instructional objectives and questions to cue students about what to expect in a lecture. The introduction also serves to help students ready themselves for the information presented during the lecture. Good and Brophy (1994) recommend the use of advance organizers for this purpose. Advance organizers help explain and interrelate the material they precede (Ausubel, 1963, p. 61).

Several types of advance organizers can be used in the lecture introduction. The *expository advance organizer* places the information to be learned into perspective with other information that is conceptually related. For example, for a lecture on the circulation of blood, an expository organizer might include a brief description of other systems in the body such as the lymphatic system and the renal/urinary system. A *comparative advance organizer* for the same lecture might compare the circulatory system with a hot water system in a house. The simplicity of a hot water system provides a concrete analogy for students to begin the study of a similar concept involving the human body. Cronin Jones (2003, p. 456) also suggests that lecturers considering using *rhetorical advance organizers,* which involve posing "a series of questions that cue students into the important topics to be covered."

The *body* of the lecture is characterized by the presentation of content in an orderly fashion, the use of visual aids to enhance the presentation, and the inclusion of questions and nonverbal cues to stimulate student attention (Kindsvatter et al., 1996). Remembering that the processing capabilities of middle school and high school students are not those of adults, it is best to have a simple plan of organization for a lecture. A complicated sequence can only cause confusion. The organization for a science lecture may show how a main idea is composed of several subordinate ones, show how ideas or events are related chronologically or through cause and effect, or show the relationship of ideas through a central unifying theory (Gage & Berliner, 1992). Line drawings, slides, graphs, photographs, models, and demonstrations are examples of visual aids that can enhance any lecture. Henson (1988, p. 92) reported that the most effective use of visual aids occurs when the "lesson is not predeveloped but built up in front of the students, who help develop the concepts . . . as the lesson develops." Nonverbal cues such as body posture, facial expressions, eye contact, gestures, and physical distance can help hold student interest and attention and stimulate their mental involvement in the lecture (Kindsvatter et al., 1996).

One other way to achieve these same ends is by telling stories. Knox (1997) recommends that science teachers consider using the storytelling formats of myth, historical narrative, and detective story to enliven their lectures and enhance student engagement. The myth of Frankenstein, the historical account of U.S. bomber pilots' discovery of the jet stream during World War II, and the Sherlock Holmes-like mystery that surrounds Watson and Crick's discovery of the structure of DNA are examples of stories that Knox believes students should hear in science classes.

Summaries within a formal lecture presentation are brief statements of important ideas. In the interactive lecture, summaries are typically question-based. An al-

ternative to summaries are lecture breaks (Olmsted, 1999), where students are encouraged to share what they have learned and provide feedback to the teacher about his or her lecture. Whether statement- or question-based, lecture summaries and breaks are intended to motivate, provide time for reflection, establish the relevancy of the material just presented, and allow for formative assessment.

The *conclusion* of the lecture is the place for the teacher to summarize major points and to ask additional questions. The success of the lecture may be gauged from students' responses to these concluding questions. The emphasis on the important points during the conclusion will help students identify relationships needed to undertake future assignments and to be involved in other activities used in the future. Unfortunately, too many lectures lack conclusions as teachers run out of time while presenting the body of their lectures, which usually implies that the lecture was too long.

Presenting Successful Lectures

The success of a lecture depends largely upon the collaboration between the teacher and students. The most successful lecture is an interaction in which the teacher offers information and receives attention, and students offer attention and receive information (Clarke, 1987). Lectures that are presented at a slow pace will bore students, while those presented at a fast pace will prevent students from understanding the lesson. A moderate pace is recommended to assure optimal learning. Your responses to the questions posed in Table 11.3 should help you gauge the overall quality of your lectures and their likely impact on student learning.

TABLE 11.3 Considerations for Preparing a Quality Lecture

- How will students be actively involved in your lecture? Will you ask and answer questions or have students engage in an activity?
- How will you make your lecture relevant and useful to your students?
- What techniques will you use to increase student interest in your lecture and attentiveness? Can humor or demonstrations be incorporated into your lecture?
- How will you link students' prior knowledge to new content during your lecture? Is your lecture organized to move from simple concepts to complex ones?
- What will you do during your lecture to prevent cognitive overload and learner shutdown?
- How will you introduce scientific vocabulary and keep scientific jargon to a minimum?
- How will you incorporate summaries or breaks into your lecture?
- What strategies could you teach students to help them improve their note-taking skills?
- What misconceptions are students likely to hold regarding the topic of your lecture? How will you confront students' misconceptions?
- How will you structure you lecture to include visual and kinesthetic stimulation in addition to auditory stimulation?

Based on information presented in Are Lectures a Thing of the Past?" by L.L. Cronin Jones, 2003, *Journal of College Science Teaching, 32*(7), 453–457.

Stop and Reflect!

Before going on, do the following:

- Select a science topic that interests you. Describe to a classmate how you would prepare a lecture to teach this topic.
- Reexamine the vignette in Box 11.1 and explain what you believe prompted Ms. Block to choose the lecture method to address the first three lesson objectives.
- Suppose that several of the students in the classes taught by Ms. Block and her colleagues are learning English as a second language. How might this knowledge likely affect their lesson preparation?

CONSTRUCTION AND USE OF ORAL QUESTIONS

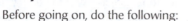

The success of a discussion, demonstration, or lecture often depends on the questions teachers ask students. Teachers must be able to formulate good oral questions. This means that questions have to be well conceived, concise, and clearly stated. Students can answer only the questions they understand. They have to understand the intent of the question in order to respond correctly.

Constructing Clear Oral Questions

Oral questions should be simple and direct so that students can grasp their meaning and intent immediately. They must be constructed using words that are familiar

to students. A word that they have not encountered before can make the question meaningless. Science teachers should take care not to overestimate their students' vocabularies and use scientific terms and other words that students do not understand.

There are many instances when a teacher can improve a question by simply replacing an unfamiliar word in a sentence with one familiar to the students.

> Original: Why does the mixture of the two chemical substances effervesce when the test tube is agitated?

> Improved: Why does the mixture of the two chemical substances bubble when the test tube is shaken?

In this example, the word *bubble* is substituted for *effervesce*, and the word *shaken* is substituted for *agitated*. The question has the same meaning but is more simply stated.

A teacher must exercise great discretion in attempting to use simple and common words when asking questions, however, because it may minimize the vocabulary and concept development of students. The technical vocabulary of science that is part of the curriculum should be taught. Just because some terms are multisyllabic or new does not mean they should be replaced by simpler terms or avoided. The vocabulary of science should be used in the context of clear and simple language.

> Original: What is your idea of an astronomical unit?

> Improved: What is the definition of an astronomical unit?

In the example given, the original question is cluttered. "What is your idea of" can be easily replaced by "What is the definition of," but the term *astronomical unit* should remain, however complicated it might appear. Astronomical unit is a basic term used in the study of astronomy, and it should be freely used.

Finally, teachers should use questions that are well structured and complete.

> Original: Proteins are made where? The equilibrium constant tells you what?

> Improved: Where in the cell are proteins made? What information does the equilibrium constant provide concerning the rate of a chemical reaction?

The original question is vaguely stated, and the students can provide many plausible answers. Rewording the question gives the students a clear understanding of exactly what is being asked.

Lower-Order and Higher-Order Questions

Many systems are used to classify different types of questions. One of the most widely used classification systems is the taxonomy of cognitive objectives developed by Benjamin Bloom and his colleagues (Bloom, 1956). The six levels of this taxonomy are presented in Table 11.4. Along with each level are the associated cognitive activities, key words, and sample questions. The knowledge and comprehension levels represent the lower levels in the taxonomy in which questions can be developed. The application, analysis, synthesis, and evaluation levels represent the higher levels of the taxonomy at which questions can be developed. The lower-order questions obviously require less thinking on the part of the learner than the higher-order questions.

Science teachers can improve their questioning skills by learning to classify their questions and by using a mixture of lower-order and higher-order questions (Rowe, 1978). Each type of question has its place in teaching science, and one type should not be used exclusively in preference to other types. Teachers may often ask recall and factually oriented questions and avoid asking questions that are thought-provoking and probing. Students should be asked oral questions that encourage them to analyze problems, synthesize ideas and make assessments, criticize, and make value judgments. Teachers should not be overly concerned about matching their questions with levels of Bloom's taxonomy, but they should recognize that there are different cognitive levels of questions and that a relationship between questions and student thinking exists (Kindsvatter et al., 1996, p. 197). By asking concise and clearly worded higher-order questions, teachers are able to increase the thought level of students' responses.

Science teachers also can help students respond to their questions at the desired level by teaching them to recognize key words often imbedded in questions (Costa & Lowery, 1989; Kindsvatter et al., 1996). For example, once taught to recognize the key words *judge* and *critique*, students would understand that when asked a question that includes one of these action verbs, they are being asked to engage in higher-order thinking, not simply to recall a fact. Key words in questions that students can be taught to recognize are shown in Table 11.4.

Probing and Redirecting Questions

Much can be gained by asking students to provide detailed responses to questions. This can be accomplished by using probing questions. Probing questions can be used to encourage students to extend, clarify, or justify their response to a question (Montague, 1987). Students should be asked to extend incomplete answers. "What comes next?" and "Please add more to what you've just said," are examples of ways to ask students to extend their answers. Seemingly memorized answers need clarification. Encourage students to clarify their responses by asking questions such as "Would you try to clarify your response to the question?" and "What does that mean to you?" and "Can you clarify what you just said?" Justification is often needed for responses to questions when none is provided. Examples of ways to ask for justification include "What evidence can you offer for that?" and "Why do you believe that is true?"

A second way to encourage detailed responses to questions and to foster student cognitive engagement throughout a lesson is by redirecting. In redirecting, the teacher asks other students to extend, clarify, or justify the response of the student to whom the initial question was directed (Montague, 1987). "What evidence supports Juan's statement that some reactions of photosynthesis don't require light?" and "Hayden, would you please expand on Kendal's answer about the relationship between adhesive forces and meniscus formation?" are examples of redirecting questions.

Wait Time and Teacher Statements

One reason why question-and-answer sessions are ineffective is that teachers tend to ask too many lower-order, rapid-fire questions. Studies by Mary Budd Rowe (1974a, 1974b) have shown that these sessions can be made more effective by using *wait time.* Wait time is defined as the duration of time between speakers. The pause that follows a question by the teacher is referred to as *wait time 1.* The pause that follows a student response to the teacher's question is referred to as *wait time 2.* Data gathered from many classroom situations indicate that the average wait time between a teacher's question and a student's response and the pause that

TABLE 11.4   A Taxonomy of Classroom Questions

Level	Cognitive Activity	Key Words	Sample Questions
1 Knowledge	Remember, recall, or recognize facts, ideas, information, or principles as they were taught.	Define, identify, list, recall, quote	1. Define photosynthesis. 2. Who discovered a cure for rabies? 3. What is the autumnal equinox?
2 Comprehension	Comprehend, interpret, or translate information or ideas.	Describe, explain, compare, summarize	1. How would you measure the distance between the Earth and a planet in the center of a neighboring galaxy? 2. How can you explain the movement of the dye in the water?
3 Application	Solve problems, find solutions, and determine answers through the application of rules, principles, or laws.	Apply, provide an example, use, determine	1. Determine the resistance in the circuits from the data given. 2. What is the molarity of the solutions, given their normality?
4 Analysis	Distinguish the parts from the whole, identify causes, find support and evidence. Construct hypotheses and drawn conclusions.	Identify causes or effects, draw conclusions, provide evidence	1. What are the effects of the two drugs in the mobility of the goldfish? 2. Present evidence that demonstrates the harm that has been caused by nuclear power plants.
5 Synthesis	Produce, design, make, and construct products. Synthesize ideas, produce ways, and determine how to . . .	Make, produce, create, write, build, design	1. Produce a scenario about life in your city if heart disease were eliminated. 2. Design an experiment to determine how much energy can be saved by using storm doors in a home in the winter.
6 Evaluation	Judge, appraise, assess, or criticize. Substantiate on the basis of a set of criteria or standards.	Evaluate, judge, critique, substantiate	1. Evaluate the government's research in tobacco from a moral and ethical point of view. 2. Judge the merits of the research based on your criteria for conducting research.

Based on data from *Taxonomy of Educational Objectives. Handbook I. Cognitive Domain*, by B. S. Bloom, 1956, New York: David McKay Co., Inc.; and *Dynamics of Effective Teaching* (3rd ed.), by R. Kindsvatter, W. Wilen, and M. Ishler, 1996, White Plains, NY: Longman Publishing.

follows students' responses is approximately 1 second (Rowe, 1974a). The term *think time* is sometimes used in place of wait time because it clarifies the "academic purpose and activity of this period of silence—to allow students and teacher to complete on-task thinking" (Stahl, 1994, p. 1).

Science teachers should strive to increase the wait time in their question-and-answer sessions when using higher-order questions. A series of lower-order questions, in general, does not necessarily require wait time between question and response. But for higher-order questions, wait time from 3 to 5 seconds should be em-

ployed to give students a chance to think and reflect. Increased wait time between teacher- and student-talk, student- and student-talk, and student- and teacher-talk will probably cause some uneasiness when first tried, but the payoffs of this change are worth the effort. Rowe (1974a, pp. 89–91) reported the following benefits when wait times were extended beyond 3 seconds:

1. The length of student solicited and unsolicited responses increased.
2. The failure of students to respond to questions decreased.

3. Student confidence and incidence of speculative responses increased.
4. The number of questions asked by students increased.

Another technique that can be used by science teachers to enhance student discourse and thinking during science lessons is the use of statements in place of questions. Although not as well researched as wait time, Dillon (1990) recommended that statements be used rather than questions because students may respond better to teacher statements than they do to their questions. Kindsvatter et al. (1996, p. 205) identify four types of teacher statements that can be used to foster classroom interactions:

- Declarative statement—reflecting on an idea related to what a student said:
   "I know what you mean. I've also seen what a tornado can do to a mobile home."
- Reflective statement—recasting or rephrasing what a student has said:
   "So you think that the winds of a tornado move in a counterclockwise direction."
- Statement of interest—indicating that you would like to hear more about what a student has said:
   "Tell me what else happened when you tried to outrun the tornado in your car."
- Speaker referral—linking a student's statement with one previously made by another student:
   "Your encounter with the tornado is very similar to Sharon's, even though yours was in Kansas and hers was in North Carolina."

Using statements to the exclusion of questions would be difficult for most teachers and might make students uncomfortable because they expect teachers to ask questions during most, if not all, lessons. Many teachers intuitively mix questions and statements during discussions, demonstrations, and interactive lectures. Making this a conscious practice is likely to increase student participation during these types of lessons.

Target Students

Discussions, demonstrations, and interactive lectures typically involve a whole class of students interacting with the teacher. However, not all students interact equally with the teacher during these types of lessons. A study by Tobin and Gallagher (1987) revealed that teachers generally ask low-level questions at random and usually direct higher-level questions to more able students—the target students. Two kinds of target students were identified: those selected because the teacher believed that these students would give responses that would "facilitate learning and content coverage," and those who raised their hands to respond to questions or called out responses. These students, typically few in number (three to seven) in each class and male, dominated class interactions.

According to Tobin, Tippins, and Gallard (1994, p. 50), target students engage in the higher-cognitive-level work of the class and in so doing reduce the cognitive demand of the work for their classmates. Non-target students listen to the interchange between the teacher and target students and then memorize correct answers. For this reason, science teachers should be very conscious of what occurs during whole-class interactions, particularly of the level of learning that takes place during instruction. They should make sure that all students are involved during instruction and that no particular type of student is disregarded or favored for any reason. Science teachers can facilitate the involvement of all students during discussions, demonstrations, and lectures through the questions they ask and the non-questioning techniques they employ.

ASSESSING AND REVIEWING

Analysis and Synthesis

1. When students have difficulty learning from lectures, it is often because they are unable to organize the information presented in a meaningful way. How could a teacher use the topic outline that follows to facilitate student learning during a lecture on vascular plants?
   I. Plants
      A. Vascular
         a. Gymnosperms
         b. Angiosperms
         c. Ferns
      B. Nonvascular

2. Why do you suppose the recitation method is used more often than either guided or reflective discussion even though research supports the superiority of discussion in facilitating meaningful learning? What actions could a science teacher take to engage students in more guided and reflective discussions than recitations?
3. Write two higher-order questions and two probing questions that you could use during a discussion, demonstration, or lecture on a science topic of interest to you.

Practical Consideration

4. Locate a description of a science demonstration that is of interest to you. Practice the demonstration and prepare yourself to guide others through the demonstration. Then, organize a science demonstration Share-A-Thon with students in your class and invite friends, family, and others to participate.

5. Arrange with a science teacher to observe an interactive lecture, a discussion, or a demonstration. Pay particular attention to the questions asked by the teacher during the lesson. Meet with the teacher after your observation to talk about what you observed.

6. List five science and social issues that lend themselves to reflective discussion. Choose one of the issues and plan a discussion that includes:

(1) the question or questions to be used to initiate the discussion, (2) questions and non-questioning techniques to be used during the discussion, (3) activities to be conducted by students in small groups or as a whole class, and (4) strategies to be used to bring closure to the discussion.

Developmental Considerations

7. Start a file of science demonstrations. Add notes to your file about your success with each demonstration after using it with students.

8. Videotape a lesson and analyze the tape for your use of probing questions and interactions with target students. Develop and enact a plan to improve your questioning and patterns of interaction.

RESOURCES TO EXAMINE

Using Think-Time and Wait-Time Skillfully in the Classroom. 1994. ERIC Clearinghouse for Social Studies/Social Science Education, Bloomington, IN. [On-line.] Available: http://www.ericfacility.net/databases/ERIC_Digest/ed370885.html.

Robert Stahl describes eight categories of periods of silence. Each category reflects a different opportunity for teacher and students to engage in on-task thinking.

"Are Lectures a Thing of the Past?" 2003. *Journal of College Science Teaching, 23*(7), 453–457.

The answer to the question asked in the title of this article is a resounding "No," according to Linda L. Cronin Jones. In making a case for using lecture as an instructional strategy, she describes 4 components of an effective lecture and summarizes 10 research-based considerations for lecturers.

Teaching and Learning Through Discussion. 1990. Springfield, IL: Charles C Thomas.

Read the eighth chapter: "Involving Different Social and Cultural Groups in Discussion." Jane White reviews anthropological research on classroom interaction involving Native American, Hispanic, and other cultural groups and suggests a variety of strategies teachers can use to engage students from diverse cultural backgrounds in productive discussions.

Invitations to Science Inquiry. 1987. Lexington, MA: Ginn Press.

Address for ordering: Science Inquiry Enterprises, 14358 Village View Lane, Chino Hills, CA 91709.

To arouse student curiosity about science, consider using discrepant events. This teacher resource manual by Tik L. Liem includes over 400 author-tested discrepant events. Many of the discrepant events are suitable for demonstration. Presented for each discrepant event is an illustration, list of materials, questions for students, and an explanation of the science behind the counterintuitive adventure.

"Questions Are the Answer." 1996. *The Science Teacher, 63,* 27–30.

Authors John Penick, Linda Crow, and Ron Bonstetter present an innovative questioning hierarchy for science teachers. The five levels of the hierarchy highlight question types that emphasize prior experiences, relationships, application, speculation, and explanation.

References

Ausubel, D. P. (1961). In defense of verbal learning. *Educational Theory, 11,* 15–25.

Ausubel, D. P. (1963). Some psychological and educational limitations of learning by discovery. *New York State Mathematics Teachers Journal, 13,* 90.

Bloom, B. S. (Ed.) (1956). *Taxonomy of educational objectives. Handbook 1. Cognitive domain.* New York: David McKay.

Clarke, J. H. (1987). Building a lecture that works. *College Teaching, 35,* 56–58.

Clermont, C. P., Borko, H., Krajcik, J. S. (1994). Comparative study of the pedagogical content knowledge of experienced and novice chemical demonstrators. *Journal of Research in Science Teaching, 31,* 419–441.

Costa, A., & Lowery, L. (1989). *Techniques for teaching thinking.* Pacific Grove, CA: Midwest Publications.

Cronin Jones, L. L. (2003). Are lectures a thing of the past? *Journal of College Science Teaching, 32*(7), 453–457.

Dillon, J. T. (1990). Conducting discussions by alternatives to questioning. In W. W. Wilen (Ed.), *Teaching and learning through discussion* (pp. 79–96). Springfield, IL: Charles C Thomas.

Eick, C., & Samford, K. (1999). Techniques for new teachers. *The Science Teacher, 66,* 34–37.

Flowerdew, J. (1992). Definitions in science lectures. *Applied Linguistics, 13,* 202–221.

Gage, N. L., & Berliner, D. C. (1992). *Educational psychology* (5th ed.). Boston: Houghton Mifflin.

Gall, M. D., & Gall, J. P. (1976). The discussion method. In N. L. Gage (Ed.), *The psychology of teaching methods: Seventy-fifth yearbook of the National Society of the Study of Education* (pp. 166–216). Chicago: University of Chicago Press.

Goldenberg, C. (1992). *Instructional conversations.* ERIC Clearinghouse for Language and Linguistics, Washington, DC. (ERIC Document Reproduction No. ED 347 850)

Good, T., & Brophy, J. (1994). *Looking into classrooms* (6th ed.). New York: HarperCollins.

Hartley, J. (1976). Lecture handouts and student note-taking. *Programmed Learning and Educational Technology, 13,* 58–64.

Henson, K. T. (1988). *Methods and strategies for teaching in secondary and middle schools.* New York: Longman.

Kindsvatter, R., Wilen, W., & Ishler, M. (1996). *Dynamics of effective teaching* (3rd ed.). White Plains, NY: Longman Publishing.

Knox, J. A. (1997). Reform of the college science lecture through storytelling. *Journal of College Science Teaching, 26,* 388–392.

Kyle, B. (1972). In defense of the lecture. *Improving College and University Teaching, 20,* 325.

McLeish, J. (1976). The lecture method. In N. L. Gage (Ed.), *The psychology of teaching methods: Seventy-fifth yearbook of the National Society of the Study of Education* (pp. 397–401). Chicago: University of Chicago Press.

Montague, E. J. (1987). *Fundamentals of secondary classroom instruction.* Upper Saddle River, NJ: Merrill/Prentice Hall.

Olmsted, J. A. (1999). The mid-lecture break: When less is more. *Journal of Chemical Education, 76*(4), 525–527.

Roby, T. W. (1988). Models of discussion. In J. T. Dillon (Ed.), *Questioning and discussion: A multidisciplinary study* (pp. 163–191). Norwood, NJ: Ablex.

Rowe, M. B. (1974a). Wait-time and rewards as instructional variables: Their influence on language, logic, and fate control. Part I. Wait-time. *Journal of Research in Science Teaching, 11,* 81–94.

Rowe, M. B. (1974b). Relation of wait-time and rewards to the development of language, logic, and fate control. Part II. Rewards. *Journal of Research in Science Teaching, 11,* 291–308.

Rowe, M. B. (Ed.) (1978). *What research says to the science teacher* (Vol. 1). Washington, DC: National Science Teachers Association.

Shepardson, D. P., Moje, E. B., & Kennard-McClelland, A. M. (1994). The impact of science demonstrations on children's understanding of air pressure. *Journal of Research in Science Teaching, 31,* 243–258.

Shulman, L. S. (1987). Knowledge and teaching: Foundations for the new reform. *Harvard Educational Review, 57,* 1–22.

Stahl, R. (1994). *Using think-time and wait-time skillfully in the classroom.* ERIC Clearinghouse for Social Studies/Social Science Education, Bloomington, IN. [On-line.] Available http://www.ericfacility.net/databases/ERICDigest/ed370885.html

Thompson, R. (1974). Legitimate lecturing. *Improving College and University Teaching, 22,* 163–164.

Tobin, K., & Gallagher, J. J. (1987). The role of target students in the science classroom. *Journal of Research in Science Teaching, 24,* 61–75.

Tobin, K., Tippins, D. J., & Gallard, A. J. (1994). Research on instructional strategies for teaching science. In D. L. Gabel (Ed.), *Handbook on research in science teaching and learning* (pp. 45–93) New York: Macmillan.

White, J. J. (1990). Involving different social and cultural groups in discussion. In W. W. Wilen (Ed.), *Teaching and learning through discussion* (pp. 147–174). Springfield, IL: Charles C Thomas.

Wilen, W. W. (1990). Forms and phases of discussion. In W. W. Wilen (Ed.), *Teaching and learning through discussion* (pp. 3–24). Springfield, IL: Charles C Thomas.

Science, Technology, and Society

STS provides students and teachers with
opportunities to study science in community settings.

The development of true scientific literacy can result only from learning experiences that go beyond those that center upon traditional science course subject matter. This goal calls for new instructional approaches that link science and technology, stressing the application of knowledge. These approaches must focus on the work of engineers and technologists as well as scientists. Consequently, they must engage students in a variety of learning activities, including those that involve the design and exploration of products, systems, and processes. The new instructional approaches must also provide opportunities for students to analyze the impact of science and technology on society, and to determine the costs and benefits associated with important issues and problems.

AIMS OF THE CHAPTER

Use the questions that follow to guide your thinking and learning about important understandings regarding the teaching and learning of science–technology–society (STS) content.

- What is the rationale for including technology as well as personal and social concerns in school science programs?

- What is technology? How is technology related to science and society?

- How can STS content related to technological products, systems, and processes be made a part of the middle and high school science curriculum?

- How can STS content intended to help students become aware of STS issues, investigate them, and make decisions regarding their findings be infused into the middle and high school science curriculum?

- What should be considered when dealing with controversial issues and personal

values in the classroom, especially related to evolution and creationism?

A RATIONALE FOR STS

The STS movement is now in its fourth decade and has had a profound effect on middle and secondary science teaching and learning. The movement arose from multiple causes, and thus has affected the science curriculum in different ways. Leading tenants of the STS movement that reflect significant shifts in thinking about the nature and purpose of science education include:

- Science education should be for all citizens not just for individuals interested in science as a career.
- Science education should focus on issues needed by citizens to take appropriate political action that addresses the environment and other aspects of life.
- Science education should be interdisciplinary rather than bound by the traditional science disciplines in order to address science-related social problems.
- Science education should stress the interrelationship between science and technology with an eye toward preparing learners for vocations. (Solomon, 2002)

These tenants resonate with the profound influences that science and technology exert on society. Every member of our society needs to understand and appreciate the interrelationship of science and technology. This is particularly true for today's youth, who will experience a multitude of scientific and technological advancements during their lifetime. A realistic understanding of the relationship between science and technology can be developed by first dealing with the unique attributes of each enterprise then addressing their implications for society. Additionally, young people need to be presented with opportunities to engage in technological design. By proposing solutions to real problems and evaluating their consequences, students can further develop their understandings of the relationship between science and technology.

Often overshadowing the need to focus on the relationship between science and technology is the demand from all sectors of society for relevance in the classroom. This societal pressure mandates that science curricula address the science-related personal and social challenges that youth face today and will likely face in the future. Students are constantly exposed to environmental and societal issues either through direct involvement or indirectly through the communications media. Some of the issues and problems to which students are exposed include drug and alcohol abuse, obesity, overpopulation, water and air quality, national defense, and hazardous waste.

In order for science education to be relevant, students must be able to examine societal issues and problems and apply scientific principles and processes to them. They must be given many opportunities to discuss their beliefs and values and to investigate and propose solutions to real-world problems. It is only through this type of exposure and instruction that students will be able to engage in meaningful discourse about science- and technology-related societal issues and problems and go on to make informed decisions about them.

WHAT IS TECHNOLOGY?

In Chapter 7 of this text, you learned about the nature of science. In this section, we briefly discuss the nature of technology. This explanation should help you clarify your understandings of technology and consider how technology is related to science and society.

Just as science is not easy to define, neither is technology. Furthermore, the differences between science and technology are not clear-cut; science and technology are inherently intertwined. As a consequence, they convey different meanings to the professional as well as to the layperson. In general, science can be regarded as the enterprise that seeks to understand natural phenomena and to arrange these ideas into ordered knowledge, whereas technology involves the design of products, systems, and processes that affect the quality of life, using the knowledge of science where necessary.

Science is a basic enterprise that seeks knowledge and understanding. It is aligned with observation and theory. Technology, on the other hand, is an applied enterprise concerned with developing, constructing, and applying ideas that result in apparatus, gadgets, tools, machines, and techniques. The products of science are often called discoveries, while the products of technology are referred to as inventions.

Technology began when humankind invented tools to make work easier and life better. Early technology was simple compared with today's high-tech products. Simple tools were made by ancient peoples to aid in hunting, farming, and fighting. Many of today's devices are complex, such as computers that present and manipulate information in amazing ways, making it possible for humans to explore the far regions of our solar system or to create new genes that perform special functions in living organisms.

However, technology is not limited to the artifacts of invention. Systems and processes are also technology. Navigation and medicine are technological systems that "encompass many pieces of hardware, and software, and know-ware," and manufacturing, the setting of priorities, and research and development are technological processes (Bugliarello, 1995, p. 228). After centuries of interplay between technology and science, there exists a myriad of designs, goods, and services that benefit humankind. Technology and science are often so intimately related that they rely on each other. This interplay of science and technology was as evident during the 1660s—when Robert Hook used the simple microscope that he designed and built to see small boxes in a slice of cork, which he called cells—as it is today in the work done in the laboratories of molecular biologists and genetic engineers.

Some technological achievements that can be addressed in school science programs are computers, digital videodisc players, digital cameras, superconducting materials, nuclear power, genetic fingerprinting, organ transplants, cellular telephones, superhighways, plastics, and the Internet. Engineers design products and services that benefit society, often drawing on scientific information to assist in their work. Their products and services have constraints that range from safety and environmental protection to the limitations imposed by materials and the weather (NRC, 1996). Engineers also engage in inquiry, use their imagination, and figure out solutions to problems. Engineers experiment, control variables, and make keen observations. These men and women possess a body of knowledge about their enterprise along with knowing many scientific disciplines. Most important, these individuals create products and processes.

In addition to the benefits of technology, the costs must be considered. Large-scale production of goods and services consumes valuable resources such as fossil fuels, forests, minerals, recreational areas, plant and animal species, and drinking and irrigation water. These resources are being depleted and are becoming more costly and difficult to obtain. Nations throughout the world must make decisions regarding the use of all resources so that this generation does not use or misuse valuable raw materials, leaving future generations without them. The problems and issues that reside with the use of natural resources that are essential to society must be part of the school science curriculum. The implications of how to apply science and make use of technology must be decided by individuals who are members of a global society. It is hoped that these individuals are well informed about critical scientific, technological, environmental, and societal issues.

STS Content in the Science Education Curriculum

There are many options available to you for incorporating STS content into your science curriculum. These options range from simply adding a brief STS encounter based on an activity described in your textbook to adopting an entire course curriculum purposefully built to provide students with a comprehensive STS experience. The development of new curriculum materials that strive to make science course content relevant and meaningful to students has encouraged the movement of STS content beyond the status of curriculum add-on. The five categories of STS science described by Aikenhead (1994) and presented in Table 12.1 highlight the levels of curricular emphasis given to STS content in many middle school and high school science classes. Studying the category descriptions will help you think about the importance that you may wish to give STS content in your students' science learning experiences.

A major impediment to any level of implementation of curriculum materials that have a strong STS orientation continues to be the felt need to cover the traditional science content among middle school and secondary science teachers. While this need is well founded, based primarily on the factual nature of the content emphasized on high-stakes tests and in district and state science curriculum standards, science teachers cannot disregard the preparation of students for life in which social, political, and economic changes in society will be affected by science and technology. A key to the success of any level of implementation is a teacher willing to recognize that an STS orientation to the curriculum may involve allowing greater student choice and self-direction, assessing STS learning outcomes, and teaching from an interdisciplinary perspective, which may mean dealing with content on the fringe of one's comfort zone.

Considered in the next two sections of this chapter are STS content options and instructional strategies for providing students with opportunities to engage in STS learning experiences. The focus of the first section is *technological products, systems, and processes*. The second section has an *issues* and *problems* focus. It is the content focus in this second section that has been the primary thrust of STS in school science and has served to guide the development of some innovative curriculum materials. STS content that has a technology or issues and problems focus is most often integrated into middle and high school science classes through one of the first three categories described by Aikenhead (1994)—Motivation by STS content, casual infusion of STS content, or purposeful infusion of STS content.

TECHNOLOGICAL PRODUCTS, SYSTEMS, AND PROCESSES

The development of useful products, systems, and processes illustrates the imagination of engineers, scientists, and technicians who attempt to affect the quality of life. Individuals who develop goods and services think, reason, and imagine in ways similar to those who theorize about natural phenomena. Often, these individuals learn to better understand basic science concepts

TABLE 12.1   Aikenhead's Categories of STS Science

1. **Motivation by STS Content**
   Traditional school science, plus a mention of STS content in order to make a lesson more interesting.

2. **Casual Infusion of STS Content**
   Traditional school science plus short study (about 1/2 to 2 hours in length) of STS content attached into the science topic. The STS content does not follow a cohesive theme.

3. **Purposeful Infusion of STS Content**
   Traditional school science, plus a series of short studies (about 1/2 to 2 hours in length) of STS content integrated into science topics, in order to systematically explore the STS content. This content forms cohesive themes.

4. **Singular Discipline Through STS Content**
   STS content serves as an organizer for the science content and its sequence. The science content is selected from one science discipline. A listing of pure science topics looks quite similar to a science course where STS control is purposefully infused, though the sequence would be quite different.

5. **Science Through STS Content**
   Science content serves as an organizer for the science content and its sequence. The science content is multidisciplinary, as dictated by the STS content. A listing of pure science topics looks like a selection of important science topics for a variety of traditional school science courses.

From "What is STS Science Teaching?" by G. Aikenhead, 1994, in J. Solomon and G. Aikenhead (Eds.), *STS Education: International Perspectives on Reform* (pp. 47–59), New York: Teachers College Press.

and principles when they develop products, systems, and processes that build upon established knowledge. Fortunately, many types of products, systems, and processes can be designed and studied by students to help develop their scientific and technological literacy.

Design and Build

Some science teachers have always engaged their students in building working models of various machines and gadgets to further their involvement in science courses. For example, middle school students can build series and parallel electric circuits, wet cell batteries, electric motors, and water clocks. Secondary students can build radios, remote-control gates, electrical generators, rockets, and simple robots. Students also like to design and build zany machines like those depicted in the cartoons of Rube Goldberg. Directions for designing and constructing these kinds of machines and many others are found in books and on the World Wide Web. For example, students can find information about the works of Rube Goldberg in *Rube Goldberg: Inventions!* by Maynard Frank Wolfe (2000) and at the Web site of the Argonne National Laboratory Educational Programs (http://www.anl.gov:80/Careers/Education/rube/rube.html).

Students also enjoy the challenge of designing and constructing gadgets or devices to achieve a particular objective. Building a bridge using linguine or popsicle sticks that will support the weight of several books or constructing a container that will hold an egg and keep it from breaking when the container is dropped from the roof of a three-story building are just two examples of challenges enthusiastically pursued by students. When pursuing these challenges, students are presented with opportunities to design a solution to a real problem, implement and evaluate their design, and communicate the stages of their work to classmates (NRC, 1996).

Other learning activities, such as planning a cafeteria menu to meet basic nutritional needs and comparing the absorbency of competing brands of paper towels or batteries, also provide students with experiences in design and analysis. Engaging in challenges of these types often leads to students applying their new understandings to other problems in their home and community. One example is the story of Ashley Kling's award-winning invention. As a ninth-grader, Ashley invented a flashing firefighter's safety boot, which makes a firefighter more visible in smoky buildings and on ladders. Ashley's invention was prompted by her concern for the safety of firefighters, like her parents who serve the city of Akron, Ohio.

Developers of the Science by Design Series at TERC (2000) recommend introducing students to the design process as a cycle of actions that are repeated until a satisfactory solution has been achieved. The seven elements that comprise the Science by Design Series design process include:

- Identify and clarify the situation
- Create the solution
- Investigate the possibilities
- Choose the solution
- Implement the design
- Evaluate the design
- Communicate the solution

Investigate and Improve

Reading, personal interviews, and site visits are other forms of inquiry that many science teachers use to help students learn about technology. These forms of investigation are appropriate for learning about technological products as well as technological systems and processes. Students can find a great deal of reading material in libraries and on the Internet to improve their understanding and stimulate their interest about technological systems and processes. They also will find that many professionals are willing to discuss the technological systems that they use in their jobs or the processes that are the backbone of important businesses and industries. For example, students can investigate the relationship between research and development in a major corporation, how computers are used in the homes of classmates or in neighborhood businesses, or the process of priority setting used by an emergency management team at the time of a natural disaster. The following list can help students organize their thinking and reporting during the study of technology and its relationship to science and society:

- Tell how the technology was invented and how the inventor's culture or situation influenced the product or solution
- Explain how the technology works and include the scientific principles upon which it is based. Include diagrams
- Give some of the beneficial uses of the technology, such as entertainment, medical, defense, education, and so on
- Describe any limitations or potential dangers of the technology

Table 12.2 lists some of the many technological products, systems, and processes that students can gather information about from reading, personal interviews, the Internet, or site visits. As a result of their investigations, students may be able to offer suggestions for improving technological products, systems, and processes. For example, the critique of a mass transit rail system in a physical science course resulted in students offering suggestions to the transit authority for increasing ridership and reducing fuel consumption in addition to learning about energy, mechanics, and motion.

TABLE 12.2   Technological Products, Systems, and Processes that Students Can Investigate

Products	Systems	Processes
Radio antenna	Air traffic control	Genetic screening
Cellular telephone	Artificial intelligence	Manufacturing
Handheld computer	Internet	Priority setting
CD player	Medicine	Research and development
Fuel cell	National laboratories	Resource distribution
Integrated circuit	Navigation	Technology utilization
Radar detector	SI-measurement	Science and economics
Smart gun	Homeland security	Trading of stocks and bonds

Stop and Reflect!

- Examine Box 12.1—Building "Mouse Trap" Cars. To what extent do you believe that Mrs. Fellabaum's class activities help students develop an understanding of technology and its relationship to science and society? Discuss your thoughts with a classmate.

STS ISSUES AND PROBLEMS

The issues and problems focus is prominently featured in the Science in Personal and Social Perspectives content standard of the *National Science Education Standards* (NRC, 1996) and the Human Society section of the *Benchmarks for Scientific Literacy* (AAAS, 1993). These guiding documents stress the importance of

Classroom Snapshot 12.1

Building "Mouse Trap" Cars

Mrs. Fellabaum describes the instructional approach she uses in her eighth-grade physical science course:

More than half of my course centers on basic physics, which includes electricity, light, motion, and sound. I begin the study of each of these topics by asking students what they know about these topics and what they would like to learn. The discussions are followed with several laboratory exercises to develop fundamental understandings of concepts and principles. With some background, the students begin to participate in design projects. When we study motion, for example, I always involve students in the construction of "mouse trap" cars. These vehicles are powered by the basic mouse trap sold at hardware stores. They are made from scratch or modified from toy cars and trucks. Since I attempt to associate this experience with speed, acceleration, and friction, one of the primary objectives is to design a vehicle that will accelerate the fastest from a stopped position to a line 2 meters away from the starting point. Another objective is to design a vehicle that will roll the farthest. Students have the option as to which type of vehicle they want to design. These activities are of high interest, and they seem to reinforce the topic we are studying.

I do not stop at the design phase of this activity because I want to further the hands-on and minds-on aspects of science and engineering. I ask all my students to write a short paper that requires them to analyze a real car and explain the features that contribute to its acceleration, speed, efficiency, and so on. Some students use their family car for the purpose of analysis, while others go to automobile dealerships and get the brochures on new cars. One of my students videotaped drag races from the Speed Channel and used the video to illustrate features that contribute to the cars' acceleration. This activity also provides the opportunity for my students to invite local guest speakers, after obtaining my permission, to discuss how people design, maintain, and repair cars. We have, on occasion, taken a field trip to a local garage where race cars are built. Surprisingly, the girls were as motivated as the boys.

students having opportunities to identify issues and problems of interest and concern, study them, and make appropriate decisions based on their inquiries.

Although the terms *issue* and *problem* often are used interchangeably within STS instruction, they have a different meaning. An issue is an idea on which people hold different beliefs and values. Whether or not to make recycling mandatory, to limit the construction of multi-family apartment buildings in a community, or to ticket drivers for not wearing seat belts are examples of issues. A problem is a situation that places a given population at risk. For example, the poisoning of fish in estuaries as a result of toxic waste from industry places the livelihood of those in the fishing industry and the health of people who eat the fish in jeopardy. Both issues and problems can be the focus of questions that spur student investigation. The study of issues and problems is becoming more commonplace in middle school and secondary science classes as teachers recognize the importance of teaching STS content.

Social studies and environmental educators have contributed much to our understandings of instruction related to STS issues and problems. They have brought to our attention the notion that different instructional approaches are needed when the purpose of instruction is conceptual enhancement, as is often the case when addressing STS issues and problems.

According to Ballantyne and Bain (1995), instructional strategies effective in enhancing conceptions are those that induce cognitive conflict and encourage learners to reconcile incompatible ideas by seeking new information or striving to reorganize their existing knowledge. It is through their efforts to reconcile incompatible ideas that students make judgments about the transforming influences of science and technology, analyze how science and technology affect beliefs and values, evaluate proposals for addressing social changes brought about by scientific and technological innovations, and formulate strategies for influencing public discussions of science and technology (National Council for the Social Studies [NCSS], 1994). Before turning our attention to instructional approaches effective in enhancing conceptions, one strategy that should not be used when addressing STS issues and problems is discussed.

Inculcation

Inculcation is not recommended for addressing issues and problems because of its inherent complications. Attempting to convince others to accept your value judgments may be misconstrued as coercion, especially if statements such as "I think you should" or "I expect" are associated with your appeals. A second complication associated with inculcation is the temptation to present only one perspective regarding a complex, multifaceted issue. The following description of Mr. Clemens' teaching illustrates this point.

Mr. Clemens teaches high school chemistry in a community where steel mills and petrochemical plants have existed for many years. He often criticizes these industries for polluting the land, rivers, and air in the community. On every possible occasion, Mr. Clemens cites how the waste materials of the steel and chemical industries are "poisoning the environment." He often invites local environmental activists to speak to his classes about the problems of the smokestack industries and their effects on urban America. Mr. Clemens requires all students to write a report on the problems of environmental pollution in their community.

This description illustrates how a science teacher attempts to inculcate students with one point of view—the evils of industry and how industry is damaging the environment. Although few would deny that industry has contributed to environmental pollution, industry has also made great progress to clean up and to protect the environment. Students need to hear both sides of issues like this one in order to make informed judgments and act responsibly.

Issue and Problem Awareness

An approach to helping students become more aware of issues and problems is through the clarification of these ideas. The clarification of personal values related to science and societal issues and problems is one approach that many science teachers might feel comfortable using when they address controversial issues. This approach provides students with an opportunity to "confront the various areas of conflict and confusion that are of specific concern to them, in a constructive and systematic way" (Simon, Hartwell, & Hawkins, 1973, p. 4). This approach also enables students to become aware of the beliefs of others, and it may help students choose what values are right for them. Issues clarification can be accomplished through discussion techniques, which might be considered safe and prudent, especially in communities where parents are very sensitive to what their children are being taught in school.

A relatively easy way to implement issues clarification is to find a newspaper article on a social issue or problem related to a science topic under study. Place the title of the article on a sheet of paper or on the whiteboard and list questions for students to answer. An example of a contemporary social issue directly related to science is "Awarding monetary damages to long-term smokers diagnosed with lung cancer." This can be discussed in a life science or biology class during the study of the human respiratory system or cell reproduction and growth. The following questions are examples of those that can be used to prompt discussion of this issue:

1. Do you smoke?
2. Does anyone in your family smoke?

3. Is it easy for people to quit smoking if they want to?
4. Is smoking a cause of cancer?
5. How can tobacco companies inform consumers of the health risks associated with smoking?
6. Should tobacco companies be held liable for the medical expenses of cancer sufferers who were long-term smokers?
7. Should the government collect money from tobacco companies to pay for the cost of treating smoking-related illnesses?

To help students assess their own values and those of their classmates about issues such as the health risks associated with smoking or the need for government intervention, some teachers use the four-corners strategy where corners of the classrooms are assigned the ratings of "strongly agree," "agree," "disagree," and "strongly disagree." Students move to the corners of the classroom that best fit their positions and offer explanations for their choices.

A second approach is to use vignettes that focus on societal issues and problems. Brinckerhoff (1986) recommends that science teachers prepare vignettes about science- and technology-related issues and problems and use these vignettes frequently throughout the school year. Many teachers have implemented Brinkerhoff's ideas as part of their daily science teaching. They distribute copies of a vignette to students or display the vignette on a screen using a projection system at the start of a class period. A sample vignette is shown in Figure 12.1.

FIGURE 12.1   Vignette on science and societal issues.

Today's Science and Societal Issue

Great advances have been made in recent years in cryogenics, the area of physics that deals with very low temperatures. Today, many animals, including goldfish, can be quick-frozen and kept alive at temperatures around −200°C and then returned to good health by slowly warming to normal temperature. All indications are that the process will work for humans. Suppose you found out that you had cancer and would die within 1 year. Would you consider having yourself frozen until a cure for cancer could be developed? If you think that having yourself frozen is a good idea, how long would you wait before being frozen? Should the government pay for the procedure, as it now pays for the treatment of many cancer patients?

Adapted from One-Minute Reading Issues in Science, Technology, and Society, *by R. F. Brinckerhoff, 1992, Menlo Park, CA: Addison-Wesley.*

Issue and Problem Investigation

The investigation and analysis of STS issues and problems goes beyond clarification in that it helps students develop deeper understandings of issues and problems. This approach stresses the organization of factual information as well as the presentation of arguments and evidence. The investigation and analysis of STS issues and problems requires students to engage in inquiry and to find out about ideas by doing library and fieldwork and using the Internet, as well as by determining other people's beliefs and attitudes. It also encourages students to separate fact from opinion and to become aware of the values held by individuals who disagree about issues or problems. The investigation and analysis of STS issues and problems culminates in students making decisions that affect their lives and the lives of others.

Two models exemplify this approach to teaching STS content. They are the analytical decision-making model developed by Oliver and Newman (1967) and Johnson and Johnson's (1988) structured controversy model. Both models are extremely useful for guiding students' examination of STS issues and problems. For example, some communities are considering whether or not to use some of their land for long-term storage of radioactive waste from nuclear power plants. This is an important decision because of the impact it can have on the local economy and because radioactive waste triggers such strong reactions from people regarding the environment and public health. The community near any proposed storage site must weigh the risks and benefits of the land use.

Students who undertake assessing whether or not the storage facility should be built near a given hypothetical community must investigate many aspects of the problem. They must learn about radiation and half-life and study the safety record of similar facilities in other states and countries. They must compare the potential danger associated with nuclear power with that of other industries. This inquiry will likely lead students to study the hazards of using coal and petroleum to produce electricity and the problems of disposing of chemicals such as polychlorinated biphenyls, lead, arsenic, and other industrial waste products that have been going into landfills.

Students must also research the beneficial effects of a storage site to the community. How will this project benefit the community economically? Local business will increase tremendously, at least during the construction of the storage site, to provide food and lodging for the construction workers, technicians, and engineers. Perhaps roads and rails will have to be improved or built. Then there will be the maintenance of the facility once it has been completed and placed in use.

The structured controversy model incorporates the unique feature of perspective reversal to help students focus on both the benefits and risks associated with a decision such as whether or not to make land available for the storage of radioactive waste. Students are paired and assigned randomly to learn either the pro or con position. After learning their assigned position and arguing forcefully in support of it, each pair is then required to learn and present the opposing position. By ensuring that all students understand both sides of the issue, reversing perspectives leads to collaborative decision making where the focus is not on winners and losers but rather on the best possible solution (Johnson & Johnson, 1988).

In order to move from factual learning to reasoned decisions, students should also investigate the attitudes and values of the people in the community regarding the long-term storage of nuclear waste. Although they cannot survey the citizens of the hypothetical community for which the proposed site is being considered, there are studies that have polled a variety of groups regarding their feelings about nuclear power and radiation. These results will surely be a significant factor in the decision to accept or reject a nuclear waste storage site in the community. If students are, in fact, investigating an issue or problem that will affect the community in which they live, interviewing people or asking them to complete a questionnaire in order to gather data on their knowledge of the issue or problem as well as their attitudes toward it would be in order.

An important learning outcome of issue and problem investigation and analysis is decision making. Given all of the information that students have gathered, what will they decide to do regarding the issue or problem they have studied? If students have been studying the feasibility of radioactive waste in their community, what do they believe should be done? Do they believe that another waste disposal area is needed but that the facility should not be constructed in their backyard? Decision making can result from a position paper prepared by students as is recommended in Johnson and Johnson's (1988) structured controversy model or from a discussion of findings and conclusions in class. Students should be asked to make these and many other types of decisions and then to take some type of responsible action if this is their desire and it is prudent to do so.

Action Learning

Another approach to bringing about conceptual enhancement of STS issues and problems is action learning. Action learning involves more than thinking, reasoning, clarifying, and decision making. It stresses taking social action in the community, which extends instruction beyond the classroom. Action learning stresses opportunities for students "to take actions toward the resolution of an STS issue and to evaluate the effectiveness of those actions" (Rubba & Wiesenmayer, 1988, p. 43).

Some science teachers have, for many years, engaged students in community learning and service projects. They have taken interested students to streams and beaches to clean up these areas and to collect samples of organisms to take back to the classroom for study. One example of this type of action learning is the Adopt-A-Stream program. Supported and directed in the state of Georgia by the Georgia Environmental Protection Division, Adopt-A-Stream involves many teachers and students in a variety of activities related to stream monitoring and cleanup. Program volunteers are encouraged to investigate the origin of water quality problems and report their findings to community officials and the regional office of the Georgia Environmental Protection Division.

Action learning is definitely a way to get students involved in issues and problems that are important to their lives and to the community in which they live. This approach helps students to become active participants in society and to perform useful services. However, considerable thought and planning must go into action learning activities. Some activities may need to be carried out after school or on weekends. Others may be potentially dangerous, and science teachers must weigh the risks and benefits. Action learning offers science teachers many ways to make science relevant and interesting for students and bring about conceptual enhancement.

Project-Based Science

Project-based science is the label associated with science learning experiences that incorporate many of the elements of issues and problems investigation and action learning. Project-based science is ideal for teaching about STS issues and problems and the science concepts and principles that underlie them. At the center of a project-based science learning experience is a question that is interesting and meaningful to students. According to Krajcik, Czerniak, and Berger (1999, p. 67), the question must also be feasible to investigate, address important science content and process, and sustain the interest of students for several weeks. Questions that meet these criteria are numerous and frequently arise from the students' day-to-day experiences and community events.

Other central features of project-based science are student collaboration, teacher-directed lessons, and student projects and presentations (Krajcik et al., 1999). Students work in collaborative groups as they carry out an investigation, with each student contributing significantly to the overall effort. Teacher-directed lessons are incorporated when appropriate to provide students with the science and social studies understandings necessary to sustain their work. The outcomes of project-based science experiences are student projects and presentations that demonstrate learning.

Project-based science, like the other approaches for addressing STS issues and problems, has been criticized for not teaching students the science content they would have learned through a more traditional approach. According to Gallagher (2004), this criticism should not be directed at the approach itself, but at the considerable variation in the clarity of teachers' goals for project-based science experiences. Research by Wheeler and his colleagues (1997) has shown that, too often, project-based science experiences highlight science issues and problems of local interest but fail to adequately address the science that underlies the issues and problems. The goal of any project-based science experience should be to help students "to comprehend the problem [or issue] and each of the alternative solutions from a scientific and social perspective" (Gallagher, 2004, p. 105). Fulfilling this instructional goal requires that students learn the science content and apply their understandings of the content to the problem or issue they are investigating. From the teacher's perspective, this is much easier to achieve when all student projects in a class focus on a single problem or issue. When using project-based science or one of the other approaches for investigating STS is-

sues and problems it is important to remember that inclusion of a social issue or problem in science instruction is for the purpose of: (1) helping students learn and understand science content and (2) enabling students to make informed decisions with regard to the scientifically based issues and problems that will confront them in life.

STS CURRICULUM PROGRAMS

The tenants of STS have been used to guide the development of a number of large-scale science programs for use with middle school and high school students. As mentioned earlier, these programs emphasize environmentally and socially relevant content in addition to important science concepts, principles, and skills. They also press students to be engaged learners, with instructional units often culminating in students making decisions regarding an STS issue or problem. Several of these innovative programs are identified in Table 12.3.

TABLE 12.3   STS-Oriented Science Programs

Middle School	High School
Issues, Evidence, and You (IEY) Grades 7–9; earth, life, and physical sciences Published by Lab-Aids, Inc. Attention to environmental issues that affect many communities, including water and energy uses and environmental impact.	*BSCS Biology: An Ecological Approach* Grades 9–10; biology Dedicated to student investigation of environmental issues and ecology in the context of a full-year biology class.
Middle School Science and Technology Grades 6–8 or 7–9; earth, life, and physical sciences Published by Kendall/Hunt Publishing Company Addresses concepts of science and technology through the themes of personal dimensions, nature of explanation, problem solving, and STS issues.	*Chemistry in the Community* (ChemCom) Grades 9–12; chemistry Published by the American Chemical Society A yearlong, activity-oriented course that highlights the relationship between chemistry and everyday life.
Science and Technology Concepts for Middle Schools (STC/MS) Grades 7 and 8; earth, life, and physical sciences and technology Published by Carolina Biological Supply Company Focuses on students' emerging abilities to understand causal relationships, patterns in data, and develop evidence-based conclusions.	*EarthComm: Earth System Science in the Community* Grades 9–12; earth science Published by It's About Time Publishing Stresses relationship of earth science to students' everyday lives and pressing environmental concerns.
Science Education for Public Understanding Program (SEPUP) Grades 7–9; earth, life, and physical sciences Published by Lab-Aids, Inc. Emphasizes increasing students' awareness of social issues, enhancing problem-solving skill, and understanding of science concepts.	*Science by Design Series* Grades 9–12; biology, chemistry, and physics Published by the National Science Teachers Association Press Emphasizes student engagement in design and testing of products—greenhouse, glove, boat, and catapult.
	Science and Sustainability Grades 9–12; earth, life, and physical sciences Published by Lab-Aids Inc. Considers local and global issues related to sustainability, including food, materials, energy, and population.

Based on information from Education Development Center, 2004, CSE K–12 Science Curriculum Dissemination Center. [On-line]. Available: *http://cse.edc.org/work/k12dissem/materials.asp#ies* (July 8, 2004).

Classroom Snaphot 12.2

Mr. Bloom's Adventure

Mr. Bloom observed a great deal of water standing in a drainage ditch located several blocks from the middle school in which he teaches life science. The ditch was an unsightly area because of the dirty water and the accumulation of trash. Mr. Bloom had a hunch that some sewage water might be seeping into the ditch because of the age of the city's sewer system, and that if they tested the water, perhaps fecal material would be found in it. When he proposed to students in his classes the idea of cleaning up the drainage ditch and analyzing the water for contamination, he got many volunteers who wanted to participate in the project.

On a Saturday in October, Mr. Bloom took a group of about 30 students, along with several parents, to the ditch to collect the cans, cups, and paper products that had accumulated there. He also directed some students to collect water samples to be given to the city water department to analyze for contamination and to be examined in the school's science laboratory.

Mr. Bloom had made prior arrangements with the city public works department for the use of their rakes, shovels, and trash bags to aid in the clean-up operation. The public works department also picked up the trash the students collected. The city water department tested their water samples for fecal material, and concluded that sewage was seeping into the drainage ditch.

The students derived a great deal of satisfaction from this project, especially when they observed the public works department digging up the broken sewage pipes and replacing them. They also benefited from examining water samples for microorganisms by using their microscopes.

Stop and Reflect!

- Read the vignette in Box 12.2 about Mr. Bloom's adventure. Indicate which of the approaches that can be used to address STS issues and problems is exemplified in the vignette. Discuss the reasons for your choice with a classmate.

- Examine student materials from one of the STS programs. How are the materials different from those found in a more traditional middle school or high school science program? How could you use the materials you examined to help students learn about an STS issue or problem and the science that underlies it?

CONSIDERATIONS FOR STS INSTRUCTION

Addressing technologies and social issues and problems in the science classroom requires careful planning and good judgment. If you are not in the position to use a whole-course curriculum with an STS orientation, you must then select topics that are directly related to your curriculum so that investigation of the relationships between science and technology and society is viewed as educationally sound. You also must select topics that are relevant to your students and that will affect their lives.

The STS approaches discussed in previous sections of this chapter suggest many ways to help teenagers see how scientific and technological knowledge can help them become better informed about themselves and the world in which they live. However, in order for any of these approaches to be successful, you must implement instruction that considers the interests and abilities of your students. In addition, you must also be knowledgeable about the technologies and social issues and problems that you wish to address in the classroom and major science understandings that underlie them. Several factors that you may wish to consider when using an STS approach are listed in Table 12.4.

EVOLUTION VERSUS CREATIONISM IN SCIENCE TEACHING

Nothing in biology makes sense except in the light of evolution. (Dobzhansky, 1973)

The influence of society on the teaching of science is clearly evident in the long and heated battle over the teaching of evolution in science courses. On many occasions during the 20th century, state boards of education or individuals have challenged or defended the teaching of evolution, creationism or, more recently, intelligent design in science courses. Some of the laws passed that restrict the teaching of evolution or promote the teaching of creationism have been rendered

TABLE 12.4   Considerations When Using an STS Approach

Relevance

- The issue, problem, or design project is related to concepts and principles that are part of the course curriculum.
- The issue, problem, or design project is meaningful to students.
- The issue, problem, or design project will hold students' attention for several weeks.

Access to Resources

- Print resources, including books, periodicals, and newspapers, that contain information about the issue or problem are available in the school.
- Students have access to the Internet to get information and communicate with experts.
- Funds are available for purchasing materials to build gadgets, models, or instruments.
- Transportation can be arranged to visit sites pertinent to the issue or problem being investigated.

Teacher's Abilities and Skills

- The teacher is knowledgeable of the science that underlies the issue, problem, or design task.
- The teacher is able to manage a student–centered learning environment and be a co-participant in the experience with his or her students.
- The teacher encourages students to discuss their feelings and beliefs.
- The teacher is a good listener.
- The teacher does not judge the responses of students or make disparaging remarks related to students' responses.

Student Development

- Students are mature enough to discuss the issue or problem with classmates and adults.
- Students have the prerequisite knowledge to investigate the issue or problem.
- Students have the reasoning skills and intellectual capacity to understand the issue or problem and possible solutions.
- Students have the dexterity and strength to build gadgets, models, and instruments.

Studying artifacts is one way to learn the relationship between science and society.

unconstitutional by the U.S. Supreme Court. A recent controversy regarding the place of evolution in the science curriculum occurred on August 11, 1999, when the Kansas State Board of Education voted to restrict the emphasis of evolution in the State's science standards. Let's review some of the most notable cases (National Academy of Science, 1998, Appendix A) and controversies over the past century, then read what the science teaching profession and the scientific community recommend to science teachers regarding inclusion of evolution in school science.

The Scopes Trial, 1925. John Scopes assigned students pages to read about evolution. In doing so, he was agreeing to test the merits of the Tennessee State law prohibiting the teaching of evolution in schools. This action resulted in a sensational event known as the "Monkey Trial." Scopes was found guilty and fined $100. However, this outcome was viewed as a victory for evolutionists. Subsequently, the verdict was overturned because of a technicality.

Epperson v. *Arkansas*, 1968, The U.S. Supreme Court invalidated an Arkansas statute that prohibited the teaching of evolution. The decision was based on the First Amendment, which says the government must be neutral in matters of religion. Consequently, the Constitution does not permit a state to require instruction that is tailored to the principles or prohibitions of any particular religion.

McLean v. *Arkansas,* 1982. Judge William Overton ruled that a "balanced treatment" statute violated the Constitution, and thus teachers did not have to give equal time to creationism when teaching evolution. Further, creationism has no scientific significance, and creationism is not science; rather it is religion masquerading as science.

Edwards v. *Aguillard,* 1987. Don Aguillard, a Louisiana biology teacher, challenged the state's equal time mandate. The statute prohibited the teaching of evolution, except when it was accompanied by instruction on creation science. The U.S. Supreme Court held that the "Creationism Act" was unconstitutional, giving science teachers the right to teach evolution without addressing creationism.

Peloza v. *Capistrano Unified District,* 1994. John Peloza claimed that his First Amendment rights were violated by the school district's inclusion of evolution in the curriculum, because he considered evolution as a "religion of evolutionism." The Ninth Circuit Court of Appeals upheld a district court finding that the teacher's rights were *not* violated when the district appropriately required the science teacher to teach a scientific theory in biology.

Kansas State Board of Education, 1999, The Kansas State Board of Education voted to greatly restrict the emphasis on evolution in the state's science standards and, in doing so, ensured that evolution would not be a part of the State's assessment tests. The State Board did not prohibit the teaching of evolution and it did not remove mention of evolution (microevolution is mentioned) from the State's science standards.

Certainly, pressures from state mandates, parents, school boards, and religious groups have had and continue to have a strong influence on teachers' motivation to address evolution in school science in order to explain changes in the earth and in living organisms over time. Science teachers can find a good rationale and recommendations for teaching evolution from U.S. Supreme Court decisions, science teacher organizations, and the scientific community.

The National Science Teachers Association's Board of Directors (NSTA, August 1997) issued its position statement on the teaching of evolution to help science teachers understand the difference between science and nonscience tenants. The Board states that "scientists seek to develop theories that:

- are internally consistent and compatible with the evidence
- are firmly grounded in and based upon evidence
- have been tested against a diverse range of phenomena
- possess broad and demonstrated effectiveness in problem-solving
- explain a wide variety of phenomena." (p. 2)

One debate concerning the teaching of evolution is not about banning such instruction but rather about providing equal time for the creation story as a valid alternative. Thus, the approach has changed, but the controversy continues. Mandates forcing science teachers to provide instruction regarding creationism strike at the heart of academic freedom. Science teachers are exercising this academic freedom and choosing not to teach creationism. Furthermore, as Skoog (1985, p. 8) points out:

> Equal time policies are not necessarily fair or educationally sound. . . . Science teachers cannot treat all knowledge equally. We must select content based on its power to explain the natural world scientifically and its ability to unify, illuminate, and integrate other facets. We should not include ideas that cannot serve these functions. . . . The courts have ruled that laws prohibiting the teaching of evolution are unconstitutional and that teachers have no obligation to shield students from ideas that may offend their religious beliefs. Furthermore, it is possible to excuse students from classes where topics, offensive to their religious beliefs, are being presented.

Science teachers must understand the history of the issues and debates surrounding the creationism/evolution controversy over the last century. Without this background, they will be intimidated and unsure of themselves in handling the teaching of evolution, especially in states that have had court cases or that have Christian fundamentalist groups who oppose the teaching of evolution. Figure 12.2 provides a set of statements that can benefit those who desire to use evolution to explain the changes that have taken place in the universe and some of the factors that have led to these changes.

We would like to end this section by indicating the tremendous support that science teachers have from the scientific community. The National Academy of Science promotes science and values the understanding that science has formulated about the universe. The Academy points out:

> In 1987 the US Supreme Court ruled that creationism is religion, not science, and cannot be advocated in public school classrooms. And most major religious groups have concluded that the concept of evolution is not at odds with their descriptions of creation and human origins. . . .
>
> Scientists, like many others, are touched with awe at the order and complexity of nature. Indeed, many scientists are deeply religious. But science and religion occupy two separate realms of human experience. Demanding that they are combined detracts from the glory of each. (Alberts, 1999, p. iv)

- Evolution means change over time and is considered a *fact* in science because of the enormous amount of evidence that has been amassed to support the changes that have occurred in the biological and physical worlds since the beginning of the universe.
- Theories are used to explain the mechanism of change and are supported by a great deal of evidence and agreement put forth by scientists. For example, plate tectonics explains the movement of the earth's crust over time. Natural selection explains the changes in biological organisms.
- Often the term *theory of evolution* is used to explain how life on earth has changed. Technically the "theory of evolution" is a contradictory term in light of the definitions given regarding the fact that evolution occurs and natural selection is the theory that explains change over time.
- Acknowledge that science is only one way of knowing about the world in which we live. Art, religion, and history are other important sources of knowledge, but science has a different goal than these enterprises, which is to understand natural phenomena.
- Instruct students about the facts, concepts, laws, and theories of science, and avoid teaching nonscience tenets.
- When teaching about physical and biological phenomena, bring into the classroom objects and materials that provide evidence for evolutionary changes that have occurred over the earth's history. Engage students in inquiry experiences with concrete materials that further their understanding of evolution and the nature of science.
- Plan ahead to determine how to deal with objections from students and parents who oppose instruction that includes evolution. Make provisions to give students alternative work in science if they wish to leave the classroom during instruction on evolution.
- The courts have upheld the right to teach evolution in science and the right *not* to teach creationism or any other religious idea in the science curriculum.
- Giving equal time to creationism or providing a forum for students to debate the merits of creationism versus evolution to determine the origin of the universe is not recommended. Instruct students about science (evolution) and leave religion (creationism) to religious instruction.

FIGURE 12.2   Ideas and recommendations for teaching evolution in the science curriculum.

ASSESSING AND REVIEWING

Analysis and Synthesis

1. The following statements describe aspects of science instruction. Which of the 8 characterize instruction that has an STS orientation? Give reasons for your choices.
   - Instruction is guided by student questions and interests.
   - Instruction is guided by a textbook.
   - Students are active participants in the learning process.
   - Instruction makes use of all available resources, both material and people, to resolve problems.
   - Instruction is teacher-centered.
   - Students collaborate to investigate issues and problems.
   - Emphasis is placed on content mastery that is demonstrated on tests.
   - Students apply science concepts to new situations.

2. Suppose you learned from your principal that parents believe that their children are not learning the content they should from your science course because of your efforts to incorporate technology- and science-related societal issues into the curriculum. Write a letter that you would send to

parents to convince them of the importance of including technology- and science-related societal issues in your course.

3. For one of the topics listed, describe a lesson in which students would build working models of a machine or gadget to further their understanding of technology.
   - Motions and forces
   - Chemical reactions
   - Geochemical cycles
   - Origin and evolution of the universe
   - The cell
   - Structure and property of matter

Practical Considerations

4. Using the vignette in Figure 12.1 as a guide, develop a vignette on a science and societal issue or problem. Then, try out your vignette with a group of middle school or high school students. Discuss your experience with a classmate.

5. Examine materials from one of the STS-oriented curriculum programs identified in Table 12.3 or another program that you know about. Write a brief critique of the program that you can share with classmates. In your critique, mention what you found to be the program's strengths and limitations relative to its content focus, instructional design, student and teacher materials, and approach to assessment. Conclude your critique by indicating whether or not you would like to use the program with classes of students and the reasons for your decision.

6. Arrange to observe a teacher's lesson that has an STS orientation. After the lesson, ask the teacher to describe the intended purpose of the lesson and how it is related to lessons that came before and those that will follow. Then, talk with classmates about your observation and discussion with the teacher. What aspects of STS are reflected in the teacher's lesson? What did you learn from observing the lesson and talking with the teacher that will likely affect your teaching?

7. Develop a lesson to teach STS content in a science class. The content focus of your lesson should be a science-related issue or problem. Teach your lesson to classmates or middle or high school students. Then, write a critique of your lesson, describing its strengths and limitations. Conclude your critique by telling what changes you would make to the lesson if you were to teach it again.

Developmental Considerations

8. Start a collection of newspaper clippings, magazine articles, and Internet sites that address technology and science-related social issues.

9. Read the *National Science Education Standards* and the *Benchmarks for Scientific Literacy* to learn more about what these documents say about addressing technology- and science-related social issues and problems within the context of science classes. In Chapter 6 of the *Standards,* check out the Science and Technology as well as the Science in Personal and Social Perspective standards; in the *Benchmarks,* examine the chapters titled "The Nature of Technology," "Human Society," "Historical Perspectives," and "The Designed World."

RESOURCES TO EXAMINE

Beyond Discovery: The Path from Research to Human Benefit. [On-line.] Available: http://www. BeyondDiscovery.org.

This site, a project of the National Academy of Science, contains a host of cases that highlight significant recent technological and medical advances and traces their historical roots. Titles currently available include: The Hepatitis B Story, Disarming a Deadly Virus, The Global Positioning System, Modern Communication, and The Ozone Depletion Phenomenon. The cases can be read on-line or downloaded using Adobe Acrobat Reader. New cases on different topics are added each year.

NSTA Pathways to the Science Standards: Guidelines for Moving the Vision into Practice. Published in 1996 (secondary edition) and 1998 (middle school edition). Arlington, VA: National Science Teachers Association.

Address for ordering: 1840 Wilson Boulevard, Arlington, VA 22201.

These edited guidebooks provide practical suggestions for enacting the *National Science Education Standards.* Of particular interest with regard to STS are the sections "Personal and Social Perspectives" and "Science and Technology" that are presented for each key area of life science, physical science, and earth and space science content standards. Ideas are offered about how to make connections between technology and society and the science content specified in the standards.

Bulletin of Science, Technology, and Society.   Journal is available in paper copy and issues since 1999 are available on-line.

This journal is published by Sage Publications. Each issue includes articles about STS teaching strategies, technological innovations, and science-related social issues and problems. Many of the articles speak directly to pre-college science teachers and offer suggestions for the infusion of STS experiences into traditional science curricula.

STS Links.   [On-line.] Available: http://www.ncsu.edu/chass/mes/stswlinks.html.

Sponsored by North Carolina State University, this site contains links to a multitude of STS-related cites. Categories under which the links are organized include: Environment and Ecology; Genetics and Biotechnology; Activist; and Publications, Journals and Newsletters.

Teaching About Evolution and the Nature of Science. 1998. Washington, DC: National Academy Press.

This 140-page paperback book by the National Academy of Science contains rationales, ideas, and activities for teaching evolution. Some of the chapter titles are: Why Teach Evolution?, Major Themes in Evolution, Evolution and the Nature of Science, Frequently Asked Questions About Evolution and the Nature of Science, Activities for Teaching About Evolution and the Nature of Science, and Selecting Instructional Materials.

Science and Creationism: A View from the National Academy of Science.   1999. Washington DC: National Academy Press. [On-line]. Available: www.nap.edu.

This is a very informative booklet that explains the importance of evolution and discusses objections to creationism in the science curriculum. This resource examines the origin of the universe, earth, and life, presenting evidence to support biological evolution. It includes answers to frequently asked questions, responses to objections to teaching evolution, and a recommended reading list for a variety of audiences.

REFERENCES

Aikenhead, G. (1994). What is STS science teaching? In J. Solomon & G. Aikenhead (Eds.), *STS education: International perspectives on reform* (pp. 47–59). New York: Teachers College Press.

Alberts, B. (1999). Preface. In the *National Academy of Sciences, Science and creationism: A view from the National Academy of Sciences,* (p. ix). Washington, DC: The National Academy Press.

American Association for the Advancement of Science (AAAS). (1993). *Benchmarks for scientific literacy.* Washington, DC: AAAS.

Ballantyne, R., & Bain, J. (1995). Enhancing environmental conceptions: An evaluation of cognitive conflict and structured controversy. *Studies in Higher Education, 20*(3), 293–303.

Brinckerhoff, R. F. (1986). *Values in schools: Some practical materials and suggestions.* Exeter, NH: Exeter Academy.

Bugliarello, G. (1995). Science, technology and society. *Bulletin of Science, Technology and Society, 15*(5–6), 228–234.

Dobzhansky, T. (1973). Nothing in biology makes sense except in the light of evolution. *The American Biology Teacher, 35,* 125–129.

Gallagher, J. J. (2004). Important goals of project-centered teaching. In T. Koballa & D. Tippins (Eds.), *Cases in middle and secondary science education: The promise and the dilemmas* (pp. 104–106). Upper Saddle River, NJ: Merrill/Prentice Hall.

Johnson, D. W., & Johnson, R. T. (1988). Critical thinking through structured controversy. *Educational Leadership, 45*(8), 58–64.

Krajcik, J., Czerniak, C., & Berger, C. (1999). *Teaching children science: A project-based approach.* Boston: McGraw-Hill.

National Academy of Science. (1998). *Teaching about evolution and the nature of science.* Washington, DC: National Academy Press.

National Council for the Social Studies (NCSS). (1994). *Curriculum standards for social studies.* Washington, DC: National Council for the Social Studies.

National Research Council. (1996). *National science education standards.* Washington, DC: National Academy of Science.

National Science Teachers Association (NSTA). (1997). *An NSTA position statement: The teaching of evolution.* [On-line.] Available: http://www.nasta.org/handbook/evolve.htm (July 11, 2004).

Oliver, D. W., & Newman, F. M. (1967). *Taking a stand.* Middletown, CT: Xerox Corp.

Rubba, P. A., & Wiesenmayer, R. L. (1988). Goals and competencies for precollege STS education: recommendations based upon recent literature in environmental education. *Journal of Environmental Education, 19*(4), 38–44.

Simon, S. B., Hartwell, M. R., & Hawkins, L. A. (1973). *Values clarification: Friends and other people: teachers manual.* Arlington Heights, IL: Paxcom.

Skoog, G. (1985). The editors corner. *The Science Teacher, 52*(1), 8.

Solomon, J. (2002). The dilemma of science, technology, and society education. In S. Amos & R. Boohan (Eds.), *Teaching science in secondary schools* (pp. 94–101). London: The Open University Press.

TERC. (2000). *Constructing a glove.* Arlington, VA: NSTA.

Wheeler, C., Gallagher, J., McDonough, M., & Sookpokakit-Namfa, B. (1997). Improving school-community relations in Thailand. In W. Cummings & P. Altbach (Eds.), *The challenge of Eastern Asia education: Implications for America* (pp. 205–220). Albany, NY: SUNY Press.

Wolfe, M. F. (2000). *Rube Goldberg: Inventions!* New York: Simon and Schuster.

Laboratory Work and Fieldwork

Laboratory work often requires special materials and equipment.

Laboratory and fieldwork are unique types of science instruction. These strategies involve *firsthand* experiences, permitting students to participate in science as a way of thinking and investigating. Laboratory and fieldwork also can help students to better understand science concepts, principles, and theories. These instructional strategies provide concrete, authentic experiences that aid students in comprehending phenomena that are discussed in the classroom. However, in order for important learning outcomes to be realized from laboratory and fieldwork, science teachers must plan them carefully and keep them focused on the specific learning outcomes.

AIMS OF THE CHAPTER

Use the questions that follow to guide your thinking and learning about laboratory and fieldwork:

- How precisely can you define the purpose of laboratory and fieldwork?

- Can you explain at least five types of laboratory approaches that should be used in science courses and develop exercises that illustrate these approaches?

- What are important elements to include when conducting prelaboratory and postlaboratory discussions?

- Can you list many teaching tips that will promote successful laboratory experiences for students?

- How would you plan a field trip for a group of students that will be instructive and safe?

WHAT IS LABORATORY WORK?

Laboratory work engages students in learning through *firsthand* experiences—interaction with the actual phenomenon being studied—not through simulations. This type of activity involves students in scientific inquiry by placing them in the position of asking questions, proposing solutions, designing experiments, making predictions, making observations, organizing data, explaining patterns, and so on. Laboratory work permits students to plan and to participate in investigations or to take part in activities that will help them improve their technical laboratory skills. Some laboratory work involves hands-on activities in which students use specialized equipment. Other laboratory work requires only ordinary equipment found in our everyday environment. Certain laboratory work is best conducted in field and natural settings where little equipment is necessary and where no intervention from the observer is required.

The science laboratory is central to science teaching because it serves many purposes. Laboratory work has the potential to engage students in authentic investigations in which they can identify their own problems to investigate, design procedures, and draw conclusions. These activities can give students a sense as to how scientists go about their work, which in turn may influence their attitudes about the scientific enterprise. Along with attitudes about science, laboratory work can help students acquire a better understanding of concepts and principles as the result of concrete experiences (Freedman, 2002). In general, laboratory work can be used to promote the following learning outcomes:

- Attitudes toward science
- Scientific attitudes
- Scientific inquiry
- Conceptual development
- Technical skills

Science laboratory work seems to leave a lasting impression on students. "Many of them [students] enjoy lab work and prefer it to other modes of learning. This is not, of course, the universal reaction of all students at all times" (Gardner & Gauld, 1990, p. 136). This statement is especially true of the middle school students who prefer active learning experiences over listening to lectures. Science teachers who are highly regarded by students frequently include laboratory exercises in their courses. These teachers believe that laboratory work enhances concept development and promotes scientific attitudes. They also realize that lab work breaks up the instructional period, which limits the amount of lecturing and adds variety to the course.

The laboratory has always been emphasized in science teaching, and during some periods in the history of science education, it has been given a dominant role. During the major science curriculum reform movement of the 1960s, for example, some science educators felt that a considerable amount of laboratory work should lead, rather than lag behind, the classroom phase of science teaching (Schwab, 1964). Curriculum planners of the 1960s placed heavy emphasis on inquiry and the processes of science by suggesting that working on problems in the laboratory is more important than drawing conclusions and that science teachers should expose their students to certain amounts of doubt in science courses even though they and the students may not tolerate ambiguity well (Schwab, 1964). Henry (1960) indicated that more emphasis should be placed on how to process data and make predictions from data, and less stress should be placed on finding exact answers. Further, Hurd (1964) recommended that the laboratory should focus on major ideas related to class work and should precede textbook assignments. Even more recently, some science educators have advised science teachers to conduct laboratory work that emphasizes hypothesizing, predicting, developing concepts, model building, and developing positive attitudes toward science. They advise that lab work should de-emphasize illustration, demonstration, and verification (Lunetta & Tamir, 1979).

The recommendation to implement inquiry-based laboratories, such as those intended by the national curriculum projects of the 1960s, may be appropriate for some students and for certain purposes. As pointed out earlier, the curriculum reform projects of the 1960s were very laboratory oriented, but they did not necessarily provide students with the experiences needed to live in a changing society. The curriculum reform projects of the 1990s, on the other hand, emphasize scientific literacy and stress the need for students to have experiences that permit them to adapt to a changing world.

Laboratory work is not a panacea for improving science education. Although most science educators promote lab work, this strategy does not necessarily produce all of the outcomes believed by many educators (Blosser, 1981; Hegarty-Hazel, 1990) for a number of reasons. For example, a great deal of the lab work that takes place in schools is "aimless, trivial, and badly planned" (Hodson, 1985, p. 44). Laboratory work that is counter to what students expect does not necessarily produce new conceptions (Rowell & Dawson, 1983). Laboratory periods are often too short, and students do not complete their lab work (Gardner & Gauld, 1990). Of course, materials and equipment are a problem in some schools where limited resources are available for this type of instruction. Some researchers who have studied the construction of scientific knowledge advise that the role of the laboratory needs to be reexamined, because student learning from firsthand experiences may not produce the intended learning outcomes that we believe them to produce (Driver, Guesne, & Tiberghien, 1985).

The ultimate success of laboratory work lies with science teachers who determine the frequency, importance, and purpose of this enterprise in a science course. If a teacher believes that laboratory work is important and has the competence and facilities to carry out this type of instruction, the chances are good that the students will frequently engage in meaningful firsthand experiences. If the teacher believes that the function of a science program is to transmit information, laboratories will be deductive in nature, occurring after textbook reading and classroom discussion; thus, the laboratory will serve only to verify existing knowledge. If the teacher believes that a science program should be investigative in nature, then some laboratories will be inductive and occur before textbook readings and teacher lectures (Pella, 1961).

Beginning and practicing science teachers should carefully formulate their professional philosophy of science teaching, taking into consideration the curriculum, the students, their approach to instruction, the facilities, and the materials available. Teachers must understand the various approaches to laboratory work so they can make good decisions regarding the type of laboratory to use with a given group of students in order to achieve a given purpose. Further, science teachers must learn to analyze laboratory manuals, related exercises, and the laboratory work taking place in their own science departments in order to evaluate their potential to promote scientific inquiry (Lazarowitz & Tamir, 1994).

Science course laboratory work can be used to achieve many different learning outcomes. Some laboratory exercises, for example, might be employed to verify a concept previously discussed in class. Other types of laboratory exercises might be used to develop particular manipulative skills that are needed for subsequent lab work. Some laboratory exercises facilitate the attainment of concepts. The desired outcomes will dictate the type of laboratory needed. Each type of laboratory approach has characteristics differentiating it from other approaches. In general, most approaches can be classified into one of five categories:

1. Science process skill
2. Deductive or verification
3. Inductive
4. Technical skill
5. Problem solving

Science Process Skill Laboratory

A major purpose for including laboratory work is to develop in students a sense for the nature of science. This aim requires that students use inquiry skills to engage in investigation. Some of the mental processes associated with science and, in particular, with laboratory work are referred to as science process skills. These skills include observing, classifying, using space/time relations, using numbers, measuring, inferring, predicting, defining operationally, formulating models, controlling variables, interpreting data, and experimenting (see Chapter 10). When the primary intent of a laboratory exercise is to help students develop the ability to use one or more science process skills, the laboratory can be classified as a science process laboratory. Certainly, science process skills are involved in all types of laboratory work, such as observing, for example. Nevertheless, some laboratory work can be used specifically to improve students' awareness and competence in using skills that are related to scientific reasoning.

There are many skills that people use to think critically and reason logically. In Chapter 10, many of the cognitive reasoning patterns were discussed, and a long list of science process skills were presented and defined. Table 13.1 provides a sample of science process skills that deserve the attention of science teachers because these are skills that middle and high school students should be capable of using.

Consider *observing* and *inferring*, which are related skills. Often, science teachers begin the school year with exercises that address these cognitive abilities. The exercise shown in Figure 13.1 is one that can stimulate students' interests in observing and inferring and give them practice with these skills. Some creativity has been put into this exercise to help students visualize these concepts. Note that definitions and background information are provided along with several examples on distinguishing observations from inferences. Just as important, students are given experiences at lab stations to help them acquire these process skills.

Figure 13.2 provides an example of an exercise that a science teacher might develop to give students practice with measurement. Note, again, that some creativity has been put into this instructional material, as noted by the title: "What Is Your Measurement Quotient (MQ)?" For this laboratory exercise, students are first given common objects to determine if they have any ideas of their mass, temperature, or length. Then they have the opportunity to check their estimates using the metric system. Both the teacher and the students can determine the degree to which the students are fluent in metric measurement, which is their measurement quotient. Of course, measuring must continue to be used throughout the year and become part of all laboratory work.

Perhaps no science course is complete unless each student has been given the opportunity to conduct an experiment. Experimenting is the most complex of the integrated process skills and one that requires students to use many process skills to test out an idea. A true experiment tests a hypothesis that states a relationship between variables. Experiments can range from simple to very complex procedures. In science teaching, experiments can be valuable activities for which students are prepared and realize their purpose. Quite often, the term *experimenting* is used loosely to mean simply "trying something out" or "messing around." Although trying something out and messing around might be encouraged, these activities should be distinguished from a true experiment.

Some science educators prefer to restrict the term *experiment* to the type of investigation known as the *controlled experiment*, in which every effort is made to control the variables involved. All factors, except for the independent variable, are held constant, and the effects of the independent variable on the dependent variable

TABLE 13.1   A Sample of Science Process Skills to Develop in Middle and High School Laboratory Instruction

Process Skill	Learning Outcome
Observing and inferring	Distinguish between observations and inferences. Make accurate observations that describe objects and events. Make plausible inferences that help to explain situations.
Measuring	Make measurements for length, mass, and volume, using SI or metric units.
Hypothesizing	Distinguish between inferences and hypotheses and know when to use each. Construct hypotheses that can be tested and for which enough data can be gathered for generalizing.
Communicating	Construct and label tables, bar graphs, and line graphs that are accurate and fit the situation. Keep a laboratory notebook and journal of activities with reflections. Write laboratory reports that are coherent and present procedures, results, and conclusions.
Experimenting	Test hypotheses and answer questions through controlled experimentation where independent and dependent variables are accounted for and properly controlled.

FIGURE 13.1 An example of an observing and inferring exercise.

Observing and Inferring Can Be a Safe Activity

An **observation** is the act of noting something that can be sensed directly or with the aid of an instrument. One can observe the color of a car, the final score of a basketball game, or the first snowstorm of the season. These and many other observations can be made, confirmed by others, and established as a matter of record. Direct observations are possible through the five senses—smell, taste, sight, sound, and touch. Although observations can be disputed, most everyday observations are accepted as fact. Indirect observations are made with instruments, such as microscopes, spectrophotometers, and multimeters.

An **inference** differs from an observation in a significant way, because it requires individuals to explain what they observe. An inference is an attempt to explain a particular event or object. It requires thinking and reasoning to make the leap from what is observed at the surface to what the observer believes is there and hidden from view or perception. An inference requires the observer to go beyond the obvious. Inferences, however, are not exactly hypotheses. A **hypothesis** is a generalization that relates to a class of objects or events, whereas an inference is related to a specific object or event. Let's develop the skill of distinguishing between observations and inferences.

Look at the illustration of the safe. Visualize yourself in a friend's home where you notice a similar safe in the master bedroom. The safe is thick, made of steel, and appears to be locked shut. Would you not wonder what is in this strong container? At best you could observe the size of this structure; however, you could not open it to see what is inside. You could infer or guess its contents. Perhaps it contains cash, jewelry, personal letters, and prized photographs. All of these ideas would be inferences made in an attempt to surmise what is inside the safe. Unfortunately, you cannot even pick up the safe and shake it to determine what rattles around inside.

Let's consider another example to distinguish between observations and inferences. Mr. Lee died on January 4, 1992, at 2:37 A.M. in San Jose, California. He was 48 years of age at the time of death. The cause of death was given as "natural" and no autopsy was performed. Mr. Lee did not indicate that he was sick. It is known that he had smoked one to two packs of cigarettes per day from the time he was 17 years old. It is easy to point the finger at cigarettes, but perhaps something else led to Mr. Lee's death. In this case, the fact that death occurred, when it happened, and where it happened is hard to refute. Many inferences can be put forth to explain his death, however, such as cigarettes, fat in the diet, or a hereditary disease that was eating away at Mr. Lee, about which he said nothing to his family and friends.

Now let's practice our observations and inferences. At lab stations 1–8 there are 35 mm film canisters in which one or more objects have been placed. You are to make many observations about each container and then infer what is inside. At the ninth lab station is a paper bag with something inside. You will be given an opportunity to smell the contents of the bag, but not to look inside. Record your observations and infer the contents. At the 10th station is a bag with objects inside. You will be given one of these objects to eat, during which time you must close your eyes and plug your nose. Record your observations and indicate what you ate. For each lab station exercise, write your observations on the left side of your lab notebook page and the inferences on the right side as shown below.

Observations   *Inferences*

Station 1:

Station 2:

Etc.

FIGURE 13.2   An exercise to develop science process skills.

What Is Your Measurement Quotient (MQ)?

Directions: For each question provide two answers. Give an estimate even if you are not sure. Then, determine a more accurate quantity than your estimate by weighing, measuring, or going to a printed source.

Equipment and materials: aspirins, dimes, balances, metric rulers, measuring cups, graduated cylinders, a metric scale, and metric balances

	Your estimate	*Actual measurement*
1. What is the mass of an aspirin tablet in grams?	_____	_____
2. What is the mass of your body in kilograms?	_____	_____
3. At what temperature does water boil in degrees Celsius?	_____	_____
4. What should your approximate body temperature be in degrees Celsius?	_____	_____
5. How many milliliters are in a 2-liter soft drink bottle?	_____	_____
6. How many milliliters are in a cup?	_____	_____
7. How many millimeters thick is a dime?	_____	_____
8. How many centimeters across is a dime?	_____	_____
9. What is the mass of a dime in grams?	_____	_____
10. On a rattlesnake hunt, six snakes were collected. The length of the snakes caught were: 35 cm, 43 cm, 62 cm, 72 cm, 85 cm, and 1.10 m.		_____
a. Estimate the average length of these snakes.	_____	
b. Compute the average length of the snakes.		_____
c. Graph the data to display the lengths of the snakes. Label the axes and give a title to the graph.		

---

are observed. For example: To determine the effect of ammonium sulfate on plant growth, two seed flats containing soil from the same lawn are seeded using a standard lawn grass mixture. One flat is watered with rainwater and the other with rainwater containing a little ammonium sulfate. The flats are kept in the same area to ensure identical conditions of temperature and light.

In this experiment, the seed flat watered with rainwater alone is called the *control.* The seed flat watered with the rain water containing ammonium sulfate (fertilizer) is called the *experimental situation,* and the ammonium sulfate is the *independent variable.* The

hypothesis being tested in this experiment is: Ammonium sulfate will increase plant growth. The *dependent variable* is the amount of plant growth.

Science teachers can use science-process-oriented laboratories to great advantage if they are sensitive to the intellectual development of their students. They should realize that there is a high correlation between the integrated science process skills and the ability to use formal operational thinking (Yeany, Yap, & Padilla, 1986). It may take considerable time to identify variables and formulate hypotheses. Thus, the less cognitively demanding skills, such as defining operationally, interpreting data, and graphing, may be the initial focus of science-process-oriented laboratory exercises for many youngsters. With some thought and planning, science process skill laboratories can be very effective in motivating students to be successful inquirers, helping them to develop important cognitive skills and subject matter knowledge. This type of laboratory may also promote the spirit of science, especially among middle school students.

Deductive or Verification Laboratory

The deductive or verification laboratory is perhaps the most common approach to laboratory work in science courses. The purpose for this type of laboratory work is to confirm concepts, principles, and laws that have been addressed during classroom discussion and reading. Most science teachers present major ideas first, through lecture, discussion, and reading, followed by laboratory work to illustrate examples of key concepts. A biology teacher, for example, might use the deductive approach to discuss different types of bacteria, such as rod-, spherical-, and spiral-shaped cells. The oral presentation might then be followed by a laboratory exercise during which students observe the different shapes of bacteria under the microscope. Or a physics teacher might use a verification laboratory to demonstrate to students how the intensity of light diminishes as the distance between the light source and the light receptor increases (Figure 8.3). In connection with the laboratory, a formula might be presented to students and problems solved on the chalkboard using various numbers to represent the distance between two points. Students are often convinced of the mathematical model of light intensity through verification of the law in the laboratory.

Many concepts, principles, and laws can be developed best through a deductive approach, whereby they are first discussed by the teacher, then followed by a laboratory activity to verify attributes and relationships. Many of the laws of physics and chemistry, which are represented by mathematical formulas, can be illustrated in laboratory work. When the formulas for these laws are first presented in class, students begin to realize their meaning. Greater meaning is acquired when students gather data and use the data with the formula to verify the law or principle under investigation.

Verification laboratories have a positive feature in that they tend to provide students with an advanced organization of an abstract idea. With this approach, students are given some notion of what they are expected to find out. Many students, especially middle school students, do not tolerate ambiguity well, and therefore they need to know what they are looking for in their laboratory work. This is why many science teachers discuss a concept or principle before they take students into the laboratory to carry out an investigation.

Consider the deductive approach used by a high school physics teacher during the study of light and electromagnetism presented in Box 13.1. You might agree from reading the description of this deductive instruction that the approach can help to reinforce subject matter content that is taken up in the classroom. In many instances, science teachers have found this method to be beneficial, first to give students a conceptual organization of the topic and then to provide them with firsthand experiences. Also, note how Mrs. Beck attempted to avoid making this experience a cookbook laboratory by helping students become familiar with the procedures so that they would not be preoccupied

FIGURE 13.3 This concept map can help students conceptualize the behavior of light through discussion and a verification laboratory exercise.

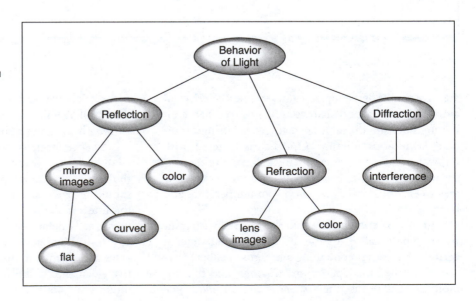

Classroom Snapshot 13.1

A Deductive Laboratory Exercise

Mrs. Beck begins her instruction on light and electromagnetism by providing students with a brief historical background and overview of this topic. She initiates this study with a lecture/discussion on three theories of light—particle, wave, and field. This segment is followed by a presentation on the work of the scientists who contributed to our understanding of these theories. Then Mrs. Beck carefully discusses the behavior of light, which she organizes in three main parts: (a) reflection, (b) refraction, and (c) diffraction. She provides students with a concept map to illustrate the order in which the behavior of light will be studied as well as the aspects of each that will be examined in the laboratory (see Figure 13.3).

After the background and overview, Mrs. Beck involves students in their first laboratory on the topic, which involves reflection. During the prelaboratory discussion, she calls on several students to explain reflection. Then Mrs. Beck specifies what the students are required to determine during the laboratory. A demonstration takes place on how to measure the angles of incidence and reflection. Again, she calls on several students to be sure that they know what to do during the laboratory experience so they will not need to constantly refer to the laboratory procedures.

The laboratory exercise requires students to work in groups and to determine the angle of reflection produced by imposing a beam of light on a reflecting surface. They are free to use many angles from which to strike the surface with a light beam. Although the students have a pretty good idea of what to expect as a result of their classroom discussions, they seem challenged by the activity because the teacher provides a variety of surfaces on which to study reflection. Some of the students display a lack of understanding about the principle, however, which is evident when they are asked to predict the reflection of a light beam that has a large angle of incidence.

with following written directions during the laboratory and by giving them some freedom to "experiment" with the angle of the incident light beam.

Inductive Laboratory

The inductive laboratory is the opposite of the deductive laboratory. The inductive laboratory provides students with the opportunity to develop concepts, principles, and laws through firsthand experiences before these ideas are discussed in the classroom. The inductive approach places students in the position to search for patterns and to identify relationships among data, after which the ideas are discussed by the teacher and applications of the concepts are provided to reinforce the learning.

Although science teachers frequently use deductive laboratories, they should also use inductive laboratories to help students acquire fundamental science concepts and principles. Examine the inductive approach taken by a high school science teacher, Mr. Fleming. Read about one of Mr. Fleming's laboratory exercises in Box 13.2, and study his laboratory worksheet in Figure 13.4 and the laboratory instructions to students in Figure 13.5. Then answer the following questions:

1. How effective is Mr. Fleming's attempt to introduce pressure through an inductive approach?
2. Contrast this inductive approach with the procedures that would be used to introduce pressure in a deductive manner.
3. Which aspects of this laboratory pertain to the *exploration, invention,* and *application* phases of the learning cycle? (See Chapter 10 for a discussion of the learning cycle.)

Technical Skill Laboratory

Good laboratory techniques are essential for conducting successful laboratory activities and gathering accurate data. They require manipulative skills that involve the development of hand-eye coordination, such as focusing a microscope, sketching specimens, measuring angles, and cutting glass. Good laboratory work also includes experimental technique and orderliness. Although laboratory work often relies on students' abilities to manipulate equipment, some is highly dependent on the use of

Classroom Snapshot 13.2

An Inductive Laboratory Exercise

The students who enroll in Mr. Fleming's chemistry course enter the 10th grade with very little understanding of basic science concepts and principles. He has had to be creative in order to provide concrete experiences that help students visualize abstract ideas and construct this form of knowledge. For example, Mr. Fleming had very little success in teaching the concept of pressure until he began to initiate the instruction in the laboratory.

Mr. Fleming begins the study of pressure with a series of stations set up around the laboratory. Students work in pairs and go to each of 10 stations where they make observations and provide explanations for what they encounter (see Figure 13.4). At each station there are familiar objects to examine or manipulate and a set of directions with information (see Figure 13.5). The 10 setups present students with a variety of situations to study, in which they receive firsthand, sensory experiences with pressure.

After the students have interacted with the instructional materials at each station, Mr. Fleming conducts a discussion of the observations, encouraging students to explain their thoughts in a thorough manner. Here is where he introduces the term *pressure* and begins to use it to help students explain the phenomena they have observed. As the discussion proceeds, Mr. Fleming develops a definition for pressure. He also calls on all of the students in the class to participate. When students are not clear about a particular occurrence or explanation, he asks them to go to a particular lab station to demonstrate what happens and to explain the events.

For the next day, Mr. Fleming asks students to bring to class one example of pressure in their everyday life and how that pressure changes. These sessions address a large range of events, from boiling water to diving into swimming pools. After a long discussion of the pressure examples that students bring to class, he sends them to the laboratory sinks where two lengths of rubber tubing have been placed. One of the tubes is twice as large in diameter as the other. Mr. Fleming asks each student to predict the pressure in the two different-sized hoses when they are attached to the faucet and the water handle is turned to the same position to let water flow into the tubes. After the students make their predictions and explain them, they test out their ideas. The findings are discussed with regard to pressure. At the end of the discussion Mr. Fleming asks the students to write about this laboratory experience and to explain pressure in a variety of situations.

"The Pressure Is On"—Lab Worksheet

Instructions: A series of stations are located around the room. You and a partner should move from station to station and examine each situation carefully. Written instructions are at each station; follow them carefully. Record your answers and observations and explain them in the spaces provided below. If you are unsure about your explanation or if you have additional questions, be sure to record those as well.

Station	Observations	Explanations
1		
2		
3		
4		
5		
6		
7		
8		
9		
10		

FIGURE 13.4   A laboratory worksheet is used for recording observations and making explanations at 10 stations set up in the laboratory.

"THE PRESSURE IS ON"—LAB STATION INSTRUCTIONS

STATION 1:

Imagine that you are in a crowded store and two women are approaching. Both are the same height and weight. One woman is wearing tennis shoes and the other high-heel dress shoes. All of you are converging on the same place in order to reach for the same item. You are certain that one of the women is going to step on your toe. Which woman would inflict more pain on your toe? Explain your answer.

STATION 2:

Each of the containers on the table is a tank filled with a different gas. All three tanks are of equal volume and all are at the same temperature. Each of the small wooden beads inside each tank represents a gas molecule in rapid motion. In which container would the pressure be greatest? How do you explain this?

STATION 3:

The container is filled with colored water. Look carefully inside and squeeze the container. Record your observations as you squeeze the container and as you release your grip on the container. Perform this squeezing and letting up many times and explain what you observe.

STATION 4:

Place your hand inside the plastic bag and try to pull the bag from the jar. What do you notice as you pull your hand out? Why does this happen?

STATION 5:

Gently pull down on the red balloon. What happens? How might this device simulate the actions associated with human breathing?

STATION 6:

Examine the marshmallow underneath the jar. Place both hands on the pump and start pumping. What is happening and how can you explain it?

STATION 7:

Fill the drinking glass with water. Place the index card over the mouth of the glass and press to form a seal. Quickly invert the glass over the sink. Yes, the sink! What happens? Explain the results.

STATION 8:

Select two clean straws from the box. Fill the drinking glass half-full with water. Hold the straws together, but place one straw inside and one straw outside the glass. Suck on both straws at once and attempt to draw up water out of the glass. Does any of the water go up the straws? Explain!

STATION 9:

Examine the tennis balls. One of these balls is new and one is old. Squeeze both of them. Do they feel different? Squeeze the can that contains new tennis balls, but do not open it. Why do you think tennis balls are stored in a pressurized can?

STATION 10:

Examine the tire. Using the tire pressure gauge, find the pressure of the tire. How does a tire pressure gauge measure the pressure of a tire?

FIGURE 13.5 These instructions are for a series of 10 stations set up in the laboratory for students to examine situations that are related to pressure.

special equipment and techniques; therefore, the emphasis of some laboratories should involve the development and use of these skills and techniques.

Science educators have placed too little emphasis upon developing proficiency in laboratory skills and techniques (Hegarty-Hazel, 1990). All students and science teachers should master many basic laboratory techniques and manipulative skills associated with the science area in which they are involved, some of which are presented in Figure 13.6. Science teachers who plan and organize laboratory experiences ahead of time can identify techniques that require special attention. For instance, the microscope is used a great deal in biology laboratory work. Most adolescents have difficulty focus-

FIGURE 13.6   Some techniques and manipulative skills necessary for science laboratory programs.

General Science

Constructing and calibrating an equal-arm balance
Determining mass with an equal-arm balance
Constructing and measuring with a metric rule
Measuring temperature with a thermometer

Measuring volume with a graduated cylinder
Determining significant figures to indicate precision
  in measurement

Life Science

Dissecting a frog or a worm
Sketching an organism
Slicing a piece of tissue for microscopic
  examination
Preparing a wet-mount slide
Focusing a microscope
Measuring dimensions under a microscope
Transferring a microscopic organism from one
  medium to another

Taking a pulse
Sterilizing instruments
Making a serial dilution
Germinating seeds
Using paper chromatography to separate chemicals
Counting the growth of microorganisms

Earth Science

Growing crystals
Orienting a map with a compass
Making and reading topographic maps
Making a profile map
Using a stereoscope
Using a Brunton compass
Testing the physical properties of minerals
Reading a classification chart for rocks

Estimating the percentage of minerals in rocks
Classifying fossils
Plotting data on a time chart
Analyzing soil
Reading an aneroid and mercury barometer
Reading an anemometer
Plotting the sun's path

Chemistry

Cutting, bending, and polishing glass
Boiling liquids in a beaker
Folding filter paper and filtering solutions
Heating liquids in a test tube
Pouring liquids from a reagent bottle and a beaker
Pouring hot liquids from a beaker
Dispensing caustic solutions

Transferring powders and crystals
Smelling a chemical
Preparing solutions of a given concentration
Titrating with a burette
Calibrating a test tube
Using an analytic balance

Physics

Soldering electrical connections
Connecting electrical devices in parallel and
  series circuits
Using electric meters
Measuring time intervals with electrical and
  water clocks
Measuring weight with a spring balance

Determining the focal length of mirrors and lenses
Locating images in mirrors
Constructing a simple telescope
Constructing a spectroscope
Setting up a siphon

Classroom Snapshot 13.3

Developing Laboratory Skills

Ms. Avrey has learned over the years that it is essential to precede the laboratory on measuring electricity with a laboratory specifically designed to teach students how to use the voltmeter and ammeter. She learned from the past that if the students misread their meters when trying to determine voltage, current, or resistance, the lab is lost. In order to measure electricity accurately, using proper technique, students must practice reading meters first, then concentrating on collecting data and making calculations. "It is too much to ask the teenagers that I have in my classes to determine the amps in a circuit before they are comfortable with the use of the meters. Remember, these youngsters do not use meters such as these in their daily lives. What makes matters worse is that the meters we use in our labs have three scales, which can be very confusing to students. Therefore, when laboratory work related to electricity is carried out in stages to develop specific competencies, my students are successful and enjoy their science experiences."

ing the microscope and centering the specimen in the microscope field. Experienced biology teachers provide their students with laboratory exercises on the care and use of the microscope. This work permits students to view such objects as newsprint and human hair under the microscope in order to learn how to focus this instrument and how to move objects into view. Because of the lens system, everything viewed is reversed, which confuses students; therefore, they need practice focusing the microscope. Beginners, for example, have a tendency to crush the glass cover slips under the objective lens when attempting to bring a specimen into clear view.

Psychomotor and mental practice are beneficial in improving the accuracy and precision of a student's laboratory measurements (Beasley, 1985). Physical practice with laboratory equipment provides concrete experience with the apparatus and procedure (Box 13.3). It gives the student a set of experiences upon which to build images that represent the skill under development. Because time is always critical to laboratory work, firsthand exposure to the equipment is essential. Then, during class time and discussion sessions, mental practice of the skill and procedures under study can ensue.

In studying electricity, for example, experienced physical science teachers might say that it is essential to precede common laboratory exercises on electricity with one that focuses solely on measuring voltage and current, using the voltmeter and ammeter. It is often asking too much of teenagers to determine the current in a circuit before they are comfortable with the use of an ammeter. Remember, adolescents do not use electrical meters in their daily lives. What complicates this matter further is that many meters used in school laboratories have multiple scales, which can be very confusing to most people. Therefore, when laboratory work is carried out in stages, some designed to develop specific

technical skills, students have a better chance of benefiting from this type of instruction.

For the concrete operational students participating in a middle school earth science class, constructing a profile map can be a challenge. Translating topographic information from contour lines to a vertical/horizontal profile is a task that requires considerable mental as well as manipulative ability. Most students need practice before they gain competence in this task and are able to realize the three-dimensional nature of a contour map.

Making sketches and drawings is an essential part of laboratory work. This type of activity not only provides a record of observations, but it reinforces visual images that pertain to essential concepts and learning outcomes in a science course. Here are some guidelines that can be used when instructing students to draw what they see in a biology class (or any other science course):

- Draw using a pencil and unlined paper
- Make the drawing large enough so that important details are easily seen
- Place the drawing near the left side of the sheet so that the labels can be placed on the right side
- Print the labels one under the other
- Use a ruler to draw lines from the labels to the drawing, and do not cross lines
- Use light stippling or dotting to shade part of a drawing
- Construct a title for the drawing at the top of the page

The preceding discussion points out that many technical skills are necessary for improving students' ability to participate in and learn from laboratory work. Students need these skills to gain the unique learning outcomes associated with the science laboratory. If students have to struggle with basic manipulative procedures, they may lose sense of what they are trying to accomplish in the laboratory. Also, if students are so unfamiliar with basic lab procedures that they need to follow them in a rote manner, they will lose much of the cognitive and affective benefits of laboratory work because they are preoccupied with following directions.

Problem-Solving Laboratory

In some instances, science teachers should engage their students in problem-solving laboratory work where students are given opportunities to identify a problem, design procedures, collect information, organize data, and report the findings. This type of laboratory investigation can involve authentic inquiry experiences for students. This approach is also recommended on psychological grounds. Because students are involved in organizing their own learning, they may be inclined to better understand what they are doing. Students take more interest in their learning when they take part in organizing it.

Consider, for instance, a set of problem-solving laboratories at the middle school level in the life sciences. The teacher might recommend that students identify an insect to study over a 1- or 2-week period. The students select an insect they wish to study, then determine questions they wish to answer about the insect. Many students will be inclined to investigate what their insect eats. Most will attempt to determine their insect's reactions to various stimuli. For example, students who elect to study meal worms might determine how these insects react to water, vinegar, salt, soap, bran flakes, cola, sandpaper, glass, electricity, sound, heat, and light. The students can be encouraged to bring from home additional materials needed to study their insect. Some students may return to the laboratory after school hours to continue their inquiry beyond the regular time set aside for in-class laboratory work.

Some science teachers use the problem-solving approach with students who wish to satisfy their curiosity about certain situations or with students the teacher wishes to motivate to study science. Science teachers can accomplish these ends outside of the regular laboratory time, usually after school when students can spend many hours engaging in hands-on experiences. For more information and examples on problem-solving instruction, study the section on problem solving in Chapter 10.

PREPARING STUDENTS FOR LABORATORY EXPERIENCES

Students must be prepared for laboratory experiences in order to benefit from them. They need to know why they are expected to participate in an activity and what they will derive from it. Science teachers who report difficulties with laboratory activities either do not prepare students for this work or do a superficial job of getting them ready. Inexperienced teachers often believe that the laboratory activity itself will carry the students through this experience and automatically produce the intended learning outcomes. Experienced science teachers have learned to plan laboratory work carefully, conduct prelaboratory discussions, give important directions, and end with a thorough postlaboratory discussion.

Prelaboratory Discussion

The prelaboratory discussion prepares students for the laboratory activity. This phase of instruction informs students as to why, how, and what they will be doing. The prelaboratory discussion is critical because it gives the students a mind-set for the laboratory. However, it does not always reveal what students should discover. This step in laboratory preparation should explain how the activity relates to the topic under study in the classroom. If, for example, a principle is being discussed in the classroom, it should be made clear to the students that the purpose of the laboratory is to examine the principle under consideration (provided it is a verification laboratory). If an inductive laboratory exercise is planned, then the prelab discussion should not present the principle, ideas, or patterns that students are expected to discover.

Consider the following discussion that might take place before a laboratory on qualitative chemical analysis to identify ions by the flame test.

TEACHER: You are going to find out how chemists and laboratory technicians determine the presence of ions. We have been discussing ions in class, and now you have an opportunity to detect them in solutions. You might think of yourselves as chemists working in a crime lab. I will write the ions on the chalkboard that you will test for in today's lab: sodium, strontium, potassium, copper, and calcium. Thomas, can you tell me what color will appear in the flame test for each of these ions?

THOMAS: I'm sorry, but I can't remember them.

TEACHER: It is not so important that you memorize the flame tests for each of the ions, but that you know where to find these tests in your textbook or on a chart, because these resources will be available to you when you are given a test on this subject. Will all of you look up the flame test in your textbooks at this time? [Pause.] Thomas, please give me the flame tests for the ions listed on the chalkboard. I will write them down.

THOMAS: Sodium is orange, strontium is violet, potassium is purple, copper is blue, and calcium is green.

TEACHER: Thank you. Now, let me show you how to test for these ions with this platinum wire. Pour a small amount of dilute hydrochloric acid into a clean watch glass. Dip the platinum wire into the hydrochloric acid and heat it in the burner flame. Why do I heat the wire first until it glows?

STUDENT: To clean the wire so that it won't be contaminated.

TEACHER: Good! Now, I dip the wire into the solution with an unknown ion and then put the tip of the wire into the flame. Maria, what ion did I have in this solution?

MARIA: Calcium!

TEACHER: That's correct. Does anyone have a question about today's lab and how to proceed?

———————————◼———————————

The prelaboratory discussion must give students the clearest possible picture and understanding of what they are to do in the lab. This will help the students concentrate to make the experience more meaningful. It also will prevent the experience from becoming a cookbook exercise in which the students must constantly refer to printed directions for guidance and thus become immersed in the mechanics of the laboratory instead of the excitement of finding out something for themselves. If special equipment and/or difficult procedures are involved, the teacher should show the students how to use the equipment and procedures and then call on some students to see how they perform these tasks. Prelaboratory discussions should be as short as possible, yet long enough to thoroughly orient the students to the laboratory.

Giving Directions

The directions for laboratory exercises must be explicit. They can be given orally, distributed in written form, or discussed during the prelaboratory session. Any combination of these also can be used. Oral directions may be adequate when one-step activities are involved and when the directions are simple enough to be remembered, such as:

> The teacher advised her earth science class that diluted hydrochloric acid reacts with substances containing carbonates. She gave each pair of students a dispensing bottle of dilute acid and a tray of assorted rocks, minerals, bones, and shells. She directed the students to test the items for the presence of carbonates.

Sometimes summarizing directions on the chalkboard that have already been given orally is helpful.

The teacher sets out test tubes, medicine droppers, a soap solution, and a liquid detergent. He showed the students how to test the effects of these solutions on hard water. He then summarized the directions on the chalkboard as follows:

1. Fill two test tubes nearly full of water.
2. Add four drops of soap solution to one test tube.
3. Add four drops of detergent to the other test tube.
4. Shake each test tube well.
5. Hold the test tubes up to the light and observe.

Written directions can be duplicated on paper and given to students, or they may be found in the laboratory manuals used in the course. Regardless of the form, the activities should be broken down into several steps. Each step should consist of a brief set of directions followed by some questions, as shown in the following example:

> Strike one of the tuning forks against the palm of your hand. Observe the fork carefully.

1. What observations can you make?
2. With which of your senses can you make observations of the vibrating fork?
3. Can you count the number of times the fork vibrates in 1 minute?

Postlaboratory Discussion

The postlaboratory discussion is a critical component of laboratory work, and it must not be conducted hastily. Often, because of short lab periods, the postlaboratory discussion is rushed at the end of the period with little gain for students. The better approach is to hold off the discussion until the next science class and conduct the postlaboratory discussion in its entirety. Considerable thought, reflection, expression, analysis, and time must be given to the postlaboratory discussion in order for students to benefit from laboratory experiences.

The postlaboratory discussion presents an excellent opportunity to focus on important learning outcomes associated with laboratory work. For example, the following may take place in a postlaboratory discussion:

1. Students' *data and observations* should be placed on the board or overhead transparencies to be viewed and analyzed. Data should be placed in tables, charts, graphs, figures, or lists in a manner that communicates clearly what was observed.
2. The data, observations, and outcomes of the lab should be *critically analyzed* to determine what it means and the extent to which it answers the questions or hypotheses under investigation. Students must *explain* the data and how it is related to the questions, methods, and interpretations. This will help students to become more logical in their thinking and cognizant of the importance of data in answering questions through scientific inquiry.

3. If the lab is designed to address *conceptual knowledge,* check on misconceptions and the extent to which these alternative conceptions are being affected. Students should be called upon to state what they believed regarding a given idea before the laboratory was initiated and what they believe now as a result of their experiences and the data collected. Ask students to write out their ideas in clear, coherent sentences and to construct concept maps to show relationships between key concepts.

4. Call upon students to identify the *science process skills* that they used to conduct their investigation and to speculate about how scientists and engineers might have conducted this laboratory exercise. These discussions will help students to gain a better appreciation for the *nature of science and technology.*

5. A science teacher can make the decision for students to *repeat laboratory work* and to perform certain parts of a lab over again. Performing a given laboratory experience only once may do very little to enhance some students' knowledge and skills. These individuals may need a considerable amount of *practice and exposure* to basic procedures and ideas, especially students who speak very little English. Also, many students do not have time to complete their lab work. Therefore, their knowledge is fragmented.

Ensuring Successful Laboratory Experiences

Science teachers must carefully plan and organize their laboratory activities in order for students to attain important learning outcomes from this work. They must give serious attention to the relevance of laboratory work, the degree of structure involved in activities, the methods by which students record and report data, classroom management, and evaluation of student work. Failure to give proper attention to these critical factors can undermine the value of laboratory activity in a science course.

Relevance of Laboratory Work

The association between classroom and laboratory work may not be evident to students during the course of daily instruction. Laboratory work often becomes a fragmented entity that seems to have little or no relation to the real world. This aspect of science teaching can become merely another activity to complete. Laboratory activities that incorporate commonplace devices and have immediate applications in the real world, however, are worthwhile to use. In laboratories where

Middle school laboratory experiences often run smoothly when the materials and procedures are well organized.

siphons, candles, electric bells, xylophones, household cleaners, mechanics' tools, over-the-counter medicines, and garden soils are studied, students rarely question the value of the work or its association with scientific principles.

Familiar objects provide a context that may be more interesting to students and serve to motivate their learning. The use of everyday materials demonstrates the applicability of science concepts and principles in daily life. These materials are usually inexpensive and easy to obtain. Often, students who are unmotivated in science classes are those who readily volunteer to bring in items for laboratory work. Also, when students study everyday phenomena in the laboratory, they are more inclined to acquire inquiry skills (Rubin & Tamir, 1988). If instruction begins with things familiar to students, the instruction is most likely to be related to the knowledge that students possess. Consequently, the instruction begins with what students know, which will facilitate their conceptual development.

Degree of Structure in Laboratory Activities

Structure refers to the amount of guidance and direction teachers give to students. It usually takes the form of written directions or questions that are prepared on duplicated sheets or in laboratory manuals. Experienced science teachers often employ highly structured laboratory exercises, especially during the first part of a science course. Highly structured exercises provide students with a great deal of guidance, which helps the teacher to manage the instructional environment. Science teachers emphasize that when they must instruct large numbers of students, short exercises that provide students with plenty of direction seem to work best.

The following comments are from science teachers regarding the structure of their laboratories:

- "Our labs are highly structured and the answers seem so obvious, but not to these sixth graders."
- "In physical science, we use highly structured labs that focus on specific objectives and reinforce specific concepts. This is important to our ninth graders who need help adapting to the high school environment."
- "The labs for many regular students are highly structured with specific instructions and questions that are close-ended because most of my students are not very science oriented. They get easily frustrated if they do not understand exactly what they are to do."

A note of caution is in order regarding highly structured laboratory work. There is a problem with using too much structure over the entire course. If the teacher uses highly structured activities throughout a course, problem solving, conceptual change, modifying misconceptions, and motivation may be limited. Structure can stifle self-directed learning and decision-making behavior. Consequently, toward the middle and end of the course, science teachers should vary the structure of their laboratory work.

After students have acquired basic inquiry skills and techniques, the teacher should give them the opportunity to identify their own problems and devise their own procedures. Over time, students will learn to conduct complete laboratory experiments. Some science teachers have suggested that students can be given more autonomy during the eighth and ninth grades than during the sixth and seventh grades, and certainly many high school students are capable of conducting their own inquiries.

Leonard (1991) suggests that science teachers should attempt to "uncookbook laboratory investigations." He claims that too many procedures and written directions for students to follow can reduce advance organization by students, thus causing them to follow directions in a rote manner and lose the meaning of the lab. Students can remember only so many directions and internalize only so much of someone else's procedures.

Student Recording and Reporting of Data

Students need assistance in recording and reporting their laboratory observations. When laboratory manuals are provided, the problem is somewhat reduced, because laboratory manuals usually provide space for student responses. When laboratory manuals are not provided, duplicated sheets or notebooks can be used to record data. Regardless of the form, recording must be kept simple. If students must devote too much time and effort to recording and reporting, they may develop an unfavorable attitude toward the laboratory.

Laboratory exercises vary in terms of their content and involvement. Consequently, recording and reporting these activities should vary. Some exercises focus on techniques and motor skills and require very little written activity. For example, exercises developing competence in using the balance, microscope, graduated cylinders, burettes, voltmeters, ammeters, force measures, and dissecting instruments require careful manipulative skills, but little is required as far as reporting the outcomes in writing.

Exercises that involve students in a great deal of inquiry and open-ended investigations may require a more extensive type of report. In these situations, students may need to identify strategies that they will use to answer research questions. They should be expected to explain the procedures used to collect data when reporting their investigations. In addition, students must report data in a form that best communicates their value to the investigation. This usually requires the use of many communication devices used in science, such as graphs, tables, formulas, and figures.

Some science teachers require very little from students regarding the procedures used to carry out an investigation, because this information is usually written in the laboratory manual or on a handout. However, these teachers require their students to prepare a thorough explanation of: (1) the results, (2) the significance of the results, (3) how the laboratory relates to the subject matter content that is under study in the classroom, (4) how the laboratory reflects the nature of science, and (5) how the concepts and principles apply to other situations. Teachers indicate that students benefit greatly from these exercises when they are required to determine the importance and derive something meaningful from their laboratory work. They also mention that this assignment is very time-consuming to grade.

A typical format for reporting science laboratory work includes the following six steps:

1. Problem
2. Materials
3. Procedure
4. Results
5. Conclusions
6. Applications

This format can become a highly stereotyped form for reporting laboratory work, however, and such an unvarying format may result in boredom and resentment from many students. Furthermore, students often mistake these steps as being synonymous with the scientific method. Science teachers are advised to vary their requirements for reporting laboratory work. Simple experiments require only simple records and reports.

Gardner and Gauld (1990) advise that teachers who emphasize correctness of data and conclusions might produce negative effects on students' laboratory performance and attitudes. They point out that students want to get the "right results" because their teachers use these results to grade them. Consequently, if students do not get good data or what is perceived to be the correct results, they may be penalized. This situation causes some students to copy data from other students so they will receive a good grade. Teachers should realize that getting the right answer can discourage curiosity and original thought. Science teachers must be acutely aware of the learning outcomes they are shaping from the type of laboratories they promote and the type of laboratory reports they require from students.

Management and Discipline During Laboratory Activities

Management is a critical factor for successful laboratory activities. This is especially true in the middle and junior high schools, where students are very active and perhaps cannot concentrate for extended periods. Laboratory room management may pose a special problem to the beginning science teacher, who may be a little lax in developing and maintaining rules for this type of activity. Some essential elements that need attention in the science laboratory include seating arrangements, grouping, discipline, and monitoring student activities. Desks and laboratory tables should be arranged so that they are not crowded, to allow for free flow of traffic. Keep students away from laboratory materials until they are ready to use them, especially during the time that the teacher is giving directions. Avoid placing work tables against walls.

Students can work individually, in pairs, or in small groups. The amount of equipment and materials usually dictates the working arrangement. Obviously, it would be best to have students work independently the majority of the time, but in most situations they must work in pairs or in small groups of approximately four students. Problems can arise when students within groups participate in very little laboratory work or when they interact between groups. Talking and fraternizing between groups usually results in a high noise level and disruptive behavior. It is best to require students to work and to talk only with those within their own group.

Noise level is a problem in open-space areas during laboratory activities. Noise creates distractions for classes in adjacent areas, causing fellow teachers to complain, and consequently resulting in negative reactions by administrators toward laboratory work. Science teachers instructing in open-space areas have had to work very hard to keep the noise level down. Those most successful at this task have instructed their students to speak quietly. These teachers help their students build a group esprit de corps, in which each group works quietly, guarding their findings, while remaining orderly.

Many laboratory activities can best be handled in groups. This is especially true for middle school students. Small-group laboratory activities will be most successful if every member is assigned a role. The following roles can be assigned to students within each group:

Coordinator: Keeps the group on task and working productively

Manager: Gathers and returns equipment and materials

Investigator: Helps conduct the investigation

Recorder: Records data and keeps notes on the investigation

Reporter: Organizes and reports the findings

The teacher should give students the opportunity to select roles that they wish to play in the investigation, giving them an opportunity to be actively involved in laboratory work. Students should rotate their roles, however, so that each is provided with a variety of experiences and responsibility for their learning. See Chapter 5 for more information on grouping and cooperative learning.

Some science teachers are more successful than others at getting students to participate in orderly and productive laboratory experiences. Although successful teachers might begin laboratory activities with a great deal of control and structure, they soon begin to encourage their students to take more responsibility for their work and conduct in the laboratory. The most successful teachers are those who spend less time controlling their students and more time structuring them and giving them more opportunities to learn on their own (George & Lawrence, 1982). These teachers maintain a classroom atmosphere in which students develop a sense of ownership and control over their work.

The teacher plays a major role in developing and maintaining a well-disciplined laboratory environment. This is essential in promoting student productivity and safety as well as avoiding complaints from other teachers and administrators. Consequently, the science teacher must keep students on task and maintain a reasonable noise level. Continuous interaction between teacher and students can facilitate this process. Walking from student to student or from group to group is also helpful. Such contact urges students to work and gives the teacher the opportunity to help students with problems. It is important to move around the entire room so that all groups of students receive the necessary attention, rather than spending too much time with any single group of students. In addition, the well-managed lab room has all of the necessary materials and equipment ready to be used. In some instances, the items should be arranged on a table where they can be taken and returned, whereas in other instances they can be placed on a cart that can be moved to where students are working.

Rules and policies regarding safety and behavior are essential to the success of the laboratory. They must be stated verbally early in the course, preferably during the first laboratory period. Once stated, they should be posted in clearly visible locations in the laboratory areas. Students should be aware that they will be expected to follow the rules consistently and without exception and that the teacher will be firm but fair about this expectation. The rules should include statements regarding conduct, safety, laboratory reports, use of equipment and materials, and grading, and they should be stated as positively as possible. Student input may be desirable when teachers are establishing rules of conduct; this will increase the probability that students will know the rules and, consequently, adhere to them. It may also be a good policy to provide a set of rules to parents so they know what behaviors the students are expected to exhibit in the laboratory. See Figure 13.7 for rules that can be used for developing a set of guidelines for science laboratory conduct.

Evaluation

Evaluation of laboratory work as a part of the total science course grade is an essential part of science instruction. There are several techniques to employ in this situation. Paper-and-pencil tests, laboratory reports, notebooks, practical examinations, laboratory behavior, and effort can all be used to determine the laboratory component of the course grade. At least nine areas regarding laboratory work can be used to evaluate students:

1. Inclination to inquire and find out
2. Ability to ask questions that can be answered in the laboratory
3. Desire to design procedures to test ideas
4. Competence and mastery of technical skills
5. Competence and mastery of science process skills
6. Ability to collect accurate and precise data

Guidelines for Conduct in the Science Laboratory

1. Do your job well and assume your share of responsibility.
2. Keep the noise level to a minimum and speak softly.
3. Work primarily with members of your group; avoid interacting with other groups' members.
4. Raise your hand if you need help from the teacher. The teacher will come to you; do not go to the teacher.
5. Horseplay is not allowed in the laboratory at any time.
6. Eating or drinking in not permitted in the laboratory.
7. Follow all safety procedures that are posted.
8. Copy the rules concerning "Safety in the Laboratory" in your notebook for reference.
9. Carefully handle all equipment and return it to its proper place.
10. Report faulty or broken equipment immediately to the teacher.
11. Do not waste materials.
12. All dangerous organisms, chemicals, and materials must be handled as directed by the teacher. If you have any questions, ask the teacher.
13. Make certain that all glassware is washed and dried before being returned to storage areas.
14. Keep your work area clean and organized.
15. Clean your tabletop before leaving the laboratory.
16. Remove litter from the floor, particularly around the areas in which you work.
17. Strive for accuracy in making observations and measurements.
18. Be honest in reporting data; present what you actually find.

FIGURE 13.7   This list of rules can be used to develop a set of guidelines for student conduct in the science laboratory.

7. Willingness to report data honestly
8. Ability to report patterns and relationships and to explain their significance
9. Thoroughness of laboratory reporting
10. Inclination to behave properly in the laboratory

Short paper-and-pencil tests are often used to evaluate laboratory work. Five to 10 items are often sufficient to assess information learned or reinforced in the laboratory. These assessments can also determine how well students have attained process skills and science concepts. Laboratory reports and laboratory notebooks are used to assess students' ability to record data and report findings.

The laboratory practical is an excellent way to assess students' knowledge of laboratory work. Laboratory stations can be set up where information or techniques can be assessed. The teacher must allow time to prepare the laboratory stations and must take care to ensure that students do not receive answers from their classmates.

Science teachers use direct observation to assess student behavior in the laboratory. Some middle school science teachers give a grade for each lab period for conduct—for example, satisfactory or unsatisfactory conduct. The effort demonstrated by students in laboratory work should be rewarded by science teachers, particularly at the middle and junior high school levels. Giving credit for demonstrated effort can develop and maintain positive student behavior in the laboratory as well as reinforce laboratory work. The teacher, of course, determines what part of the total grade should reflect effort in the laboratory. In general, laboratory work accounts for 20% to 40% of the report card or course grade, and effort should be a part of this percentage.

FIELDWORK

Science teachers should incorporate fieldwork into their curricula because it offers authentic learning experiences for students, giving them greater understanding of the natural and technological world in which they live. Field trips are perhaps the most enjoyable and memorable of academic experiences for students. Generally, field trip sites are somewhat familiar to students, which causes them to take a special interest in these events. Today, there is renewed interest in field experiences because of their potential to contribute to the improvement of scientific literacy.

Planning Field Trip Experiences

Field trips permit firsthand study of many things, both natural and man-made, that cannot be brought into the classroom. Hospital operating rooms, electrical power generating plants, petroleum refineries, space centers, sewage treatment plants, observatories, and wildlife refuges are field sites that students can benefit from visiting. A trip to these and many other sites rivals any video presentation or in-class lecture that students might receive about the activities that take place at these locations.

The Curriculum

When science teachers entertain the idea for including field trips in their courses, they must examine the curriculum and decide which experiences relate directly to the course. Field trips require much time to arrange and conduct, so selection must be based on the goals and content of the curriculum. The question should be asked: Which topic(s) ought to be taught or reinforced by taking students into the field? If a science teacher can identify a topic in the curriculum that students should study outside of the classroom, the chances are good that she or he can make a case for organizing a field trip to that location.

Surveying Possible Sites

Students should study indoors the things that are best studied indoors and study outdoors the things that are best studied outdoors. It should be obvious that far too much instruction takes place within the classroom walls. Fortunately, within and around most schools there are hundreds of things worthy of study—resources far more valuable than those available in the school science laboratories. Common objects and events are often the best to study in their natural environment. Science teachers can begin planning by making a list of field sites, beginning in the school, moving to the school grounds, streets, neighborhoods, community services, rural areas, small businesses, museums, hobbies, small manufacturing plants, and large industrial facilities. The places listed in Figure 13.8 present a large number of field sites, many of which are rather easy to access.

Administrative Policy

Field trips within the confines of the school property are usually easy to arrange. However, even for these experiences it is advisable to consult with the school administration so that you are informed about school policy. Further, incidents may have occurred in the past that the teacher should be aware of, because these events may have caused the administration to be concerned about field trips, even on school grounds. Excursions off school property will certainly require administrative permission. Science teachers need to be fully informed of school and district policies regarding field trips to locations that require transportation. Liability is always a consideration. Policies governing trips away from school have usually been established. Some principals may possess negative attitudes about these events, however, because of problems that they have encountered. Science teachers should be aware of these matters. Most school policies require written notice, which includes purpose, location, times of depar-

FIGURE 13.8   Examples of field study locations and related sites.

School Building

Heating and cooling areas: heat, condensation, temperature
Electrical system: safety, wiring, voltage, current
Automobile shop: batteries, engines, brakes, safety
Cafeteria: food, nutrition, diet
Kitchen: hygiene, cooking, fire
Music department: sound, music
Auditorium: acoustics

School Grounds

Lawn: plants, animals, habitats, ecology
Shrubs: effects of light and shade
Trees: seasonal changes, identification, classification
Flagpole: measurement, position of sun, seasons

Streets

Vehicles: types, stopping distances
Traffic: safety, patterns, intersections, lights
Pedestrians: patterns of walking and crossing
Streets: type of pavement, maintenance
Utility lines: service, safety

Residential Dwellings

Gardens: topsoil and subsoil
Flower beds: identification, classification, conditions
Lawns: organisms, fertilizers, shade and light
Insulation: type, amount
Roofs: composition, pitch

Community Services

Fire station: equipment, simple machines, ladders
Police car: computers, radar, engine, safety
Hospital: operating room, diet, sterilization
Nursery: plants, classification, seasons
Water works: purification, pipes, computer system

Small Businesses

Supermarket: food, labeling, refrigeration
Building supply: materials, machines, tools
Dry cleaners: chemicals, cleaners, safety
Electronic repair: electronics, computers, recorders

Manufacturing and Utility Plants

Bakeries: baking, receipts, packaging
Dairies: refrigeration, pasteurization, production, packaging
Chemical plants: refining, production, transportation, research
Electricity: furnaces, nuclear reactors, turbines, generators

Outside of the City

Beaches: wave action, marine life
Ponds: plant and animal specimens
Fields: flowers, birds, insects
Hillsides: erosion effects
Rivers: energy, sediments, movement
Woodlands: trees, classification, soil, succession

Other Sites

Botanical gardens: flowers, reproduction
Museums: archeology, geology, natural science, medicine, space science
Planetariums and observatories: planets, stars, solar system, universe
Zoos: ecology, diversity, evolution

ture and return, names of students, and so on. Written permission from parents is usually required as well. Figure 13.9 presents a list of important items that must be considered when taking students off-campus to participate in a field trip.

Conducting a Field Experience

Since taking a field trip is viewed as a big event, considerable preparation is invested in this undertaking. Planning and instructional activities take place prior to the trip so that students are well informed of what they will be doing. The teacher and the students know precisely what to do once at the site. After they return to the classroom, there are follow-up activities to maximize the value of the experience.

Preparation

Once a field trip has been decided upon, considerable planning should take place to ensure maximum benefit. Instruction is part of the preparation phase so that students have a clear idea of what they will be expected to observe and learn. Students need to develop the proper mind-set for this event so that they will be concentrating and learning important skills, procedures, and information. Read the vignette in Box 13.4 to get an idea of how a high school biology teacher approached a field experience.

FIGURE 13.9   A checklist of important field trip considerations.

_____	Permission granted by school administration
_____	Arrangements made with field trip site personnel
_____	Determination of admission fee to field trip site
_____	Date, and departure, arrival and return times established
_____	Transportation arrangements
_____	Parent consent forms
_____	Parent and other teacher chaperones secured
_____	Preparation of several lists of students who will participate, leaving one with principal
_____	Emergency medical forms for students who require them
_____	Identification of cellular or other telephones for emergency use
_____	Lunch, snacks, and other meal arrangements
_____	Need for special clothing or equipment
_____	Determination of lavatory facilities

Classroom Snapshot 13.4

Planning the Field Trip

Ms. Walker spent three class periods getting her students ready for a field trip to a large pond located on the grounds of the school district's Science Center. During the first period, she described the purpose of the field trip and informed the students that parental permission is required for those who would be going to the center by bus. In the second class period, Ms. Walker introduced the study of ecology with a brief lecture on some major principles of the topic. Then students were given practice in identifying a small number of organisms that they might collect on the field trip day. They seemed to require a great deal of practice focusing on specimens under the microscope, especially those that are moving across the field of view. During the third period, the teacher organized the students into cooperative groups and gave all students a task to perform during the trip.

At the Field Trip Site

As soon as they got off the bus, Ms. Walker and her students entered the main building of the Science Center for a brief orientation by one of the staff members. Safety and student conduct were addressed. Then Ms. Walker reviewed the purpose for the trip and performed a check to determine if each student knew his or her task. Then students were taken to the pond and the center's staff member recommended techniques to collect specimens. When the students completed all of their work at the pond and returned to the center, they entered a large room with 15 microscope stations where they could view macroscopic as well as microscopic organisms. The staff member and Ms. Walker circulated among the students answering questions and guiding them in their work.

After the Field Trip

Ms. Walker devoted two instructional periods to the pond trip back in her classroom. She used the first period for laboratory work to give each student more time to examine the organisms that he or she gathered as well as those that others collected. Ms. Walker also set up four microscope stations with specimens for students to identify and for them to explain the role of biotic creatures in the pond's ecosystem. The second class period was devoted to group presentations to discuss the ecology of this aquatic biome. This session offered students another opportunity to construct more knowledge about important ecological concepts and principles.

ASSESSING AND REVIEWING

Analysis and Synthesis

1. Interview a few new and a few experienced teachers to obtain their views on the purpose and importance of laboratory work in the courses they teach. Also, determine the frequency of the laboratory work in their courses. Discuss this information with other members of your science methods class.

2. Analyze the laboratory activities for a science course and classify the laboratories into one of the following categories: process skill, deductive, inductive, technical skill, or problem solving. Evaluate the laboratory activities based on their variety and appropriateness for the students who are using them. Discuss your evaluation with other class members.

Practice Considerations

3. Develop an instrument to evaluate how a science teacher conducts a laboratory. Include ideas discussed in this chapter, such as the prelaboratory discussion, applicability, structure, recording/reporting, management, and evaluation. Establish a set of criteria from which you can make a

judgment regarding the degree of inquiry that takes place during a laboratory exercise.

4. Survey how science teachers and science coordinators in a school district conduct inventories, order supplies and equipment, and maintain and store laboratory equipment, chemicals, and supplies.

5. Discuss with the other members of your science methods class the science teaching facilities that you believe are good or exemplify effective science teaching.

6. Develop a laboratory exercise illustrating one of the five types of laboratories described in this chapter. Conduct the laboratory with a group of peers or with middle or senior high school students enrolled in a science class.

Developmental Considerations

7. Plan a field trip for several science classes of middle or high school students to a site in your community. Address the aspects of fieldwork that were discussed in this chapter in order for the trip to be a productive and safe event.

RESOURCES TO EXAMINE

Science Education for Public Understanding Modules. Sargent-Welch *VWR Scientific*, 911 Commerce Court, Buffalo Grove, IL 60089. Phone: (800) 676–2540.

This is one of the companies that distributes the Science Education for Public Understanding (SEPUP) modules that are described in Chapter 2. The 12 modules were produced at Lawrence Hall of Science at the University of California at Berkeley to improve the public's understanding of chemicals and their relationship to everyday life. Each module contains many hands-on laboratory activities for middle school students (or high school students and adults). Some representative titles are *Risk Comparison, Investigating Ground Water, Toxic Waste: A Teaching Simulation, Plastics in Our Lives,* and *Household Chemicals.* These instructional materials are interesting and important to the lives of students.

National Association of Biology Teachers. 11250 Roger Bacon Drive #19, Reston, VA 22090.

This national biology teacher organization has produced many instructional materials for teaching

biology. The following are among its publications that you should consider for your professional library:

Favorite Labs from Outstanding Teachers, Monograph VII (1991)

Favorite Labs from Outstanding Teachers, Volume II (1993)

Biology Labs That Work: The Best of How-To-Do-Its (1994)

Flinn Scientific, Inc. P.O. Box 219, Batavia, IL 60510. Phone: (800) 452–1261.

The *Flinn Chemical Catalog Reference Manual* contains a very large number of instructional materials that relate to teaching chemistry and basic science along with important information and listings of equipment, apparatus, and materials. This publication will be very useful to those who use chemicals in their instruction, especially chemistry teachers.

Kendall/Hunt Publishing Company. 4050 Westmark Drive, P.O. Box 1840, Dubuque, IA 52004. Phone: (800) 258–5622.

Kendall/Hunt produces a large number of instructional resources for science teachers. This company, in particular, publishes innovative science curriculum projects that generally stress laboratory work and student activity.

The Exploratorium. 3601 Lyons Street, San Francisco, CA 94123. [On-line.] Available: http://www.exploratorium.org/

The Exploratorium is one of the finest science museums and has provided leadership in educational programs of learning via museums. The facility has permanent as well as changing programs of high interest to teachers, students, and the general public. The museum features a "Teachers Institute" that offers hands-on activities that are based on Exploratorium exhibits, which include content discussions and classroom materials. The "Institute for Inquiry" provides workshops and on-line support for inquiry learning as well as professional development for science teachers interested in ideas for inquiry-based science. Science teachers should visit this Web site and visit the museum if they are in or near San Francisco.

REFERENCES

Beasley, W. (1985). Improving student laboratory performance: How much practice makes perfect? *Science Education, 69,* 567–576.

Blosser, P. E. (1981). *A critical review of the role of the laboratory in science teaching.* Columbus, OH: ERIC/SMEAC Clearinghouse.

Driver, R., Guesne, E., & Tiberghien, A. (Eds.). (1985). *Children's ideas in science.* Philadelphia: Open University Press.

Freedman, M. P. (2002). The influence of laboratory instruction on science achievement and attitude toward science across gender differences. *Journal of Women and Minorities in Science and Engineering, 8*(2), 191–199.

Gardner, P., & Gauld, C. (1990). Labwork and students' attitudes. In E. Hegarty-Hazel (Ed.), *The student laboratory and the science curriculum* (pp. 132–156). New York: Routledge.

George, P., & Lawrence, G. (1982). *Handbook for middle school teaching.* Dallas: Scott, Foresman.

Hegarty-Hazel, E. (1990). *The student laboratory and the science curriculum.* New York: Routledge.

Henry, N. B. (Ed.). (1960). *Rethinking science education: Fifty-ninth yearbook of the National Society for the Study of Education, Part 1.* Chicago: University of Chicago Press.

Hodson, D. (1985). Philosophy of science, science and science education. *Studies in Science Education, 12,* 25–57.

Hurd, P. D. (1964). *Theory into action.* Washington, DC: ERIC/SMEAC Clearinghouse.

Lazarowitz, R., & Tamir, P. (1994). Research on using laboratory instruction in science. In D. L. Gabel (Ed.), *Handbook of research on science teaching and learning* (pp. 94–130). Upper Saddle River, NJ: Merrill/Prentice Hall.

Leonard, W. H. (1991). A recipe for uncookbooking laboratory investigations. *Journal of College Science Teaching, 21*(2), 84–87.

Lunetta, V. N., & Tamir, P. (1979). Matching lab activities with teaching goals. *The Science Teacher, 46*(5), 22.

Pella, M. O. (1961). The laboratory and science teaching. *The Science Teacher, 28*(5), 29.

Rowell, J. A., & Dawson, C. J. (1983). Laboratory counter-examples and the growth of understanding in science. *European Journal of Science Education, 5,* 203–215.

Rubin, A., & Tamir. P. (1988). Meaningful learning in the school laboratory. *American Biology Teacher, 50,* 477–482.

Schwab, J. J. (1964). *The teaching of science.* Cambridge: Harvard University Press.

Yeany, R. H., Yap, K. C., & Padilla, M. J. (1986). Analyzing hierarchical relations among integrated science process skills. *Journal of Research in Science Teaching, 3,* 277–291.

14

Safety in the Laboratory and Classroom

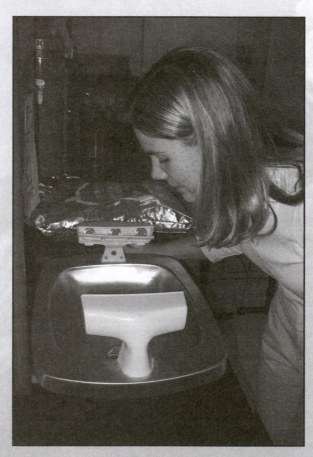

Students' familiarity with laboratory safety equipment will ensure its proper use when needed.

Safety is one of the most important factors to consider in science teaching. The science laboratory and classroom are places where accidents can occur as a result of the mishandling and use of apparatus, equipment, chemicals, and certain live materials that are often maintained in these teaching environments. A program of safety should be in place that includes the training of teachers, students, and other personnel who may be involved in science instruction. Certain standard safety procedures should be implemented as a matter of course before, during, and after instruction, and these safety procedures must be given high priority to ensure a continuous and effective safety program. Not only must students be safe in school science activities, but they must understand about safety and why there are certain rules and procedures.

AIMS OF THE CHAPTER

Use the questions that follow to guide your thinking and learning about inquiry-based science instruction and how you can be successful in implementing it:

- Can you summarize what the laws state regarding the necessity to provide safe learning environments for students?

- Where would you find national, state, and district safety guidelines pertaining to where you are teaching or would like to teach science?

- What are the responsibilities of students and teachers for maintaining safety in the classroom, field, and laboratory?

- Can you list many preparations that should be made by science teachers before the school year begins to ensure a safe learning environment in the classroom and laboratory?

- What are the safety guidelines for teaching biology, chemistry, earth science, and physical science courses?

- Why is it important to teach a laboratory safety unit to students and for teachers to participate in safety workshops and seminars?

INTRODUCTION

Current national standards stress the importance of a scientific and technologically literate society. The science education reform movement supports this goal by encouraging investigative science instruction whereby students are actively engaged in learning about phenomena. This type of science curriculum places great responsibility on the teacher to provide safe and productive learning environments. Student safety must be ensured at all times.

Science teachers have a moral obligation to promote safety awareness in the science classroom, laboratory, and field. It is important that they recognize the legal implications when students are not properly supervised and when students are not trained to be responsible for their own safety and the safety of others. The teaching of safety and the use of appropriate laboratory procedures for safety should be an integral part of all science instruction. An accident or injury can spoil an enjoyable science learning environment.

SAFETY AND THE LAW

The science teacher must be aware of the legal responsibilities regarding safety in the classroom. The very nature of the science classroom and laboratory increases the probability of student accidents, and teachers must take every precaution to ensure the safety of the students and themselves. If an injury occurs in the classroom or in the laboratory, what do the courts commonly look for? First, the courts ask if there is a duty (responsibility) owed. And the answer to that is *yes*. Next, the courts want to know the standard of care that was provided. Three areas determine the standard of care in education. A teacher owes his or her students:

1. Active instruction regarding their conduct and safety in the classroom
2. Adequate supervision
3. Consideration of potential hazards

Merely posting rules in a classroom is not enough. Science teachers must instruct students about the rules, proper conduct, and potential hazards and assess their knowledge in these areas (Vos & Pell, 1990).

The teacher must be well acquainted with state regulations regarding liability. Each state has specific statutes and requirements. If an accident occurs as a result of a teacher's noncompliance with such regulations, then the teacher is vulnerable to a legal suit, which injured students may choose to initiate. Such procedures can result in heavy fines or even the loss of a teacher's job. In addition to state regulations, the local board of education may have explicit policies and rules regarding the teacher's responsibilities. Very often, courts uphold such policies, even though they may not appear in the teacher's contract, and the science teacher is held liable for breaches pertaining to the health and safety of students.

Science teachers should also *carefully read their contracts* and take special note of any responsibilities concerning student health and safety. Thus, the first and most obvious step the diligent teacher must take is to carefully investigate safety regulations that have been specified by state statutes, school board regulations, and the individual teacher's contract. Omitting this step is foolish because any accidents that result from noncompliance may leave the teacher legally responsible.

Another source of teacher responsibility with regard to safety is common law, which refers to law that has been established by judges in actual courtroom cases. The law of negligence (which is the primary governing standard) derives mainly from common law. Because most states have waived common law immunity, the school board is usually named as the defendant in a suit, although it is not uncommon for a teacher to be sued based on common law (Vos & Pell, 1990, p. 38).

If an injured student sues the teacher on the grounds of negligence, the teacher can raise a legal defense called **contributory negligence,** which holds that the injured student behaved in a manner that contributed to the injury. The teacher must, however, offer evidence to show that the injured student's behavior constituted gross disregard for his or her own safety. If such behavior can be established, traditional common law would prevent the student from recovering damages from the teacher. However, in some states, this type of defense is being compromised by the doctrine of **comparative negligence,** which states that when contributory negligence is involved, both the plaintiff and the defendant will be held liable for damages consistent with their respective shares of the negligence. For example, if the plaintiff (student) committed 80 percent of the negligence, she or he could recover only 20 percent of the total damages from the defendant (teacher). Whatever the case, the teacher must be in a position to prove that he or she took every possible precaution to ensure the safety of the students.

Science teachers must always be prudent and demonstrate ordinary care in their teaching duties. During instructional activities in which certain safety hazards are known to exist, as in the use of corrosive or explosive chemicals in a laboratory exercise, for example, teachers must use *extraordinary care* to avoid any mishap that could injure a student. The teacher must prepare students for the activity, pointing out the dangers and stressing the importance of behaving properly in the laboratory. They also must supervise students during the activity so that they carry out their procedures safely.

The best way for a teacher to avoid legal suits is, of course, prevention. Teachers must make a calculated effort to anticipate accidents and potentially risk-laden situations. In addition, the teacher should keep complete records of maintenance work, safety lectures, and specific safety instructions given during particular activities. This time and effort can reduce the teacher's liability. More important, the teacher can reduce the occurrence of classroom and laboratory accidents.

All science teachers must become knowledgeable about teacher liability and indemnification (protection against damages, loss, or injury). They can begin by requesting to see documents in the local school district(s) pertaining to this area. In addition, they should acquire information on these topics from such sources as the *Laboratory Safety Workshop* (James A. Kaufman & Associates) and Flinn Scientific, Inc., which are described at the end of this chapter in the section "Resources to Examine." *Safety in School Science Labs* (Wood, 1991) speaks directly to science teachers and is very informative with regard to liability and safety rules and procedures.

GENERAL SAFETY RESPONSIBILITIES

Science teachers are responsible for safety in the science teaching environment; however, many take the charge lightly. It is not unusual to find many potentially hazardous violations. Inoperable fire extinguishers, safety showers, overhead sprinklers, or eyewash fountains; inadequate lighting; unlabeled chemicals; and faulty equipment are but a few common hazards found in the laboratory. Teachers must be aware of such problems in order to maintain a safe environment. They must be alert about what constitutes a safety hazard.

Accidents that occur in the laboratory are usually minor. The most common types are cuts and burns from glass and chemicals. Students will touch broken glass, handle hot vessels, and fail to wear safety glasses—all unsafe practices that can be avoided if teachers give students proper instruction and supervision. In addition, some students have a tendency to taste substances used for laboratory exercises. This is obviously dangerous. A general lab rule is no eating or tasting unless directed to do so by the teacher.

The teaching of safety must be done systematically and constructively. Many teachers introduce safety units at the very beginning of the school year. They instruct students on laboratory safety and how to conduct themselves during science classes. This approach is successful because it increases student safety knowledge and reduces the number of unsafe behaviors in the laboratory. Teachers also should become educated on safety and attend special courses and seminars on safety, enroll in first aid and CPR courses, talk with other science teachers about safety problems, and read articles on safety.

Preparation Before the School Year Begins

Before the school year begins, the teacher should inspect the classroom and laboratory to determine sites of potential danger. A checklist (inventory) such as the one shown in Figure 14.1 can serve as a guide for this purpose. A checklist ensures that the inspection will be

FIGURE 14.1   Checklist for safety inspection of science facilities.

	No Attention Needed	Attention Needed	Comments
Gas valves and shutoffs			
Water valves and shutoffs			
Electrical lines and shutoffs			
Electrical outlets			
Exhaust fans			
Chemical storage			
1. Temperature of storage area			
2. Aisles cleared			
3. Chemicals properly stored			
4. Age of chemicals within expiration date			
Fire extinguishers			
1. Placed properly			
2. Label and seal show recent inspection			
3. Special type available for chemical fires			
4. Special type for electrical fires			
5. Type for ordinary fires not due to electrical or chemical causes			
Fire blankets			
1. Recent inspection			
2. Strategically placed			
Safety showers			
Eyewash fountains			
Sand buckets			
Student laboratory positions			
1. Gas outlets for leaks			
2. Water outlets for leaks			
3. Sinks have proper drainage			
4. Electrical outlets are functional and properly grounded			

organized and systematic and that critical safety aspects will not be forgotten. At the same time, the teacher has a record of direct responsibility and concern for safety in the event that litigation should arise in the future.

Conducting an inspection requires the cooperation of the school principal and must be coordinated to include the services of maintenance personnel, electricians, plumbers, and other skilled individuals. The teacher, in concert with the appropriate personnel, should inspect the laboratory and classroom areas for malfunctions involving gas lines, water valves, electrical lines and outlets, exhaust fans and hoods, and temperature controls in storage and classroom areas. Eyewashes, fire blankets, fire extinguishers, and safety showers also require inspection. It is best to engage qualified individuals to detect and rectify problems in laboratory facilities. It is not the teacher's responsibility to correct electrical or plumbing problems; such problems must be handled by qualified personnel.

Before the school year begins, have fire extinguishers inspected and placed in areas where they are visible and accessible. Examine labels and seals on fire extinguishers to determine when they have been inspected and if they are perceived to be operable. Special types of fire extinguishers should be available in the laboratory—those that extinguish ordinary fires not due to electrical or chemical causes and those that control electrical and chemical fires. Fire blankets are important in certain laboratory situations—particularly the chemistry laboratory. Place these blankets in strategic areas in the laboratory and check them often to see that they are in good condition.

Safety showers and eyewash fountains that have not been used for a period of time tend to malfunction because of corrosion. The teacher is responsible for seeing that they are clean, functional, and available in various areas in the laboratory in case of emergency.

Sand buckets can be useful in case of fire. Periodically check them during the school year to see that they are clean, full of sand, and readily available in areas where fires are likely to occur. In general, sand buckets are considered standard equipment in chemistry and physics laboratories but not in the biology facility. We strongly recommend that sand buckets be standard equipment in **all** laboratories, regardless of the science discipline.

Inspect students' laboratory stations for gas leaks and electrical problems. All electrical outlets must be properly grounded and in good condition at all times. The teacher must correct electrical problems, preferably by engaging a qualified electrician. Gas leaks are detected by placing a soap solution around outlet joints and watching for the appearance of bubbles. Remember that merely "sniffing" the area is never adequate for detecting small gas leaks. Do not try to rectify gas problems without the help of qualified personnel.

Teachers must have easy access to master controls for gas and electrical sources in the laboratory in order to prevent serious mishaps when it is essential to cut off the power or gas supply quickly. The design of older facilities may make it difficult to satisfy this requirement, but if controls are accessible, their location should be known to the teacher.

Safety Responsibilities During the School Year

The science teacher is responsible for promoting safety awareness once the school year begins. This responsibility has to be taken very seriously, particularity if students will be involved in activity-centered science. More accidents are likely to occur when students are exposed to hands-on activities during laboratory work. Consequently, more care and supervision is required when students are handling equipment, chemicals, apparatus, live animals, poisonous plants, and other hazardous items.

Class size must be considered when planning laboratory activities. Classes that exceed the recommended number of students for the available space pose a safety hazard (Rakow, 1989). Unfortunately, few states have legislation that mandates class size in the science laboratory. Guidelines for lab space and class size are available from Flinn Scientific, Inc. (see "Resources to Examine" at the end of this chapter).

Pitrone (1989) suggests the implementation of a safety learning center to teach safety issues to middle school students. The safety learning center consists of four stations where the students participating in the center: (1) learn rules of laboratory safety and common hazard symbols, (2) learn to identify some basic laboratory equipment, (3) practice some simple laboratory procedures, and (4) take a quiz on safety and sign a safety contract. The safety contract is meant to be proof that safety procedures were stressed in case such evidence is needed.

There are certain inexpensive general precautions that a teacher can take to ensure a safer instructional environment during the school year. The following are some suggestions regarding implementation of these procedures:

1. Develop a set of general safety rules to be in effect at all times in the laboratory. These rules should include a code for laboratory dress that requires safety goggles and gloves at appropriate times and should forbid careless activity, horseplay, and the wearing of contact lenses during certain activities.
2. Safety posters are necessary in the science teaching environment. Posters that stress particular safety precautions are available commercially, but homemade posters may be more pertinent to the situation.

3. Schedule periodic safety inspections in the laboratory during the school year. Examine fire extinguishers, safety showers, fume hoods, and eyewash fountains. Check student laboratory stations to see that gas and water outlets and electrical sources are functioning properly.

4. Inspect storage areas regularly to see that aisles are clean and chemicals are properly stored and labeled. Remember to store chemicals by class and then alphabetically.

5. Arrange laboratory furniture to allow enough working space for students to conduct activities. Inspect furniture to see that it is functional and not defective. Ask students to report any problems.

6. Inspect apparatus, equipment, and electrical devices before allowing students to use them. Electrical equipment and appliances must meet certain specifications and be approved by Underwriters Laboratories or another known organization. Homemade electrical devices can be hazardous.

7. Report problems in lighting immediately to the appropriate personnel. Good lighting is necessary for a safe working environment.

8. Monitor ventilation in the laboratory regularly. Again, report malfunctions as soon as possible. Do not conduct laboratory procedures requiring good ventilation while the system is functioning improperly.

9. Instruct students in the use of safety equipment. Point out the location of such equipment and periodically demonstrate the use of fire extinguishers, safety showers, and eyewash fountains. Allow students to practice using the equipment.

10. Require students to behave in the laboratory. Ask them not to engage in horseplay or other careless activity and constantly supervise students to see that their behavior is consistent with your expectations.

11. Demonstrate and stress the correct procedures before permitting students to use certain types of equipment, materials, and supplies. Describe the procedures while students are seated at their desks, but do not place an array of laboratory instruments in front of each student and then attempt to explain the procedures.

12. Prohibit students from performing unauthorized experiments or activities. Do not allow them to use materials, equipment, or supplies unless instructed to do so. Never allow students to open chemical storage cabinets, refrigerators, and so on. Only the teacher has this privilege.

13. Perform potentially dangerous student activities as a teacher demonstration before allowing students to engage in the activity. Point out possible hazards and show students how to avoid certain pitfalls that may occur while they are conducting the exercise.

14. Report and describe all accidents, even minor ones, to the administration. Keep details on file for reference in case of future inquiries or litigation. Request witnesses to supply their signed versions of the accident, including the circumstances that caused the accident, if known. Ask them to include the names of the individuals involved and a description of the supervision the teacher provided during the time the accident occurred.

15. Do not allow students to transport chemicals outside of the laboratory without permission. Chemicals, equipment, and apparatus should be used only in areas that are constantly supervised by the teacher.

16. Control the use of chemicals by storing them in safe places and allowing only required amounts to be available in the laboratory as needed.

17. Include first-aid kits as standard equipment in all science classrooms. Kits should be large enough to hold the proper materials and arranged to permit quick access to items without unpacking the entire contents.

18. After reviewing first-aid procedures with students, post a list of the procedures near the storage rooms and other strategic areas. Do not allow students to use first-aid kits without permission. In the event of a serious injury, avoid the use of any medication or manipulation of the victim until the school nurse or a physician is consulted. The materials in first-aid kits should be used only for minor injuries, burns, cuts, or other conditions that are not serious.

SAFETY GOGGLES AND EYE PROTECTION

The eye is a precious organ and obviously is irreplaceable. It is formed of soft tissue and exposed to the environment outside of the body. We must do everything possible to avoid situations that might result in any type of an eye injury. Because of the serious nature of protecting students' eyes, eye protection is *mandatory*.

Safety goggles are the standard eye-wear protective device. They are designed to prevent the following from coming in contact with the eyes:

- Corrosive gases and fumes
- Irritating vapors
- Corrosive liquids
- Hot liquids
- Sharp objects
- Small particles
- Fire and heat

Science teachers *must require* students to wear safety goggles whenever the possibility exists that foreign material may come in contact with the eye. **That is the law!** Safety goggles must be available, in good condition, and fit students properly. When the elastic bands break or become stretched so that they no longer hold the goggles to the face, they should be replaced or new goggles purchased. After students use the goggles, they should be placed in a goggles sanitizer that uses UV radiation to destroy organisms that may be transferred among the students. If a UV sanitizer is not available, use an appropriate disinfecting agent to clean the areas of the goggles that come in contact with the skin.

Contact lenses are generally not allowed in science laboratories (Segal, 1995). The belief is that vapors, liquids, and tiny particles can lodge between the contact lens and the eye, causing irritation and even damage. Also, soft contact lenses present a risk because they can absorb and retain chemical vapors. It also may occur that when foreign materials are splashed into the eye, removing the contact lens may become a problem. Irrigating or washing the eye can be a problem if a person is unconscious and you are not aware that he or she is wearing contact lenses. Science teachers must have a list of students who wear contact lenses and make sure they remove the contact lenses and use eyeglasses during a laboratory activity that requires the use of safety goggles.

Safety goggles must be worn and maintained properly.

"Numerous industries, educational authorities, and organizations have arbitrarily restricted the use of contact lenses within their respective administrative domains" (Cullen, 1995, p. 24). Therefore, today the absolute requirement forbidding the wearing of contact lenses is being relaxed, because in some situations contact lenses may benefit the wearer in that he or she can see better with them than without them. Cullen (1995) urges us to weigh the situation to assess the risks:

> It is improbable that the corneal response to volatile substances would be affected significantly by the wearing of a rigid contact lens, because these substances would be eliminated rapidly by tear flow; however, water-soluble gases, fumes, and substances capable of binding to or being absorbed into, hydrogel lens materials would be expected to produce prolonged exposure resulting in a more severe or chronic response.
>
> Contact lens wearers who experience symptoms should not wear their lenses in such environments and they should ensure that their lenses are properly cleaned and rinsed before reuse. Severely soiled lenses must be replaced. (p. 23)

Many school districts prepare a form to advise parents about the potential risks involved if their child wears contact lenses in the lab. The parents must read and give their disposition on whether to permit the child (a) to wear contacts along with safety goggles or (b) not to wear contacts along with safety goggles. This form also helps to identify which students wear contact lenses. Remember, regardless of the decision about wearing contacts in the science laboratory, **safety goggles must be worn in the laboratory and other settings when eye-wear protection is necessary.**

See Flinn Scientific for an excellent discussion on contact lenses in school science laboratories (http://www.flinnsci.com/).

In the elementary school and middle school, one can observe students using safety glasses with side shields for laboratory activities that do not involve chemicals. In these situations, the teachers are trying to protect students eyes from sharp objects or impact. However, you should check with school and district policies when using safety glasses rather than safety goggles.

SPECIFIC SAFETY GUIDELINES FOR BIOLOGY

Precautions for Using Animals

Animals such as rats, mice, guinea pigs, hamsters, and rabbits must be handled gently and with thick rubber or leather gloves. There is always a danger that animals will become excited as they are being handled, particularly if they are injured or pregnant, or if foreign materials are being introduced into the cage. Animals should not be provoked or teased. If animals feel threatened, they will defend themselves, sometimes to the point of biting or scratching. Animals will exhibit violent behaviors if poked with fingers, pens, and other objects through the wire mesh of their cages. Discourage such actions because they can result in the injury of an individual or an animal.

Only those who know how to handle animals should be responsible for them. This means that before giving students the responsibility for handling animals, the teacher must instruct students in their proper care and maintenance.

It is illegal to use for instruction animals that are poisonous or known carriers of disease. Avoid using poisonous snakes, scorpions, and Gila monsters. If snakes are used, be certain that they are not dangerous to individuals concerned. In general, do not use wild animals that are known carriers of rabies and parasites unless reasonable cause can be shown. In such cases, the animals must be inoculated before they are permitted in the classroom or laboratory. Obtain mice, rabbits, rats, guinea pigs, and gerbils from reputable supply houses that will guarantee inoculation against rabies.

Teachers should weigh the advantages and disadvantages of using animals for science instruction.

A teacher should have good reason for keeping animals and insects in the classroom or laboratory. Safety, feeding requirements, replication of natural environments, and unjustified confinement must be considered before using animals in classroom work, all of which make the proper maintenance of animals in cages a problem. Maintain all animals in clean cages and feed and water them on a daily basis or as required. Make provisions for feeding animals on weekends and vacation periods. Often, teachers or responsible students take animals home over extended periods of time to ensure their proper care.

All animals used in teaching must be acquired and maintained in accordance with federal, state, and local laws. Most states require permits to acquire and maintain wild animals in captivity. If permission is granted to maintain a wild animal in the laboratory, it is important that the animal be returned to its natural environment as soon as its use is not required.

Perhaps the best known set of guidelines for animal use in precollege education is from the Institute of Laboratory Animal Research (ILAR). The ILAR has published the 10 principles that are shown in Figure 14.2. These principles clearly delineate the responsibilities of those desiring to use animals for instructional purposes. You should note the restrictive use of vertebrates for animal study. The *Principles and Guidelines for the Use of Animals in Precollege Education* from ILAR are endorsed by the National Association of Biology Teachers (NABT). Although the ILAR guidelines are rather restrictive, NABT acknowledges the importance of animal studies and their use for science instruction. See NABT's Web site for its position statement on the use of animals in biology education.

Science teachers must become more knowledgeable about the use of animals, particularly vertebrates, in the study of biology. Only then will they be able to guide instruction that achieves optimal educational value, but not at the expense of inhumane treatment of animal life. Orlans (1995) encourages science teachers to acquaint themselves with a large range of animal investigations that do not involve harming or destroying life.

The three R alternatives to using animals in research are *replacement, reduction,* and *refinement* of experimental procedures. This approach is being taken by more and more biological research institutions as well as companies that produce products requiring toxicity testing. Zurlo, Rudacille, and Goldberg (1994, p. vi) point out "that *in vitro* methods act together with whole-animal and clinical (human) studies to advance science, develop products and drugs, and treat, cure, and prevent disease." For more information (newsletters, booklets, technical reports, etc.) on this topic, contact the Center for Alternatives to Animal Testing, Johns Hopkins School of Public Health, 111 Market Place, Suite 840, Baltimore, MD 21202-6709.

FIGURE 14.2 Ten principles for the use of animals for instructional purposes.

The humane study of animals in precollege education can provide important learning experiences in science and ethics and should be encouraged. Maintaining classroom pets in preschool and grade school can teach respect for other species as well as proper animal husbandry practices. Introduction of secondary school students to animal studies in closely supervised settings can reinforce those early lessons and teach the principles of human care and use of animals in scientific inquiry. The National Research Council recommends compliance with the following principles whenever animals are used in precollege education or in science fair projects.

Principle 1

Observational and natural history studies that are not intrusive (that is, do not interfere with an animal's health or well-being or cause it discomfort) are encouraged for all classes of organisms. When an intrusive study of a living organism is deemed appropriate, consideration should be given first to using plants (including lower plants such as yeast and fungi) with no nervous systems or with primitive ones (including protozoa, planaria, and insects). Intrusive studies of vertebrates with advanced nervous systems (such as octopi) should be used only when lower invertebrates are not suitable and only under the conditions stated under Principle 10.

Principle 2

Supervision shall be provided by individuals who are knowledgeable about and experienced with the health, husbandry, care, and handling of the animal species used and who understand applicable laws, regulations, and policies.

Principle 3

Appropriate care for animals must be provided daily, including weekends, holidays, and other times when school is not in session. This care must include
   a. nutritious food and clean, fresh water;
   b. clean housing with space and enrichment suitable for normal species behaviors; and
   c. temperature and lighting appropriate for the species.

Principle 4

Animals should be healthy and free of diseases that can be transmitted to humans or to other animals. Veterinary care must be provided as needed.

Principle 5

Students and teachers should report immediately to the school health authority all scratches, bites and other injuries, allergies, or illnesses.

Principle 6

Prior to obtaining animals for educational purposes, it is imperative that the school develop a plan for their procurement and ultimate disposition. Animals must not be captured from or released into the wild without the approval of the responsible wildlife and public health officials. When euthanasia is necessary, it should be performed in accordance with the most recent recommendations of the American Veterinary Medical Association's Panel Report on Euthanasia (*Journal of the American Veterinary Medical Association, 188*(3): 252–268, 1986, et seq.). It should be performed only by someone trained in the appropriate technique.

Principle 7

Students shall not conduct experimental procedures on animals that
   a. are likely to cause pain or discomfort or interfere with an animal's health or well-being;
   b. induce nutritional deficiencies or toxicities; or
   c. expose animals to microorganisms, ionizing radiation, cancer-producing agents, or any other harmful drugs or chemicals capable of causing disease, injury, or birth defects in humans or animals.

In general, procedures that cause pain in humans are considered to cause pain in other vertebrates.

Principle 8

Experiments on avian embryos that might result in abnormal chicks or in chicks that might experience pain or discomfort shall be terminated 72 hours prior to the expected date of hatching. The eggs shall be destroyed to prevent inadvertent hatching.

Principle 9

Behavioral conditioning studies shall not involve aversive stimuli. In studies using positive reinforcement, animals should not be deprived of water; food deprivation intervals should be appropriate for the species but should not continue longer than 24 hours.

Principle 10

A plan for conducting an experiment with living animals must be prepared in writing and approved prior to initiating the experiment or to obtaining the animals. Proper experimental design of projects and concern for animal welfare are important learning experiences and contribute to respect for and appropriate care of animals. The plan shall be reviewed by a committee composed of individuals who have the knowledge to understand and evaluate it and who have the authority to approve or disapprove it. The written plan should include the following:

   a. a statement of the specific hypotheses or principles to be tested, illustrated, or taught;

   b. a summary of what is known about the subject under study, including references;

   c. justification for the use of the species selected and consideration of why a lower vertebrate or invertebrate cannot be used; and

   d. a detailed description of the methods and procedures to be used, including experimental design; data analysis; and all aspects of animal procurement, care, housing, use, and disposal.

Exceptions

Exceptions to Principles 7–10 may be granted under special circumstances by a panel appointed by the school principal or his or her designee. This panel should consist of at least three individuals, including a science teacher, a teacher of a nonscience subject, and a scientist or veterinarian who has expertise in the subject matter involved.* At least one panel member should not be affiliated with the school or science fair, and none should be a member of the student's family.

April 1989

---

* In situations where an appropriate scientist is not available to assist the student, the Institute of Laboratory Animal Research (ILAR) might be able to provide referrals. For more information write to the ILAR, National Research Council, 2101 Constitution Avenue NW, Washington, DC 20418, or call (202)334-2590.

Principles and Guidelines for the Use of Animals in Pre-College Education, produced by the Institute for Laboratory Animal Research, National Research Council, of National Academies. Go to http://www. national academies.org/ilar

Precautions for Specific Biology Procedures and Activities

Certain procedures and activities carried out in the biology laboratory require special mention. Activities involving the use of dissection instruments, sterilizing equipment and instruments, decayed and decaying plants and animal material, pathogenic organisms, and hypodermic syringes must be carefully monitored by the teacher. Activities involving blood-typing and field trips also have unique problems that can cause them to be potentially dangerous.

Care During Animal Dissections

Certain cautions and procedures must be observed when conducting animal dissections. Use only rust-free instruments that have been thoroughly cleaned and sterilized. Dirty instruments are not safe and may cause infections. Instruct students thoroughly in the proper use of the instruments. Scalpels are generally used for dissection; if none are available, single-edged razor blades can be substituted. Some teachers recommend using scissors instead of scalpels. The teacher should demonstrate the proper techniques for using scalpels and dissecting probes before permitting students to use them. It should be stressed when students use a cutting instrument such as a scalpel that the direction of the incision must be away from the student's body.

Cuts can occur during the cleaning of scalpels and needles, so use care during the cleaning process. The use of rubber gloves while cleaning equipment will protect the student against cuts and infection.

Using Live Material

The following list describes procedures and precautions to follow when using live material in the biology lab:

1. Do not use decayed or decaying plant or animal material unless every precaution is taken to ensure its proper handling. Improper handling may expose students to infection or accidental ingestion.
2. Warn students not to touch their mouths, eyes, or any exposed part of their body while using decayed or decaying material. Disposable gloves and forceps should be used to prevent physical contact.
3. Store decayed or decaying material in the refrigerator if it is to be used over a period of several days.
4. Use fungi with care to avoid the release of spores into the classroom environment. Spores may cause some students to have allergic reactions upon exposure.
5. Avoid weeds and plants that may induce hay fever and other pollen allergies. Large amounts of plant pollen can produce adverse effects.
6. Do not maintain cultures of pathogenic bacteria, viruses, or fungi in the laboratory. To do so may expose students to infection, particularly if they are not trained in proper laboratory techniques for handling microorganisms.
7. Avoid the use of blood agar, which can induce the growth of pathogenic bacteria.
8. Avoid the use of viruses in the laboratory because they may infect other living organisms in the school building.
9. Do not allow students to inoculate bacterial plates with human oral material. This simple exercise involves certain risks because it could lead to the production of pathogenic organisms.
10. Warn students to be extremely careful when using pipettes to transfer microorganisms. It is best to use safety bulbs instead of pipettes.
11. Use precautions when transferring by inoculating needles or loops. When a heated needle or inoculating loop is placed in a culture medium, the material tends to splatter and produce aerosols, causing the release of microorganisms into the air. Instruct students to remove as much of the culture material as possible before sterilizing the loop or needle.

Sterilizing

A pressure cooker is excellent for sterilization purposes if an autoclave is not available. An improperly operated pressure cooker may pose certain dangers, however, so it is important to thoroughly understand the directions for operating a cooker before attempting to use it. Clean the safety valve on a pressure cooker and make sure it is operable before using it. Strictly follow the safety limits indicated in the directions or on the pressure gauge. Turn off the heat so that air pressure in the cooker will gradually be reduced to normal level before removing the cover. Do not remove the cover until the pressure is at a safe level. Do not allow students to operate a pressure cooker without proper supervision.

In the absence of an autoclave, sterilize glass Petri dishes and test tubes that have been used for culture growth by placing them in a strong solution of Lysol, creosol, or other chemical disinfectant for a period of time before washing. Wear rubber gloves when washing glassware or instruments used for inoculation.

The disposal of cultures in glass Petri plates can be a problem if an autoclave is not available. Use disposable Petri plates instead of glass plates for laboratory exercises in which students carry out their own procedures.

Body Fluids and Tissues

Samples of human body fluids and tissues are often used for biology laboratory investigations. Blood, check cells, and saliva are commonly used to illustrate biological concepts and principles. However, great care must be taken when gathering and using body substances. They are considered a biological hazard and can cause the spread of disease and infection. Conducting blood-typing on student subjects is risky. This practice is not recommended, given the current health problems with AIDS and hepatitis.

Precautions During Field Trips

Field trips have inherent problems that require special attention to safety. Biology field trips take place in different types of environments, each of which has a unique set of problems. Consequently, it is essential that the teacher know beforehand what precautions are needed to conduct a safe field trip. This requires that the teacher first visit the area to evaluate it for potential hazards.

Students need a list of specific rules of conduct to follow during the course of a field trip. Each trip will probably require the development of a specific set of rules. The following are some general safety guidelines for a biology field trip:

1. Brief students about the area they will visit. Instruct them about the areas that they are prohibited from visiting without supervision, such as ravines, cliffs, and bodies of water.

2. Tell students the type of clothing they are permitted to wear or take with them. Appropriate footwear is essential to avoid accidents.

3. Instruct students about the plants they should not touch, such as poison sumac, poison ivy, and certain mushrooms. Familiarize the students with poisonous plants that they may encounter on the trip. If possible, bring specimens of such plants into the classroom before the trip so that students can learn how to identify them. Warn students not to touch specimens in the classroom.

4. Warn students not to touch or pick up reptiles or other animals or touch dead carcasses of animals or birds.

5. Caution students about eating any plant material in the field unless it is identified by an expert as safe. Poisonous plants often appear very similar to edible ones, and even experts can make serious mistakes in identification. Alert students not to touch fungi and decaying material unless they are informed to do so.

Additional Considerations for Safety in Biology Teaching

Some additional safety considerations that apply to biology teaching are listed here:

1. Use indirect sunlight or a lamp when viewing with a microscope. Avoid direct sunlight on the mirror, which could cause damage to the eyes while viewing.

2. Avoid the use of alcohol burners in the laboratory; they are hazardous. Use Bunsen burners or hot plates instead.

3. Require that appropriate clothing be worn during the laboratory period and especially avoid long-sleeve or loose garments. Lab coats or aprons are advisable when students are working with caustic materials.

4. Require students to wash their hands after using chemicals and at the end of every laboratory session to avoid ingestion of chemicals.

SPECIFIC SAFETY GUIDELINES FOR CHEMISTRY

A number of activities commonly conducted by students in the chemistry laboratory are potentially hazardous. The teacher must weigh the risks involved before allowing the students to perform certain activities. If the risks are too high, there are alternatives. If alternatives are not possible, then abandon the activity or perform it as a teacher demonstration. In some cases, even as a teacher demonstration, the risks might still be too great.

Chemistry Safety Precautions

The majority of accidents in science instruction involve activities in the chemistry laboratory or the use of chemicals in other areas of science. Many accidents occur because teachers are careless about requiring students to wear goggles. In some instances students might be requested to remove contact lenses, yet required to wear safety goggles, during laboratory activities. Proper dress and use of laboratory aprons are often disregarded. The teacher should check students' attire to see that they are not wearing loose jackets, neck-ties, or sandals.

The precautions listed here are further suggestions for a safe environment when using chemicals in the laboratory:

1. When inserting glass tubing into a rubber stopper, always lubricate the glass with glycerin beforehand. Otherwise, the glass tube is likely to break, possibly sending tiny glass fragments into the eyes or skin.

2. When bending glass tubing, keep the burner flame low and heat the material gently. Do not force the glass to bend; it may suddenly break or shatter, possibly causing injury to an individual.

3. When using a match to light a Bunsen burner, always light the match *first,* then turn the gas on *slowly.* Turning on the gas before lighting the match can result in accumulated gas, which might be explosive. Keep arms, hair, face, and other body parts as far away from the burner as possible while it is being ignited.

4. When heating any substance in a test tube, point the mouth of the tube away from the body. Boiling often occurs quickly and without warning, causing the boiling substance to spew the hot vapor on individuals in the vicinity.

5. Clean used test tubes meticulously. Residue left in test tubes could sabotage future experiments, either by altering results or, worse, by causing unexpected dangerous reactions.

6. Clean chemical spills immediately. There are potential dangers if laboratory tables are not cleaned. For instance, if spilled hydrochloric acid is not cleaned from the surface, an individual could lean on the table, causing burns to clothing or skin. A spilled substance also could accidentally be mixed with another spilled substance, which may result in a violent reaction.

7. Make absolutely certain that students do not attempt to remove a beaker, test tube, porcelain dish, or other glassware from a flame without using proper utensils. Tongs, test tube holders, and heat-resistant gloves are designed precisely for this purpose. No student should use bare hands during these tasks.

8. When diluting acids, always add the acid to the water, and not the reverse. The reaction of acid with water is exothermic—that is, large quantities of heat are released. If water is added to the acid, the water will tend to remain on the surface of the acid because it is less dense and, consequently, will not mix. It may produce a violent reaction, which in turn may cause the acid to splatter into the eyes or onto the skin of individuals nearby. To add the acid to the water safely, place a stirring rod in the water and hold it at an angle. Pour the acid slowly down the length of the rod above the water. This procedure prevents splashing while pouring. Be sure to wear safety glasses.

9. When heating materials, always use open vessels during the heating process. Do not heat vessels that have been stoppered. When heating liquids, it is good practice to use boiling chips to prevent bumping.

10. When evaporating a toxic or dangerous solvent, use a well-ventilated fume hood.

11. Avoid subjecting flammable materials to any open flame. Open flames are dangerous in the presence of flammable substances.

All laboratory activities or demonstrations, whether performed by students or the teacher, must be considered potentially dangerous. Before using an activity, the teacher must first weigh whether the educational benefits are worth the risks that may be involved. The teacher must exercise extreme care no matter how many times he or she has performed the demonstration or conducted the laboratory.

Storing and Using Chemicals Safely

Many accidents occur in the classroom or laboratory because of improper storage and use of chemicals. Those who use chemicals in their teaching must be knowledgeable about what substances are potentially dangerous. To avoid unforeseen problems, know what facilities are required for storage of chemicals, the safety procedures to employ when using them, and the safety procedures to use to properly dispose of them.

Today, many chemicals should not be used or even stored in a science laboratory because of the growing concern for people's health and better understanding of the potential risks involved with these chemicals. Science teachers who are not experienced with chemicals should discuss their use and storage with experienced chemistry teachers, and they should become familiar with the literature recommended at the end of this chapter.

Combustible substances, poisonous materials, acids and bases, and other dangerous chemicals have special storage requirements and, in most cases, must be securely stored to avoid potential accidents. Always securely lock combustible substances, such as methanol and ethanol, in metal cabinets. Acids and bases should be stored on the proper type of shelving, such as metal, in cabinets or in a closet. Do not store in the same area chemicals that may react with each other; their caps may corrode so that they cannot be removed. In addition, acids and bases must be stored close to the floor to minimize the possibility that they might fall, crashing onto the floor, spattering their contents on someone. Glycerin and nitric acid, acids and cyanides, potassium chlorate, and organic substances should not be stored in close proximity.

Science teachers must refer to accepted organizational schemes for organizing and storing chemicals, for example, the one developed by Flinn Scientific (see "Resources to Examine" at the end of this chapter). Teachers must not organize a chemical storage area by placing chemicals in alphabetical order because some chemicals can react with each other. The categorization of organic and inorganic compounds, volatile liquids, and acids and bases have been worked out by experts and should be followed.

There is a list of poisonous substances that by law cannot be maintained or used in the lab, including substances such as benzedrine, benzene, arsenic, vinyl chloride, and asbestos. Other poisonous substances that are considered to be carcinogenic cannot legally be part of the chemical inventory, including formaldehyde, carbon tetrachloride, phenol, xylene, and lead compounds. Again, refer to the sources at the end of this chapter to determine what chemicals to use and store and how to inventory them.

Teratogens cause physical or functional birth defects and should not be stored or used in the science curriculum. Teachers must warn students of possible harmful effects of these substances. Some teratogenic substances include aniline, phenol, carbon tetrachloride, and xylene. A list of toxic substances, teratogens, and carcinogens is given in Table 14.1.

Carcinogens are cancer-causing substances. Do not store or use chemicals that are suspected of mutating cells. Warn students of the possible harmful effects of such substances.

Other Suggestions for Safety

All chemicals must be treated as if they are potentially dangerous. Do not downplay the problems that can result if chemicals are exposed to the skin or caustic fumes are inhaled. Neither should the teacher allow situations that may result in explosions or fires. The precautions needed to avoid potential hazards require knowledge about the nature of the chemicals stored in the labora-

TABLE 14.1   Some Hazardous Chemicals

Toxic Substances	**Teratogens**
Ammonium dichromate	Aniline
Ammonium thiocyanate	Benzene
Arsenic and arsenic compounds	Carbon tetrachloride
Barium salts	Lead compounds
Benzene and benzene compounds	Phenol
Beryllium	Toluene
Bromine	Xylene
Cadmium and cadmium salts	
Carbon disulfide	**Irritants**
Carbon tetrachloride (also possible carcinogen)	Ammonium dichromate
Chloroform	Borane
Chromic acid	Ether
Chromium trioxide	Hydrogen peroxide
Cyanides (water soluble cyanides)	Methylene chloride
Dimethyl sulfate	Nitrogen dioxide
Hydrogen chloride	Toluene
Hydrogen fluoride	Xylene
Hydrogen iodide	Zinc chloride
Hydrogen sulfide	
Lead and lead compounds	**Carcinogenic Substances**
Manganese compounds	Asbestos
Mercury and mercury compounds	Benzene
Molybdenum compounds	Carbon tetrachloride
Naphthalene	Formaldehyde
Nickel and nickel compounds	Lead compounds
Nitrogen dioxide	Nickel and nickel compounds
Styrene	Phenol
	Xylene
Corrosive substances	
Bromine	
Hydro–halogens	
p-dichlorobenzene	
Sodium	

tory as well as common sense in their use. The following suggestions can help prevent potential problems:

1. Keep the laboratory and other areas where chemicals are stored or used well ventilated and maintain a relatively cool temperature.
2. Use approved safety cans and metal cabinets to store flammable liquids.
3. Store cylinders of compressed gases by type and mark them as highly toxic, corrosive, or flammable. Store in cool and well-ventilated areas. Limit the amount of flammable liquids and gases maintained in the laboratory.
4. Store large bottles of acids and bases on shelves that are no more than 2 feet above the floor, and store them away from each other to prevent corrosion and other chemical reactions.
5. Inspect chemicals annually to see whether they are properly identified or outdated. Properly dispose of contaminated, unlabeled, and deteriorated chemicals.
6. Do not leave chemicals in areas where students are working unless they are going to use the chemicals.
7. Keep chemicals in storage until they are ready to be used.

8. Store only small quantities of flammable substances in areas where they will be used. Large quantities are difficult to handle in case of a fire or accident.

9. Do not concentrate large quantities of flammable substances in any area in the laboratory.

10. Do not store chemicals in hallways and other heavy-traffic areas. Students are often curious about what is stored in boxes and cabinets. Mishandling can cause accidents.

11. Do not store chemicals on shelving above eye level unless there is easy access with ladders or stools. Individuals trying to remove chemicals from out-of-reach shelves run the risk of dropping chemicals and causing mishaps.

Disposing of Chemical Wastes

To avoid unnecessary risks, remove from the laboratory waste materials that accumulate as a by-product of scientific investigations and become useless because they are improperly labeled or have aged. Chemicals that are no longer used or needed also must be properly removed from the inventory.

Disposing of chemicals requires certain important procedures. Before disposing of chemicals, consider the federal, state, and local rules and regulations, the effect of the chemicals on the environment, their level of toxicity, and the degree to which they are hazardous. In addition, consult with an experienced chemistry teacher, a science supervisor, or use the reference information given at the end of this chapter. The following suggestions might be useful when disposing of chemicals:

1. Do not pour strong acids and flammable liquids down a drain without first diluting them. Do not dilute acids by pouring water into them; pour acids into the water for dilution. Neutralize or dilute all hazardous wastes before disposing of them.

2. Do not pour volatile substances and chemicals that produce noxious odors down the drain. They may lodge in interconnected drains located in other areas of the building, causing odors in these areas.

3. Always label solid wastes as such and place them in suitable containers, making certain that the containers will not react with the wastes.

4. When there is doubt about the proper handling of solid wastes, seek advice from scientists at universities or nearby industries or call commercial disposal firms. Chemical supply houses also are good sources of information.

5. Use care when disposing of carcinogens, radioactive materials, and other hazardous substances. If you do not know the procedures for handling these materials, seek help from the science coordinator, principal, or local fire department. They may provide the proper disposal method or suggest someone who knows.

SAFETY IN THE EARTH SCIENCE LABORATORY

In addition to safety practices normally involved in all secondary science laboratories, possible hazards associated with the teaching of earth science require special attention. Teachers are under the misconception that nothing dangerous can possibly be associated with the activities that occur in the earth science laboratory, but rocks and minerals commonly used in the laboratory can and do present certain health hazards. The tasting of minerals and rocks, chemical procedures and analysis, crushing procedures, and the mere handling of rocks and minerals in the laboratory are potentially dangerous activities.

Minerals containing arsenic and several that contain calcium, copper, lead, or zinc arsenates are poisonous (Puffer, 1979). Acute arsenic poisoning can produce gastrointestinal disturbances, muscle spasms, dizziness, delirium, and coma. Minerals containing lead also present health hazards because lead is poisonous in all forms. The ingestion of lead minerals in large quantities can produce cramps, muscle weakness, depression, coma, and even death. Lead poisoning can be cumulative, and effects can range from moderate to very severe (Puffer, 1979).

Inhalation of certain mineral and rock dusts also can cause certain health problems. Minerals containing manganese, asbestos, and quartz are hazardous in dust form, so avoid inhalation. Manganese dust can induce headaches, weakness in the legs, and general irritability when inhaled. Silica dust can cause silicosis (a lung disease), which has symptoms similar to those of tuberculosis. Asbestos dust fibers are known to cause cancer and asbestosis in human beings.

The following safety guidelines pertain to earth science laboratory practices. The teacher should use them whenever appropriate:

1. The teacher and students should wear goggles when crushing rocks with a hammer or other instruments.

2. Do not crush rocks or other minerals unless they are wrapped in a cloth. This precaution prevents rock fragments and dust from being dispersed in the laboratory area and may prevent injuries to the eyes and other parts of the body.

3. Require students to wear gloves when handling large rock samples, particularly when moving or crushing the samples. Jagged rocks can produce both surface and deep wounds.

4. Do not allow students to lift heavy rock samples alone. Instruct students to help each other when lifting large or cumbersome samples. Use dollies or other equipment to move large and awkward objects.

5. Warn students not to wear open-ended shoes or sandals during field trips. Require them to wear long pants for protection. Gloves are essential when collecting materials on field trips.
6. Before taking a field trip, provide a special set of rules regarding the conduct of students during the trip. Oral directions are not substitutes for written directions. Written rules are constant reminders to students and ensure proper behavior in the field.

SAFETY GUIDELINES FOR PHYSICS AND PHYSICAL SCIENCE LABORATORIES

Accidents from electrical sources in physics and physical science laboratories are not uncommon. The mishaps can range from minor burns to death. Burns caused by electrical sources are usually slow to heal and often require several months of treatment for recovery. Thermal burns caused by high temperatures near the body, such as those produced by an electric arc, are similar to sunburn and are usually not severe unless the body has been exposed for long periods of time.

Impulse and electric shocks are not only unpleasant; in some cases, shock intensities produced by higher currents passing through the chest or nerve centers may produce paralysis of the breathing muscles. Excessively high currents will cause death. Currents that blow fuses or trip circuit breakers can destroy tissue and produce shock and damage to the nervous system. It only takes a small amount of current, on the order of 0.1 amperes, to stop the beating of the human heart. The following safety procedures are guidelines for working with electricity:

1. Know the total voltage and current of the electrical circuit before using a piece of electrical equipment.
2. Use extension cords that are as short as possible, properly insulated, and of a wire size suitable for the voltage and current involved.
3. Service electrical apparatus and devices only when the power is turned off. Make certain that power is not accidentally turned on during servicing.
4. Do not permit students to service electrical equipment or apparatus.
5. Do not permit students to be in the vicinity of electrical apparatus or equipment being serviced.
6. Do not turn power on after servicing until all students are moved to a safe area. Notify students when it is safe to return to their positions.
7. Use properly insulated, nonconducting tools that are in good condition when working with electrical equipment. Use only appropriate tools—those that have specifications indicating that they can be employed for servicing electrical devices.

8. Properly mark all electrical equipment, using letters 2 or 3 inches high to indicate the voltage.
9. Make sure electrical contacts and conductors are enclosed at all times to avoid accidental contact and check them periodically for compliance.
10. Periodically inspect electrical outlets to see that they are in good order. Constant use may cause wear and loosening of outlets.
11. Avoid using metallic prongs, pencils, and rulers when working on an electrical device.
12. Do not wear rings, metal watchbands, or metal necklaces in the vicinity of an activated electrical device.
13. Never handle activated electrical equipment with wet hands or while the body is wet or perspiring.
14. Do not use highly volatile or flammable liquids to clean electrical equipment. There are cleaning solvents that can be used safely, but investigate whether they are suitable for electrical devices.
15. Allow only qualified electricians to perform electrical wiring and maintenance of electrical outlets and devices. Do not allow students or unqualified teachers to perform these functions.
16. Do not store volatile and flammable liquids in the vicinity of activated electrical equipment. The heat generated by equipment may cause a fire or explosion.
17. Do not handle electrical equipment that has been in use for a long period of time. It may be very hot and could cause serious burns; or the hot equipment may be dropped, causing damage to some of its parts.
18. Use electrical appliances that are approved by Underwriters Laboratories or another known laboratory.
19. Have homemade equipment inspected by a licensed electrician before using it. Always regard homemade equipment as potentially dangerous until checked by the electrician.
20. Use indoor equipment inside, not outside. The same is true for indoor and outdoor outlets and indoor and outdoor electrical wires. Do not use outdoor equipment or wire when the ground is wet or when it is raining.
21. Service tools that have shocked anyone or that have emitted sparks. Do not use such tools until they are in good working order.
22. Have all electrical devices properly grounded. Grounding can be complicated and must be done by a licensed electrician.
23. If possible, have ground fault interrupters (GFI) installed to prevent possible electrocution. Many state electrical codes now require outlets to have a GFI.
24. Teach electricity concepts in the laboratory using low-voltage sources in the range of 1 to 6 volts.

RADIATION SAFETY

Secondary school biology, physics, and chemistry courses include topics that involve radiation. Physics and chemistry courses involve experiments that deal with radiation emission of radioactive isotopes, x-ray diffraction apparatus, Crookes tubes, Laser beams, ultraviolet rays, infrared rays, and microwaves. Biology courses sometimes involve experiments exposing biological materials to radiation sources. Apparatus and materials that generate radiation can be hazardous.

The inclusion of laboratory activities that involve radioactive materials in secondary school science is controversial; some feel that such activities are inappropriate at this level. This is not the place to discuss the pros and cons of such activities. However, the teacher should carefully weigh the benefits of these types of activities against the potential dangers of subjecting students to radioactive sources.

In any event, it is imperative that teachers know how to handle apparatus and materials so that the laboratory is a safe place for teachers and students to work. Teachers should be properly trained in the use of materials and apparatus before attempting to use them in the laboratory. Self-taught teachers must be certain that their teaching techniques are safe and appropriate. Radiation experts and scientists, university professors, and other qualified individuals can provide invaluable assistance for formally trained and self-taught teachers. Furthermore, permission from the school administration to use radiation sources in teaching may be required. Some school districts have regulations that prohibit the use of such materials.

Suggestions for Use of Non-Ionizing Radiation

Using non-ionizing radiation requires special precautionary measures (Mercier, 1996). A list of these measures follows, including some special recommendations for using laser beams:

1. Laser beams are very dangerous. If the intensity is high enough, severe burns can result. Preventive measures are extremely important because laser beams can cause blindness in less than 1 second. The teacher must become skillful in handling the equipment and know the safety measures required. The following are safety recommendations for the use of laser beams in the classroom:
   - Keep students away from all sides of the path of laser beams.
   - Warn students and other individuals not to look into the laser beam.
   - Do not aim laser beams directly into the eyes.
   - Do not allow laser beams to hit the exposed skin of an individual.
2. Ultraviolet radiation is harmful below 310 nm. Mercury arcs and other sources can produce radiation below 310 nm, and the teacher should take care to use proper shielding and adequate filtering materials.
3. Radiation from microwave ovens can cause severe damage. Although high frequencies cause heat sensation on the skin, low frequencies do not, and thus an individual is not aware that tissue damage is taking place. Microwave ovens should be equipped with adequate interlock mechanisms.
4. Ultrasonic beams of high intensity also can be extremely harmful; use them with caution.

SAFETY UNITS FOR STUDENTS

The work of Dombrowski and Hagelberg (1985) suggests that a unit on laboratory safety increases students' safety knowledge and reduces the number of unsafe behaviors. Safety units that can develop student awareness and responsibility toward safety are best presented during the early stages of a laboratory course. Throughout this period, students can learn how to use safety equipment such as safety showers, fire extinguishers, eyewash fountains, and fire blankets. They can be indoctrinated to use laboratory coats, eye goggles, and gloves at appropriate times. They can be shown how to handle broken glass, chemicals, and electrical equipment and how to light a Bunsen burner. Stress the importance of housekeeping as well as the necessity of maintaining a clutter-free work environment. During the course of the unit, the students can develop a set of safety rules, which the teacher can supplement.

The unit can vary in length, but three or four class periods would probably suffice. The unit should be general, dealing with aspects of safety that apply to the laboratory course that will be offered. The use of visual aids, demonstrations, and hands-on activities will meet the unit objectives. Active student involvement is necessary to make this unit an effective experience. Other safety considerations specific to a laboratory exercise can be dealt with as the course progresses.

The teacher can administer pretests and posttests using questions similar to those in Figure 14.3 before and after the unit to determine whether the unit improves students' safety awareness, knowledge, and sensitivity. The same questions can be used for both tests, or questions can vary, depending on what has been stressed.

After teaching the unit, require students to sign a safety contract such as the one in Figure 14.4. The

FIGURE 14.3 Sample laboratory safety quiz.

Laboratory Safety Quiz

Directions: The following questions are either true or false. In the blank to the left of each statement, write the letter *T* if the statement is true, or *F* if the statement is false.

_____ 1. It is required by law to wear safety goggles in the area where chemicals are stored.

_____ 2. When diluting acids, water is always poured into the acid.

_____ 3. A chemical is considered dangerous only if it is toxic or flammable.

_____ 4. The teacher is the only individual responsible for safety in the laboratory.

_____ 5. A fire that involves a solvent should be extinguished with a carbon dioxide fire extinguisher.

_____ 6. The disposal of chemical wastes produced from an exercise should be done by flushing the material down the drain.

_____ 7. Prescription glasses can be used instead of safety glasses when working in the laboratory.

_____ 8. It is permissible for students to use beakers for drinking purposes after they have been sterilized.

_____ 9. It is permissible for responsible students to remove chemicals from the storage areas.

_____ 10. The student should be able to operate various types of fire extinguishers.

_____ 11. In general, it would be permissible for students to substitute one chemical for another in the case of a shortage of a particular substance.

_____ 12. It is permissible to store reagents and chemicals in student lockers.

FIGURE 14.4 Sample student safety contract.

Student Safety Contract

I agree to follow all my teacher's instructions regarding safety procedures during laboratory work. I will conduct myself in responsible ways at all times while working in the laboratory and not engage in any horseplay.

While in the lab I will do the following:

1. Carry out the required housekeeping practices.

2. Know the location of fire extinguishers, safety showers, eyewash stations, and safety blankets and learn how to operate and use them.

3. Wear appropriate safety goggles when performing potentially hazardous activities.

4. Wear appropriate dress, as required by the teacher, during laboratory activities.

5. Know where to get appropriate help in case of emergency.

6. Agree to follow all printed and verbal safety instructions as given by the teacher and/or principal.

7. Agree to take and pass the safety test administered by the teacher.

I have carefully read this contract and agree to its conditions. My parents have read and signed this contract, and fully understand the implications of its contents.

_____   _____
Signature of student   Signature of parent

---

students should not take the signing of the contract lightly. It is an agreement that the students will behave as required to maintain a safe environment. To make the document more meaningful, it is suggested that the parents read and sign the contract as well, so they, too, understand the implications of its contents. The safety contract is a valuable record for the teacher to have in case of future litigation. It will show that the teacher has been responsible in attempting to instruct, promote, and maintain a safe working environment for all concerned.

The teacher can effectively teach safety only with the proper background. Units cannot be presented in a haphazard fashion; they must be well organized and taught by knowledgeable individuals. A teacher's background knowledge should be extensive before embarking on a safety unit. Safety knowledge can be strengthened by attending courses, workshops, and lectures as they are offered by safety experts. Background also can be acquired by talking with science teachers, scientists, fire marshals, and others who have the expertise on particular aspects of safety.

ASSESSING AND REVIEWING

Analysis and Synthesis

1. From recall, make a list of safety hazard inspections you would undertake before the school year begins. Check your list with what is described in the chapter about these safety hazards and modify your list accordingly.

2. Design a safety contract that would be suitable for students taking middle school science. Compare the contract you have designed with the one found in this chapter. What are the differences? Discuss the differences between the two contracts with the students in your methods class. What did you stress in the contract you prepared that was not stressed in the one found in this chapter?

3. Write a few paragraphs stating the safety precautions that must be taken to protect the eyes. Be sure to include the guidelines for wearing contact lenses.

Practical Considerations

4. Prepare an inventory of the possible storage hazards associated with any one or more of the following courses: physics, chemistry, biology, earth science, and physical science. After preparing the inventory, visit a local school and seek permission to examine the storage areas associated with the course you chose to teach.

5. Outline a safety program that you would institute if you were the chairperson of a science

department in a middle or secondary school. Ask a science chairperson in a local school to critique the program. Discuss the results with your methods class.

6. Prepare the safety rules you would post in a prominent place in one or more of the following areas: (a) a chemistry laboratory, (b) a physics laboratory, (c) an earth science laboratory, (d) a biology laboratory. Prepare an example of the poster you would use for one of the areas. Ask a member of the class to make suggestions for improving the poster.

7. Observe a middle school or high school science laboratory activity while students are performing hands-on activities. What safety practices are obviously in effect? What safety hazards are evident while students are working? What precautions do students take to avoid accidents? Discuss the observations with members of your methods class.

Developmental Considerations

8. Make a list of questions regarding science safety that you would like answered. Go to the Web sites given in section "Resources to Examine" at the end of this chapter. Determine the answers to your questions from these electronic sites, and gather other information as well.

American Chemical Society   1155 16th Street NW, Washington, DC 20036. Phone: (800) 227-5558. [On-line.] Available: http://www. acs.org/

The American Chemical Society provides a wealth of information regarding chemical safety. Its pamphlets and books are useful resources for science teachers who desire to learn more about the proper use and storage of chemicals.

Flinn Chemical Reference Manual   Obtain the most current edition. Flinn Scientific, Inc., P. O. Box 219, Batavia, IL 60510-0219. Phone: (800) 452-1261. Fax: (708) 879-6962. [On-line.] Available: http://www. flinnsci.com/

Flinn is a recognized company that provides schools with equipment, information, and assistance to make their science program safe and successful. Some of the information and supplies that a science teacher can obtain from Flinn's catalog or by contacting the company are:
- Safety equipment, such as goggles, cabinets, sanitizers, eye washers, showers
- Student safety contracts, labels for chemicals, safety posters
- Material safety data sheets (MSDS) that provide important information about chemicals
- Federal Right-to-Know Law or Hazardous Communication Standards
- Standards and designs for school science laboratory facilities
- A scheme for organizing, labeling, and storing chemicals
- Procedures for identifying unlabeled laboratory chemicals
- Suggested laboratory chemical disposal procedures

Laboratory Safety Workshop   James A. Kaufman and Associates, 101 Oak St., Wellesley, MA 02181. Phone: (617) 237-1335. Fax: (617) 239-1457. [On-line.] Available: http://www.labsafety.org/

Professor Kaufman has produced many useful materials to help science teachers and industrial workers better understand hazardous materials and situations that place people at risk. He and his associates conduct safety workshops across the country to educate workers and professionals about safety in the workplace. Dr. Kaufman visits school districts to assess their lab facilities and chemical inventories. He also publishes a safety newsletter.

National Safety Council   1121 Spring Lake Dr., Itasca, IL 60143. Phone: (708) 285-1121. [On-line.] Available: http://www/nsc.org/

This organization provides a large assortment of printed matter regarding many aspects of safety that pertains to schools, the workplace, and homes. It produces magazines and pocket handbooks that are appropriate for the lay audience. The site provides information and data on safety from vehicles to chemicals.

National Association of Biology Teachers   11250 Roger Bacon Drive #19, Reston, VA 22090-5202. Phone: (800) 406-0775 or (703) 471-1134. [On-line.] Available: http://www.nabt.org/

This is an important organization for providing information regarding the use of animals and all organisms. Periodically, the NABT Board issues position statements on teaching biology, such as the use of human body fluids and tissue products in biology teaching, the use of animals in the classroom, and the dissection of animals. Its periodicals, *The American Biology Teacher* and *News & Views* (a newsletter), are very informative.

Investigating Safely: A Guide for High School Teachers.   By Juliana Texley, Terry Kwan, and John Summers. National Science Teachers Association Press. 1840 Wilson Boulevard, Arlington, VA 22201-3000. [On-line.] Available: www.nsta.org

This is a handy guide to classroom, laboratory, and field safety. It discusses many aspects of proper and safe conduct in science programs. The book addresses setting the tone for safety, equipping the lab, living organisms, field studies, and many other topics related to science safety.

Occupational Safety & Health Administration   200 Constitution Ave., Washington, DC 20210. Phone: (202) 523-7075. [On-line.] Available: http://www.osha.gov/

This governmental organization has produced many regulations and guidelines for safety in the workplace. OSHA has many documents that pertain to all aspects of safety hazards. In some states, OSHA's regulations hold for public schools, whereas in other states OSHA's regulations are superseded by the state's Hazardous Communication laws and standards. There are many regional offices across the United States that a science teacher can contact for assistance.

REFERENCES

Cullen, A. (1995, January–February) Contact lens emergencies. *Chemical Health & Safety,* pp. 22–24.

Dombrowski, J. M., & Hagelberg, R. R. (1985). The effects of a safety unit on student safety, knowledge, and behavior. *Science Education, 69,* 527–534.

Mercier, P. (1996). *Laboratory safety pocket guide.* Natick, MA: James A. Kaufman & Associates.

Orlans, F. B. (1995, October). Investigator competency and animal experiments: Guidelines for elementary and secondary education. *Lab Animal,* pp. 29–34.

Pitrone, K. (1989). Safety: A learning center. *Science Scope, 13*(3), S22.

Puffer, J. H. (1979). Classroom dangers of toxic minerals. *Journal of Geological Education, 27,* 150.

Rakow, S. (1989). No safety in numbers. *Science Scope, 13*(3), S5.

Segal, E. (1995, January–February). Contact lenses and chemicals: An update. *Chemical Health & Safety,* pp. 16–21.

Vos, R., & Pell, S. W. (1990). Limiting lab liability. *The Science Teacher, 57*(9), 34–38.

Wood, C. G. (1991). *Safety in school science labs.* Natick, MA: James A. Kaufman & Associates.

Zurlo, J., Rudacille D., & Goldberg, A. M. (1994). *Animals and alternatives in testing.* New York: Mary Ann Liebert.

Computers and Electronic Technologies

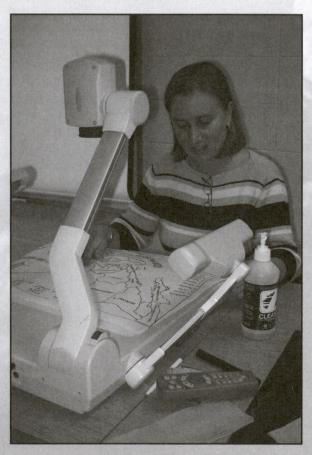

Teachers can use electronic technologies to communicate with students about science concepts and theories.

Computers and other electronic technologies have become important elements in efforts to improve science teaching and learning. Computers play a multitude of instructional roles from personal tutor and information source to data organizer and communication tool. In recent years, the power and versatility of the computer have been significantly enhanced with the coming of age of multimedia systems and telecommunications capabilities. The amount of software available for use by science students is growing almost exponentially, and what can be accessed via the Internet is virtually limitless. In addition, recent advances in video, audio, and photographic technologies have extended sensory experiences associated with science learning. It is important that science teachers learn about the capabilities of computers and other electronic technologies and consider how to best use them to enhance the science learning experiences of their students.

AIMS OF THE CHAPTER

Use the questions that follow to guide your thinking and learning about some fundamental aspects of using computers and other electronic technologies to support your science teaching:

- What changes in science instructional practices are associated with the use of computers and electronic technologies?

- What is a computer multimedia system? What kinds of electronic media can be used to support science learning?

- How can the Internet be used to enhance science instruction and student learning?

- What are some possible applications of computers and electronic technologies in science instruction?

- What aspects of software and electronic media should be considered when contemplating their use in science lessons?

MODERN TECHNOLOGY FOR SCIENCE TEACHERS AND STUDENTS

The number of computers in schools has increased dramatically over the last 10 years. The typical school today may have one computer for every four students, with some schools providing laptop computers with wireless Internet connections to every student. The machinery is relatively trouble-free, there is a wealth of available software, and more is known about the capabilities of computers and telecommunications. In addition, today's teachers are technology savvy, many having developed their own Web pages.

Recent advances in our understanding of learning have also led to changes in the ways in which technology is used for instruction. Uses of technology based on a transmission model of teaching, such as drill-and-practice and tutorials, are decreasing, while uses of technology that support instruction grounded in constructivist thinking are increasing. This is evident in science instruction, where the most common uses of computers and related technologies are in support of students gaining access to information, analyzing information, and communicating with others about their learning (Becker, Ravitz, & Wong, 1999). All science teachers must be prepared to meet the challenges and revel in the excitement associated with making technology an integral part of their science instruction.

Technology Infusion

Technology infusion in the science classroom is being called for at the national, state, and community levels. According to Adams, Krockover, and Lehman (1996, p. 66), it involves "access to information via the Internet, the use of electronic technology for simulations and laboratory-based experiences, and the retrieval of media sources via CD-ROM or digital videodisc." This level of infusion cannot possibly be achieved with only a single computer and a floppy disk drive. Much more is required.

At the very least, computers used for science instruction must have a CD-ROM drive and be capable of supporting a number of peripherals. Ideally, more than one of these computers should be readily accessible in the science classroom, not just available in a computer laboratory that is shared with other science and nonscience classes.

Additionally, the science classroom should be minimally equipped with a computer-based laboratory system with multiple sensor options and a large color monitor or liquid crystal display (LCD) panel or projector (Adams et al., 1996). More and more classroom computers are being connected to the Internet via broadband local area networks.

The infusion of computers and related technologies into the science classroom is best accomplished when a need for the technology is established. It is wise to establish a technology infusion strategy before purchasing hardware, software, and Internet service. Ball (1996) advises science teachers to

- Begin with a vision, not machines
- Use technology to do something different
- Start locally and then go global

A vision for what you want to accomplish leads to fiscally responsible purchases. This vision often becomes clear when you take advantage of the many opportunities available through school districts, universities, and science teacher associations to learn about the different technologies and their capabilities for enhancing science instruction. Using the technology for something that cannot be done without it tends to generate excitement and enhances its educational benefit. Beginning small with one program or a single Internet site will allow you and your students to learn how to use the technology effectively. And it is a strong start that helps build the confidence needed to tackle more demanding and far-reaching learning opportunities. Ball's advice is well worth following to avoid the pitfalls of apathy and obsolescence that can be associated with technology infusion efforts.

Benefits Associated with Technology Use

The benefits associated with computer use in science instruction are many, and the list of benefits continues to grow as teachers explore new uses for emerging technologies. When computers and related technologies are used wisely by teachers to support instruction, student science achievement is improved and students view computers and other technologies more favorably (Berger, Lu, Belzer, & Voss, 1994; Flick & Bell, 2000). The improvement in science achievement is most pronounced for authentic, complex learning experiences. It is in these learning experiences that students are challenged, engage in productive inquiry, make use of prior knowledge and higher-order thinking skills, build conclusions from data, collaborate with other learners, and reflect on their experiences (Papanastasiou, Zembylas, & Vrasidas, 2003; Stern, 2000). Additionally, the use of computers and related

technologies complements school and science education reform in that it encourages and facilitates eight instructional shifts noted by Collins (1991):

- A shift from whole-class to small-group instruction
- A shift from lecture and recitation to coaching
- A shift from working with better students to working with weaker students
- A shift toward more engaged students
- A shift from assessment based on test performance to assessment based on products, progress, and effort
- A shift from a competitive to a cooperative social structure
- A shift from all students learning the same thing to different students learning different things
- A shift from the primacy of verbal thinking to the integration of visual and verbal thinking (Berger, et al., 1994, p. 473)

SCIENCE TEACHING WITH MULTIMEDIA

The computer and other electronic technologies can be combined to provide some of the most powerful curriculum resources that science teachers can have at their fingertips. In a computer multimedia system, the computer serves to link other media forms so that the utility of the system is greater than that of any one element operating alone. For some years, science teachers have used computers to control the delivery of multimedia via floppy disk, videodisc, and CD-ROM. But without question, a computer connected to the Internet now provides the most inexpensive and easiest way for teachers to make use of the vast array of multimedia-based materials available for science instruction. Students can engage in multimedia experiences individually, in small groups, and, with the aid of a computer projection system, as an entire class. Making multimedia highly desirable for use in science instruction is its capability to not only present useful and interesting information but to encourage student active engagement in the science learning process.

There are a number of media formats available that you can use to enhance your instruction, and all are available on the Internet. Seven formats described by Houghton (2003) are: still images, audio, video, animation, 3-D virtual reality, electronics and remote control, and text. Each of these different media formats can make a unique contribution to your teaching and your students' science learning. Collectively, multimedia can help you be successful in the classroom by enabling your students to use modalities that are most comfortable to them and by increasing their motivation for the subject and for learning (Tileston, 2004).

Still Images

Science teachers have long used photographs, drawings, and diagrams to communicate understandings that words alone cannot convey. The images used to support student science learning were often ones that the teacher had gathered over time or those provided with textbook programs.

Today, a plethora of science-related images can be accessed easily on the Internet. By using the "Images" option available on search engines such as Google (http://google.com) and AltaVista Images (http://www.altavista.com) you can access these images in a matter of seconds. Additionally, you and your students can use a digital camera to capture still images for use during science lessons. All digital cameras have some means for transferring the images as electronic files to a computer, where the images can be viewed, incorporated into a multimedia presentation, or printed on paper.

Audio

There are some things that students just have to hear to comprehend. The call of a mockingbird, the growl of a black bear, and the sound of a tornado are among the many audio recordings available on cassette tape and compact disc (CD). Additionally, these audio recordings are accessible on the Internet, as are many others, including interviews with famous scientists such as astronomer Carl Sagan and ecology guru Rachel Carson. A search for audio recordings that can be used to augment your science lessons can be easily conducted by clicking the audio button on DOGPILE (http://www.dogpile.com) or another Internet search engine. To enable all students to hear the audio recordings, we recommend that a set of classroom speakers be used or headphones for individual students be connected to the computer.

Video

Video is perhaps the most compelling of all media systems available to science teachers. Middle and high school students have grown up surrounded by video—in games, at the movies, and on television. Many videos useful for science instruction are available in digital videodisc (DVD) format and can be shown using a DVD player to a class on a large monitor or through a projection system. Individual students or pairs of students also can watch videos on desktop computers equipped with DVD player software.

With the growing availability of faster Internet access and free video player software, more and more science teachers also are incorporating video from the Internet into their science instruction. Because of the bandwidth required for retrieving high-quality video from the Internet, most video is no more than a few minutes in length. Even with this limitation, there are video clips available on the Internet related to just about all science topics.

Animation

Animation is typically constructed by sequencing still images that show different positions of inanimate objects. Often built to simulate events and structures that cannot be seen or easily experienced by other means, animations can be particularly useful for helping students construct understandings about difficult and abstract science concepts. Animations that illustrate DNA transcription and translation, hydrogen bonding, muscle contraction, carbon-14 decay, and evaporation are among the many that are available at commercial and government Internet sites.

A growing number of the science animations found on the Internet are large files and require fast Internet access, much faster than possible through a telephone modem. Some have unusual file names that make them difficult to locate and may require special players for viewing, such as *Flash Plug-In* available for free from *Macromedia* (http://www.macromedia.com). Internet sites to check out for animations that you may wish to use in your science lessons included: *Scientific Illustration and Animation* (http://www.imagecyte.com), and *North Hampton College's Science Animation* page (http://science.nhmccd.edu/b101/ap1int.htm).

3-D Virtual Reality

3-D virtual reality (VR) makes use of powerful visualization techniques that enable learners to place themselves in virtual environments that mimic aspects of the physical and living world. Virtual environments allow learners to engage in near-natural interactions with objects and organisms and to change perspective. The *Virtual Solar System Project* and the *Virtual Gorilla Modeling Project* (http://lpsl.coe.uga.edu/projects/ele.asp) are just two of the many development efforts underway to produce high-quality 3-D/VR materials for use in science classrooms.

Slowing the immediate use of 3-D/VR materials in science classrooms is the necessary high Internet bandwidth required and the absence of a dedicated Internet search engine for VR files (Houghton, 2003). Without a doubt, 3-D/VR represents an important next step for middle and high school science education because it allows for situated learning experiences, including those that involve interacting with concepts and principles that are not normally accessible and where learner safety may be a concern (Winn & Jackson, 1999).

Many standard and innovative laboratory investigations can be carried out using sensors attached to calculators.

Electronics and Remote Control

There are a host of electronic devices, in addition to desktop computers, readily available to support science laboratory work and fieldwork. A growing trend in industry and science education is the use of calculators and hand-held computers to gather, display, and analyze scientific data. Calculators are ubiquitous, cheap, and the programmable models are extremely powerful. Hand-held computers having multiple integrated functions are controlled by modern operating system software and are becoming more affordable.

Sensors that convert chemical or physical changes to electrical signals can be connected to both of these devices. When sensors are suspended in the air, they can detect changes in such variables as temperature, wind speed and direction, oxygen and carbon dioxide levels, barometric pressure, light intensity, and relative humidity. Data collected using sensors can be displayed on a calculator or hand-held computer or brought back to the classroom and downloaded into a desktop computer for further analysis. Once set up, some sensors can be left unattended in the field or as part of a laboratory experiment. Data captured by these sensors can be re-trieved by connecting directly to a computer or accessed using wireless technology.

The Internet is a portal to real-time data collected by sensors all over the world. For example, you and your students can access water level data collected at sites across the United States by researchers working with the U.S. Geological Survey (http://waterdata.usgs.gov/nwis/rt). Alternatively, you may find it useful to have your students interact with a remote garden full of plants at the Telegarden (http://telegarden.aec.at), where they can monitor the effects of their remote manipulations of such variables as water and light. The number of opportunities available for students to engage in scientific data collection and analysis via the Internet continues to grow.

Text

Text is the most basic of all media, but nonetheless a very powerful tool for science teaching. To a greater or lesser extent, text supports all other media. Text is often used to explain a still image or to guide learners' interactions with audio, video, and other forms of media. In its own right, text also can lead to learner understandings impossible to reach by other means.

Text was the only system of communication on the Internet in its early days, primarily because of the limits of the technology. Today, however, you and your students can access countless text-based scientific documents via the Internet at the push of a button. E-mail, listservs, and newsgroups are also convenient ways to communicate with others about scientific topics and issues.

As you think about these seven media forms and their capabilities, it should be clear to you that multimedia is transforming science teaching and learning in ways not considered possible even a decade ago. The Internet is a significant tool in this transformation due to its ability to merge all media (Houghton, 2003). At one Internet site, you and you students can read text, listen to an interview, view a video clip, collect data, and much more. Your use of multimedia will enable you to do a better job of teaching science and will likely provide you with the means to teach differently than you would have without it.

Stop and Reflect!

- Select a biology, physics, chemistry, or earth science topic that interests you. Then, explain to a classmate how multimedia might be used to help students learn about the topic.
- Check out one of the Web sites identified in this section about multimedia. Write a brief description that can be shared with classmates about what you found.

TEACHING SCIENCE USING THE INTERNET

More and more science teachers are making use of the Internet to support student learning. It is indeed a unique computer-based electronic system in its capability to incorporate multimedia and facilitate communication. The Internet permits students to retrieve information in the form of text, images, sound, and numeric data and to communicate with others living in different locations around the world. When used advantageously, the Internet also enables teachers to help students develop the important skills of organizing, analyzing, composing, and problem solving needed for an information-based society. Now it is possible for schools, planetariums, museums, educational centers, and other facilities to share resources and exchange ideas through this network.

A computer, modem, telephone line, and telecommunications software are the basics needed to gain access to the Internet. Internet access can be gained through commercial Internet service providers such as America Online, BellSouth, NetZero, and EarthLink. Commercial services provide the necessary telecommunications software and hardware and charge a user fee. Colleges, universities, and many school districts are also Internet service providers, typically offering free Internet access to staff and students. The Internet service provided by these noncommercial institutions tends to be through a dedicated connection and is usually of the same high quality available through commercial Digital Subscriber Line (DSL) service. The broadband connections used by noncommercial institutions and available to individuals with DSL service allow for faster transfer of information than is possible through a dial-up modem attached to an ordinary telephone line.

In exploring the various features of the Internet and their application for science instruction, it is helpful to think of the Internet as a mega shopping mall where each store provides a different product or service. And as in a shopping mall, some stores attract more business than others. The parts of the Internet that have attracted the most business from science teachers and their students are electronic mail and the World Wide Web. This is primarily due to the quick and inexpensive communication function of electronic mail and the Web's multifunctional, point-and-click access. In recent years, the Web has functioned much like a large department store that has just opened in the mall—pushing smaller and older specialty stores out of business. Internet users are finding few reasons to use programs such as file transfer protocol (ftp) and Gopher to access information on the Internet because of the Web's increasing versatility and ease of use.

Electronic Mail

Electronic mail, or e-mail, facilitates the sharing of information between computer users. E-mail can be accessed on the Internet using programs such as Eudora and Pine or Internet browsers such as Netscape Communicator and Internet Explorer. An exciting use of e-mail is to have individual students or whole classes exchange messages about science topics under investigation. For example, a science class in Texas can use e-mail to share data on weather patterns or bird migration with other science classes anywhere around the world. Students also can use e-mail to contact scientists and other science experts to ask questions about the patterns observed in their data or to learn more about something presented in a textbook or at an Internet site. Student enthusiasm remains high when using e-mail because the time between messages is reduced to minutes compared to the days or weeks required for the exchange of messages via the postal service.

An easy way to get started using e-mail in science classes is to identify individuals, often called keypals, or partner classes that are interested in or studying the same science topics as your students. There are many Internet sites for doing this and most do not charge a fee. The sites that follow can serve as starting points for locating keypals and partner classes as well as seeking advice from science experts.

- *eMail Classroom Exchange* (http://www.epals.com/) This site provides e-mail addresses for teachers and their students in more than 100 countries and an instant translator to allow communication with students and teachers whose first language is not English. A search using the key words *chemistry for ages 14 through 18* turned up classes in the United States, Venezuela, Japan, and Romania interested in corresponding about different kinds of chemical analyses and science fair experiments.
- *Mighty Media Network Keypals Club* (http://www.teaching.com/keypals/) This is an excellent site for connecting classrooms to classrooms and students to students. The mailing lists available at this site can assist with locating classroom partners and provide insights about intercultural e-mail communication.
- *Pitsco's Ask an Expert* (http://www.askanexpert.com/) Through this site, you and your students can obtain the e-mail addresses of hundreds of science experts, ranging from aerospace engineers and forensics scientists to plasma physicists and zookeepers.
- *Global School Net Internet Project Registry* (http://gsn.org/gsh/pr/). This site provides a searchable database of teacher-developed collaborative projects, some requiring

technology (e.g., Web-based videoconferencing) but most require only the most basic e-mail capabilities. A science teacher can, for instance, search by specific key words or find all projects involving science at a given level of technological complexity.

E-mail also can be exchanged among groups of people who share a common interest using *listservs*. A listserv is simply a computer-based mailing list to which many people subscribe. Subscribing to a listserv typically involves sending an e-mail message to the list's address that includes the word *subscribe,* the list's name, and your first and last name. Many listservs related to science education exist where comments, questions, rebuttals, and opinions are posted on a daily basis. Several science education-related listservs are identified in Table 15.1. While most of the listservs in this table are appropriate for use by teachers, students also may be encouraged to use them.

When introducing students to listservs, it is always a good idea to encourage them to "lurk" or read the list for a week or two before posting any messages (Leu & Leu, 2000). This strategy will allow students to gain insights into the topics being discussed as well as learn about protocols followed by the user group. Also, Dock-

erman (1998) recommends saving the confirmation message received when first subscribing to a listserv because it contains directions for unsubscribing in the event that the amount of mail becomes overwhelming or the topics being discussed are no longer of interest. Because lists do change and new ones start up almost every day, the mailing list directories at http://directory. google.com/top/computers/Internet/E-mail/mailing_ lists/directories.com, http://www.edweb.org, and http:// tile.net/lists/ may help you and your students stay connected to useful lists.

Many science teachers also find newsgroups valuable sources of up-to-date information on topics of interest. Using newsgroups, you can read and post messages just as on listservs. However, you have to log on to a newsgroup each time you want to access the posted messages or add a message of your own. This can be an advantage over listservs because postings from newsgroups are not sent to your e-mail address and will not accumulate in your mailbox. A limitation associated with some newsgroups is that messages are deleted after only a couple of days due to the high volume of daily postings. Newsgroups that may be of interest to you and your students are presented in Table 15.2. Other science education-related newsgroups may be located by search-

TABLE 15–1   Science Education-Related Listservs

APPL-L (listserv@vm.cc.torun.edu.pl) Computer applications in science and education

BIOPI-L (listserv@ksuvm.ksu.edu) Biology and education discussion

CHEME-SAFETY (majordomo@list.pitt.edu) Chemical safety discussion

CLIMATEEDUCATION (climate-educate-l@listserv. icfconsulting.com) Environmental Projection Agency climate change education list

GRANTS-L (listserv@jhuvm.hcf.jhu.edu) National Science Foundation grants list

GEOED-L (listserv@uwf.cc.uwf.edu) Geology and earth science discussion forum

INFORMAL-L (ISEW-ASTC-L@Home.EASE.lsoft.com) Informal Science Education Network

MOLBIO-L (listproc@lists.missouri.edu) Molecular biology discussion

OUTDOOR-ED (listserv@latrobe.edu.au) Outdoor education list

PHYS-L (listproc@atlantis.cc.uwf.edu) Physics educators list

PHYSHARE (listserv@lists.psu.edu) High school physics resource list

SCIEDDISCUSS (listproc@listproc.bgsu.edu) Science education discussion

TABLE 15–2   Science Education-Related Newsgroups

alt.folklore.science	Discussion of folklore related to science
bionet.biophysics	Science and profession of biophysics
k12.ed.science	Science curriculum in grades K–12
misc.education.science	Discussion of issues related to science education
school.subject.science	Discussion about physics, computer science, and chemistry
sci.skeptic	Skeptics discussing pseudo-science
soc.history.science	History of science and related topics

ing the listings posted at http://tile.net/news/. Directions for accessing newsgroups can also be found at this Internet site.

World Wide Web

The World Wide Web is the newest of the Internet services and is responsible for much of the Internet's current notoriety. It is unique among Internet services in two important ways. It provides hypertext links between documents and access to movies, audio, on-screen pictures, and full font and styles for text (Engst, 1995). World Wide Web search engines such as Yahoo, WebCrawler, Lycos, and Google can simplify locating and downloading files by searching through databases of locator addresses and descriptors located at various Internet sites. However, for many science teachers and their students, searching the Web using search engines such as these can be frustrating and not very productive. For example, the results of a search for *bird migration* using Google returned more than 441,000 hits, and the vast majority of these would be of little immediate use to middle and high school science students and teachers. A more effective strategy for science teachers who wish to begin using the Web with their students is suggested by Leu and Leu (2000). They recommend that teachers and their students start by exploring a few central sites that provide information and resources specifically for science education.

Central Science Sites

Central sites have much in common with the large department stores in shopping malls. By visiting one or two department stores you can find much of what you are looking for and save time in the process. By using a few central science sites, similar benefits can be realized. Some of the most useful central Web sites for science education are associated with federally funded projects and provide a number of resources for science teachers and their students. Others that are just as useful are the products of private efforts or the work of local or regional consortia that involve partnerships between museums, businesses, and schools. Central cites that are highly recommended by many who have carefully examined the Web with science education in mind are described here.

The premier site for science education resources is the *National Science Digital Library* (http://nsdl.org). This site is presented by the Eisenhower National Clearinghouse and is organized to support science education from kindergarten through graduate school. All resource collections and services accessible through NSDL have been carefully scrutinized for their scientific merit. The NSDL portals provide access to selected audience-specific resources. For example, it is possible to browse the NSDL Middle School Portal by subject topic as well as by National Science Education standard. The soon to be opened *Teachers' Domain Pathways to Science Portal* will provide access to multimedia resources for science teaching and independent study, many of which come from educational public television.

Also an excellent site to consider as a starting point for exploring the Internet is the *National Aeronautics and Space Administration* (NASA) (http://www.nasa.gov) site. This site contains a wealth of information about many NASA projects, a multimedia gallery that features some wonderful photographs and video clips, details about upcoming broadcasts by NASA television, and an education section. The education section includes information about NASA education programs, education news, an education calendar, resources for teachers, and resources for students.

Another highly recommended site is the *Eisenhower National Clearinghouse for Mathematics and Science Education* (http://www.enc.org:80/). A click on the "Digital Dozen" button on the site's homepage will lead you to a collection of 13 carefully reviewed Internet sites that change every month. Past sites are archived and can be searched using a resource finder at the site. Other sections under the "Web Links" label allow access to hundreds of science lesson plans and activities organized by topic and brief stories about science teachers making a difference with students. In addition, this site includes a section where you can ask questions of science education experts and one where you can read a number of science education articles and other publications.

A favorite site of many science teachers is *Frank Potter's Science Gems* (http://www.sciencegems.com/). Initially launched as a resource for earth science teachers, this site has expanded to include thousands of links to teaching resources for all science subjects. The resources are organized into categories by science subject and topic. Special features available at this site include links to science lesson plans that use Internet resources and a guide to great science discoveries of the last decade.

San Francisco's Exploratorium is one of the most highly regarded science museums in the world, and the *Exploratorium Home Page* (http://www.exploratorium.edu/) provides access to many of the museum's excellent exhibits and science instructional resources. The site includes a number of highly engaging activities through which users can explore the science of various sports, build geodesic structures with gumdrops, or investigate the inside of a floppy disk. Additionally, over 100 scaled-down versions of the Exploratorium's exhibits, called *Science Snacks,* are available at the site. These exhibits can be constructed using inexpensive materials and used to engage students in some very exciting science activities and demonstrations.

Other sites worth visiting are *Access Excellence* (www.accessexcellence.org/) and *Science Learning Network* (http://www.sln.org/). Affiliated with the National

Health Museum and the pharmaceutical company Genetech, Access Excellence is for biology and life science teachers. The site includes an activities exchange, on-line science mysteries, directory of on-line projects, and a separate section for AP biology. The Science Learning Network is supported by Unisys and the National Science Foundation. Its guiding theme is inquiry-based science education. Contained within the Network site are links to "Ten Cool Sites" that are updated monthly, activities and other resources from an international network of science museums, and connections to teachers at the six Science Learning Network schools.

Of course, there are many more sites that you could use to begin your exploration of science education resources on the Internet. However, starting with a few central sites will make the job of finding ideas for science learning experiences, whether they make use of the Internet or not, easier and more enjoyable.

Internet Activities, Projects, Inquiries, and WebQuests

Wishing to take full advantage of the vast resources available through the World Wide Web, more and more science teachers are introducing their students to the Internet as a tool for finding answers to their own science questions. Studies of these efforts at on-line inquiry suggest that students are not always prepared to take full advantage of this new learning tool (Hoffman, Krajcik, & Soloway, 2004). They have difficulty navigating the Internet, judging the credibility of Internet sites, and synthesizing the information found at multiple sites. Science teachers need to provide their students with other experiences using the Internet before involving them in on-line inquiry. Leu and Leu (1999) recommend that science teachers first engage their students in Internet activities and projects.

Internet Activities

The resources of the Internet can be used to develop engaging science activities for students. The process of developing science activities using the resources of the Internet is no more difficult than when using printed materials. First, find an Internet site that contains content that can be used to achieve your learning objectives. You can bookmark the site so that it can be easily found by students or download the entire site to a computer's hard drive. Downloading the site eliminates the potential hassle of trying to access the Internet during class and gives you control over what students are able to access. Next, develop directions and questions to guide students' use of the site and assessments to determine what they have learned.

Internet resources that can be developed into science class activities can be found at many sites, but we recommend that you begin your search with the central sites identified in the previous section. *Welcome to The pH Factor!* (http://www.miamisci.org/ph/) is a site from the Miami Museum of Science that we located through the Eisenhower National Clearinghouse's Digital Dozen. It is ideal for helping middle school students develop an understanding of pH as part of an introductory chemistry unit. Similarly, the *Mystery of the Poison-Dart Frog* (http://www.ncmoa.org/costarica), which we located through the Science Learning Network, is a great site for middle school life science teachers interested in having their students solve a mystery as they learn about the animals and plants that live in the forests of Costa Rica. The on-line resources available for constructing Internet activities seem to be limitless.

Internet Projects

Internet projects involve students or classes of students working collaboratively to investigate real-world problems. Some projects can be completed in a class period or two and involve little preparation, while others necessitate a larger commitment of classroom time and may involve the purchase of special equipment for data collection or reporting. Of course, Internet access is a central feature of any Internet project, but many projects require only one computer with e-mail access. Through participation in Internet projects, students do real science, develop understandings about the nature of science, and improve their communication skills in addition to learning how to use the technology (Noonan, Undated).

Internet projects take many forms, ranging from those coordinated by university researchers to those developed and facilitated by a single teacher. A number of projects, such as *The International Boiling Point Project* and *The Albatross Project,* take advantage of the ability of the Internet to facilitate data sharing around the globe by focusing on phenomena that vary geographically. When selecting Internet projects for your classes, it is a good idea to make sure that the projects' driving questions are (1) meaningful to students, (2) based in real-world experiences, (3) worthwhile in terms of the science content that can be addressed, (4) open-ended. It is also important that they lead to long-term investigations (Krajcik, Czerniak, & Berger, 2003). A sampling of the many questions around which Internet projects have been developed are: What is the effect of acid rain on our rivers? How do airline pilots find their way? What is the frequency of the TPC allele in the human population? How do pollen types and counts change with the seasons?

Many Internet project sites may be accessed through the central science sites identified earlier. For example, *Access Excellence's Classrooms of the 21st Century* (http://www.accessexcellence.org/21st/TE/AO/) and *NASA's On-line Interactive Projects* (http://quest.arc. nasa.gov) provide indexes and access to dozens of ongoing projects. Additionally, the *CIESE On-line Class-room Projects* (http://www.k12science.org/currichome.html) and *The Center for Highly Interactive Computing in Education* (http://www.nice.org) are good sites to search for partners and projects that match your interests and those of your students.

Internet Inquiries

In Internet inquiries, students seek answers to their own questions, sometimes working in pairs or larger collaborative groups. Internet inquiries provide students with opportunities to take full advantage of the Internet along with other electronic technologies. They can gather information from Internet sites and other sources, analyze and make sense of the information, and then develop a presentation of their findings and conclusions (Leu & Leu, 2000). The findings and conclusions of the inquiry could be communicated to others and debated via e-mail or at a personal Web site.

Student participation in Internet inquiries usually requires additional scaffolding beyond that provided through engaging in Internet activities and projects. Students need help to generate questions from phenomena they find interesting and to develop their questions into ones that will lead to meaningful and sustainable inquiries (Feldman, Konold, & Coulter, 2000). Students also need help searching for information using on-line search engines, finding resources pertaining to their questions, and analyzing and synthesizing the resources they find on the Internet, according to Hoffman et al. (2004).

To help address these challenges, Hoffman and his colleagues recommend that teachers model search techniques, talk with students about the appropriateness of search terms, and allow class time for students to demonstrate and discuss their on-line search strategies. They also recommend that students be reminded of the loosely configured organizational structure of the World Wide Web, the complex nature of research, and that answers to research questions often emerge from synthesizing information found at multiple sites and in other resources, including books and journals. Finally, they encourage teachers to support student evaluation and synthesis of on-line resources using the following strategies:

- Provide contradictory articles from the World Wide Web for learners to evaluate
- Model and discuss appropriate evaluation and synthesis skills
- Encourage learners to share resources and content summaries with peers
- Require multiple information sources from student final reports (Hoffmanet et al., 2004, p. 220)

WebQuests

Combining aspects of Internet activities, projects, and inquiries, WebQuests engage students in challenging and motivating Internet-based learning opportunities. As conceived by Bernie Dodge in the mid-1990s, a Web-Quest follows a basic lesson format and may be completed in a couple of class periods or extended for several weeks. There are five basic elements to most WebQuests: an *introduction* that includes background information, a *task* that can be accomplished by the students, a description of a *process* that involve students interacting with information sources to complete the task, *guidance* provided in writing or orally by the teacher about how students should organize and synthesize the information gathered, and a culminating experience that brings *closure* to the quest (Dodge, 1995). In addition, a Web-Quest typically has an accompanying rubric that can be used to evaluate students' accomplishments.

WebQuests most suitable for use with science classes are those that focus on science-related problems that call for creative solutions and science topics about which there is genuine disagreement (Brooks & Byles, 2000). Topics that meet these criteria and around which WebQuests have been designed include acid rain, scientific and ethical uses of Antarctica, designing amusement park rides, and protecting the Galápagos from human encroachment. Many WebQuests are becoming popular science instructional resources. Locations to begin your search for science WebQuests include Bernie Dodge's WebQuest site (http://webquest.org) and Tom March's site (http://www.bestwebquests.com). Information about constructing WebQuests and a WebQuest template can be found at *A WebQuest About WebQuests* by Bernie Dodge (http://www.internet4classrooms.com/wq_wq.htm).

Considerations When Using the Internet

Inappropriate use of the Internet and school computers is a concern of many teachers when engaging students in Internet explorations like those discussed. Using on-line search engines, it is possible for students to access pornography and other information unsuitable for adolescents. Personal privacy, misuse of information found on the Internet, and Internet etiquette are among the issues that teachers find themselves addressing when their students use the Internet. In addition to using blocking software that limits students' access to sites based on the presence of certain words, more and more schools and school districts are developing policy statements to guide students' use of the Internet and school computers. According to Leu and Leu (2000, p. 63), most acceptable use policies include the following components:

- An explanation of the Internet and its role in providing information resources to students

- A description of acceptable and unacceptable behavior that emphasizes student responsibility when using the Internet
- A list of penalties for each violation of the policy
- A space for all parties (including student, parents/guardians, and teacher) to sign the agreement

For information about a school district's Internet and computer acceptable use policy, contact the technology coordinator for the district or check the district's Web site.

Stop and Reflect!

- Explore two or more of the central science sites described in this section. Discuss what you find at these sites with a classmate.
- Examine the vignette in Box 15.1. What recommendations can you make about using multimedia and the Internet that might enhance the science learning experiences of Ms. Roper's students?

Classroom Snapshot 15.1

Technology in Motion

The presence of computers and other electronic technologies is not a novelty at Stonewall Jackson High School. The use of instructional technology has been strongly encouraged by school administrators and well supported with local monies and several privately funded projects. The high school media center and science department are well equipped when it comes to technology. Many software and multimedia programs have been purchased in recent years for use in science classes, along with a DVD player and two CD-ROM players. All science classrooms have at least three microcomputers, a 25-inch monitor, and high-speed Internet access. Parents and visitors marvel at the amount of up-to-date technology available at the school for science instruction.

Despite the plethora of equipment, most Stonewall Jackson High science students see the use of computers and other electronic technologies as "just a different way for teachers to teach the same boring stuff." Given this prevailing student attitude, most of the school's eight science teachers have become disillusioned with the promise of instructional technology and are using it less than they were even 1 year ago. A view held by many of the school's science teacher is: "Why incorporate technology into science classes if it does nothing to motivate students to learn science?"

Ms. Roper is one teacher who does not share this view. She thought hard about how she could get students interested in using technology to learn about "motion and forces," the next topic in her curriculum. She was concerned about connecting abstract science concepts with what her students knew and had an interest in. She knew that the technology available at her school could help her, but she didn't want to use it in a way that would turn students off.

An idea came to her. Why not begin the unit on motion and forces by allowing my students to use the Internet to learn more about the concepts that will be addressed, such as speed, velocity, and acceleration? She knew that her students were interested in many activities to which these concepts could easily be related, so she presented it to them in this way:

Ms. Roper: I have written on the board several activities: car racing, gymnastics, dancing, baseball, sailing, volleyball, and space travel. What do they all have in common?

Dava: They all would be fun to watch or do.

Kendal: Some use special equipment or machines, but all involve quick movement.

Pete: I think that car racing is the most exciting of them all.

After several more students expressed their opinions, a class consensus developed that they all involved people moving, sometimes with the help of machines. Other activities were added to the list until about 30 were identified.

Ms. Roper: To start this unit, I would like you to form three-member teams and use the Internet to find out what you can about one of these activities. To access the Internet, you can use the computers in the media center or the one here in the room. As you browse the Internet for information on your topic, save what you find about motion, speed, velocity, and acceleration. And don't forget to check for bulletin boards related to your topic. Let me know when your team has decided on a topic, so that we don't have two teams working on the same one.

Two days later, the student groups presented what they found. The teams were encouraged to use the projector connected to one of the classroom computers to show some of the Internet sites and bulletin board messages that were considered particularly interesting and informative. The wealth of information that the students collected in just 2 days surprised even Ms. Roper. The student presentations led to a number of questions related to motion and forces that the students now had a reason to find answers for.

That afternoon, Ms. Roper told two of her fellow science teachers about the success she had found with her physical science classes. Her enthusiasm caused the other teachers to wonder if they could do what Ms. Roper had done. It also led Ms. Roper to wonder about how she might use sensors linked to her classroom computers, WebQuests or Internet inquiries, and toy cars such as Hot Wheels to help students answer some of the questions that were raised during their presentations.

USES FOR COMPUTERS AND ELECTRONIC TECHNOLOGIES IN SCIENCE INSTRUCTION

There is virtually no limit to the ways in which computers and electronic technologies can be used in the science classroom, as the previous sections of this chapter indicate. They can be used as a presentation tool, an individualized learning center, or to facilitate group interaction and problem solving (Dockerman, 1998). Another way to describe their uses is in terms of the investigative processes that are at the heart of all inquiry-based science learning. When confronted with the need to know, science students, with guidance from their teacher, 'can use computers' and other electronic technologies to *find out* about ideas and information, *analyze* information, *compose* a representation of their newly constructed understandings, and finally *communicate* with others about what they have learned or what to learn (Leu & Leu, 1999).

When finding out about ideas and information, students may use sensory instruments interfaced to the computer to extend their senses or access resources well beyond those available in textbooks by coupling computers to CD-ROMs or connecting to the Internet. Computers equipped with well-designed software or linked to other electronic technologies can also facilitate the organization, analysis, and interpretation of ideas and information. Computer spreadsheets and graphing and presentation software also provide ways for students to construct meaning from their learning experiences and to share their knowledge with others through various presentation modes. Figure 15.1 shows examples of the many applications of computers and electronic technologies in science instruction.

Stop and Reflect!

- Study the examples listed under each of the four applications of computers and electronic technologies in Figure 15.1. What other examples can you add to the four lists?

- Again examine Box 15.1, "Technology in Motion," and discuss with a classmate which of the four application categories are demonstrated in the vignette.

FIGURE 15.1 Applications of computers and electronic technologies.

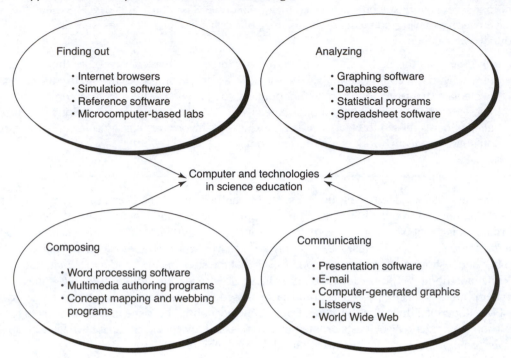

SELECTING QUALITY SOFTWARE AND MEDIA

Instructional software and multimedia are available on floppy disk, CD-ROM, and digital videodisc or can be accessed via the Internet. The quality of instructional software and multimedia is a major factor in determining the benefits derived from them. The quality must be high—easy to use and instructive—otherwise the computer and other electronic technology will make little contribution to science education. Many education software and multimedia programs are available, and the number of Internet sites continues to grow, but not all of them are effective for instruction. A number of programs and sites appear to be useful when first examined, but a closer look may lead you to conclude that they have little educational value. It is easy for software and multimedia developers, regardless of the delivery platform, to make colorful, flashy-looking programs that appear useful; however, in the final analysis, these teaching tools have little instructional significance. Careful analysis of software and multimedia programs and Internet sites is essential before they are used in science instruction.

Perhaps the first thing that you should do before selecting a program or Internet site for use is to reflect on the course you are teaching or will be teaching. Identify the key concepts, principles, laws, and other understandings and skills that you want students to master or what aspects of the nature of science and technology that you would like students to explore. This process will give purpose to your search for quality software and multimedia and should help you incorporate computer technology into the curriculum as opposed to using them because it seems to be the thing to do.

When examining a piece of software or Internet site, you should read the developer's description of the purpose. What will the program help students learn or do? Based on our discussion in the previous sections of this chapter, you should recognize that some programs and Internet sites are designed to help students find out about something, others will assist them to analyze and make sense of information, and still others will enable students to compose representations of their science understandings or communicate with other people about what they know or want to know. In some instances, all of these capabilities will be incorporated into a single program or Internet site. Also, from the program description and by personally exploring the software or Internet site, you should be able to determine for whom it is intended. Usually the grade level and content focus for the program or site is specified, but often the information given is too general. In addition to determining the merits of various important aspects of the software, you may want to consider its cost.

Teachers reviewing software or multimedia regardless of the delivery platform should seek answers to the following questions:

- Is the software or multimedia accurate and current?
- Is the language used clear and concise?
- Does the program enhance motivation and maintain interest?
- Does the program engage the learner as an active participant?
- Is the software of high technical quality?
- Can the developer provide evidence of its effectiveness?
- Is the program free from objectionable bias?
- Are the program's teacher's guide and documentation of high quality?

- Are clear directions provided for loading the software and using it for the first time?
- Does the program stimulate creativity? (Heinich, Molenda, Russell, & Smaldino, 1996, p. 277)

Computer technology and the right software or multimedia package can assist teachers in enhancing their instructional programs. Nevertheless, science teachers must be keenly aware of the technical and the instructional quality of the software or multimedia they wish to use. Technically, it must be easy to use, and the screen display and graphics must be easy to view. Instructionally, the content of the program must be accurate and appropriate for the students. Good software and multimedia can be selected only through systematic inquiry into what is available and careful evaluation of it for a given group of students.

ASSESSING AND REVIEWING

Analysis and Synthesis

1. Indicate your agreement or disagreement with each of the following statements. For those with which you disagree, write a brief paragraph to convince others of the need to agree with your position.
   a. All science teachers need to develop a basic level of understanding in using sensors to collect data that can be displayed on a calculator or computer.
   b. When selecting software or multimedia, science teachers should begin by asking the question, "What concepts and skills are addressed by the program that match those addressed in my science course?"
   c. Sooner or later, science teachers will need to be able to develop software.
   d. Computers should be incorporated into science lessons whenever possible.
   e. 3D virtual reality will become less useful to science teachers and their students in coming years.
2. Identify three to five possible shortcoming or limitations that you associate with using computers and electronic technologies to support science teaching and learning. Then, develop strategies for overcoming these shortcomings or limitations.
3. Describe the differences between Internet activities, Internet projects, and Internet inquiries.

What student learning outcomes would you expect from an Internet inquiry that you would not expect from either an Internet activity or Internet project?

Practical Considerations

4. Use sensors connected to either a calculator or hand-held computer to collect and display data from the laboratory or field. Discuss your experiences with a classmate and decide on strategies that could be used to overcome any problems you encountered.
5. Assemble a collection of images, audio tracks, and video clips that you could use to aid your teaching of a particular science lesson. For each image, audio track, and video clip, briefly describe how you would use it in the lesson.
6. Work through a WebQuest of interest to you from the many identified at Bernie Dodge's or Tom March's WebQuest sites. Write a brief critique of the WebQuest and share it with your classmates.
7. Work with a classmate to interview two middle school or high school science teachers about their uses of computers and electronic technologies to support instruction. What did you learn from your interviews that you would make a part of your own teaching practice?

Developmental Considerations

8. Work with a classmate to set up a listserv for your science methods class. Encourage all of your classmates to use the listserv during student teaching and beyond to discuss ideas and information related to science teaching and learning, including successful lessons and useful science teaching resources.

9. Keep a log of your favorite Internet sites. Include in your log the Web address for each site and how you used the site to support your teaching.

RESOURCES TO EXAMINE

Does World Wide Web Surfing Guarantee Learning?
2004. In *Cases in Middle and Secondary Science Education: The Promise and Dilemmas,* edited by T. Koballa and D. Tippins (pp. 212–221). Upper Saddle River, NJ: Merrill/Prentice Hall.

Joseph Hoffman and his colleagues present the case of Mary, a ninth-grade physical science teacher who engages her students in Internet inquiries as a way to make the study of weather phenomena meaningful to them. Revealed through the case are strengths and limitations associated with this kind of science learning experience. Suggestions derived from the University of Michigan Digital Library project for helping students prepare for and take advantage of opportunities to engage in Internet inquiries follow the case.

Science on the Internet: A Resource for K–12 Teachers. 2003. Upper Saddle River, NJ: Merrill/Prentice Hall.

Prepared by Jazlin Ebenezer and Eddy Lau, this four-chapter handbook is a valuable resource for science teachers because of the hundreds of science-related Web sites identified and briefly described. The topics of Internet surfing strategies, ways of using the Internet for science instruction, links to science activities, and science curricular frameworks serve as organizing themes for the chapters.

EDThoughts: What We Know About Science Teaching and Learning. 2001. Aurora, CO: Mid-Continent Research for Education and Learning.

Included in this edited volume are research-based responses to questions asked by teachers regarding the uses of computers and related technologies in science classrooms. Among the questions addressed are: How does using instructional technology affect science inquiry teaching and learning? How can using instructional technologies make science learning more science-like? How can students learn to assess the credibility of Internet information? Each response includes discussion of best practice and classroom implications.

Vernier Software and Technology. 13979 SW Millikan Way, Beaverton, OR 97005. [On-line.] Available: http://www.vernier.com

Vernier Software and Technology has been in business for more than 20 years and is a premier supplier of science data collection tools and software. Probes available from Vernier can be used with desktop computers as well as with calculators and hand-held computers. Some of Vernier's newest probes connect directly to a computer's USB port. In addition to an on-line catalog and purchasing directions, the Vernier Web site provides access to technical support, information about future training sessions, downloadable sample programs, and an on-line discussion board for uses of Vernier products.

REFERENCES

Adams, P. E., Krockover, G. H., & Lehman, J. D. (1996). Strategies for implementing computer technologies in the science classroom. In J. Rhonton & P. Bowers (Eds.), *Issues in science education* (pp. 66–72). Arlington, VA: National Science Teachers Association.

Ball, J. (1996). Technology infusion strategies. *The Science Teacher, 63*(3), 51–53.

Becker, H. J., Ravitz, J. L., & Wong, Y. (1999). *Teacher and teacher-directed student use of computers and software, Report # 3, Teaching, learning and computing: 1998 national survey.* Center for Research on Information Technology and Organizations. University of California, Irvine. [On-line.] Available: http://www.crito.uci.edu/tlc/html/findings.html (February 20, 2005).

Berger, C. F., Lu, C. R., Belzer, S. J., & Voss, B. E. (1994). Research in the use of technology in science education. In D. L. Gabel (Ed.), *Handbook of research in science teaching and learning* (pp. 466–490). Upper Saddle River, NJ: Merrill/Prentice Hall.

Brooks, S., & Byles, B. (2000, November). Using a WebQuest in your classroom. [On-line.] Available: http://internet4classrooms.com/using_quests.htm (June 16, 2004).

Collins, A. (1991). The role of computer technology in restructuring schools. *Phi Delta Kappan, 73*(1), 28–36.

Dockerman, D. A. (1998). *Great teaching in the one-computer classroom.* Watertown, MA: Tom Snyder Productions.

Dodge, B. (1995). WebQuests: A technique for Internet-based learning. *Distance Educator, 1*(2), 10–13.

Engst, A. C. (1995). *Internet starter kit for Macintosh* (3rd ed.). Indianapolis: Hayden Books.

Feldman, A., Konold, C., & Coulter, B. (2000). *Network science, a decade later: The Internet and classroom learning.* Mahawah, NJ: Lawrence Erlbaum.

Flick, L., & Bell, R. (2000). Preparing tomorrow's science teachers to use technology: Guidelines for science educators. *Contemporary Issues in Technology and Teacher Education* [On-line serial], *1*(1). Available: http://www.citejournal.org/vol1/iss1/currentissues/science/article.htm (February 20, 2005).

Heinich, R., Molenda, M., Russell, J. D., & Smaldino, S. E. (1996). *Instructional technologies and learning.* Englewood Cliffs, NJ: Prentice Hall.

Hoffman, J., Krajcik, J., & Soloway, E. (2004). Using the World Wide Web to support student inquiry. In T. Koballa & D. Tippins (Eds.), *Cases in middle and secondary science education: The promise and dilemmas* (pp. 216–221). Upper Saddle River, NJ: Merrill/Prentice Hall.

Houghton, R. S. (2003). *Rationale for multimedia use and instruction in education.* Western Carolina University. [On-line.] Available: http://www.ceap/Houghton/MM/RationaleMMframes.html (June 18, 2004).

Krajcik, J., Czerniak, C., & Berger, C. (2003). *Elementary and middle school classrooms: A project-based approach.* New York: McGraw-Hill.

Leu, D. J., & Leu, D. D. (1999). *Teaching with the Internet: Lessons from the classroom* (1999 ed.). Norwood, MA: Christopher-Gordon.

Leu, D. J., & Leu, D. D. (2000). *Teaching with the Internet: Lessons from the classroom* (3rd ed.). Norwood, MA: Christopher-Gordon.

Noonan, K. (Undated). All about online projects. [On-line.] Available: http://www.accessexcellence.org/21st/TE/AO (June 15, 2004).

Papanastasiou, E. C., Zembylas, M., & Vrasidas, C. (2003). Can computer use hurt science achievement? The USA results from PISA. *Journal of Science Education and Technology, 12*(3), 325–332.

Stern, J. (2000). The design of learning software: Principles learned from the computer as learning partner. *Journal of Science Education and Technology, 9*(1), 49–65.

Tileston, S. W. (2004). *What every teacher should know about media and technology.* Thousand Oaks, CA: Corwin Press.

Winn, W. D., & Jackson, R. (1999). Fourteen propositions about educational uses of virtual reality. *Educational Technology, 39*(4), 5–14.

chapter

16

Long-Term Planning and Assessment

Long-term planning is made easier by attending to important elements of teaching.

Effective teachers plan well. They have solid ideas about what they want students to know or be able to do and how their lessons will help students achieve these instructional outcomes before they begin teaching. Consequently, teachers who organize their courses into units and plan them with the end in mind will be better able to provide meaningful learning experiences for their students than science teachers who follow a curriculum that others have organized and planned. The process of planning science units gives teachers opportunities to think deeply about what they want students to know and be able to do and how they will teach in ways to actively engage students and help them learn. Unit planning expands the basic lesson planning process in scope and time, but remains consistent in its consideration of general learning goals, instructional objectives, instructional strategies, and approaches to assess student learning. In addition, planning gives teachers ownership of the curriculum and empowers them to be creative in their teaching. Few activities are as useful for science teachers as organizing their own instruction through unit planning.

AIMS OF THE CHAPTER

Use the questions that follow to guide your thinking and learning about important understandings regarding long-term planning and assessment:

- How has science education reform influenced long-term planning and assessment?
- What elements should be considered when constructing a science unit plan?
- What resources are available to science teachers for planning instructional units?
- What are the characteristics of learning assessment that comprise a multifaceted science assessment system?

- What are some useful procedures and techniques for scoring science learning assessments and assigning grades?
- How should one go about planning a science instructional unit and assessing its potential for promoting scientific literacy among adolescent learners?

UNIT PLANNING AND SCIENCE EDUCATION REFORM

According to science education reform documents (AAAS, 1993; NRC, 1996), science teaching should take on a different form from the one where students sit in straight rows, receive information during most class periods, and take part in laboratory work once a week. Instruction must be initiated by questions that are meaningful to students, stimulating them to search for answers over extended periods of time. Science should be taught as inquiry, which focuses on the learning of ideas that can be tested against established scientific knowledge (NRC, 1996). Thus, students will be constructing their own knowledge and explanations, testing their ideas against reality, and comparing them with established conceptions.

Moreover, the evaluation of student achievement and progress should be based on a more authentic assessment system (Clark & Star, 1996). Many learning outcomes should be measured in situations in which the knowledge and skills will actually be used. If students are expected to use metric measurement in everyday situations, they should be assessed using 2-liter soft drink bottles, for example, which they encounter frequently in grocery stores and homes. Assessment must occur with real-life objects rather than substituting paper-and-pencil measures for the sake of convenience. Projects should be common products in science courses and judged using rubrics, checklists, and other criteria that are agreed upon by teacher and students. Portfolios also should be used to show students' work, evidencing their achievement and charting their academic growth.

When considered from the perspective of science education reform, there are many points to consider when constructing a science teaching unit. Fortunately, many are similar to those considered when developing effective lesson plans. The principle difference is the scope of the planning effort. Rather than planning for a lesson that may take one or two class periods, you will now be planning for student learning experiences that may last for 10 class periods or more. Important considerations in unit planning include *general learning goals, instructional objectives, during and end-of-unit assessments,* and *learning activities.*

General Learning Goals

When planning a unit of instruction for a middle school or high school science course, the first place to look for guidance is the general learning goals for the course. These general learning goals will likely be found in the form of content standards and the more precisely worded benchmarks that help explain the standards. The *National Science Education Standards* (NRC, 1996), as well as standards developed at the state and school district level, describe what students should know and be able to do as a result of science instruction. Your examination of these standards should allow you to group them by topic or theme into coherent clusters. If you are new to a school, check with other science teachers to see if work has already been done to group standards associated with a single course into clusters. Seeing the organizational schemes developed by other teachers may help you to decide the appropriate structure for instructional units you develop.

Instructional Objectives and Assessments

Once you have selected the standards that will be addressed in a unit, it seems that the next logical step is to collect instructional materials or pull materials from a resource unit related to the selected standards. While gathering instructional materials is a necessary activity at this stage of unit development, it is not the only activity to which you should devote your energies. You will also want to consider developing instructional objectives for your unit. Recall from Chapter 6 that instructional objectives serve to link standards to learning assessments. Because of this relationship, we recommend that you give considerable thought to how you will assess student learning associated with the unit. In fact, we urge you to make decisions about your unit assessments first, before writing your instructional objectives and making final determinations about your instructional activities. Through the process of developing your assessments, you will make explicit what students should know or be able to do by the end of the unit. Making explicit what you want students to learn will make writing instructional objectives a snap and will make deciding on instructional activities that much easier.

The sequence of constructing assessments, then writing instructional objectives, and finally organizing instructional activities is not as linear as it might first appear. As you engage in the process of unit development, you will undoubtedly find yourself tweaking or changing your assessments and instructional objectives to ensure alignment with your chosen instructional activities. You may find an activity or learn of a different way of helping students learn the content and skills included in the unit. It is perfectly fine to make adjustments to your assessments, objectives, and instructional activities. In fact, it is very much a part of the unit planning process. But, it is most important that your assessments, objectives, and activities stay true to the standards that served as your starting point for unit development. Units that stray from course standards may not adequately prepare students to perform well on high-stakes assessments, such as graduation tests and end-of-course tests, that are keyed to these standards.

Choices for assessing students' learning related to a unit of instruction extend far beyond paper-and-pencil tests. Contemporary assessment involves the use of many data-gathering formats, including portfolios, journals, concept maps, observation, drawing, and open-ended problems. These various formats and many more are called *alternative assessments* because they offer alternatives to traditional paper-and-pencil tests. Alternative assessments are not meant to replace paper-and-pencil tests but to supplement them and are often described as authentic. Alternative assessments are *authentic* if they "require students to apply scientific knowledge and reasoning to situations similar to those they will encounter in the world outside of the classroom, as well as situations that approximate how scientists do their work" (NRC, 1996, p. 78). More information about different forms of assessment is presented later in this chapter.

Learning Activities

Ideas for learning activities are most important when planning a teaching unit. For those individuals with many years of teaching and curriculum experience, these ideas come to mind quickly. For those who are new to teaching, however, ideas do not just appear; they are produced only after much searching and thinking. While textbook materials can be the source of great ideas, they should not be the sole source of information around which teaching units are built. The following list identifies useful resources for unit planning:

- Experienced science teachers
- University science and science education professors
- Scientists working in industry
- Public relations managers for science-and technology-related industries
- Laboratory manuals
- Science paperback books
- Professional science organizations
- Aquariums
- Museums

- Planetariums
- Nature centers
- Public libraries
- Science-and technology-related Internet sites
- Local utility companies and municipal treatment plants
- National Science Teachers Association publications
- Science magazines such as *ChemMatters, Scientific American, Science News, The New Scientist, Science Digest, Discover,* and *Technology Review*
- Science magazines for secondary school students, such as *Current Science*
- "Science Times" section of the *New York Times*
- Television programs such as *Nova* and those on the Discovery Channel

Planning instruction is a key factor in effective teaching. In constructing science units, a teacher should begin by examining the science course for which it is intended. The standards must be studied carefully to determine the content, scope, and sequence of the course. Based on consideration of the standards, appropriate assessments can be planned and resources can be gathered. Completion of these tasks leads naturally to the description of instructional activities. The focus of the instructional activities must be student achievement as determined by the assessments.

Figure 16.1 shows a list of the elements typically included in a complete teaching unit plan. Again, it must be emphasized that the elements listed are not developed in the order presented during the construction of a unit plan and that detailed instructional planning,

Paper-and-pencil tests should not be the only means of assessing student understanding of science.

most often in the form of lesson plans as described in Chapters 3 and 6 of this textbook, complement and extend the elements presented here.

FIGURE 16.1   Elements of a science teaching unit plan.

1. Place a **cover page** at the front that gives the title of the unit, the subject, and the course or grade level for which it is intended. Also include your name, professional affiliation, and address.

2. On the next page, write one or more paragraphs about the **purpose** and **scope** of the unit.

3. Construct a **concept map** or another type of **visual** to show the concepts, principles, theories, and skills that will be addressed in the unit.

4. Construct a **time frame** that provides an overview of the major activities and learning objectives to be addressed for each day of instruction. Begin with Day 1, Day 2, Day 3, and so on. The time frame elements can serve as the major activities for each day of instruction.

5. Describe the **instructional plans** for each day or lesson associated with the unit. The instructional plan for each day or lesson may take the form of a lesson plan and include the following elements:
   instructional **objectives**, instructional **activities**, including questions, and estimated **time** to complete the activities; **homework assignments**; instructional **materials** and **equipment**; and lesson **assessments** that correspond with the lesson objectives and **scoring specifications**.

6. Prepare summative **unit assessments** and **scoring specifications**. The unit assessments should build on and extend lesson assessments and may include unit tests as well as alternative formats that provide opportunities for students to show what they know and can do in authentic situations.

MULTIFACETED ASSESSMENT

Science education reform places assessment as the centerpiece of science teaching. Developing unit plans without careful consideration of assessment is like planning a dinner party without thinking about the food. Neither teaching nor the dinner party can exist without these central elements. Understanding assessment as part of the unit planning process means that testing and assessment are not synonymous. Paper-and-pencil tests have long stood as the hallmark of assessment in middle and secondary school science classes. However, teachers are finding that the multiple-choice, fill-in-the-blank, and short-answer questions included on these tests are not assessing *all* the science understandings that students are learning in science classes. The important work for science teachers when constructing teaching units is to select appropriate assessments that match their instruction and standards for student learning and use the assessment well to obtain information that enables them to make accurate inferences about what students know and can do.

Rather than abandoning paper-and-pencil tests altogether and using only alternative assessments, many informed teachers have chosen to employ multifaceted assessment systems. A multifaceted assessment system makes use of alternative assessments along with the more traditional forms of assessment to gather information about what students know and are able to do in science, according to Doran, Chan, Tamir, and Lendhardt (2002). The assessment formats that comprise a multifaceted assessment system are many and range from those that involve students working independently or in small groups to those that require a high degree of direct teacher involvement. Included in a multifaceted assessment system are assessment formats that emphasize student performances, visual representations, written products, oral presentations, and constructions (Lewin & Shoemaker, 1998). Making the various assessment formats important to the science teaching and learning process is the fact that they serve as vehicles for students to make their science understandings and skills explicit and available to teachers for evaluation.

We recommend that the assessments that comprise a teacher's multifaceted assessment system be viewed as the recipes in a cook's favorite cookbook. Just as the cook selects the recipe that best matches the occasion and the palettes of her guests, the teacher should select the assessment format that best matches her curricular aims and provides the desired information to chart student capability and progress. Because of their familiarity to readers of this text, traditional assessment formats, those typically found on paper-and-pencil

tests, will not be addressed. What follows is a discussion of alternative assessment formats and scoring guidelines appropriate for science instruction in the middle and secondary grades.

Alternative Assessment Formats

Alternative assessment formats provide teachers the opportunity to assess process in addition to product and to gain richer understandings of what students are thinking and how they construct meaning. Reasons for the increased interest in alternative assessments include their ability to reflect real student learning, create equity in assessing students, and bridge the apparent chasm between teaching, learning, and assessment (Oppewal, 1996). Many alternative assessments focus on student performance and on task authenticity by asking students to use skills and abilities that are applicable to real-life situations and problems. Several alternative assessment formats are described in Table 16.1.

Developing alternative assessments is quite different from constructing tests, and in many respects more demanding. Doran et al. (2002) point our that today's teachers must select appropriate task formats from among the myriad available and consider the intended purpose of the assessments when making these selections. They may need to write the assessment tasks themselves or modify existing tasks to make them usable along with developing suitable sets of scoring criteria that will be used to score students' performance. In addition, according to Doran and his colleagues (2002), teachers must make decisions about the amount of help that they provide learners as they engage in assessment tasks.

Concerns associated with these new assessments tend to be more apparent than is the case with tests. The authenticity and complexity of the tasks increase the possibility for students to misinterpret the directions and questions. Scoring inconsistencies also are possible when scoring criteria are poorly developed or employed by teachers unfamiliar with their use. Also, unfamiliarity with the nature of the tasks or with special tools or language may disenfranchise certain groups of learners or discriminate against them. For these reasons and others, the development of assessment tasks requires time and attention to details.

Fortunately, a growing number of educators are building alternative assessment tasks and using them in science classes. Their successes and failures provide insight into the process of task development and guidance for teachers wishing to use alternative assessments with their own students. Pioneers in the area of alternative assessment recommend a systematic approach to the development and modification of assessment tasks. The step-by-step process described by Lewin and Shoemaker (1998, p. 29) is similar to the approaches recom-

TABLE 16.1   Alternative Assessment Formats

Concept Map

A concept map graphically shows meaningful relationships among scientific concepts. When students are asked to construct concept maps, the concepts may be provided for them, or they may be asked to generate them without assistance. Students also may be provided with partially completed concept maps and asked to fill in the missing concepts. The technical design challenges that some students associate with concept map construction can be lessened through the use of Inspiration Software (www.inspiration.com). Scoring guidelines for concept maps are found in the assessment materials that accompany many textbook programs.

Drawing

Drawing exercises are extremely useful for assessing the understandings of students for whom English is their second language and for students who have reading and writing difficulties. Students can be encouraged to annotate their drawings or to write brief descriptions of pictures. When presented as storyboards, drawings can also reveal a wealth of information about the scientific explanations that students apply to everyday events.

Interview

An interview may be open-ended or partially structured (Martin, 2000). In an open-ended interview, the teacher asks few questions and listens carefully to what the student has to say. A partially structured interview is organized around a set of questions written by the teacher ahead of time. Responses to questions tell the teacher what the student is thinking and understands in addition to suggesting areas where remediation might be needed. To save time, Berenson and Carter (1995) recommend interviewing three or four students at one time, conducting short individual interviews while other students are working, and tape recording student-to-student interviews.

Inquiry-Oriented Investigation

To carry out an investigation, students are provided with familiar materials and clear directions. Depending on the nature of the investigation, students may be allowed to seek guidance from the teacher or classmates. Some teachers organize investigations into planning and execution phases. Examples of inquiry-oriented investigations along with suggestions for individual accountability during group assessment can be found in *Science Educator's Guide to Laboratory Assessment* by Rodney Doran, Fred Chan, Pinchas Tamir, and Carol Lenhardt (2002, NSTA Press).

Journal

A journal may include responses to questions given by the teacher, questions written by students that they wish to have answered, reactions to class activities and homework, or spontaneous reflections. Diagrams and drawings also may be included in journals. To help keep journals from becoming a burden, consider reading only a dozen or so randomly selected journals a week or having students read each others' journals and provide feedback. Appropriate uses for journals include becoming better acquainted with your students and helping them to succeed as science learners.

Laboratory Performance Task

When engaging in a laboratory performance task, a student works to generate a product that illustrates certain understandings or skills. To overcome some of the logistical and management problems associated with this type of assessment, Berenson and Carter (1995) suggest that performance tasks be set up at stations around the classroom and that students alternate between visiting the stations and working on written assignments at their seats. The checklist for a laboratory performance task is shown in Figure 6.3.

Laboratory Report

The traditional model for lab reporting includes sections for the Purpose, Materials, Procedures, Data, Data Interpretation, and Conclusion. An alternative to the traditional model is the narrative lab report. The format for this kind of lab report is like that of a letter to a parent or friend in which the student describes the laboratory experience. Licata (1999) recommends the following questions as prompts to guide students' writing of narrative lab reports: What was I looking for? How did I look for it? What did I find? What does it mean?

Portfolio

A portfolio presents evidence of student capability or progress and can be used in formative assessment, to stimulate student and teacher reflection, or as a summative evaluation of student work for a semester or an entire course. A portfolio may include items that make use of many of the assessment formats described in this table. Students often write captions to accompany the items included in a portfolio. The captions explain how the items serve as evidence of learning (Barton & Collins, 1997). To make a portfolio a useful assessment tool, it must be made accessible to students and attended to on a regular basis.

mended by others and is based on their own task-building experiences:

- Be clear about your target: the skills and knowledge students will demonstrate and the standards that they will be expected to meet
- Be familiar with the critical traits and key concepts of a strong performance
- Create and describe a context for the task that will make it more meaningful and engaging
- Write a short description of the task
- Rewrite the task in a clear and concise manner
- Assign the task to students
- Develop a step-by-step work plan (for students)
- Provide a sample from past years (if possible) to show students what "good" looks like
- Provide instruction
- Score the task and then make necessary revisions for its use next time

This step-by-step process provides an excellent framework for developing assessment tasks and modifying them for use in science classes, but it does not tell the whole story. Most of the alternative assessment formats in use by science teachers emphasize student performance in and outside of the laboratory. These performance assessments are most often modified versions of science instructional activities. In many cases, the transformation of an instructional activity into a performance assessment involves coupling the activity with a suitable set of scoring criteria. The set of scoring criteria for a performance assessment is called a *rubric* or *checklist*. When students engage in science instructional activities, they generate models and visuals, propose solutions to problems, design and conduct experiments, and construct written responses that involve the application of critical thinking skills. When married with the appropriate rubric or checklist, these instructional activities can become performance assessment tasks.

Scoring the many possible science performance tasks requires making explicit the criteria by which student work will be judged. This typically involves the development or refinement of a scoring rubric or checklist. It is important for you to know that there are a number of resources from which to draw on when developing science assessment tasks, including the accompanying scoring rubrics and checklists.

Locating Alternative Assessment Tasks

The first place to look for assessment tasks that make use of the various formats described earlier in this chapter are middle and high school science textbooks and the supplementary materials provided by publishers of these textbooks. For example, in *Holt Chemistry Visualizing Matter* (Myers, Oldham, & Tocci, 2000), alternative assessment tasks recommended in the teacher's

edition include having students engage in performance tasks, develop portfolios, and write responses to critical thinking questions. This program also comes with a CD-ROM that contains additional assessment resources and scoring rubrics. Similarly, Prentice Hall's middle school program *Science Explorer* (Padilla, Miaoulis, & Cyr, 2000) includes multiple performance assessments, application questions, and a long-term project in every chapter. Additional performance assessments that emphasize student drawing, writing, and oral presentations along with scoring rubrics for chapter projects are provided on a CD-ROM.

Science assessment tasks also can be found on the Internet. An excellent site to begin a search for assessment tasks is the Center for Technology in Learning's *Performance Assessment Links in Science* (PALS) (http://www.pals.sri.com). This site is a resource bank of science assessment tasks that is continually updated. The tasks are indexed to the *National Science Education Standards* and to grade-level bands and content areas. Information about each assessment task is presented under the headings of student directions and response forms, administrative procedures, scoring rubric, examples of student work, and technical quality data from field testing. The tasks found at this site may be used as presented or modified by teachers to better match their assessment needs. Links to a host of other international, national, state, and school district Web pages that include samples of science assessment tasks can be found at the *Performance Assessment Tasks* site (www.col-ed.org/smcnws/assesstask.html) maintained by the Science and Mathematics Consortium of Northwest Schools. Sample assessment tasks found at Web pages linked to this site use a number of assessment formats, including portfolios, journals and logs, concept maps, laboratory performance assessments, and inquiry-oriented investigations.

In addition, science teachers and college-level educators have written many trade books and journal articles about alternative assessment in recent years. These books and articles are another source of assessment tasks that can be used with middle and secondary school science students. The National Science Teachers Association (NSTA) and the Association for Supervision and Curriculum Development (ASCD) frequently publish trade books on issues of assessment and include assessment articles in their journals, *The Science Teacher, Science Scope,* and *Educational Leadership.*

Scoring Rubrics and Checklists

Scoring rubrics and checklists present the set of criteria by which a student's work will be judged. For a rubric, the criteria are shown as lists of descriptors along a numbered scale. The scale for most scoring rubrics has between three and five points. On a scale that runs from 1 to 5, a score of 5 would represent the highest level of performance, and a score of 1, the lowest level of performance. Most teachers set a minimal acceptable level of performance, such as 3 on a 5-point scale.

A checklist consists of a description of the desired performances and a scale to score the performances. The typical scale includes only "yes" and "no" options to indicate whether or not the performance was observed. Other checklist formats include space for comments about the performance and scales that provide a range of options to score the performance.

Before a rubric or checklist can be developed, the task to which it will be applied must be known. Specified in the task description are the standards that students are expected to meet. Students are usually given the task and the scoring rubric or checklist at the same time. Doing this makes the scoring criteria explicit and eliminates the need for students to ask what they need to know or be able to do to perform well on the assessment task. Figure 16.2 shows the description of a phase change task, the setup used in the task, and the standards in the areas of collaborative work, scientific literacy, and systems analysis. In this example, the task is designed to assess student performance in three areas; thus three sets of rubrics are presented.

The rubrics shown in Figure 16.2 are *holistic* in design, in that they evaluate all of the criteria specific to each of the three topics at one time. Good preparation for this assessment task would make use of instructionally embedded assessments of students' understandings and behaviors relative to each of the topics using *analytic* rubrics. An analytic rubric provides a rating for each criterion individually. For example, the analytic rubric for "Collaborative Worker" would rate the criteria of: (a) staying on task, (b) offering and defending ideas, (c) taking on various group roles, and (d) participating separately rather than lumping them all together. The individual ratings of the teacher on each of these criteria would provide helpful diagnostic feedback to students.

Figure 16.3 shows a checklist that can be used to assess students' use of the microscope and the preparation and staining of materials for observation. This checklist provides a range of options—excellent, adequate, and inadequate—for scoring the performance. It is a task-specific checklist that would be of little use for assessing other laboratory understandings and skills.

The process of developing a task-specific scoring rubric or checklist can be greatly simplified by starting with a rubric or checklist template and modifying the template to match the task. Rubric templates from which task-specific rubrics can be developed for assessing a variety of performances are available at the *Rubistar* Web site (http://rubistar.4teachers.org), at *Rubrics.Com* (http://www.rubrics.com), and at *Teach-nology* (http://teachers.teach-nology.com/web_tools/rubics). Visitors to these sites may select from a number of rubric templates developed by teachers and university educators and then modify these templates on-line to match their own performance tasks. At the Rubistar site, rubrics are available for laboratory reports, experiments, and scientific drawings in addition to other performance areas germane to the science classroom, including historical role-play, interview, debate, storyboard, and video production. Teach-nology provides additional rubric templates useful to science teachers, and Rubrics.Com includes tools for designing performance tasks and aligning them with standards.

Checklist templates can be found at the *Project Based Learning* Web site (http://pblchecklist.4teachers.org/checklist.shtml). Checklists of potential use to middle and high school science teachers include those that pertain to laboratory work, laboratory safety, experimental research, cooperative group work, relating concepts, and science background research. Additional checklists and information about the use and development of checklists can be found at the *Western Michigan University's Evaluation Center* Web site (www.wmich.edu/evalctr/checklists). The developers of these sites that contain rubrics and checklist templates present their work as tools to help teachers develop high-quality assessments who do not have the time to develop them from scratch.

The true value of scoring rubrics and checklists lies in their ability to communicate to teachers and parents what students know and can do as well as provide students with understandable performance targets (Marzano, Pickering, & McTighe, 1993). Scoring rubrics and checklists must be clearly worded and match the standards set forth in the tasks. They can be developed to render a holistic judgment or an analytic judgment, based on careful ratings of individual parts of the work. Regardless of the type of judgment sought, well-crafted scoring rubrics and checklists allow students to answer for themselves the questions, "How will we be graded?" and "How am I doing?"

Stop and Reflect!

- Think of a science instructional activity that you really enjoyed as a student. How could the activity be transformed for use as a performance task?

- Look back over the assessment formats described in Table 16.1. Try to identify the outcomes for which scoring criteria could be developed for a task that uses one of these assessment formats. It may help to think about the outcomes in terms of performances, oral presentations, written products, and visual representations.

FIGURE 16.2   Scoring rubric for phase change task.

Task: This is a three-day activity in which students observe and perform a distillation to demonstrate phase change, explain energy transformation, and identify key components in the system. On day one, a group of students writes a description of the distillation equipment that is placed in a location that the other class members cannot see. The rest of the class assembles the equipment laying on the lab tables according to this description. On day two, the lab groups use the setup to experiment with the phase change of water from liquid to gas and back to liquid. Each group writes their own statement of the problem, hypothesis, procedure, data table, and conclusion. On day three, each student describes individual components of the setup and explains how each part is used to cause water to change phase.

Rubric:

Topics	Scores			
	4	**3**	**2**	**1**
Collaborative Worker: Student can take charge of his/her own behavior in a group	Student stays on task; offers useful ideas and can defend them; can take on various roles; participates without prompting.	Student stays on task; offers useful ideas and can defend them; can take on various roles; rarely requires prompting to participate.	Student does not attend to the lab. Student accepts group view or considers only his/her own ideas worthwhile. Student needs regular prompting to stay on task.	Student does not respond to the group. Student is not involved or may try to undermine the efforts of the group.
Scientific Literacy: Student uses processes and skills of science to conduct investigations.	Student identifies the question, forms a possible solution, writes out steps to test the possible solution, designs a data chart, collects data, and concludes about the validity of the possible solution.	Student identifies the question and forms a possible solution. Procedure and data chart are complete but lack clarity and/or creativity. Student concludes about the validity of the possible solution.	Student identifies the question but does not form a complete solution. Procedure and data chart are incomplete and the conclusion does not speak to the possible solution.	Student does not identify the question. No possible solution is given. Procedure and data chart are incomplete or missing. The conclusion is incomplete or missing.
Systems Analysis: Student describes how a system operates internally and how it interacts with the outside world.	Student identifies how parts of the system interact and provides personal insight into the interacting of the parts. Student relates how the system interacts with the outside world.	Student identifies how parts of the system interact and relates how the system interacts with the outside world.	Student does not identify some parts of the system. Student does not understand how the parts interact and does not relate how the system interacts with the outside world.	Student incorrectly identifies the parts and cannot describe how they interact either within or outside the system.

Distillation setup:

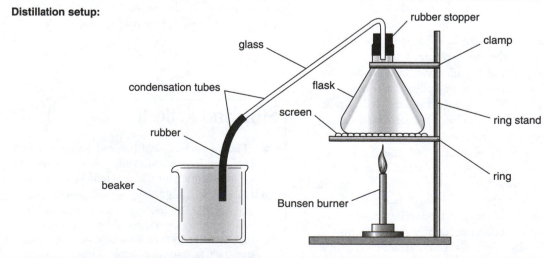

Reprinted with permission of NSTA Publications from "Effective Rubric Design", by K. Jensen, from The Science Teacher, *62(5), 1995, p. 36, published by the National Science Teachers Association, Arlington, Virginia.*

FIGURE 16.3   Example of a checklist to assess students' use of the microscope.

E = excellent; A = adequate; I = inadequate

Gross body movements

1. Removes microscope from its case or space in the storage cabinet. Grasps the arm of the instrument with one hand and places the other hand under the base.   E   A   I
2. Sets the microscope down gently on the table with the arm toward student and stage away from student. The base should be a safe distance from the edge of the table.   E   A   I
3. Uses a piece of lens paper to wipe the lenses clean.   E   A   I
4. Clicks the lower power objective into viewing position.   E   A   I
5. Adjusts the diaphragm and mirror for the best light.   E   A   I
6. Places a prepared slide of human hair on the stage so that it is directly over the center of the stage opening.   E   A   I
7. Secures the slide in place with the stage clips.   E   A   I
8. Looks to the side of the microscope and slowly lowers the low-power objective by turning the coarse adjustment wheel until the objective almost touches the slide.   E   A   I
9. While looking through the eyepiece, with both eyes open, slowly turns the coarse adjustment so that the objective rises. The hair should become visible.   E   A   I
10. Brings the hair into sharp focus by turning the fine adjustment wheel.   E   A   I
11. Shows the properly focused slide to teacher.   E   A   I
12. Focuses the hair under high power and shows this properly focused slide to teacher.   E   A   I
13. Prepares to return microscope to storage area; turns the low-power objective into viewing position and adjusts it approximately 1 cm above stage.   E   A   I
14. Returns the microscope, handling by the arm and base, to storage place.   E   A   I

Finely coordinated movements

The following observations are made by the teacher, who judges how well a student can prepare and stain materials for observation under a microscope.

Preparation and staining of an onion cell wet mount slide

1. Rinses a microscope slide with water and wipes both sides with a clean, soft cloth.   E   A   I
2. Rinses and dries a cover glass.   E   A   I
3. Cuts an onion lengthwise and removes a thick slice.   E   A   I
4. Peels the delicate tissue from the inner surface.   E   A   I
5. Uses a medicine dropper to place a drop of water in the center of slide.   E   A   I
6. Places a small section of onion tissue in the drop of water.   E   A   I
7. Lowers the cover glass over the onion skin.   E   A   I

8. Staining the specimen: adds a drop of iodine stain along the edge of the cover glass.   E   A   I
9. Places a small section of a paper towel on the opposite side of the cover glass. This will draw the stain across the slide by capillary action.   E   A   I

UNIT PLANNING IN ACTION

Making decisions about what students should learn from a unit of instruction and selecting appropriate assessment strategies to document what they have learned are indeed important aspects of the unit planning process. However, there are other considerations associated with unit planning to which science teachers must also attend. The unit planning experiences of Mr. Zimble, a third-year science teacher, highlights considerations of assessment as well as other considerations that link assessment to learning experiences. Before reading on, examine Box 16.1 to learn about Mr. Zimble's ideas for addressing the planning challenge brought to him by his principal.

Without a doubt, Mr. Zimble's situation is unique. The new course he was asked to design has no well-articulated standards associated with it to guide his planning. In a way, this lack of direction makes planning difficult, but it also allows for great flexibility. In cases such as this, the teacher should seek guidance from experienced colleagues and consult other sources, including national science education reform guidelines. But, in the end, the teacher must rely on his or her own

Classroom Snapshot 16.1

Mr. Zimble's Water Unit

For over 25 years, most of the freshmen at North Rockcreek High have taken physical science, which consists of a half-year of basic physics and a half-year of basic chemistry. The principal believes that a change is needed in order to provide students with a more interesting interdisciplinary experience as an introduction to high school science. He also believes that changing this introductory course will encourage more students to take high school chemistry and perhaps even physics as science electives before graduating.

After overcoming the shock of being given the big assignment to develop a new course, Mr. Zimble began to reflect on this task. He recalled the science methods course that he was required to take for certification and the unit plan that he had to prepare for the course. One idea that stuck in his mind was the instructor saying repeatedly to the class: Teach students fundamental science within a relevant context. In other words, teach basic ideas and make them meaningful to students. With fundamentals and relevance on his mind, Mr. Zimble decided to form a list of unit topics that he could draw from to form the new science course.

Mr. Zimble began to brainstorm ideas for the course. In the process, he contacted many science teachers for their recommendations. He talked with biology, chemistry, and physics teachers in his school building as well as a few high school science teachers in other schools. Mr. Zimble also contacted a middle school science teacher who had given a dynamic district inservice workshop at the beginning of the school year. He borrowed as many innovative curriculum materials as he could find as well as the state's new science curriculum framework and the national science reform guidelines: *Benchmarks for Science Literacy* (AAAS, 1993) and *National Science Education Standards* (NRC, 1996). It did not take long before ideas for the course topics and units began to flow. The following is a list of science-related topics that represents his initial thinking:

- Electrical power generation
- Building supplies and materials
- City parks and gardening
- Water in the community
- Dry cleaning and laundering

- Medical diagnosis with x-rays and MRIs
- Beauty supplies and cosmetics
- Climate, weather, and atmosphere
- Vehicles, transportation, and safety
- Health and sanitation

With these topical ideas for starters, Mr. Zimble realized their potential to integrate biology, chemistry, earth science, and physics for teaching fundamental science concepts that relate to phenomena that are familiar to students.

Mr. Zimble could not wait to finalize the list of topics because he wanted to start planning immediately a unit on water. He believed that water would be the ideal topic to begin the new integrated science course. Mr. Zimble quickly gathered many resources for ideas with which to plan the first unit.

---

understanding of the purpose of the course in the context of promoting scientific literacy along with the interests and dispositions of the students who will take the course. Mr. Zimble seems to have sought guidance from different sources and carefully thought about the course's purpose and the needs of ninth-grade learners as he started planning his unit on water.

Let's take a closer look at Mr. Zimble's unit planning efforts as he considers what students will learn, how their learning will be assessed, and the learning activities that will facilitate students' construction of science understandings. While these aspects of the unit planning process will be addressed as if they occur in a linear sequence, be assured that they do not. As mentioned earlier

in this chapter, unit planning is not at all linear. Moving back and forth between considerations of assessment, learning activities, objectives, and the concepts and skills to be learned is a natural part of the unit planning process.

Learning Activities

One of the recommendations that Mr. Zimble recalled from his methods course was the instructor's emphasis on the importance of first identifying activities for students that would teach them important ideas. This prompted him to examine the resources that he had gathered and to begin to list instructional activities, sequencing them as shown in the time frame in Figure 16.4. He wanted to

FIGURE 16.4 This time frame shows the scope and sequence of instructional activities for the science unit centered around water in a community.

Time Frame
"Water in Our Community"

Day 1
- Initiate the study of water with a puzzling situation for students to figure out, which will stimulate student interest in water and illustrate important properties of this chemical compound. All students are requested to place a drop of water on a piece of wax paper and to determine if the water rolls or slides across the waxed surface.
- Discuss structural, chemical, and physical properties of water.
- Conduct a brainstorming session to list all of the uses of water in the community, leading to the purpose and overview of the water unit.

Day 2
- Continue the study of water with a laboratory exercise about the adhesive and cohesive properties of water. Each student is requested to predict how far the water will rise in glass tubes of different diameters, then to test their predictions while working in small groups.
- Continue to discuss structural, chemical, and physical properties of water.
- Present the class with the assertion from an angry citizen who claims the local drinking water is not fit to drink. Use this situation to plan investigations to study water in many areas of the community.

Day 3
- Continue the study of surface tension of water with a laboratory activity. Each student is given the challenge: Determine if you can float a small, medium, and large paper clip on the surface of water.
- Continue to discuss structural, chemical, and physical properties of water.
- Continue planning activities to study water in the community and formalize the investigative groups.
- Plan for a laboratory exercise to filter dirty water. Ask students to bring some of the equipment and materials needed for the lab in order to increase their involvement.

Day 4
- Discuss the class field trip to the municipal water treatment plant.
- Ask students to list the steps in the water purification process, which represent those used at the municipal water treatment plant. Urge students to think logically, express themselves clearly, and then build on what students say.
- Conduct a laboratory exercise to purify dirty water.

Day 5
- Discuss the filtration and purification of water from the laboratory exercise of the day before and relate it to what is likely to be observed on the field trip to the municipal water treatment plant.
- Conduct a lecture/discussion of structure of water molecules and solution chemistry.

Day 6
- Continue to conduct the laboratory exercise to purify dirty water.

Day 7
- Review the chemical and physical properties of water to check on students' understanding of these ideas.
- Place students in their investigative groups and help them to plan their water studies.
- Prepare for the field trip to the water purification plant. Ensure that all students know what to do and have ready the questions they want to ask. Check for signed parental approval forms, permitting students to take the field trip.

Day 8
- Take field trip to the municipal water treatment plant. Bus leaves school at 8:30 A.M. and arrives back at school for the last lunch period at 12:20 P.M.

Day 9
- Discuss the field trip by reviewing the treatment plant's filtration process and the properties of water. Address student beliefs and issues associated with the sanitary conditions of the community's drinking water.
- Plan for students to collect water samples throughout the city and community to analyze in the science laboratory.

Day 10
- Present a short lecture on the importance of water on earth that leads into acid/base chemistry.
- Conduct a short laboratory exercise on determining the acidity and basicity of solutions.

Day 11
- Continue with a lecture/discussion of the importance of water on earth and acid/base chemistry.

(continued)

FIGURE 16.4   *Continued*

Day 12	■ Conduct a laboratory activity to determine the pH of an assortment of items found in the home, e. g., soft drinks, fruit juices, liquid detergents, hand soaps, shampoos, floor cleaners, etc.
	■ Lecture on ions in solution, focusing on metal ions, salts, cations, and anions.
Day 13	■ Conduct a laboratory on the identification of metal ions in solution.
	■ Review the properties of water, water purification, pH, and ions in solution.
	■ Remind students to bring in water samples from various parts of the city and rural areas.
Day 14	■ Administer the quiz on properties of water, water purification, pH, and ions in solution.
	■ Begin the laboratory investigation to determine the impurities, pH, ions, etc., of the water samples taken from various parts of the city and adjoining areas.
Day 15	■ Continue the laboratory to determine the impurities, pH, ions, etc., of the water samples taken from various parts of the city and adjoining areas.
	■ Return the quiz and discuss basic chemistry and the chemistry of water.
Day 16	■ Conduct a lecture discussion of elements, compounds, ions, and the periodic chart. Practice naming some common elements and compounds.
	■ Set out examples of elements, compounds, and ions for students to examine and identify.
	■ Give students a homework sheet for naming elements, compounds, and ions, and for writing symbols and formulas.
Day 17	■ Continue lecture/discussion of elements, compounds, ions, and the periodic chart. Practice naming some common elements and compounds.
Day 18	■ Continue building students' knowledge of elements, compounds, and ions.
	■ Plan for a mock town hall meeting regarding the water purity of the drinking water in the community.
Day 19	■ Conduct a laboratory investigation to examine and identify the microorganisms in the water samples collected from ponds, drainage ditches, rivers, and streams.
Day 20	■ Permit the investigative groups to plan for the town hall meeting. Urge students to construct charts and tables to convey their data and to present logical arguments.
Day 21	■ Conduct a recitation and review session on the properties of water, steps in the water purification process, ions in solution, microorganisms living in water, and naming and writing the formulas for basic elements and compounds.
Day 22	■ Continue to review the important ideas studied during the unit. Help students to find personal meaning in what they have been learning.
Day 23	■ Administer the unit test.
	■ Plan for the town hall meeting to address the purity of the municipal water supply.
Day 24	■ Conduct the town hall meeting to discuss the municipal water supply and the claim by one of the citizens that the water is unsafe to drink.

start the unit with an attention grabber that he remembered from his science methods class. For his introduction to the study of water, Mr. Zimble would conduct the "Drop of Water" activity, whereby all of the students are given a piece of wax paper and requested to place one large drop of water on it. Students are then instructed to tilt the wax paper in order for the water drop to move over the paper. Mr. Zimble would pose the following question:

> Does the drop of water roll or slide across the wax paper?

The teacher believes strongly that the students would be challenged by this puzzling situation and would want to figure out the answer to the question. Further, he believes that the exercise would stimulate student interest and the desire to study water. (Refer to Appendix A for a detailed description of how to conduct this simple activity, which you should try out and include in your science teaching resource file.)

On Day 1, Mr. Zimble would follow the "Drop of Water" activity with a discussion of the structural, chemical, and physical properties of water. He planned a question-and-answer session on adhesive and cohesive properties of water that would help students to understand the action of water on the surface of the wax paper and its ability to rise up narrow glass tubes, which would occur in the laboratory exercise scheduled for Day 2.

Along with introducing the properties of water, Mr. Zimble planned to address common uses of water in everyday life, which would open up the learning environment for considering science and societal issues that might be relevant to the study of water in their community. Note that this new science teacher has several science education strands running throughout the unit, such as knowledge of fundamental chemistry, investigation of ideas, and consideration of societal issues.

Mr. Zimble feels strongly about requiring students to participate in small-group investigative projects, because he believes this will make the study of water more meaningful and serve to integrate fundamental science into the instruction. He came up with a plan for the group projects after considerable thought. He would bring up the assertion of an irate citizen who claims that the city's tap water is not fit to drink because it is contaminated. After students react to this issue, Mr. Zimble will ask the class to examine all of the water in the entire community. During this process, they will collect data needed to debate the drinking water purity question. For this investigative inquiry, he will organize the class during Day 3 into five groups—Tap Water, River Water, Lake Water, Pond Water, and Swimming Pool Water—and inform them that they will analyze samples of water from a particular part of the community. The results discovered by the entire class will provide an overall picture of the contents and quality of the water for the entire community. Further, each group will perform many basic water tests, which will give them practice with a variety of analytical procedures.

On Day 3, Mr. Zimble planned to conduct another hands-on laboratory activity, also pertaining to adhesive properties of water and surface tension. For this exercise, students will be challenged to float paper clips of different sizes on the surface of water. This activity will require manual dexterity. It also will cause students to think more deeply about the bonding of water molecules, especially after they are instructed to add a drop of liquid detergent to the water and observe what happens to objects that are floating on its surface.

On Day 4, Mr. Zimble planned to carry out another laboratory exercise to filter dirty water. Before reading on or discussing the filtration process, he planned to ask students to generate an ordered list of processes that they believe are used to filter and purify muddy water. He will show the class a sample of disgusting-looking water that he has placed in a large glass container on the demonstration table. Students will be urged to figure out ways to remove debris and contaminants from the muddy water. They will be requested to order the steps in the process of purifying the water, similar to the process used at the municipal water treatment plant. Mr. Zimble will permit students to change their proposed filtration process many times. After giving students time to modify their steps, he will make a PowerPoint presentation about the filtration process used by the local water treatment plant.

Skipping ahead to Days 10, 11, and 12, Mr. Zimble planned to address acids and bases because of their direct relationship with water and solution chemistry. He saw this as an opportunity to present a short lecture on the importance of water and its intimate relationship with fundamental chemistry. Mr. Zimble's organized lecture on water addresses four key points: the role of water in human civilization, water as part of the biosphere, the role of water in the human body, and water as the medium through which acids and bases manifest their characteristics. He uses this final point as segue for introducing common acids and bases and their relations to human activity.

Following this lecture, one of the activities that Mr. Zimble planned to do with students is to assess the concentration of several common acid and base solutions, including acetic acid ($HC_2H_3O_2$), carbonic acid (H_2CO_3), hydrochloric acid (HCl), ammonium hydroxide (NH_4OH), and calcium hydroxide ($Ca(OH)_2$). The students will be using at least seven indicators to produce color reactions. For this activity, Mr. Zimble will ask each group of students to prepare the color indicators that they will be using. In this manner, the students will gain experience in combining chemicals. He suspects the students will be interested in the vivid colors that are produced from acid/base indicators derived from common food products, such as grape juice, tea, and red cabbage juice.

Mr. Zimble will gather several water quality and water testing manuals that the students can use for reference when they study their water samples. These manuals will help them in their analytical chemistry work on Days 11, 12, and 13. He will also borrow a few water analysis test kits from a science teacher who teaches an environmental science course in another high school in the district. Some of the tests that the students can carry out are as follows:

Odor	Iron
Color	Magnesium
Turbidity	Nitrate
Acidity	Nitrite
Alkalinity	Phosphate
Ammonia-nitrogen	Salinity
Dissolved oxygen	Hardness

Mr. Zimble will make available microscopes and reference material for students to use in identifying pond life and microorganisms that may be in their water samples. In addition, he will ask the municipal water treatment plant lab supervisor to perform fecal coliform tests on the water samples collected by all of the groups.

Mr. Zimble expected that by the time Days 19 and 20 arrive, the students would be prepared to demonstrate their knowledge of fundamental water chemistry and address the question regarding the purity of drinking water. Remember, he organized the group investigations so that the class would study water from many places in the community—water pipes, rivers, streams, ponds, lakes, and swimming pools. Further, students would examine many aspects of water, from its structural properties to the microorganisms that often inhabit it. Mr. Zimble believed that the mock town hall meeting would be an excellent activity to end the water unit.

Instructional Objectives and Assessments

Mr. Zimble had to think deeply about the assessment process because it must help him to achieve the goals of the new interdisciplinary course that he was assigned to develop. One of the main goals of the course is to help students develop more positive attitudes toward science during their first year in high school. In order to accomplish this aim, the first unit that the ninth graders study must set the tone for their high school science course experiences. If the assessments are too easy, the students will take science too lightly, and they will not be challenged intellectually. If the assessments are too difficult, many of the students will be turned off to science.

As Mr. Zimble reflected on the discussions that occurred during his teacher education courses, the words *authentic assessment* and *portfolio assessment* came to mind. He remembered that instruction and assessment should be closely associated, and they should reflect real-life situations. He realized that the group investigation could serve as a vehicle to begin a portfolio for the students that would contain evidence of what they had learned during their high school science courses (Collins, 1991). Students would be assembling many items for their group investigations that would start a good portfolio, such as photographs, maps, and diagrams of where they obtained their water samples; charts and tables constructed to present water analysis data; sketches of microorganisms that live in the water samples collected; written arguments regarding the purity of the community's water used during the mock town meeting; and an overview of the inquiry. Mr. Zimble believed that the investigations and the town hall meeting would provide an ideal stimulus to motivate students to do their best work; thus, he would give the same weight to participation in the group investigation as he would for the unit test. With the help of another teacher, and after some discussion with students, Mr. Zimble developed a rubric for grading each student's work and contribution to the group investigation.

With some of his assessments and instructional activities prepared and others in various stages of development, Mr. Zimble found it relatively easy to write instructional objectives. The instructional objectives would be incorporated into lesson plans that outline in greater detail Mr. Zimble's planning efforts. The following list contains some of the objectives initially constructed by this teacher for his water unit, some of which would likely be modified as Mr. Zimble continues to plan instruction for individual lessons:

1. Predict the behavior of water moving across, up, or down various surfaces and explain the reasons for these occurrences based on the structural and molecular properties of water.
2. Demonstrate capillary action of water and its tendency to rise up in narrow tubes and explain this action based on the structural and molecular properties of water.
3. Show the effects of surface tension of water and how it can permit objects to float.
4. Given a list of water filtering and purification processes, order them in a sequence that most likely would be used by municipal water treatment plants to make water safe for drinking.
5. Define an acid and a base and give uses for at least four common acids and four common bases.
6. Given a list of common household products, match the products with their corresponding pH values.
7. Explain what an ion is and give an example of a metal, salt, acid, and base ion.
8. Given the symbol of a common element or the formula for a common compound, name the element or compound. Also, when given the name of a compound, write the formula.
9. Participate in a group investigation to analyze water taken from a particular place(s) in the community. Provide a written report of the investigation, giving the reason for conducting the inquiry, the procedures followed, the information gathered, the analyses of the data, and the conclusions.
10. When presented with an article from a newspaper or magazine, or one that would likely appear in these printed sources, interpret the information and evaluate it for factual accuracy and usefulness to the general public.

A final consideration related to assessment is the evaluation of students' work and the assignment of grades. Mr. Zimble planned to evaluate the success of the water unit by assessing student performance in a variety of ways. He believes that by using many assessment techniques, a realistic idea of student learning can be ascer-

FIGURE 16.5   This concept map highlights the important content contained in the unit, "Water in Our Community."

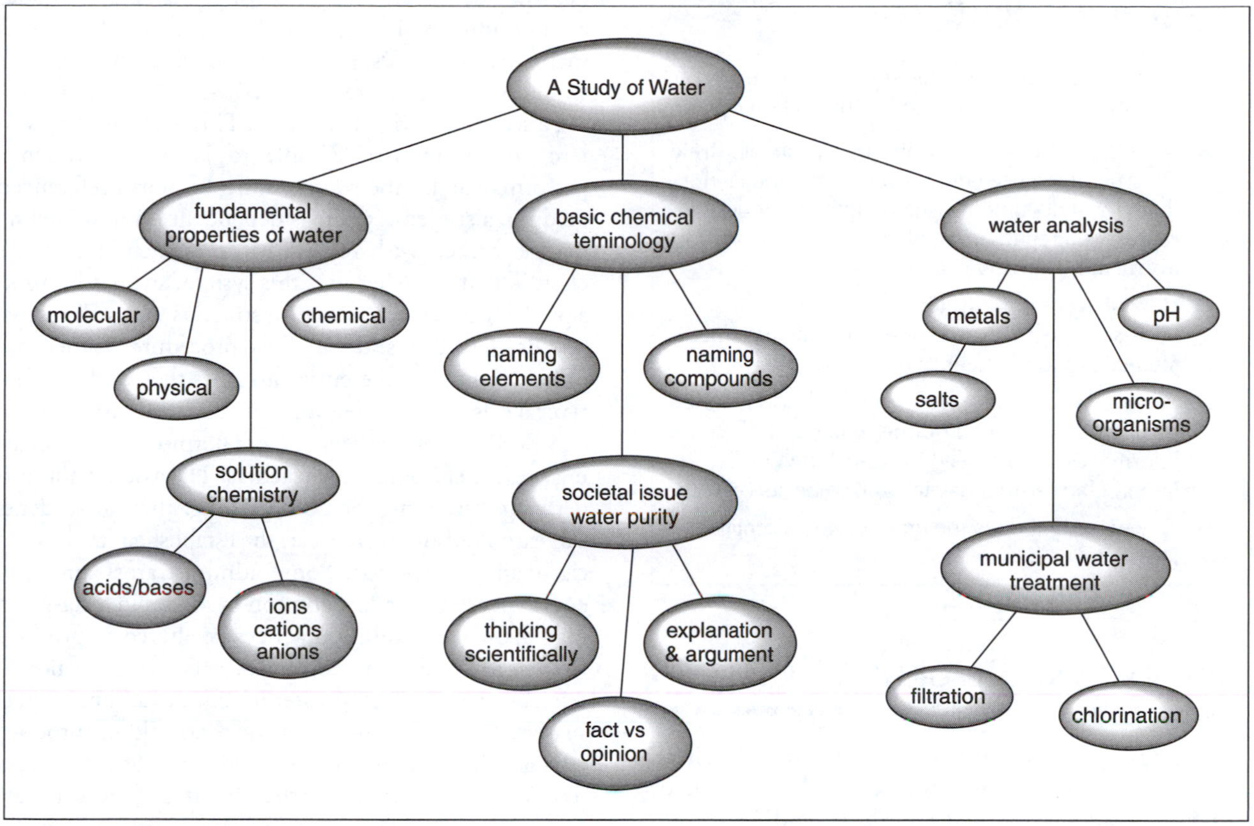

Unit Content

tained. Further, he believes that the measures he was going to use would reinforce authentic learning as well as help him to evaluate how much students learned from the study of water. The grading scheme that Mr. Zimble planned to apply is presented here. More will be said about grading and reporting grades in the final section of this chapter.

Quiz (properties of water, water purification, pH, and ions)	15 points
Laboratory exercise (capillary action of water)	5 points
Laboratory exercise (filtration and purification of water)	5 points
Laboratory exercise (determination of pH in common solutions)	5 points
Unit test (chemical and physical properties of water, acids and bases, and water purification and analysis)	35 points
Group investigation	35 points
Maximum possible points:	100

When all is said and done, what will the students learn from the water unit? Mr. Zimble pondered this question as he thought about the new science course he was responsible for developing and the first unit that he had just planned. He wondered if there were too many activities in the water unit and how his ideas for the unit could be operationalized as lesson plans that provide additional detail about student learning experiences and daily assessments. Mr. Zimble's thoughts about the number of activities raised questions in his mind about whether the many activities might cause the students to focus on the excitement of doing and finding out but miss the science he wanted them to learn. This introspection motivated him to construct a concept map (shown in Figure 16.5), giving a visual picture of the important content that he believed was embedded in his unit plan. Do you believe the teacher included enough basic chemistry in this unit, which was designed to familiarize students with some fundamental terms and concepts of solutions chemistry and basic chemistry? In addition, will the students learn some valuable information about water in general?

Stop and Reflect!

As you think about the water unit conceived by Mr. Zimble, what is your reaction to his instructional plan?

- Does the "Water in Our Community" unit illustrate the type of science education recommended in the reform documents (see Chapter 1), or does it represent a repackaging of traditional science instruction with few changes?

- How relevant is the water unit for early adolescent learners, and does the unit introduce students to fundamentals of schemistry?

- Suppose you were called on to teach Mr. Zimble's class on Day 2, 3, or 11 of his water unit. What information would need to be included in his lesson plan for that day for you to be successful?

- To what extent does the unit develop scientific literacy?

GRADING AND REPORTING GRADES

A serious responsibility for all science teachers, whether developing a new course like Mr. Zimble or teaching a well-established course, is grading and reporting grades. Teachers grade student work in order to communicate with students and their parents about students' performance. Grades serve as indicators of student learning and thus "should be based on solid, high-quality evidence about student achievement" (Brookhart, 2004, p. 11). However, not all of what students do in a science class should be graded. While student ability, effort, attendance, and attitudes do influence achievement and should be assessed, most teachers agree that these factors should not be considered in determining grades. Nonjudgmental, formative feedback to students about these achievement-related factors is best provided through written or oral means. Grades are meaningful and defensible when they are derived from assessments, either tests or alternative formats, that match the curricular aims in terms of content, level of required thinking, and mode of response (Brookhart, 2004).

Criterion-Referenced and Norm-Referenced Grading

An important consideration of teachers when thinking about grading is whether grades should reflect what a student has actually learned or how the student's performance compares with the performance of classmates. This is the main difference between criterion-referenced and norm-referenced grading. In criterion-referenced grading, student achievement is judged relative to an established set of criteria. Following this system, grades are not adjusted in any way. The teacher will allow as many As, Bs, Cs, Ds, and Fs as students earn. The same would be true for scores of 1, 2, 3, 4, and 5 obtained using a scoring rubric or checklist. This is the grading system chosen by Mr. Zimble to judge his students' performance in the water unit. In norm-referenced grading, a student's grade is dependent on how well he has performed with respect to other members of the class. When a teacher uses this system, she has in mind a predetermined percentage of students who will receive As, Bs, Cs, Ds, and Fs. This procedure, sometimes called grading on the curve, assumes that students in a typical class can be categorized in a normal distribution.

Both criterion-referenced and norm-referenced grading present challenges for teachers. The assumption underlying criterion-referenced grading, that all students can earn As if they achieve at the established level, is occasionally questioned. Some administrators and parents expect to see a distribution of grades in a class and may insist that grading practices be altered to produce Bs, Cs, Ds, and Fs. In contrast, the criticisms of norm-referenced grading are greater in number and more persuasive. One criticism is that teachers seldom produce tests or other assessments that yield normally distributed scores. Another criticism is that the sizes of most middle and high school classes in which the procedure may be used are too small to expect a normal distribution. This is particularly true in advanced classes where students are homogeneous, with similar aptitudes. More importantly, norm-referenced grading does not match the model of science learning proffered in the *National Science Education Standards* (NRC, 1996), where all students are given the opportunity to achieve at high levels. If all students master the expected learning standards, how can a teacher justify giving the majority Cs, Ds, and Fs? Clearly, the criticisms of norm-referenced grading make criterion-referenced grading the preferred choice for middle and high school science teachers.

Assigning Report Card Grades

Ideally, when using criterion-referenced grading, the teacher would identify the standards and describe the students' performance relative to the standards. This approach would yield written statements of students' attainment on report cards rather than As, Bs, and Cs. While a few middle and secondary schools use criterion-referenced report cards to indicate student progress toward specific standards, the vast majority of schools require that students' grades be reported as numerical scores or letter grades.

The numerical or letter grade recorded on most report cards is a summary score, derived from the combination of several scores. This summary score is intended to provide the best representation of the teacher's evaluation of a student's performance. Combining scores of different kinds, whether percentages from tests or rubric scores from projects and lab work, to arrive at a summary score is indeed a challenging task. Fortunately, there are several methods for arriving at a report card grade that teachers may consider.

One is the median method. As described by Brookhart (2004), this method involves ordering a student's equally weighted grades from lowest to highest and counting to the middle to find the median. The median score is recorded on the report card as the summary grade. In the case where one assignment carries twice the weight of other assignments, it should be counted twice and both scores for the assignment should be included in the ordered list of scores. The median is easily determined when there is an odd number of scores, but it also can be used with an even number of scores by considering the median as the grade between the middle two scores. The median method is most appropriate when the grades in a report period are from rubrics, but the resulting numeric score (e.g., 1, 2, 3 or 4) or letter grade may not be easily translated into the percentage score (e.g., 90%) required on many school report cards.

Woolfolk (1995) offers other systems for combining grades from different assignments to arrive at a numeric grade—percentage grading and the point system. Percentage grading involves assigning grades based on the percentage of an assignment a student has accomplished or mastered. Using this system, the teacher gives percentage scores for class tests, performance tasks, and other assignments, then he or she computes an average for these scores to arrive at a final grade. Suppose a student's test score was 85%, her lab report score was 93%, and her microscope performance score was 61%. Her average grade is 78% and would be recorded as a C if the following percentage categories were applied:

A	90–100%
B	80–89%
C	70–79%
D	60–69%
F	below 60%

Applying this system with rubric scores is problematic. For instance, a rubric score of 2 on a 4-point scale may indicate a performance much better than the 50% this score would generate by percentage grading.

In contrast, the point system is adaptable for use with grades generated from tests as well as rubrics. When using the point system, a total number of points are awarded for each assignment, determined by its value (Woolfolk, 1995, p. 578). For example, a maximum score of 15 points could be awarded for a performance task worth 15% of the term grade; a maximum score of 20 points could be awarded for a unit test worth 20%; and a maximum score of 30 points could be awarded for a portfolio worth 30%. A portfolio meeting all the criteria would be given a score of 30 points, while one that meets some but not all of the criteria would be given less than 30 points. To calculate report card grades using this system, the teacher would simply add up the points for each student. Letter grades could be given by using an established scale. If required, a percentage grade could be calculated using this system by dividing a student's actual points by the maximum possible points and multiplying by 100. An established scale might look something like this:

TERM SCORING SCALE
Maximum possible points = 250

A	250–200 points
B	199–150 points
C	149–100 points
D	99–50 points
F	below 50 points

Before adopting any grading system, it is important for you to understand the expectation regarding grading placed on you by the school where you are employed. Much can be learned about those expectations by studying the school's grading policies and examining the report card format used to communicate student grades. Grading policies tend to specify what should be taken into account when grading—whether grades are reported as letters, numbers, or written descriptions of performance—and how final exam grades should be weighted in calculating course grades (Brookhart, 2004). In addition, a school's grading policy often provides information about how grades should be interpreted (e.g., A = Excellent) and informs teachers about how grades are reported to the school administration. The report card provides other useful information including the number of grading periods; if a mark for conduct, effort, or attitude must be reported; and whether a space for teacher comments is provided. All of the information gleaned from these sources is vitally important to you in considering decisions about grading and grade reporting practices.

Brookhart (2004) urges teachers to not allow grading to be an afterthought, but to think about it well in advance of the deadline for turning in report cards. In addition to communicating with students about what is expected of them to achieve at high levels, she suggests that teachers reflect about their own grading practices and offers the following questions to guide that reflection:

- How do you assess tests, quizzes, lab reports, performance tasks, homework, class participation, effort, cooperation, etc.? How do these items contribute to a report card grade?
- What methods do you use to calculate or assign report card grades?

- What meaning do you try to encode in your grades? Student achievement? Student progress? Student improvement?
- What do you do when a student's grade is just below (or above) the borderline or cutoff for a letter grade?
- How should failure, Fs, and zeros be handled in determining final grades?

Grading, regardless of the system used, is always a challenge for teachers. Students are concerned about their grades and want to know how they will be graded. Grades can motivate students as well as turn them against science and science teachers. It is important that teachers inform students about their grading system and explain to them why the system is fair.

ASSESSING AND REVIEWING

Analysis and Synthesis

1. Construct or locate several examples of different types of assessments that correspond to a content standard for a science course you would like to teach. Discuss the assessments with classmates to determine how well they are constructed, focusing on clarity, ambiguity, and correspondence with the standard.

2. Suppose a teacher told you that she does not have time for diagnostic or formative assessment in her science classes. What would you say to try to convince her to include these forms of assessment in her teaching plans?

3. Scientific literacy is a central idea discussed in this middle and secondary science methods textbook because science educators have used the term for over 50 years to promote the ideals of science education. In Chapter 7, "The Nature of Science," a definition of science is presented along with four themes of scientific literacy. For the definition of science and each of the themes, identify key terms to help you recall their meaning. Then, evaluate the extent to which Mr. Zimble's water unit reflects these aspects of science teaching, which are:
   a. What is science?
   b. Science as a way of thinking
   c. Science as a way of investigating
   d. Science as a body of knowledge
   e. Science and its interactions with technology and society

Practical Considerations

4. Examine a school's grading policy and report card format. What do these sources of information tell you about the grading system used by a teacher employed by the school?

5. Use an on-line design tool to build a rubric or checklist for a particular performance task. Test the rubric or checklist with a class and solicit student feedback regarding its appropriateness. Then, revise the rubric or checklist based on the students' feedback.

Developmental Considerations

6. Read an article from *Science Scope* or *The Science Teacher* that focuses on assessment. Discuss the article with others interested in science assessment. Devise a plan to implement a suggestion from the article in your teaching.

7. Work with colleagues to develop new units or revise existing units for the science courses you teach.

RESOURCES TO EXAMINE

The Problem with Tyler's Grade.   2004. In *Cases in Middle and Secondary Science Education: The Promise and Dilemmas* (2nd ed.), edited by T. Koballa and D. Tippins (pp. 247–251). Upper Saddle River, NJ: Merrill/Prentice Hall.

In this open case, chemistry teacher Dava Coleman describes her attempt to explain to a student how she scored his laboratory report using a scoring rubric and the difficulties that arose in the process. A response on the case by David Radford offers detailed feedback regarding how to help students understand rubrics and their applications.

Science Educator's Guide to Laboratory Assessment. 2002. Arlington, VA: National Science Teachers Association.

Rodney Doran, Fred Chan, Pinchas Tamir, and Carol Lenhardt describe a host of alternative assessment formats and provide assessment examples from the areas of biology, chemistry, physics, and earth science. They also discuss considerations to keep in mind when developing assessments and how to make use of laboratory performance assessment results.

Science Activities: Classroom Projects and Curriculum Ideas. Published quarterly by Heldref Publications, 1319 Eighteenth Street, NW, Washington, DC 20036. Phone (202) 296-6267.

Science Activities are indexed by ERIC in the Current Index to Journals in Education and Media Review Digest. Microform editions of Science Activities are available from Bell and Howell Information and Learning, Series Acquisition Department,

300 N. Zeeb Rd., Ann Arbor, MI 48106. [On-line.] Available: http://www.umi.com

Science Activities is a resource for teachers containing experiments, explorations, projects, and curriculum ideas. These activities and ideas have been used by experienced teachers and in science classrooms in elementary grades through high school. Each edition also cites many materials and places that one can go to for additional science teaching resources.

Classroom Assessment and the National Science Education Standards. 2001. National Academy Press: Washington, DC 20055.

A supplement to the *National Science Education Standards,* this book makes a case for strengthening assessment in the science classroom. It contains sections on summative and formative assessment, school-system-level support for assessment, and teacher professional development for improving science classroom assessment.

REFERENCES

American Association for the Advancement of Science. (1990). *Science for all Americans.* New York: Oxford University Press.

American Association for the Advancement of Science. (1993). *Benchmarks for science literacy.* New York: Oxford University Press.

Barton, J., & Collins, A. (1997). Starting out: Designing your portfolio. In J. Barton & A. Collins (Eds.), *Portfolio assessment* (pp. 1–10). Menlo Park, CA: Addison-Wesley.

Berenson, S. B., & Carter, G. S. (1995). Changing assessment practices in science and mathematics. *School Science and Mathematics, 95*(4), 182–186.

Brookhart, S. M. (2004). *Grading.* Upper Saddle River, NJ: Merrill/Prentice Hall.

Clark, L. H., & Star, I. S. (1996). *Secondary and middle school teaching methods.* Upper Saddle River, NJ: Merrill/Prentice Hall.

Collins, A. (1991). Portfolios for assessing student learning in science: A new name for a familiar idea? In G. Kulm & S. M. Malcolm (Eds.), *Science assessment in the service of reform* (pp. 291–300). Washington, DC: American Association for the Advancement of Science.

Doran, R., Chan, F., Tamir, P., & Lendhardt, C. (2002). *Science educator's guide to laboratory assessment.* Arlington, VA: NSTA Press.

Lewin, L., & Shoemaker, B. J. (1998). *Great performances: Creating classroom-based assessment tasks.* Alexandria, VA: Association for Supervision and Curriculum Development.

Licata, K. P. (1999). Narrative lab reports. *The Science Teacher, 66*(3), 20–22.

Martin, D. (2000). *Elementary science methods: A constructivist approach* (2nd ed.). Albany, NY: Delmar.

Marzano, R. J., Pickering, D., & McTighe, J. (1993). *Assessing student outcomes.* Alexandra, VA: Association for Supervision and Curriculum Development.

Myers, R. T., Oldham, K. B., & Tocci, S. (2000). *Chemistry: Visualizing matter.* Austin, TX: Holt, Rinehart and Winston.

National Research Council. (1996). *National science education standards.* Washington, DC: National Academy Press.

Oppewal, T. (1996). Science portfolios: Navigating uncharted waters. In J. Rhoton & P. Bowers (Eds.), *Issues in science education* (pp. 114–122). Arlington, VA: National Science Teachers Association.

Padilla, M. J., Miaoulis, I., & Cyr, M. (2000). *Science explorer program.* Upper Saddle River, NJ: Prentice Hall.

Woolfolk, A. E. (1995). *Educational psychology* (6th ed.). Boston: Allyn & Bacon.

Appendix A

Little Science Puzzlers

A DROP OF WATER

A Puzzling Situation

Purpose

Many aspects of science involve problem solving. Scientists often attempt to figure out how nature acts as it does or how things work. Further, they must explain what they find out. Water is an interesting substance that can stimulate curiosity, provide a context to learn more about fundamental science, and engage students in problem solving. For example, if you place a drop of water on a piece of wax paper and ask the question, Does the drop of water roll or slide across the paper? you will have a puzzle that needs to be resolved and explained.

Materials

a piece of wax paper (approx. 8 cm × 8 cm) for every person

water and a dropper to distribute one drop to each person

a small amount of black pepper

liquid detergent and a toothpick for each person

Procedure

1. Distribute a piece of wax paper to all participants and request that they place a drop of water on the paper.
2. Instruct participants to tilt their wax paper so that the drop of water moves across it. Pose the question:

   Does the drop of water roll or slide across the paper?

   Encourage participants to work on this puzzle by themselves to find a way to support their answer to

the question and to determine for certain how the drop of water moves across the paper.

3. Circulate among the participants to observe how they are examining the movement of the drop of water across the wax paper. Ask them to give a statement regarding how the water moves—rolls or slides—and to demonstrate that this is, in fact, the way it occurs.

   HINT: By placing a speck of black pepper or chalk dust on the drop, one can readily see that the drop is rolling.

Discussion

When most or all of the participants have solved the puzzle, ask them to explain the reason why the water rolls across the wax paper. Discuss the following concepts:

- **Adhesion:** the force of attraction between unlike molecules
- **Cohesion:** the force of attraction between like molecules

In this situation, we observe the cohesive effects of water molecules permitting a drop of liquid to form and maintain a spherical shape that will roll on a surface without breaking apart.

1. What happens when you place the tip of the toothpick into the detergent and then touch it to the drop of water?
2. How do you explain what happens to the drop of water?

   HINT: One end of the detergent molecule bonds to the water molecule and disrupts the adhesion between water molecules at the surface of the drop, causing it to break apart.

HOT IS HOT!

A Little Puzzler

The sun is a gigantic fireball approximately 93 million miles from earth. This star produces enormous amounts of heat generated by its nuclear furnace, where hydrogen fuses to form helium. These nuclear reactions produce high temperatures in the core of the sun and a spectrum of radiation that spreads out into space. Humans can detect some of the sun's radiation in the form of white light, which makes it possible to see during the daylight hours. We can also detect its heat, especially during the summer months.

If you could extract a pinhead-sized portion of the superheated material from the sun's core, would a person feel this heat source on earth from a distance of 1 mile, 10 miles, or 100 miles?

ANSWER: At 100 miles, the heat would be so intense that it would kill a person.

Source: Adapted from *The Cosmic Mind-boggling Book* by N. McAleer, 1982, New York: Warner Books.

HOW STRONG IS STRONG?

A Science Puzzler

$-$ ⟵――――――――――⟶ $+$

30 meters

Ask the participants to tell you what they know about electromagnetic force. They should indicate that electromagnetism is one of the four fundamental forces that have been ascribed to nature by science. The four forces are called gravity, the weak nuclear force, the electromagnetic force, and the strong nuclear force. These ideas are used to describe the interactions that take place between the various types of matter: protons, neutrons, electrons, and so on.

Conduct a thought experiment whereby you ask the participants to visualize two bits of very dense matter, each with a diameter of 1 millimeter. Imagine that you can transform all of the particles in one of these bits of matter into negative charges and all of the particles in the other bit into positive charges, as indicated in the diagram. Further, you separate the two bits of matter by a distance of 30 meters. Ask the following question:

At 30 meters will there be an attraction between the two bits of very dense matter?

ANSWER: Solicit responses from many of the participants. Most individuals will say that there is a small attraction between the two bits of matter. However, they will indicate that the force of attraction is very small because of the distance. They may mention the relationship that holds for gravity and electrostatics, which says that the force of attraction is equal to a constant times the product of the masses of the two objects divided by the square of the distance between them. These are small pieces of matter, and the distance of 30 meters is rather large.

The participants will be shocked when you tell them that the force of attraction between the two bits of matter, each with an opposite charge, is 3 million tons. Yes! Three million tons of force is pulling the bits of matter toward each other. Wow! Now do you believe that electromagnetic forces are STRONG?

THICK AND THIN LIGHT BULB FILAMENTS

A Little Science Puzzler

40 watts

75 watts

Have you ever wondered how light bulbs are constructed so that some give off more light than others? The bulb on the left is rated at 40 watts and the one on the right is 75 watts.

Tell which bulb gives off more light and explain your answer.

ANSWER: The 75-watt light bulb produces more light. The main reason for this is the size of the filament inside the glass bulb. The 75-watt light bulb has a slightly thicker filament than the 40-watt light bulb. The larger-size filament permits more electrical current to flow through it; thus, it uses more energy and produces a brighter light than a lower-wattage bulb. Examine the filaments inside light bulbs rated at different wattages and note the thickness of each filament.

THE EGGCITING EGG HUNT

A Puzzling Situation

Context

It was the week before Easter and Mrs. Barefoot and her 5-year-old daughter, Caroline, were decorating eggs for the annual Easter egg hunt. They had just hard-boiled a dozen eggs and were preparing to boil a dozen more when the phone rang. Mrs. Barefoot went to answer the phone while Caroline stayed in the kitchen. Upon her return to the kitchen, Mrs. Barefoot saw that Caroline had mixed the hard-boiled eggs with the raw ones.

How can Mrs. Barefoot tell the difference between the hard-boiled eggs and the raw eggs?

Materials

hard-boiled eggs

raw eggs

Procedure

1. Spin each egg on a smooth flat surface.
2. Quickly stop each egg from spinning and then at once allow it to spin again.
3. Observe the behavior of each egg. Group the eggs into two piles based on their behavior.

4. Raw eggs spin when released, whereas hard-boiled eggs do not.

Questions & Answers

How can you explain the different behavior of the raw and boiled eggs?

ANSWER: When the shell of the rotating raw egg is briefly stopped, its fluid will still be rotating.

RAISINS ON THE MOVE

A Puzzling Situation

Context

It's snack time and two friends, Jan and Mike, are enjoying their raisins and sparkling soda as they sit and talk. All of a sudden, they are bumped by a passer-by and some of Jan's raisins spill into Mike's cup of sparkling soda. Within a few minutes, they witness a strange occurrence. Raisins are moving up and down in the cup of sparkling soda. What causes the raisins to behave like this?

Materials

raisins

clear plastic cup or drinking glass

sparkling soda (club soda, Sprite, or 7-Up)

Procedure

1. Fill the plastic cup about two-thirds full of sparkling soda.
2. Gingerly add four to six raisins one at a time to the cup.

3. Watch the raisins and write down what you observe.
4. Come up with an explanation for the movement of the raisins.

Discussion

When the raisins are first put into the cup, they sink to the bottom. While at the bottom of the cup, bubbles in the sparkling soda attach to the raisins. These are carbon dioxide bubbles. As the bubbles attach to a single raisin, they function like tiny life buoys, bringing the raisin to the surface. The carbon dioxide bubbles burst when they reach the surface, causing the raisin to sink. This process is repeated over and over until most of the carbon dioxide gas escapes from the sparkling soda and the soda becomes flat.

Appendix B

Science Demonstrations

BERNOULLI'S PRINCIPLE

A Discrepant Event Science Demonstration

Purpose

Discrepant events create surprise and cause students to concentrate on what is taking place. Many science demonstrations present contradictions in our thinking, because they illustrate laws and principles that are not immediately understood by observation. Bernoulli's principle, which pertains to air pressure, is such an idea. Fortunately, there are many discrepant event demonstrations that can be conducted in the science classroom to help students learn about Bernoulli's principle and many other principles.

Materials

   two thick books of similar size and one sheet of
      8 1/2-by-11-inch paper (for "Blow under a
      Sheet of Paper")

   one shoe box (or any container or bowl of similar
      size) and several playing cards (for "The Falling
      Card Trick")

   a spoon and a water faucet (for "Squirting Water
      on the Spoon")

Procedure for "Blow under a Sheet of Paper"

1. Set the two books on a table so they are approximately 5 inches apart.
2. Place one sheet of paper lengthwise so each end rests on one of the books. Center the paper between the two books (see illustration).

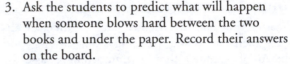

3. Ask the students to predict what will happen when someone blows hard between the two books and under the paper. Record their answers on the board.
4. Ask for a student volunteer to blow under the paper.

Questions & Answers

1. **What happened when the air passed swiftly under the paper? Is this what you predicted?**

   ANSWER: The paper bent down toward the table. Many students will have predicted that the paper will rise up or be blown off the books.

2. **Why did the paper bend toward the table?**

   ANSWER: When someone blows under the paper, that air is moving much faster than the air above the paper. The air moving rapidly across the underside of the paper produces less air pressure than the air above the paper, according to Bernoulli's principle. This action results in more air pressure above the paper, which forces the paper to bend down to the table. Bernoulli's principle states that the faster air moves across a surface, the less pressure it exerts on that surface.

3. **Predict what should happen if you hold a sheet of paper to your chin and blow across it. Why do you think so?**

   ANSWER: The paper should rise. Let students try this out for themselves at their desks. The moving air on top of the paper has less air pressure than the air underneath the paper, thus the paper will lift.

Procedure for "The Falling Card Trick"

1. Place a shoe box (or other container) on the floor directly in front of you.
2. Hold a playing card horizontally directly over the box and drop it into the box. Do not point out to the students the angle at which you release or hold the card.
3. Ask several students to come up and try to drop a card into the box.

Questions & Answers

1. **Which cards fell into the box and which cards did not?**

   ANSWER: The observant students should see that the cards that were initially held horizontally and dropped fell straight down into the box. The cards held vertically or at other angles drifted away from the box.

   Some students might have trouble seeing this. You could make this a game where you predict whether each card dropped will fall in or not. After doing this a few times, through questioning, invite students to discover how you are holding each card as you drop it.

2. **Why do the cards that are held horizontally drop straight into the box?**

   ANSWER: As the card falls, the air pressure above the card drops. Since the card is horizontal, the air pressure affects the card uniformly. This can be drawn on the board as follows:

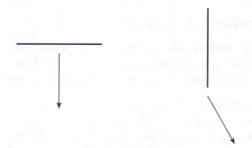

3. **Why do the cards dropped at an angle drift away?**

   ANSWER: As in the example, when the card is released horizontally, the air pressure above the card decreases as it falls. However, when the card is at an angle, there are differences in air pressure around the card. The air pressure is the lightest over the lowest part of the card. The lighter pressure does not cause that end of the card to lift because it is still falling, but the lighter pressure does cause that end of the card to fall more slowly than the other end. The difference in the speed at which each end of the card falls causes it to drift away and often to tumble end over end. This too can be illustrated on the board.

Procedure for "Squirting Water on the Spoon"

1. Turn on a water faucet to get a fast stream of water.
2. Loosely hold a spoon by its handle with the curved end 3 or 4 inches away from the stream of water. Ask the following question:

   What will happen when I bring the curved underside of the spoon in contact with the fast-moving stream of water?

3. Let several of the students hold the spoon and feel it jump into the stream of water.

Questions & Answers

1. **What caused the spoon to jump into the water?**

   ANSWER: The fast-moving water causes a decrease in the air pressure on the *bottom* of the spoon. Because the pressure on the bottom of the spoon is less than the air pressure on the top, the greater pressure pushes the spoon into the water.

2. **Can you think of examples of everyday occurrences that demonstrate Bernoulli's principle?**

   EXAMPLE A: Airplane wings, hang gliders, and so on. The wings of an airplane are curved to form an airfoil. This shape creates an area of lower pressure over the wing when the plane moves through the air. The greater pressure underneath forces the wing upward, creating lift for the airplane.

   EXAMPLE B: Baseball pitchers throw curve balls and drop balls by putting spin on the ball. When a great deal of spin is given to a baseball, it causes the air on one side of the ball to travel faster. This, in turn, causes a pressure change that pulls the ball to the side with the least pressure.

   EXAMPLE C: When a semitrailer rig travels down the highway, it creates an area behind its large cargo trailer that has lower air pressure than one normally experiences driving down the highway. When a vehicle travels at close proximity behind the trailer, the vehicle will be pulled along by the reduced air pressure that it experiences between it and the trailer.

   EXAMPLE D: Many internal combustion engines use a carburetor to mix air and gas together to facilitate combustion. The air traveling through the carburetor is channeled into a narrower passage, causing it to speed up. The reduced pressure in the air channels "pulls" the gas into the carburetor where it mixes with the air. Again, we observe Bernoulli's principle in effect.

THE NO-POP BALLOON

A Science Demonstration

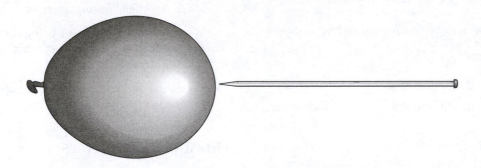

Purpose

You can demonstrate the property of a particular polymer by piercing a balloon with a sharp object and observing that the balloon does not pop. The rubber-like material that is used to manufacture balloons is composed of chains of carbon-based molecules. These polymers are very flexible and rather loosely structured, so a thin, sharp object can slip between the sheets of polymer chains and not disrupt the material. By following the directions and with some practice you can present an attention-getting demonstration that will cause the audience to think more deeply about polymers and the wonders of man-made chemical products.

Materials

    several large, good-quality balloons (i.e., balloons with heavy rubber walls)

    a long, thin, sharp object to push into the balloon (an 8- or 10-inch length of coat hanger wire with one end sharpened or an upholstery needle)

    some lubricant (cooking oil or liquid soap)

Procedure

Remember, you should practice this demonstration a few times before you present it to the class.

1. Inflate the balloon to only about one-half its capacity and tie the end. You do *not* want the balloon to be filled to capacity with air so that the rubber walls are stretched tight, ready to burst at the touch of a sharp object.
2. Take the wire or needle and lubricate the sharp end that will be pushed into the end of the balloon. You want to slip the point between the polymer chains.
3. Locate the end of the balloon, opposite the tied-off end. You may notice that this region is not stretched as much as the middle area. Now gently push the needle into the balloon with a twisting motion until it penetrates far into the interior of the balloon.

Questions & Answers

1. **Explain why the needle does not cause the balloon to pop or the air to rush out through the hole that the needle is making in its wall.**

   ANSWER: The needle is squeezing between the sheets of molecules that are held tightly against the needle. The air pressure in the half-filled balloon is not strong enough to disrupt this careful separation of rubber polymer.

2. **Do people bleed or feel the fine needles that are pushed into their skin when receiving acupuncture treatments?**

   ANSWER: Acupuncture is a similar process to inserting the needle into the balloon between the polymer chains. Skin is a polymer composed of protein-based tissue.

BRUISING FRUIT

A Science Demonstration

Have you ever wondered why an apple is sometimes brown on the inside when you bite into it or cut it open? If you examine the apple, in many instances you will notice that the skin has a slight indentation that indicates that the apple was hit or bruised, thus causing the flesh under that area to turn brown and mushy. When an apple or other fruit is bruised, oxidative enzymes are activated that catalyze oxidation-reduction reactions. These enzymes are found in the cells of fruit. They react with oxygen to decompose the cells of the fruit, which causes the darkening of the fruit. You can retard this process and illustrate it with a demonstration[*] by adding a common chemical to fruit.

Vitamin C, also called ascorbic acid, is well known as an important nutrient for humans. It is found in many citrus fruits and is used as a preservative and nutritional supplement. Vitamin C is a reducing agent. It belongs to the family of chemicals called antioxidants. As an antioxidant, vitamin C reacts with the oxidative enzymes in the fruit cell before they can destroy the fruit cell. The molecular formula for ascorbic acid is $C_6H_8O_6$.

Purpose

You can conduct the following demonstration to illustrate how to retard bruised fruit from browning.

Materials

   vitamin C tablets
   fruit juice
   a few apples
   six small beakers or cups

Procedure

1. Prepare the following setup of equipment and materials to illustrate how to retard the browning of bruised fruit with the addition of vitamin C. Either place a copy of the table on a chalkboard or on an overhead transparency to summarize the results and observations (see table on next page).

   Note that this is a set of experimental conditions that can be used for this demonstration. You can formulate other variables and conditions that may be even more illustrative of the ideas under study.

2. Slice an unpeeled apple (or pear) into six or more large pieces. Then bruise each piece of fruit by smashing it with your thumb. Place a bruised piece into each beaker and add the ingredients shown in the table on the next page. Then cover all of the beakers, except number 1.

3. Wait 25 minutes, then empty the beakers and make observations on the color of each piece of fruit.

Questions & Answers

1. **How does the fruit slice in beaker 1 compare to the others?**

   ANSWER: It should be darker in color.

2. **How does the fruit slice in the fruit juice compare to that in the vitamin C solution?**

   ANSWER: It should be about the same color.

3. **How does mother nature protect her fruit from the oxidative enzymes?**

   ANSWER: Apples and pears have protective peels or skins.

4. **If you make a fruit salad, how does squirting it with lemon or lime juice help prevent browning?**

   ANSWER: Lemon and lime juice both contain vitamin C, an antioxidant that retards the chemical reactions that lead to browning of fruit.

Source: Adapted from "The Chemistry of Bruised Fruit" by T. Anthony, 1987, in E. L. Chiappetta (Ed.), *Ideas and Activities for Physical Science* (pp. 2-14–2-15), Houston: College of Education, University of Houston with permission from Tom Anthony.

Beaker	Observation of Fruit	
	Beginning	End
1—no liquid, uncovered		
2—no liquid, covered		
3—filled with water, covered		
4—filled with boiled water, covered		
5—filled with vitamin C solution, covered		
6—filled with fruit juice, covered		

PULL IT OR YANK IT—WHAT IS THE DIFFERENCE?

A Science Demonstration

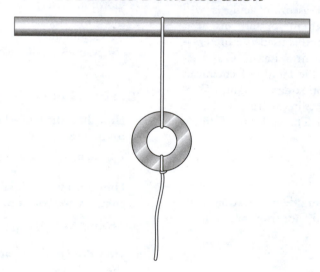

Purpose

Whether you pull or yank on a string that is attached to an object that you wish to move makes a big difference. In an attempt to move an object, you (the force) must overcome its **inertia.** According to Newton's first law of motion, or inertia, a body at rest tends to remain at rest and a body in motion tends to remain in motion unless acted on by a force. Certainly the mass of an object determines how easy or difficult it is to move the object or stop it if it is in motion. Here is a simple demonstration that illustrates the law of inertia.

Setup

Obtain some light string or heavy thread for this demonstration. You need a line that can be snapped or broken by pulling on it. Get a small barbell weight (a two-and-one-half-pound weight works well). Tie the string to the weight in two places as shown in the illustration. The top end must be secured to something strong, such as the end of a desk or a broom handle.

Procedure

1. Arrange the students so they are close to the apparatus and can see any changes that occur in the strings.
2. Alert the students to observe the strings as you pull down slowly with an even force on the bottom string. The string above the weight will snap.
3. Alert the students to observe the strings as you yank down quickly and forcibly on the bottom string. The string will snap this time between the weight and your hand.

Questions & Answers

1. **Why does a slow continuous downward force break the string *above* the weight?**

   Answer: When you pull down slowly the barbell weight actually moves down with this force and it adds to the stress placed on the upper string. Thus, the upper string has more force on it than the lower string and consequently it breaks first.

2. **Why does a sudden increase in the downward force break the string *below* the weight?**

   Answer: When you yank on the lower string, the barbell weight and the upper string are at rest and tend to remain at rest. Therefore, the lower string has to overcome both of their masses or inertia, according to Newton's first law. The lower string absorbs the full force of the downward motion of the hand.

   Call on participants to repeat this demonstration to give them a feel for this inertial experience.

HOW DOES A WEATHER VANE WORK?

A Science Demonstration

Background

Knowledge of the direction from which winds are blowing is an important aspect of weather forecasting. In the Northern Hemisphere, winds move in a clockwise direction around centers of HIGH pressure and counterclockwise around centers of LOW pressure. Skies in a HIGH pressure area tend to be clear with generally fair weather, whereas skies in LOW pressure areas tend to be cloudy with stormy weather. By noting the direction from which the winds are blowing, the movements of HIGH and LOW pressure areas can be tracked and the next day's weather can be forecast.

Observations of wind direction can be made using a weather vane. Students are taught that a weather vane points in the direction from which the wind is blowing. This can lead to students forming a misconception about how a weather vane functions. Students tend to focus on the weather vane's pointing tip and neglect its size and shape. Which should be larger, the weather vane's tip or its tail? Does the shape of the weather vane affect its accuracy? These are the questions explored in this demonstration.

Materials

- five 3-by-5-inch index cards
- five plastic drinking straws
- five straight pins
- five pencils with erasers
- scissors
- cellophane tape
- a metric ruler
- a large fan or powerful hand-held hair dryer

Procedure

Weather Vane Construction

1. Cut one large and one small triangle out of an index card. The larger one should be about twice as large as the smaller one.
2. Cut two slits about 2 cm long at both ends of a plastic straw. Cut the slits so that the triangle index card pieces fit into the straw as shown in the illustration. Tape the index card pieces to the straw to hold them securely.

3. Find the weather vane's pivot point by balancing the straw on your index finger. Push a straight pin through the pivot point and into the eraser of a pencil. The weather vane should now spin freely on the pin and is ready to use.
4. Construct four more weather vanes that match the designs shown here. Mark the ends of each weather vane with the letters *a* and *b* as shown.

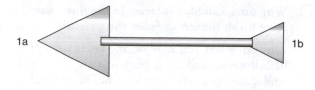

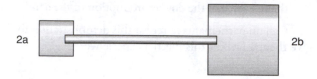

5. Copy the illustration of the four designs onto the chalkboard or prepare an overhead transparency of it.

Weather Vane Testing

6. Put the first weather vane constructed in front of a fan or hair dryer. Test it in the stream of moving air until its performance becomes predictable. Have students verify that the point of the weather vane is pointing in the direction from which the wind is blowing.

7. Show the students the other four weather vanes. Ask them to predict which of the following statements describes the performance of each in the stream of moving air. Tally the students' responses.

   ■ With respect to vane 1, is the wind coming from direction 1a or 1b?

   ■ With respect to vane 2, is the wind coming from direction 2a or 2b?

   ■ With respect to vane 3, is the wind coming from direction 3a or 3b?

   ■ With respect to vane 4, is the wind coming from direction 4a or 4b?

8. Put each of the four weather vanes one at a time in the stream of moving air and observe its performance. Compare the students' predictions with the observations for all four of the weather vane designs tested.

Questions & Answers

1. **What happened when vane 1 was placed in the stream of moving air? Is this what students predicted?**

   ANSWER: End *b* pointed in the direction from which the wind was blowing. Many students will have predicted that the point of the weather vane, or end *a*, will point in the direction from which the wind is blowing.

2. **What happened when the three other weather vane designs shown in the figure were placed in the stream of moving air? Did the observations match the predictions?**

   ANSWER: For weather vane 2, the one with the squares, end *a* pointed in the direction from which the wind is blowing. For weather vanes 3 and 4, end *b* pointed in the direction from which the wind was blowing.

3. **Write a rule that fits the observations of the weather vane designs tested.**

   ANSWER: Examples of rules that fit the observations are:

   a. The small end of the weather vane points in the direction from which the wind is blowing, regardless of the shape of the tip and the tail.

   b. The point is not the critical variable; the critical variable is the surface area of the ends of the vane.

4. **Compare the rules written by the students.**

5. **Build and test a weather vane design not presented in this demonstration that fits the rule.**

MAKING A CLOUD

A Science Demonstration

Background

Clouds form when moisture in the air condenses. But what causes the moisture in the air to condense, and what does the moisture condense on? These are questions for which too few students have answers. In this demonstration the contributions of air pressure, condensation nuclei, and moisture to the formation of clouds are examined.

Materials

one clear, two-liter plastic bottle with cap

water

matches

overhead projector (or other light source)

Safety

This demonstration requires the use of fire. Perform the demonstration away from flammable materials. Wear safety goggles.

Procedure

1. Seal the bottle with its bottle cap and rest it on top of a lighted overhead projector. Direct the students to look into the bottle and not at the image projected by the overhead projector.
2. Repeatedly squeeze and release the bottle to change the pressure inside. (The air pressure inside is increased when force is applied by pressing on the outside of the bottle and decreased when the bottle is released.)
3. Add a couple of milliliters of water to the bottle, seal it again, and then repeatedly squeeze and release the bottle.
4. Put a lighted match inside the bottle and seal it. Then, repeatedly squeeze and release the bottle to change the air pressure inside.

Questions & Answers

1. **What did you observe?**

   ANSWER: A cloud did not form when the empty bottle was squeezed or when it was squeezed with water inside. Only after the match was dropped inside the bottle containing water and the bottle was squeezed did the cloud form.

2. **Did the cloud form when the bottle was squeezed or when it was released? How do you explain your observation?**

   ANSWER: The cloud formed when the bottle was released. Releasing the bottle causes the air pressure inside to be reduced.

3. **Based on what you observed, what conditions are needed for a cloud to form?**

   ANSWER: Moisture, condensation nuclei, and pressure change. (In this demonstration, smoke served as the condensation nuclei. Dust particles are the most abundant condensation nuclei in the air.)

4. **Explain how a cloud might form in nature.**

   ANSWER: Water evaporating from a lake or the ocean puts water vapor or moisture into the air. Dust particles and smoke in the air provide the condensation nuclei necessary for the water to condense on. With moisture and condensation nuclei in the air, a cloud would form when air pressure is reduced, such as when air is heated and rises.

Appendix C

Science Laboratory Activities

THE DIFFUSION OF MOLECULES AND IONS

A Laboratory Exercise

Purpose

Diffusion is a fundamental principle that is present in our everyday world. It is the tendency of molecules or ions to move from areas of higher concentration to areas of lower concentration until the concentration is uniform throughout the system. Diffusion explains how gases in the air spread out when released from one location where the concentration of their molecules is higher than in the space surrounding their source. Diffusion also explains how ions and molecules in solutions spread out through the liquid in a container or how nutrients move across a cell membrane.

Materials

bottle of perfume, cologne, or other odorous liquids, and cornstarch solution (rather dilute solution)

Lugol's iodine solution

plastic sandwich bags (fold-over type, not zipper type), one for each group

beakers or large cups, one for each lab group

Demonstration

Take a bottle of any perfume or liquid that students will be able to smell when you remove the cap and pour some on a cotton ball. Ask participants the following questions:

1. How long did it take to detect the odor of the liquid once it was exposed to the air in the room?
2. How did the vapors of the liquid get from the cotton ball or the open container to your nose?

How do the molecules of the liquid travel from the source to your nose, in a straight line or zigzag path or some other type of motion? Require the participants to draw a diagram of the phenomenon.

In the discussion that follows these questions, bring up the term **diffusion,** explain it, and list many situations in which diffusion occurs in everyday life.

Procedure

Organize participants into lab groups in order for them to carry out the diffusion exercise whereby iodide ions move through a plastic membrane.

1. Pour about 50 milliliters of cornstarch solution in each plastic sandwich bag and tie the top with a rubber band or string.
2. Place the bag of cornstarch solution into a beaker half-full of iodine solution (Lugol's solution).
3. It will take about 15 to 20 minutes before you begin to see the cornstarch turn blue-black. If you wait 1 day, the reaction takes place to a greater extent and the color is more dramatic.
4. Ask the participants to devise tests to determine if other substances besides the ingredients that make up the iodine solution diffuse through the walls of the plastic sandwich bag.

Questions & Answers

1. **What does the color change inside the bag signify?**

   ANSWER: A chemical passed through the walls of the plastic bag into the starch solution. The chemical was iodine. The iodide ions were small enough to pass through spaces in the plastic and interact with the starch, giving the characteristic blue-black color that shows the presence of starch.

2. **Were the water molecules able to diffuse through the plastic bag into the starch solution?**

   ANSWER: The water molecules are probably too large to diffuse through the plastic membrane.

OSMOSIS AND A CHICKEN EGG

A Laboratory Exercise

Background

Life is maintained by an intricate balance of substances passing into and out of a cell through a membrane. Water, glucose, amino acids, carbon dioxide, and many other chemical elements and compounds pass through cellular membranes to maintain the proper nutrition that a cell must have in order to function. This dynamic process is partly explained by diffusion, which is the spreading of molecules from an area of greater concentration to an area of lower concentration. A type of diffusion associated with water is called osmosis. Osmosis is the diffusion of water through a selectively permeable membrane from an area of greater concentration to an area of lesser concentration. Osmosis is an essential process that takes place in all cells, with water molecules moving through the cell membrane.

Purpose

This activity illustrates osmosis taking place through the membrane of a chicken egg. A chicken egg is ideal for this exercise because it is large and has a cell membrane that becomes visible when you remove the shell in a particular manner. Although you may not have noticed, there is a membrane between the shell and the yolk/white part of the egg. If you remove the shell of an egg, the membrane can be observed surrounding the liquid material on the inside. With only the membrane to keep an egg intact, the effects of osmosis can be observed when the egg is placed in water where the concentration of water is greater on the outside of the egg than on the inside.

Procedure

This exercise takes approximately 3 days and can be conducted as a take-home laboratory exercise. During the first 24-hour period, the shell of one egg is removed by placing it in vinegar, which dissolves the calcified shell.

1. Each participant should obtain two eggs of the same size and place each egg in a separate cup. In the first cup, pour in enough water to cover the egg. In the second cup, pour in enough white vinegar to cover the egg. The liquid level in both cups should be at least 3 centimeters above the egg. Let stand for 24 hours.

2. On the second day, make and record observations on both eggs. Remove the vinegar in the second cup and rinse the egg—carefully. Then pour in enough water to cover the membrane-exposed egg so that the water level is 3 centimeters above the egg. Leave for another day.

3. Make observations of the intact egg in the first cup with water and the egg with the shell removed in the second cup with water. What are the similarities and differences between the two eggs?

Conclusion

Write a few paragraphs describing what took place in this experiment and the science behind the events.

RADIOACTIVE HALF–LIFE

A Laboratory Simulation Exercise

Purpose

The purpose of this laboratory simulation is to illustrate some concepts related to radioactive half-life. Radioactivity is an important process that occurs all the time in nature. It is occurring among some of the elements in our bodies every second of our life. The laws of chance are also illustrated in this simulation because radioactive decay is a random process similar to tossing a coin. This exercise is designed to review important background information that is necessary to understanding radioactivity and the atom.

Materials

shallow square cardboard boxes with covers (approximately 5-by-5 inches), one for every two students. You can make square boxes from rectangular ones by cutting off the long dimension and restoring the sides with tape.

unpopped popcorn, approximately 1 pound

felt-tip pens

graph paper, one sheet for every two students

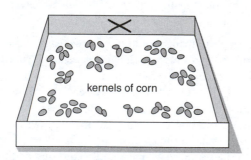

kernels of corn

Students will work in pairs. Each pair will be given one box, and 100 pieces of corn will be placed into each box. You can facilitate the preparation of this lab by asking a few students to help you count out the 100 pieces of corn for each box. A simple way to do this is to arrange the corn in rows and columns of ten, producing a ten-by-ten matrix, making it easy to see when you have 100 pieces of corn.

The boxes can be obtained at department stores, gift stores, or box stores. Mark an X on one of the inside walls of the box. Place a rubber band around each box to secure the cover so the corn does not spill.

Prelaboratory Discussion

Review some basic concepts related to radioactive decay with students by asking:

1. **What happens when a radioactive element decays?**

   ANSWER: The nucleus of the element gives off rays or particles. In some instances this release of matter and energy changes the mass of the element by reducing the number of protons and neutrons in the nucleus, thus forming a new element with a lower atomic mass (equation A). In other instances it results in the transformation of a neutron into a proton, thereby increasing the atomic number by one (equation B) while maintaining the same atomic mass.

   A. $^{226}_{88}\text{Ra}$ $\rightarrow$ $^{222}_{86}\text{Rn}$ + $^{4}_{2}\text{He}$
      radium   radon   alpha particle

   B. $^{210}_{83}\text{Bi}$ $\rightarrow$ $^{210}_{84}\text{Po}$ + $^{0}_{-1}\text{e}$
      bismuth   polonium   beta particle

   When a neutron transforms, it forms a proton and an electron (or a beta particle). Yes, it is strange to have a situation where energy and matter are given off, yet you end up with an element that has a greater atomic number—another unusual facet of nature.

2. **Why are some elements unstable and decay?**

   ANSWER: When elements have too many particles or neutrons versus protons in the nucleus, they have an abundance of energy in their nucleus. This excess energy causes the atom to be unstable and give up energy in the form of particles so that it can stabilize. Remember, everything in nature wants to become stable.

3. **How can you tell if a substance is radioactive?**

   ANSWER: Radioactive substances give off particles, rays, or energy that can be detected and measured accurately.

4. **What is half-life?**

   ANSWER: Since a radioactive isotope is constantly changing into something else, a very useful question is, How long will the isotope last before all the atoms in it have changed to something else? Half-life is the time it takes for one-half of the radioactivity to be given up. One way to tell how many atoms of a radioactive isotope are left is to use an instrument, such as a Geiger counter, that measures radioactivity by measuring the number of alpha, beta, or gamma rays emitted. Generally, the less radioactive material there is, the weaker the radioactivity will be.

5. **Why do radioactive substances behave this way?**

    ANSWER: Whether an atom is going to decay or not in the next second is a matter of chance. It might decay now, or it might not decay for another million years. As with flipping a coin, there are only two possible outcomes, the atom either decays or it doesn't. The chances that an atom will decay in the next second are a lot greater with an isotope that has a short half-life than one with a long half-life.

6. **How can you illustrate a 50-50 chance occurrence?**

    ANSWER: Flip a coin many times, each time recording whether a head or tail appears. What is the chance of getting a head or a tail? If you flip the coin only 10 times what do you get? Flip the coin 30 or 40 times and you will find that the 50-50 probability becomes more apparent. Radioactive decay is a similar process.

Tell the students that they are going to perform a half-life laboratory activity using kernels of corn. Each box has 100 kernels of corn. Go over the following procedure before you permit students to begin the activity.

Procedure

1. Pass out the boxes, each containing 100 kernels of corn. Note that each kernel of corn has a pointed end. When the corn is in the box, the pointed end will point to one of the four sides of the box. What are the chances of a particular kernel pointing to the side marked X? (Answer: one in four).
2. With the cover securely on the box, shake it five or six times. Place the box on the table and remove the cover.
3. Remove the kernels that are pointing to the side with the X. Remember the kernels can be pointing to any part of the side with the X, not just directly at the X itself. If some of the kernels are pointing exactly at the X-side's corners, take one-half of those out. Do not put any of the kernels back into the box.
4. Record the number of kernels taken out and the number left. Repeat this activity for 10 trials.

Data table of half-life graph

Trial	Started with	Took Out	Number Left
1	100		
2			
3			
4			
5			
6			
7			
8			
9			
10			

5. After the 10 trials, graph the results: number of kernels remaining versus trials. Ask the students to label axes of the graph; they need practice in this skill. Connect the points with a smooth line rather than using a ruler.
6. Use the figures from the class totals to construct a composite graph on the chalkboard from everyone's results.

Postlaboratory Discussion

1. Call on many groups of students to hold up their half-life graphs and compare the curves. Discuss the variation in the graphs. Point out that this is not due to students' errors, but to the fact that the smaller the sample, the greater the variation. Note that the composite curve produced from everyone's results is generally smoother because the number of trials is greater on this curve than on any individual group's curve. In an experiment measuring the radioactivity of actual materials, the curve would be very smooth because the sample of material would contain millions of atoms.

2. **Ask why a curved line was obtained instead of a straight line.**

    ANSWER: When you take one-half of a quantity, you get something even though it may be very small. In other words, you do not just end up with nothing quickly.

3. **Define half-life.**

    ANSWER: Half-life is the time it takes for one-half of the radioactive atoms to disintegrate.

4. **During radioactive decay, when does an element decrease its atomic number? Increase it?**

    ANSWER: When the nucleus of an element gives up an alpha particle, it loses four atomic mass units—two protons and two neutrons—and forms a lighter element. When one of the neutrons transforms into a proton and a beta particle, it forms a new element with a larger atomic number. (See the examples given earlier.)

5. **What is the significance of a long half-life versus a short half-life?**

   ANSWER: An element with a long half-life gives off matter/energy slowly; therefore, its radioactivity is not very intense. Consequently, it is generally not very dangerous but will be around a long time as a radioactive element. An element with a short half-life gives off matter/energy very quickly; therefore, its radioactivity is intense. It will not be around as long, but it may be very dangerous because of the rate at which it gives off radioactivity.

6. **How many trials did it take to use up half the kernels?**

   ANSWER: Usually two or three.

7. **How many trials did it take to use up half of the 50 kernels that were left?**

   ANSWER: Usually four or five.

RESPIRATION IN YEAST

A Laboratory Exercise

Background

Yeasts are single-celled fungi that form chains of cells. They belong to the class of fungi called Hemiascomycetes, which contains more than 30,000 species. The energy-releasing process that enables yeasts to live, grow, and reproduce is called cellular respiration. A principal source of energy used to carry on respiration is sugar ($C_6H_{12}O_6$), which may be derived from other multicarbon compounds.

Yeasts of the genus *Saccharomyces* are used to make alcohol in the production of cider, beer, and wine. Alcohol and carbon dioxide are produced when the yeast is grown in vats that contain little or no oxygen. Respiration under these conditions is called fermentation. A different strain of *Saccharomyces* is used in bread making. Here, the process is the same, but yields different results. As the sugar in the bread dough is used by the yeast cells, carbon dioxide is released, which makes the dough rise. Heat from the oven drives out the carbon dioxide gas and evaporates the alcohol, leaving the fluffy textured bread.

The equation for fermentation (anaerobic respiration) in yeast is

$$C_6H_{12}O_6 \rightarrow 2C_2H_5OH + 2CO_2 + 2\text{-}P$$
$$\text{(2 phosphate groups)}$$

Purpose

In the experiment that follows, yeast will be grown in the presence of little oxygen. The purpose of the experiment is to determine the effect of different amounts of sugar on yeast respiration rate.

Materials

six 250-milliliter clear glass or plastic bottles

six 200-milliliter clear glass or plastic cups

six pieces of aquarium hose, each about 30 cm long

two 6-ounce containers or bars of modeling clay

100 grams of table sugar

two packages of dry baker's yeast

600 milliliters of warm distilled water

1/2- and 1-teaspoon size measuring spoons

six graduated cylinders

50 milliliters Bromthymol blue (BTB) (*Caution:* BTB will stain clothes and skin.)

Procedure

1. Write the question, What is the effect of different amounts of sugar on the respiration rate of yeast? on the chalkboard.

2. Have students construct hypotheses related to the question before beginning the investigation. Ask them to provide reasons for their hypotheses. Proceed with the investigation once two or three hypotheses have been generated and discussed. An example hypothesis is: As the amount of sugar is increased, the rate of respiration will decrease.

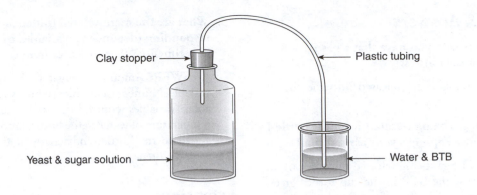

Clay stopper ⟶

Plastic tubing

Yeast & sugar solution ⟶

⟵ Water & BTB

Assembling the Experimental Apparatus

3. Label the 250-milliliter bottles 1, 2, 3, 4, 5, or 6 to correspond with the treatment condition to which your group has been assigned. (Treatment groups are specified in the accompanying table. All treatment conditions should be represented in the class.)
4. Assemble the stopper apparatus for your bottle by rolling clay around the aquarium hose.
5. Pour 100 milliliters of warm distilled water into your bottle.
6. Add table sugar to your bottle in the amount indicated in the table. (5 grams = approximately 1 teaspoon)
7. Add 2 grams of yeast to your bottle. (2 grams = approximately 1/2 teaspoon)
8. Using the stopper apparatus, seal the top of your bottle. Make sure that the tubing is *not* touching the sugar solution.
9. Place the other end of the tubing in a cup of tap water to which two to three drops of BTB has been added.
10. Swirl the sugar and yeast solution in the bottle, then allow the experimental apparatus as illustrated to set for 10 minutes.

Data Collection

11. Count the number of bubbles released into your cup of water in 5 minutes. (All groups should start and stop counting bubbles at the same time.)
12. Then calculate the number of bubbles released per minute from the bottle by dividing the number of bubbles that you counted by five.
13. Copy the table and graph (as illustrated) onto a sheet of paper.
14. Record the number of bubbles per minute released from your group's bottle and the bottles of other groups in the appropriate spaces in the table.
15. Complete the graph using your class data.

Table

Bottle	Amount of Sugar	Number of Bubbles per Minute
1		
2		
3		
4		
5		
6		

Graph

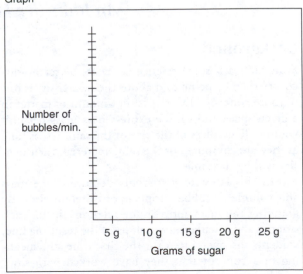

Number of bubbles/min.

5 g   10 g   15 g   20 g   25 g

Grams of sugar

Questions & Answers

1. **What evidence do you have that a gas is produced in the bottles?**

   ANSWER: Bubbles are released into the cup of water.

2. **What is the gas being released from the bottles? What evidence supports your assumption?**

   ANSWER: The gas being released must be carbon dioxide because the BTB in the cup turned green or yellow, indicating that the water has become more acidic.

3. **How does the amount of sugar affect the amount of gas produced?**

   ANSWER: Answers will vary depending on results. The typical results show that more gas is produced when more sugar is added. A limit to the number of bubbles produced per minute is eventually seen when amounts in excess of 25 grams of sugar are added to the experimental apparatus. When the available sugar exceeds that which can be metabolized by the yeast in a fixed period of time, a leveling off of the respiration rate is seen.

4. **Do the results of the experiment support your hypothesis?**

   ANSWER: Answers will vary.

5. **What are the manipulated (independent) and responding (dependent) variables in this experiment? What variables were controlled?**

   ANSWER: Amount of sugar is the manipulated variable. Number of bubbles is the responding variable. Variables controlled include amount and temperature of water in the bottle, amount of yeast added to the bottle, and length of time bubbles were counted.

Extensions

1. Use the graph of class data to estimate the number of bubbles released per minute when 30 grams and 12 grams of sugar are added to the experimental apparatus. Check your estimates by repeating the experiment using these amounts of sugar.

   NOTE: Estimates beyond the range of available data are called **extrapolations** and estimates within the range of data are called **interpolations.**

2. Determine the approximate amount of sugar in grape or apple juice. Substitute 100 milliliters of juice for the sugar solution. After adding yeast and letting the apparatus set for 10 minutes, count the bubbles for 5 minutes and then calculate the average bubble count per minute. Using the graph prepared from class data, estimate the amount of sugar in the juice.

MASS AND VOLUME RELATIONSHIPS

An Inductive Laboratory Exercise

Background

Students learn some science concepts better by discovery than by being told about them. Density is one of those concepts. Density is the amount of matter in a given space and can be expressed as mass per unit volume. Regardless of the size of the samples, as long as they are composed of the same material, their density will be the same.

In this laboratory students determine the mass and volume of rubber stoppers of different sizes. By graphing the mass and volume relationship for each stopper and calculating the slope of the resulting line, students discover, often for the first time, the meaning of a concept that they have worked with since middle school.

Materials

five solid rubber stoppers of different sizes (*must be the same type*) per group

two or three graduated cylinders per group, sized to contain the different stoppers

one balance per group

graph paper

tap water

Procedures

1. Tell students that the purpose of the lab is to determine the relationship between mass and volume experimentally.

2. Instruct students to copy the table presented below onto a separate sheet of paper.
3. Give five different rubber stoppers to each group. Instruct the groups to determine the mass and volume of each stopper and then record their data in the table. (Mass may be determined using the balance and volume by the displacement method.)
4. Next instruct them to construct a graph like the one shown below on a sheet of graph paper, making sure that the scales on the x and y axes are appropriate for their data.
5. Then instruct students to plot their mass and volume data for each stopper on the graph and draw a **line of best fit** through the data points.

Table

Stopper No.	Mass of Stopper	Volume of Stopper

Questions & Answers

1. **Describe the relationship between mass and volume shown on your graph.**

   ANSWER: Answers will vary, but should indicate that as mass increases, volume also increases.

2. **Calculate the slope of the line on your graph using two points on your line of best fit. Then calculate the slope a second and a third time using different combinations of points on your line of best fit. [Slope $\Delta y/\Delta x$, or $(y_2 - y_1)/(x_2 - x_1)$]**

   ANSWER: The slope of the line should be greater than 1 and all three calculations of slope should be the same, or nearly so.

3. **What science concept (physical property) does the slope represent? You may wish to consult your physical science, earth science, or chemistry text for help in answering this question.**

   HINT: You are looking for something that shows the relationship between mass and volume.

   ANSWER: Density.

4. **How do the data collected in this laboratory verify the definition of this concept?**

   ANSWER: The data show that the density of the rubber stoppers is the same regardless of the size of the stopper.

Graph

Y-axis

Mass (g)

Volume (mL)

X-axis

Appendix D

Scoring Key for Science Teaching Inventory Found in Chapter 1

SCORING KEY
For Science Teaching Inventory Found in Figure 1.2

Directions: Circle your answers from the inventory in the following columns. Then, count the number of items circled in each column and multiply the total for each column by 8.33. Use the blanks that follow to record your column totals and product.

Column 1	Column 2
1A	1B
2A	2B
3A	3B
4B	4A
5B	5A
6A	6B
7A	7B
8A	8B
9B	9A
10A	10B
11A	11B
12B	12A

Total number of responses in Column 1 _____ × 8.33 = _____
Total number of responses in Column 2 _____ × 8.33 = _____

Explanation: The product obtained from your responses to Column 1 is an approximate percentage of how often your beliefs reflect an uninformed view of science teaching, whereas the product obtained from your responses to Column 2 is an approximate percentage of how often your beliefs reflect an informed view of science teaching.

Index